# ARMS CONTROL AND MILITARY FORCE

The Adelphi Library

# Arms Control and Military Force

THE ADELPHI LIBRARY 3

*edited by*
**CHRISTOPH BERTRAM**
*Director, IISS*

Published for
THE INTERNATIONAL INSTITUTE FOR
STRATEGIC STUDIES
by
Gower and ALLANHELD, OSMUN

*Published by*

Gower Publishing Company Limited,
Westmead, Farnborough, Hampshire, England
and
Allanheld, Osmun & Co. Publishers, Inc.
6 South Fullerton Avenue
Montclair, New Jersey 07042, USA

*British Library Cataloguing in Publication Data*

Arms control and military force—
    (Adelphi Library)
1   Arms, control
I   Bertram, Christoph   II International Institute
    for Strategic Studies   III Series
    327.174    JX1974
ISBN 0-566-00344-9

0 566 00344 9 (UK)
0/916672/70/0 (US)

# CONTENTS

# INTRODUCTION

As a conscious effort of policy, arms control has been an invention of the 20th century. It was the horror over new, highly destructive arms in the late 19th century that fathered the attempts to seek, through a series of international conventions just before the Great War, restrictions on the use of certain weapons and the imposition of laws of warfare. The horror of World War I, coupled with the idealism of the League of Nations, led to new attempts in the 1920s and 1930s to reduce the number of major weapon systems and to encourage political accountancy of the dynamics of arms races through an international registry of arms expenditures and arms exports—early forms of what are today known under the term of "confidence-building measures". After the Second World War, it was the emergence of the atomic weapon—more terrible than any of the many destructive means so far conceived by mankind—which spurred the desire to seek, through negotiated limitations, a barrier against disaster. In much of post-war history, therefore, arms control has been closely associated with *nuclear* weapons, and linked to the general effort to reduce the risk of war between the two major nuclear coalitions, the Soviet Union in the East and the United States and its allies in the West.

In spite of the considerable political appeal of arms control and the intellectual investment in the field over the years, the record has not been very impressive. The difficulties that have to be faced by any arms control policy and any particular approach are indeed daunting: states do not arm themselves in order to facilitate the placing of limitations on themselves; what seems rational to one side may seem dangerous to the other; balances of forces are difficult to construct and maintain; and the verification of agreements—so essential in

democratic countries for the acceptability of any arms control agreement with the Soviet Union—is at best imperfect, at worst ineffective. In the past decade, two major obstacles in particular have presented themselves, one political, the other technical. Politically, arms control agreements between two opposing sides require a minimum of consensus on the state of their general relationship and, if possible, on the desired state of force relations that arms control should help to support; the fact that the Soviet Union has undertaken both military programmes and international activities which seem designed not to maintain but to change the *status quo* in the Soviet favour has in itself strained the basis on which arms control—always a compromise—can be pursued with any optimism. Technically, the rapid change in the quality of military means—both conventional and nuclear—over the past 10 years has tended to undermine agreements for limitation—since the missions that they sought to restrict by imposing limits on specific weapon systems could be undertaken by other, non-restricted weapons. If for no more than these two reasons, there is today a widespread scepticism over the utility and relevance of arms control between East and West.

The Adelphi Papers and articles in this volume represent the essence of the Institute's research and publications in the arms control field over the past five years. They thus do not seek to trace the history of arms control as such but to provide analyses, ideas and proposals on how to approach the thorny task of controlling the competition in arms against the background of past experiences and new challenges. These contributions deal primarily with the problems of East-West arms control efforts, which reflect the underlying political realities of the negotiations conducted, particularly in the

1

Strategic Arms Limitation Talks (SALT) between the United States and the Soviet Union and in the Talks on Mutual Force Reductions (MBFR) between countries of NATO and the Warsaw Pact. Joseph Coffey's study on Arms Reductions in Europe (Adelphi Paper No.105) sets out the range of methods for negotiated arms control in the European context; of all the papers represented here, it is perhaps the most optimistic as to numerical restrictions. Uwe Nerlich's paper on Nuclear Weapons and East-West Negotiations (Adelphi Paper No.120) introduces the political asymmetries between East and West into the consideration for arms control, particularly in that area—theatre nuclear forces—which has since become known under the general term of "grey area weapons".

SALT is examined both as a general approach—Beyond SALT II (Adelphi Paper No.141)—and as an example for the limitations of the quantitative method of East-West arms control (Arms Control and Technological Change, Adelphi Paper No.146). Both papers argue that the traditional approach to arms limitations is increasingly flawed and suggest new ways of controlling military capabilities in a rapidly changing technological environment. The nature and extent of this technological change is shown in the brief excerpt from *Strategic Survey*, the Institute's annual assessment of major strategic developments.

The direction for new efforts in arms control that emerges from these studies is this: unless arms control can come to terms with the new complexity of military power it will fail. Purely quantitative weapons and force restraints will be insufficient, and arms control must again be integrated into national security policies. It cannot be allowed to live a life separate from other security concerns. The "mission approach" suggested in Adelphi Paper No.146—to limit what military forces can do rather than concentrate on the specific weapons at their disposal—is closely related to the more political perspective of Confidence-Building Measures which are examined, not only for

the East-West context, in Adelphi Paper No.149. These are, clearly, more modest notions of arms restriction than those nourished in the heyday of arms control enthusiasm; the complexity of the problem requires complex answers. But if the controversy in recent years over SALT, MBFR or the "grey area" are any guide, we must think in new directions if arms control as a contribution to security is not to be discredited.

The difficulties and shortcomings of the more quantitative approach ot arms limitation may be particularly evident in the East-West context, where highly advanced industrial countries with competing notions of stable security confront each other. In other areas—the Middle East for example (see Yair Evron's Adelphi Paper No.138)—the more fluid military and political situation may be susceptible to solution by methods that are no longer appropriate to curb the military competition between East and West. And yet, even in a regional context, we are reminded of a fundamental condition for arms control: it is a servant of political agreement and an indicator for the level of political compromise reached rather than a method to promote, in itself, political compromise.

This does not alter the fact that arms control remains an important approach to security policy. It does, however, put it in perspective. And it does point to the test that arms control must be subjected to in the future if it is to be an effective instrument of national security policy in general. Arms control is not, even if agreements can be reached—and the past decade has shown how difficult it is to reach agreements—an end in itself. Only if we succeed in devising methods by which arms control can promote or accommodate political interests and give visibility, substance and durability to these interests will arms control remain effective.

The studies included in this volume are the Institute's contribution to this debate.

Christoph Bertram

2

# 1 NEW APPROACHES TO ARMS REDUCTION IN EUROPE

J. I. COFFEY

## INTRODUCTION

For almost thirty years the United States and her North Atlantic Treaty Organization (NATO) allies have confronted the Soviet Union and her fellow-members of the Warsaw Treaty Organization (Warsaw Pact) in the centre of Europe. Over this period both sides have expended vast sums on the development of new weapons and the maintenance of large forces in an effort to ensure their security. In the process they have once again turned Europe[1] into an armed camp: a million NATO soldiers, sailors and airmen in West Germany and the Low Countries confront a million Warsaw Pact troops in East Germany, Poland and Czechoslovakia, while hundreds of thousands more armed men are ranged against each other in southern and in northern Europe.

Those endorsing this build-up of military power insist that it is essential. They argue that the presence of armed men along the line of confrontation discourages encroachments and so stabilizes the political situation. They maintain that the availability of back-up forces inhibits attempts to exploit weak spots, and that the deployment of nuclear-armed units inhibits larger-scale military operations as well. They also point out that the existence of cohesive alliances serves to avoid misunderstandings about the consequences of employing force, thereby helping to preserve peace in Europe.

[1] Technically, Europe extends from the Urals to the mid-Atlantic (taking in the Azores in the south and Iceland in the north) and from the North Cape to the Bosphorus. However, since Turkey spans the Bosphorus, its territory in Asia is included in this Paper under both the geographic and the political definitions of Europe. Conversely, the Union of Soviet Socialist Republics is not considered here as politically part of Europe but as a separate entity. Thus, the phrase 'European security' refers to the interests and the problems of the thirty-one states west of the Soviet border, six of which are allied with the Soviet Union, thirteen of which are members of NATO, and twelve of which do not formally belong to either grouping.

These are weighty arguments and must be given due consideration; however, not even those who advance them would list military power as the sole factor contributing to peace. Moreover, whatever the contribution of military power, it has not achieved the larger goal of ruling out threats to the territorial integrity, economic viability and political freedom of choice of the countries of Europe – that is to say, it has not sufficed to ensure European security.[2]

[2] As used in this Paper, the phrase 'European security' means two things:

(1) The preservation of the territorial integrity, economic viability and political independence of the countries concerned – the most vital of all national interests;

(2) Reasonable confidence that threats to use force, pressures backed by force, or the actual employment of force cannot adversely affect these national interests.

This definition has a number of important implications which should be made explicit. One is that 'security', as defined here, is a minimal concept which does not include objectives such as the maintenance of a given power position, the enhancement of national prestige, the extension of national influence and similar vaguely defined aims. Another is that it differentiates between specific objectives essential to security (as access to Middle East oil may be to the countries of Western Europe) and those which are merely desirable (such as obtaining that oil on favourable economic terms). A third is that it does not set up perfectionist requirements; thus a country may find its political independence limited because it has made a partial surrender of sovereignty to extra-national organizations such as the European Economic Community, because of ideological, political, and cultural ties with other countries, or simply out of prudence (Denmark's 'freedom of choice', for example, is unlikely to extend to torpedoing Soviet ships as they pass through the Sound). A fourth is that it concentrates on inhibiting the use of force or threats to use force, rather than on precluding all forms of conflict among states, or all ways of exercising pressure; for example, a naval blockade would, under my definition, constitute a 'threat', whereas an embargo on oil, whatever its impact on economic viability, would not. Finally, this concept of 'security' extends – as it must – to perceptions of security (which do, after all, determine whether it in fact exists – were security based solely on relative military capabilities Canada would live in mortal fear of the United States, and Uruguay would arm against Brazil).

3

The sense of insecurity derives in part from the mere presence of armed forces in large numbers, which heightens awareness of particular military threats (such as a Soviet amphibious landing on the north coast of Norway or a NATO nuclear strike against targets in Poland) and increases concern about the intentions of those who have deployed these forces. It also derives from the fact that much of Europe is divided into two blocs with opposing ideologies, differing socio-economic systems and conflicting interests. The feelings of insecurity created by this division are intensified by the fact that the leaders of these two blocs, the United States and the Soviet Union, see Europe not only as a prize of great value but as an arena within which to compete for power, influence and prestige. Finally, these feelings are enhanced because the United States and the Soviet Union have not hesitated to use their overwhelming power to achieve political gains or avoid political losses – even to the extent of using force or the threat of force.

Perhaps the most significant contribution to the sense of insecurity is the awareness that if either of the super-powers chose to unleash its full might, no country in Europe could stand against it. For one thing, only the most advanced states possess the technical knowledge required to develop modern weapons and the industrial base needed to build them. For another, few such states can afford to produce in quantity the range of equipment used by armed forces today; even countries like France and Britain must concentrate on a few types of weapons, while Italy – which spends less on defence research in a year than the United States spends in a week – is literally priced out of the market. Furthermore, not even West Germany, the most populous country in Europe, could match the numbers of troops available to the super-powers (which have three or four times as many men to draw on), so that – even if they wanted to – the individual nations of Europe could not create armed forces comparable with those that could be brought against them.

The two super-powers muster not only powerful conventional forces but even more powerful nuclear ones as well, with delivery vehicles numbering in the thousands. If even a few of these weapons were ever employed they could devastate any country on the face of the globe.[3] Even the lesser nuclear powers are at a disadvantage compared with the United States and the Soviet Union, since they can hope to deter only gross and direct threats (such as that of a disarming strike or an all-out assault by conventional troops) and then only by threatening actions which could result in their own annihilation. Those countries relying solely on conventionally-armed units are at even more of a disadvantage, since such units are so vulnerable to nuclear weapons and so incapable of coping with their means of delivery that in the event of all-out war they can, in the words of General André Beaufre, 'only disperse, dig in, and take part as best they can in . . . rescue operations'.[4] Most of the nations of Europe are therefore exposed to threats which they themselves have no means of deterring or countering.

Obviously, not all threats to the security of the countries of Europe derive from the confrontation between East and West or from the presence on the continent of the two super-powers (Cyprus may be more worried about the military potential and behaviour of her neighbours than those of the Soviet Union or the United States). Broadly speaking, however, it is the division of Europe into opposing armed camps that constitutes the greatest threat to the greatest number of countries, and it is the imbalances between the capabilities of the two super-powers and those of the states of Europe which makes it so difficult for the latter to assure security and to protect their national interests. (As President de Gaulle put it, the continued military predominance of the United States and the Soviet Union would either 'paralyse and sterilize' the rest of the world or place it 'under the yoke of a double hegemony'.[5]) The fundamental question for these countries is, therefore, how to change the present situation to one in which the threats posed by the super-powers and

---

[3] By way of illustration, 200 1-megaton (MT) warheads delivered on the United States could kill 80 million Americans; a similar number dropped on the Soviet Union could kill 40 million Russians. In each case, 200 MT equivalents represents about 5 per cent of the deliverable megatonnage available.

[4] André Beaufre, *Deterrence and Strategy*, translated by Major-General R. H. Barry (New York: Praeger, 1966), p. 123.

[5] *Speeches and Press Conferences*, French Embassy in the United States, no. 253A, 28 October 1966, p. 6.

their respective alliances would be reduced in magnitude, in likelihood, or both.

There are, of course, a number of ways of attaining these goals, ranging from the transformation of the international system to the establishment of new centres of power in Europe. Unfortunately, the developments most likely to alleviate threats to the peace of Europe, such as the establishment of the rule of law, the creation of effective collective security organizations, and so on, are the least likely to be attained. Even more unfortunately, the more likely alterations in the international or the regional system may also be the less productive; for example, the development of a (Western) European Nuclear Force might enhance the security of some countries at the expense of others – notably those in Eastern Europe. Thus, whatever their long-term objectives or aspirations, the states of Europe may in the short run have to look to less sweeping and more balanced ways of reducing the threats to their security.[6]

One way of doing this would be energetically and meaningfully to pursue the search for accommodation between East and West, with a view to resolving differences which could lead to a clash of arms, creating vested interests in the maintenance of good relations, and changing perceptions of the adversary's behaviour. To some extent this process is already under way, as is illustrated by the efforts of both sides to expand mutual trade, increase technical and economic interchanges, normalize political relations and devise a new framework for future co-operation in these areas and that of European security. Moreover, in addition to joint measures of this kind, the United States and the Soviet Union have also sought to rule out the use of force against each other, their respective allies or any other country 'in circumstances which may endanger international peace and security'.[7]

General moves towards *détente* and specific agreements to seek political change by peaceful means can inhibit the use of force, and so contribute to European security. However, while they certainly increase the costs of military action, they do not necessarily preclude it, since some regimes may be comparatively insensitive to such inhibitions. Others may be so convinced of the importance of the interests at stake as to be willing to pay the price of using force, as was the Soviet Union when she sent troops into Czechoslovakia in 1968 and the United States when she landed marines in the Dominican Republic in 1965. It is thus understandable that some Europeans should seek not only to strengthen inhibitions regarding the use of force but also to reduce others' ability to use it, should they choose to do so: in short, that they should seek to limit and control armaments.

### Security Through Arms Control

The great merit of arms-control measures[8] is that, unlike efforts to improve East–West relations and create obstacles to the use of force, they do affect military capabilities (which are the most direct and effective instruments by which one country can undermine the security of another). This is not, however, their sole advantage. By constraining military capabilities, arms-control measures influence decisions to

[6] For a more detailed discussion of ways of, and difficulties in, transforming the present order, see J. I. Coffey, *Arms Control and European Security* (London: Chatto and Windus for the IISS, to be published in 1975).

[7] Nixon–Brezhnev Agreement on the Prevention of Nuclear War, *The Times* (London), 23 June 1973, p. 4. For an earlier (if less specific) understanding concerning limitations on the use of force see the First, Second and Third Articles of the 'Basic Principles of Relations between the United States of America and the Union of Soviet Socialist Republics', 29 May 1972, in *Weekly Compilation of Presidential Documents*, vol. 8, no. 23

(5 June 1972), pp. 943–44 (Washington: Office of the Federal Register, National Archives and Records Service, 1972).

[8] As used here, 'arms control' includes any measure limiting or reducing forces, regulating armaments or restricting the deployment of troops and/or weapons which is intended to induce responsive behaviour, or which is taken pursuant to an understanding with another state or states. This definition covers indirect controls, such as budgetary ceilings, as well as direct ones, such as constraints on the size of missiles. It includes unilateral (as well as bilateral or multilateral) measures – provided they are designed to enhance the possibility that other countries will keep the peace or to induce reciprocal reduction and restrictions, and are not intended simply to improve a country's force posture or to ease the burdens of defence. As well as explicit agreements it covers tacit understandings – for example, the apparent 'understanding' that, as part of the overall settlement of the Cuban missile crisis in 1962, the United States would remove her intermediate-range ballistic missiles (IRBM) from Turkey. It also leaves the way open both for formal agreements and for informal ones, such as the simultaneous announcements by the late President Johnson, Sir Alec Douglas-Home and Mr Krushchev of cut-backs in the production of plutonium for nuclear weapons.

employ force and also strengthen inhibitions regarding the use of force (to use force would be to acknowledge the failure of a nation's chosen policy). In both these ways they can alleviate perceptions of threat, and thereby facilitate the improvement of relations among states. If progress towards *détente* is in some sense a precondition for arms control, arms control is also a means of furthering and speeding up progress towards *détente*.

Furthermore, arms control can have other beneficial effects. It can dampen arms races, which both feed on and induce tensions. It can reduce the economic and social costs of defence – an item of concern to virtually every country in Europe. It can create vested interests in maintaining good relations – otherwise one of the participants may invoke the escape clauses which are implicit in any agreement and explicit in most. And it can, if long continued, alter both the nature of the international system and the relative influence of states within that system, thereby partially achieving the objectives of many European countries.

Whether arms control will in fact enhance security (and achieve any desirable side effects) depends in part on the sources of concern about security and in part on the scope and nature of the measures adopted. For example, the May 1972 agreements between the United States and the Soviet Union on the limitation of strategic armaments may have ratified a rough balance between the two super-powers but they did not reduce their capabilities *vis-à-vis* the countries of Europe; in fact their relative advantages with respect to other nuclear powers have increased, despite the SALT agreements.[9] Moreover, these agreements generated new fears that parity in strategic forces between the Soviet Union and the United States might give one or both of the super-powers greater freedom to employ other kinds of forces, inside or outside Europe, in ways potentially detrimental to European security.

Nor are the current negotiations in Vienna on the reduction of NATO and Warsaw Pact forces in Central Europe likely to alleviate these and other fears. For one thing, the interests of the participants in these negotiations are so different, and their proposals so divergent, that any measures adopted are likely to be limited in scope and slow in implementation. Secondly, these measures are likely to leave untouched not only the forces in other parts of Europe but also those outside it. The latter are seen by some Europeans as a direct threat (which is how the Western allies view the Soviet tank divisions and other mobile units inside the Soviet Union, and the East Europeans see the strike aircraft aboard American carriers), by more as an indirect threat (they could precipitate conflicts which might spill back into Europe, like the colonial wars between France and England in the eighteenth century), and by many as perpetuating the enormous military advantages of the super-powers (whose relative strength might increase as mutual force reductions began to affect European troop strengths and weapons levels). This last suspicion could enhance European concern that imbalances between European forces and those of the super-powers might enable (or even incite) the exercise of political pressures. It could strengthen the belief that Europeans do not count for much in the eyes of the super-powers, so that their interests can be disregarded with impunity. And it could exacerbate the feeling that the smaller powers are being asked to make all the sacrifices, while the super-powers go their own military ways – a feeling clearly evident during discussion of the Treaty on the Non-Proliferation of Nuclear Weapons.

Such concerns, beliefs, and feelings could adversely affect the acceptability to Europeans of arms-limitation measures: we might get through Stage I of Mutual Force Reductions, which concerns possible force reductions by the super-powers, but not through Stage II, which would involve cuts by the European countries. More importantly, they might induce the Europeans (particularly the West Europeans) to seek to build up their own military power so as to secure a voice in decisions which affected them – and, while one could scarcely fault them for choosing this option if no other were available, its potential implications for *détente*, and for the security of Europe as a whole, suggest that other options should be tried first.

One possible alternative would be to seek to alleviate these concerns through the imposition of overall restrictions on the armaments of

---

[9] For an assessment of the technical and strategic implications of SALT I see J. I. Coffey, 'The Savor of SALT', *Bulletin of the Atomic Scientists*, vol. XXIX, no. 5 (May 1973), pp. 9-15.

countries belonging to the Western Alliance or to the Warsaw Pact. Hopefully, such restrictions could reduce both direct and indirect threats to European security and complement the limited kind of measures now being discussed at Geneva and at Vienna, which would affect only some kinds of weapons and some types of forces. Conceivably, they could also set the stage for controls over the armaments and military establishments of both the non-aligned states in Europe and non-European powers – controls which must be adopted at some stage if the controls affecting the NATO and Warsaw Pact countries are to continue in effect.

The purpose of this Paper is to develop this alternative, by looking at:

(1) Limitations on the size and the capabilities of NATO and Warsaw Pact forces, which might alleviate concerns about military imbalances, both quantitative and qualitative;

(2) Restrictions on the deployment of at least some components of these forces, which might hinder the kind of action that could threaten European security.

# I. LIMITATIONS ON THE SIZE AND CAPABILITIES OF ARMED FORCES

Overall limitations on armed forces may afford the best – if not the only – way of precluding worrisome improvements in an opponent's defence establishment. They may also be more flexible in their application, and hence more acceptable to the countries concerned, than specific restrictions on particular forces and weapons. They may have an impact on the military capabilities of the super-powers which could not be achieved by regional arms control measures and, even if they do not, may erode the political utility of those capabilities by placing limits on the numbers of guns, ships and other symbols of power.

There are a number of ways of holding down the size of armed forces and constraining their capabilities, including limiting the number of men under arms, imposing ceilings on classes of weapons, restricting the amounts which can be spent for defence and controlling certain important activities, such as research and development. Each has its merits and its difficulties; each will apply unequally (and perhaps inequitably) to different countries; and each will be viewed differently by those countries. We will look first at the feasibility of each type of measure (i.e., its advantages and disadvantages), leaving its acceptability – and hence its implications – for later consideration.

## The Establishment of Force Levels
In the discussions on general and complete disarmament, which took place in the late 1940s and the early 1950s, each side put forward a seemingly endless series of proposals and counter-proposals for limitations on the number of men under arms. The initial concept took the form of proposals for percentage reductions in the existing forces, but it foundered over the question of verifying existing force levels as a prelude to making reductions – a procedure which the Soviet Union described as 'inspection without disarmament'. This led to suggestions for force ceilings which would be lowered during successive stages of disarmament until each state was left with only those forces required to maintain internal security.[10]

There is an aura of attractiveness about proposals to set force levels. They impose constraints on a highly visible and very important component of military power – the number of men under arms – and force levels are apparently simple and clear-cut. Moreover, such proposals seem equitable, gradations in power being accompanied by differences in force levels, and they allow flexibility in the allocation of manpower to different components of the armed forces.

In practice, however, many of these advantages turn out to be illusory. For instance, force levels are not simple and clear-cut. Should these levels apply only to members of the armed forces or to all militarized units, like the CRS (*Compagnies Républicaines de Sécurité*) of France or

---

[10] See, for example, the statement of principles of the Soviet bloc submitted to the Ten-Power Disarmament Committee on 8 April 1960, and that of the Western powers, submitted on 26 April 1960, cited in Bernhard G. Bechhoefer, *Postwar Negotiations for Arms Control* (Washington: The Brookings Institution, 1961), pp. 541–43.

the Border Guards of Czechoslovakia? Should one count only men on active duty or those in the reserves as well? Should one count only men in uniform, ignoring civilian workers, civilian contractors and civilians employed in aircraft factories and other facilities? Moreover, how does one count all these various components? Should they be counted on an equal basis or on a sliding scale?

If ceilings on force levels do not apply to border guards and similar para-military formations, which are commonly equipped with light infantry weapons and frequently trained for combat rather than police missions, countries having such units would gain an advantage which could in some cases be significant: for example, the number of East German Border Guards and Security Troops is four times more than those of West Germany and is equal to almost a quarter of the number in the West German Army. In addition, unless ceilings were applied to such para-military units, they could be strengthened to a degree which could largely offset reductions in military manpower. Alternatively, they could be used to train recruits, thereby facilitating the rapid expansion of the regular forces or enabling them to circumvent force ceilings – which would normally apply to trainees as well as to long-service soldiers. On the other hand, ceilings which did include para-military forces would penalize countries possessing them, since, whatever their utility in combat, it is not likely to approach that of trained soldiers or experienced seamen. In any case, such ceilings would be difficult to define (how should one count the Danish Home Guard and the Hungarian Workers' Militia?), hard to verify and virtually impossible to enforce. The best answer would probably be to settle for unilateral restraints on the size and equipment of para-military units, leaving each country free to adjust to changes in the forces of others.

As far as reserves are concerned, these can add considerably to the military capabilities of a country. Some states, like Switzerland and Sweden, design their armed forces around reservists. Some, like the United States, supplement their active duty forces with whole divisions drawn from the organized reserve, while others rely heavily on reservists to fill out units kept at cadre strength, as does the Soviet Union. Still others use them as West Germany does, to secure rear areas against raiders and saboteurs, or to replace men who may fall in combat. In general, reservists will be less well-trained than men on active duty and less ready for employment, but differences in prescribed roles, levels of training and stockpiles of equipment will make some countries' reservists much more effective than others'. Moreover, geography and communications nets will affect the speed with which they can be deployed, a factor of considerable importance in any confrontation in Europe.

Counting reservists would therefore impose severe constraints on some countries; not counting them would give considerable advantages to others; while counting them only in part would lead to endless arguments, as was the case during the disarmament negotiations of 1928–32. These considerations, plus the difficulty of verifying numbers of reservists, argue for leaving them untouched, at least for the present.

An even greater difficulty with curbs on military manpower is the fact that civilians can substitute for soldiers in a variety of roles, from barber to weapons artificer, and can perform almost every administrative task required for the armed services; in fact when the allies limited the *Reichswehr* to 100,000 men, at the Treaty of Versailles, they included in that figure civilian administrators, who were an integral part of the German logistic system. Attempting to count civilians does, however, considerably complicate the problem of verifying levels of manpower and could also cause inequities, because of the budgeting and personnel practices of the various countries (for instance, civilian teachers in schools for American children in West Germany are carried on the Department of Defense payroll). Moreover, counting those civilians on the payroll would not rule out other means of substituting for men in uniform. For instance, services for military establishments may be sub-contracted, either because it is cheaper or because it enables the mobilization of skills and resources not otherwise available (the radar research station at Orfordness, in England, was manned by American and British employees of the Radio Corporation of America under contract to the United States Air Force). It is questionable whether one could control this and other means of substituting civilians for soldiers without intrusive inspection, almost complete access to records and an impartial tribunal to hear complaints – none of which seems likely in the near future. Even then one would not touch the vast industrial enterprises which carry on research and development, conduct tests, manufacture equipment, maintain and upgrade weapons and otherwise perform the functions which in an earlier and simpler age were carried out by military arsenals.

All this means that prescribing levels of men under arms is not simple and may not be effective in precluding the development of military capabilities. Moreover, force ceilings could create inequities, with advanced nations better able to shift to civilian support than underdeveloped ones, and totalitarian societies better able to do so clandestinely (e.g., by detailing tractor repairmen to work on tanks or providing laboratory facilities for military research). Further inequities may arise from disparities between the status of a state (and hence the force levels it is allocated) and the size of the territory it must defend, others from a state's geographic position between two hostile powers (like those of Poland in the eighteenth century, Germany in the latter part of the nineteenth century and the Soviet Union in the twentieth century). Furthermore, various states may combine in alliances, thereby aggregating their manpower totals, and presumably their military capabilities – for example, until 1949 the troop strengths of Britain, France and (possibly) of Nationalist China could be reckoned with those of the United States, whereas the Soviet Union stood virtually alone. A further inequity may stem from the fact that some powers will have more responsibilities than others, arising either from the retention of territories in various parts of the globe or (as in the case of France) from special relationships with former colonial states.

The fact that inequities result from the establishment of symmetrical force levels suggests a considerable amount of bargaining before any ceilings on forces, equal or unequal, are accepted – if they ever are. But this does not mean that their imposition would not be useful. Force ceilings could have considerable symbolic importance, particularly if set below present levels; they could head off build-ups in armed forces by countries whose military strength is comparatively low; and they could affect the cutting edge of military capabilities (i.e., those men armed, organized and trained for employment in combat). They could also be accompanied by other measures – such as ceilings on classes of weapons – which could offset some of the disadvantages and make some of the constraints resulting from ceilings on forces more meaningful.

## Ceilings on Classes of Weapons

Rather than attempting to control military capabilities indirectly – by establishing force levels, imposing budgetary restrictions and so on – one could move directly to set ceilings on types of weapons. This was the method used in the Interim Agreement on the Limitation of Strategic Offensive Arms, which, together with the Agreed Interpretations and Unilateral Statements of both sides, prescribed the total number of inter-continental launchers the United States and the Soviet Union could have, how many could be light and how many heavy, the circumstances under which ICBM could be converted to SLBM, and so on.[11]

Interested powers could similarly restrict tanks, planes, warships and other kinds of weapons. There are, however, greater difficulties here. Most of these weapons, unlike ICBM and SLBM, have multiple roles – the same basic aircraft serving as interceptor, fighter-bomber and reconnaissance plane. Moreover, qualitative differences in other kinds of weaponry may be even greater than qualitative differences among missiles: the capabilities of destroyers, for instance, vary not only with size but also with age, armament, electronic equipment, and so on. Also, while missiles are highly visible and easy to count, other weapons systems – particularly smaller and more mobile weapons, such as tank and artillery pieces – are not. Finally, tanks and

---

[11] The Interim Agreement between the Union of Soviet Socialist Republics and the United States of America on Certain Measures with Respect to the Limitation of Strategic Offensive Arms, 26 May 1972, will be found in the *Weekly Compilation of Presidential Documents* (*op. cit.* in note 7), pp. 927–29; and in *Survival*, July/August 1972, pp. 195–99. Details concerning the numbers of missiles authorized will be found in Dr Kissinger's news conference of 27 May 1972 (*Weekly Compilation . . . , op. cit.*, pp. 932–37), while the Agreed Interpretations and Unilateral Statements are reprinted in *The New York Times*, 14 June 1972, p. 18, and in *Survival*, *op. cit.*

aircraft, unlike ICBM, may be found not only in active units but also in the hands of reserve forces, in storage and in the process of production – so that cut-off points are much more difficult to determine.

Furthermore, attempts to impose ceilings on non-strategic weapons may encounter some of the same difficulties that marked the SALT talks, perhaps in exaggerated form. Although the number of ICBM at hand may be more than sufficient to carry out their wartime missions, the same cannot be said of the numbers of tanks, planes or guns, and ceilings on these kinds of weapon may induce (as the limitations on strategic armaments did) a shift to qualitative improvements, which might be even more meaningful in the case of conventional weapons than in that of nuclear ones. Since such ceilings would strike at many more elements of the armed services and their associated interest groups than did limitations on strategic armaments, they might also be correspondingly more difficult to introduce.

Nevertheless, increases in numbers of weapons can be perceived as threatening, as evidenced by the West German reaction to the introduction of some one thousand additional Soviet tanks into East Germany in 1973.[12] Moreover, in circumstances such as limited conventional operations numerical advantages could make a difference to the outcome and may be pursued for this reason. Such pursuit could be costly and could induce counter-actions by potential adversaries, thereby generating new tensions. There is thus reason for attempting to head off arms build-ups and to inhibit shifts in regional or local military balances.

Unfortunately, some weapons which are viewed as threatening, or which figure heavily in regional balances, are hard to control. For example, verification of ceilings on tanks would require some means of ascertaining with reasonable accuracy not only those weapons in the hands of both active and reserve units but also those in repair shops, depots and the factories producing them. It would also require fair knowledge of both the capacity of these factories and the percentage of this capacity being utilized – otherwise production could be stepped up both quickly and with little evidence that this was taking place. It might mean concentrating production in designated plants. Certainly it would require some means of tracing the movements of the tanks produced and, more importantly, some indication of what was done with existing tanks – which could be retained in units, stockpiled for use in replacing combat losses, shipped overseas or scrapped, all with varying effects on weapons ceilings, military capabilities and political influence. Moreover, while normal sources of intelligence and (expanded) satellite reconnaissance could provide some insight into what was happening, it is questionable whether they would satisfy everyone that the prescribed ceilings were being honoured, and even more questionable whether they would provide evidence strong enough to support a charge that the ceilings were being violated.

In varying degrees this is also true of other weapons systems which are viewed as 'threatening'. Rockets and short-range missiles are larger, less numerous and presumably produced in fewer factories, and so somewhat easier to verify. However, even here the number allocated to reserve units or in stockpiles may not be known with any precision, and the possibilities of exceeding ceilings without being detected – or (worse) leading opponents to believe that ceilings are exceeded when in fact they are not – may be quite high. Aircraft are obviously easier to monitor, despite their mobility, but may be more difficult to differentiate by type and armament, the problem here being not so much one of numbers as of capabilities. (For instance, conversion of the Soviet Air Defence Forces' fighter-interceptor aircraft to multi-purpose planes could have the effect of increasing the combat potential of the Soviet Tactical Air Force by 60 per cent.)

Thus, unless and until some forms of inspection are accepted, or extensive measures for providing reassuring information are adopted, the number of weapons systems on which ceilings can be placed will be relatively small.

One possibility would be to start with naval forces. In general these take a long time to build and are hard to conceal, and for both these reasons are relatively easy to control. They are useful militarily and also for the exercise of political pressures in what has come to be called

---

[12] These reactions were observed by the author, who in May 1973 was interviewing Federal Government officials in Bonn.

'gunboat diplomacy'. Additionally, many of the current concerns of NATO and the Warsaw Pact centre around naval forces, with the West worried about the build-up and redeployment of the Soviet Navy and the Soviet Union unhappy about the world-wide presence of the United States Navy. Finally, ceilings on naval forces could head off costly and perhaps unsettling arms races, since the Soviet Navy is continuing to build new vessels, and the United States Navy is scheduled to increase the number of attack submarines currently available and to reverse the six-year decline in major combat surface ships in operation.[13]

One way to impose a ceiling on naval forces would be to limit the numbers of ships by class, as was done at the Washington Naval Conference of 1922. This, however, would be very difficult, because the naval forces of the major powers are less homogeneous today than they were then, and differ markedly from one another. The imposition of limitations by class would require a definition of each class, as well as considerable bargaining over what each limit should be. An alternative which avoided this difficulty would be to set limits on tonnage, as was done for cruisers at the London Naval Conference of 1929, thereby enabling each signatory to build what ships it chose. Such ceilings would favour countries with large numbers of small but deadly patrol craft and few requirements for deep-ocean operations.

Another problem is that ceilings on the forces of each country would ignore both the existence of alliances and the effects of geography, which almost automatically give the Warsaw Pact predominance in the Baltic and the Black Sea. If, however, ceilings took into account alliance relationships, either by adjusting national limits to reflect them or by setting totals for each side, NATO would either have to be granted much higher ceilings than the Warsaw Pact, thereby perpetuating its advantage, or it would have to make drastic reductions in naval forces. Ceilings by region might pose equal difficulty, in that the Soviet Union would have nowhere but the Pacific to deploy ships withdrawn from Europe,

whereas NATO could presumably transfer West German or Italian warships to the North Atlantic and could certainly add to those of the United States in home waters.

This suggests that any comprehensive arrangements for ceilings on naval vessels would be complex in nature and almost certainly asymmetrical in their impact, even if they simply froze navies at present levels. It also suggests that formal agreements to constrain naval vessels would be difficult to negotiate and slow in coming. For these reasons, it is recommended that one look instead to tacit understandings rather than formal agreements, to measures which would affect primarily the United States and the Soviet Union rather than to more widespread controls, and to concentration on a few types of ships rather than to comprehensive limitations. Since it is easier to halt further build-ups than to scrap existing warships, this approach might be tried first.[14]

**Constraints on Military Budgets**

Another measure which might be considered for limiting armed forces is the imposition of constraints on military budgets. Such constraints would be popular, since the cost of defence is increasing pretty well everywhere, even if not at the same rate as gross national product.[15] It is also at first sight a simple measure, since cutting the resources available to the military will obviously reduce military capabilities. For both these reasons, and because money saved on defence could be reallocated either for domestic purposes or for development aid to the Third World, there has been widespread support for this measure.

In fact, constraints on military budgets are one of the most complex and difficult kinds of controls to apply. Firstly, not all expenditures for military purposes are found in the budgets of the defence ministries. In the United States, for example, some 40 per cent of the annual budget of the Atomic Energy Commission goes towards the production or upgrading of nuclear weapons, while it is believed that in the Soviet Union as

---

[13] *Statement by Admiral Thomas H. Moorer, USN, Chairman, Joint Chiefs of Staff, before the Defense Appropriations Subcommittee of the House Committee on Appropriations on 3 April 1973* (hereafter cited as *Moorer Statement, 1973*), mimeograph (Washington DC: USGPO), pp. 37–38, 40.

[14] One reason for this is, of course, that it does not so directly threaten service interests. Another is that it enables modernization, through the construction of new ships and the retirement of old ones, and hence may be more acceptable – if less valid.

[15] *The Military Balance 1974–1975* (London: IISS, 1974), appendix 2, table 2, pp. 78–79.

11

much as 70–80 per cent of the All Union Science budget may be concerned with defence. Secondly, these budgets themselves include costs incurred on behalf of other agencies, with the American Navy providing both ships and men for the United States Hydrographic Service. Finally, it is very simple not only to hide items within the defence budget (as is commonly done for the intelligence services of most countries) but also to provide hidden subsidies to the military establishment, by, for example, the attachment of personnel without cost to the defence ministry, by the procurement of goods and services by other agencies, through measures for the remission of taxes, and in many other ways. All this means that verification of constraints on military budgets requires a considerable knowledge of the budgetary procedures of other countries, access to their records, the right to raise questions concerning the correlation between these records and what actually went on, and not least a limited right of inspection of both military and supporting facilities. And, even then, such verification can only be of an approximate nature.

Even if these problems were overcome, constraints on military budgets would still affect countries in different ways. Money used for military purposes does not have the same purchasing power as that spent in the open market: sometimes, as in countries with controlled economies, it will buy more, and frequently, as in countries with 'free' economies, it will buy less. The purchasing power of the defence dollar (or rouble) will also vary with what it buys; in some countries soldiers are paid very little, whereas in other countries, which rely on volunteers, they are paid considerably more, both actually and in relative terms. (For instance, it is estimated that manpower costs account for 56 per cent of the American defence budget as against 30–35 per cent for the Soviet, even though the Soviet Union has almost 50 per cent more men under arms.)[16] This suggests that one should consider constraints on military budgets which would hurt rather than cripple, which would be general rather than detailed, and which could conceivably withstand some of the stresses already noted.

One such measure might be a freeze on military budgets as a percentage of gross national product (GNP). This would affect directly only those countries planning new defence programmes of such an order as to require major increases in expenditure, as may be true of the Soviet Union and is likely to be true of the United States.[17] Such a freeze might also pinch when the cost of defence is rising faster than GNP, either because of inflation or because of 'gold-plating' weapons and equipment (i.e., incorporating refinements in design which are of marginal utility). Since the percentages of GNP allocated to defence by the NATO countries and those of the Warsaw Pact have in most instances either remained constant or declined, this type of freeze would not be unduly restrictive and for this reason might be acceptable. There are, however, problems in determining GNP over and above those incidental to verifying any constraints on military budgets. For example, the Soviet Union uses instead a concept called net material product (NMP), which does not allow for depreciation of capital equipment or for services. Even in those countries declaring their GNP, its true value is obscured by taxes imposed at various stages of production and by subsidies. Thus, both economists and accountants might have their work cut out to verify a measure of this sort.

An alternative approach would be to freeze budgets in terms of constant dollars (or roubles or marks), as this would more seriously constrain defence programmes. Such a freeze would largely mean that new programmes would have to be adopted at the expense of old ones, or as the outgrowth of more efficient administration of military establishments. It would also mean that an inflation of defence costs greater than that of the economy as a whole would have an adverse effect on defence programmes – more markedly so in 'free' economies than in controlled ones, where prices can be manipulated and where inflation tends to be hidden rather than reflected in the cost-of-living indices. Moreover, since

[1] 'The Military Balance 1973–1974 (London: IISS, 1973), pp. 8 and 9 for costs, 2 and 5 for force totals.

[17] According to the Brookings Institution, research on new weapons, cost escalation in procurement and additional pay-rises could increase the American defence budget for FY 1977 from its projected total of $87 billion (in 1973 dollars) to a total of as much as $95 billion. At this level, the share of defence in GNP would rise from the current 6·4 per cent to 7·0 per cent. Charles L. Schultze et al., Setting National Priorities: The 1973 Budget (Washington: The Brookings Institution, 1972), p. 81.

very different programmes are undertaken within each defence establishment, the rate of cost increases is not the same as for the country as a whole, which raises the question of how to adjust for this – if, indeed, it is possible to do so. Even if these technical problems could be resolved, and effective controls instituted, they would probably have more of an impact on some countries than on others, and thus might not be acceptable.[18]

A more extreme measure would be to freeze budgets at their present levels, regardless of future increases in GNP or in costs. This would probably affect NATO much more than the Warsaw Pact, although even there the costs of equipment have been rapidly rising.[19] It would, moreover, have a serious effect on programmes requiring increased expenditures for personnel, like the American switch to an all-volunteer army. And while the Soviet defence budget has ostensibly shown a slight falling off over the last few years, one might expect that a budget freeze would also 'pinch' the Soviet Union, already engaged in an extensive programme of modernization. Partly because of the asymmetrical effects, partly because countries which control prices can evade it, such a freeze may not meet with universal approval.

Another possibility would be to freeze only one budget item, such as procurement costs or all capital expenditures. This would allow expenditure for pay and allowances to increase and would equalize major cost differences between the countries of Eastern and Western Europe – although at some risk that expenditures earmarked for personnel could be diverted to other purposes. It would hit hardest those countries with new weapons under development or with large forces in need of modernization, consequently having a marked impact on programmes of vital concern and serving as a useful complement to other means of limiting modernization, such as controls over R & D. It would, of course, be less effective than an overall freeze, especially as regards manpower. Moreover, additional problems might be expected in determining procurement budgets or the costs of capital expenditures. In fact, current American practice is to estimate the Soviet budget from the number of weapons produced and the types of facilities constructed, and, if this remains the only way of verifying a freeze on procurement budgets, it might be simpler to attempt to limit production in a direct manner.

If various types of 'freeze' on defence budgets are difficult to apply, reductions in defence budgets are an even worse problem. Defence expenditures are so uneven, both in absolute and in relative terms, that cuts which one country could absorb with little difficulty would impinge heavily on the military capabilities of another. Again, the greater strains resulting from tighter curbs on defence budgets may increase the pressures to offset these by manipulating prices and adjusting taxes, or by outright 'cheating' on the agreement. A further difficulty is to choose a basis for reductions which would not have an unequal impact on the two Alliances – thereby violating the principle of 'undiminished security'.[20]

In general, therefore, it is impossible to be optimistic about the practicality of constraints on military budgets, which are bound to be complicated, inequitable, intrusive, and difficult to apply in any satisfactory manner. This does not mean that budgetary constraints may not be imposed on a partial and voluntary basis, only that formal agreements to this effect are unlikely. Nor does it mean that countries may not make token reductions – perhaps in the form of mutual announcements of budget cuts, perhaps in the form of payments to the UN which would

---

[18] For example, French defence expenditures increased by more than 25 per cent between 1968 and 1972, but the real value of expenditures fell by at least 3 per cent (*The Military Balance 1973–1974*, table 3, p. 76).

[19] The price of tanks has risen 250 per cent in the last ten years, of aircraft 320 per cent, and of motor torpedo boats almost 500 per cent, according to Siegfried Schönherr, in *Wirtschaftswissenschaft* (East Berlin), 8 August 1969, pp. 1161–74, cited in John Erickson, *Soviet Military Power* (London: Royal United Services Institute for Defence Studies, 1971), p. 103.

[20] Although each side started out by stating its objectives differently, the Soviet Union and her associates seeking 'equal security' and the United States and her allies 'the present degree of security at reduced costs', both have apparently adopted the phrase 'undiminished security' as a guiding principle – even though they may interpret it differently. See, in this connection, the article in *Pravda*, 17 December 1973, reported by *The New York Times*, 18 December 1973, p. 3, and the opening statement by the head of the American delegation to the talks on Mutual Force Reductions, Ambassador Stanley R. Resor, in United States Arms Control and Disarmament Agency public information release 73-9, 31 October 1973 (mimeograph), p. 4.

amount to a fixed percentage of expenditures for defence[21] – it means only that budgetary constraints offer little promise of having any major impact on the control of armaments.

## Controls on Research and Development

An alternative way of limiting the capabilities of armed forces would be to place constraints on research and development (R & D) which would slow down the process whereby new weapons are introduced into national armouries. Since R & D leads not only to the design of new weapons systems but to alterations leading to greater efficiency and speed of production, constraints on research will obviously adversely affect military capabilities. They will also affect other advantages gained from R & D, such as the ability to guard against advances which an adversary might achieve, the possibility of getting round the legal and political inhibitions on certain types of weapons (for example, by developing nauseous gases instead of toxic ones), and the capacity to influence allies and neutrals by the sale of advanced weapons and the transfer of military technology. Expenditure on R & D also serves to maintain a technological base which can support defence programmes and can strengthen and placate various interest groups benefiting from these. Thus, constraints on R & D can result in a variety of consequences, some desirable, some undesirable.[22]

One reason for imposing constraints upon R & D is that these could alleviate concerns about the possible development of weapons which could upset the military balance, with MIRV (Multiple Independently Targetable Re-entry Vehicles) and MARV (Manoeuvrable Re-entry Vehicles) as prime examples.[23] Another is that they might head off 'research races' between adversaries which could lead to suspicion as to

each other's motives and intentions, creating further obstacles to the improvement of East–West relations – to say nothing of the prospect for agreements on the limitation of armaments. A further reason is that they could to some extent lessen the discrepancies between the resources and skills which the super-powers devote to military R & D and those available to the countries of Europe, consequently improving the relative position of European countries. And, as side benefits, constraints may reduce costs and enable civilian authorities to gain a tighter control of programmes for weapons development.

There are a number of problems to be dealt with in any attempt to constrain R & D. Firstly, research in itself is hard to control, since it is impossible to tell what knowledge may be relevant in an uncertain future and to prevent people from having ideas which may affect that future. (How could one conceivably have prevented Einstein developing his equation $E = MC^2$ for the conversion of matter into energy?) Again, if one attempts to impose constraints on a broad front, these will affect a wide range of activities, and lead to consequences which may not be intended, whereas to impose constraints on a narrow field requires accurate knowledge of the 'state of the art' in that field – including the state of the enemy's art. Another difficulty is that asymmetries in both knowledge and methods of research make it hard to design and install measures which would be mutually effective, and hence have any chance at all of being accepted.

The imposition of constraints on development would be just as difficult. Many weapons are being developed for civilian as well as military uses, like nauseating gases, or are the subject of research in both civilian and military laboratories, as is the case with the utilization of lasers for air and missile defences. Furthermore, some of the work on weapons systems carried out in military laboratories might have civilian applications, for example in the use of radar for tracking aircraft. And even if one could differentiate between military and civilian applications it would be impossible, without opening every laboratory to an adversary, to assure him that work on weapons development was not being carried on.

This suggests that new weapons should be caught in the stages between development and testing, or between testing and procurement.

[21] The advantage of this proposal is that it would penalize those countries which keep up or increase their expenditures for defence, whereas the proposals to pay to the United Nations a percentage of monies cut from defence budgets would penalize those which reduce these expenditures.

[22] For many of the ideas in this and subsequent paragraphs I am indebted to Dr Harry G. Gelber of Monash University, Clayton, Victoria, Australia. See Harry G. Gelber: 'Technical Innovation and Arms Control', *World Politics*, vol. XXVI, no. 4 (July 1974).

[23] For a fuller discussion of weapons which could be destabilizing, and why, see Coffey, *Arms Control and European Security*, *op. cit.* in note 6, Chapter III.

Those in the first stage are harder to catch but easier to stop, those in the second easier to catch but more difficult to stop, because one reason for tests is to enable decisions on procurement to be made.

A method of halting development before the testing stage would be by discussing with an adversary those innovations in weaponry which could be destabilizing – as could those leading to a first-strike capability. However, such a method would necessitate revealing to an adversary one's knowledge of potential weapons and concern at their implications, and doing this would imply a significant level of trust in the adversary – which might not necessarily be present. Alternatively, one could pass to that adversary reassuring information about development programmes, and perhaps permit him to monitor certain weapons tests on a reciprocal basis. This, again, might make him a free gift of one's own knowledge and techniques, and it assumes a degree of reciprocity which might be unreal, at least so far as major weapons systems are concerned.

Another possible approach would be to open defence laboratories, on an expanding and reciprocal basis, to visits from and exchanges of scientists and technicians, to the transmission of reports, and so on, as has been suggested by Dr Herbert F. York.[24] If successful, this would have two consequences: it would bring back into the mainstream of scientific endeavour those now engaged in military research; and it would insure both sides against military-technical 'surprises'. Such success would, however, depend on a high degree of trust, on a more or less symmetrical application of the principle, and on a change of heart such that no country would build secret laboratories in unsuspected areas.

All this suggests that, whatever the desirability of measures intended to inhibit weapons development, they may be neither feasible nor acceptable. It also suggests that one must rely primarily on stopping these weapons at the test stage. There are essentially two ways of achieving this. One way is to impose limits on the number of tests or to ban certain types of tests; this would ensure that particular weapons cannot be developed to the point where they could be 'destabilizing' – this being the rationale for constraints on the

testing of MIRV.[25] This can only be effective if it is known which weapons systems are to be headed off. The other way is to permit tests of new weapons, perhaps under conditions and circumstances which would make monitoring by other nations easier, with the aim of precluding production and/or deployment rather than development. This approach has also been taken up at the Strategic Arms Limitations Talks, where both the United States and the Soviet Union undertook to discuss and negotiate limitations on ABM systems based on different physical principles from those now in operation.[26] This, however, allows competition in the development of weaponry until such weapons have been tested, until both sides agree that they may be destabilizing, and until the side with the weapon decides that it is unlikely to secure a significant military or political advantage by going ahead with procurement. While this coincidence of interests may extend to laser missile defences, it remains doubtful whether it will extend to many other weapons.

An alternative approach would eschew openness and selectivity in favour of broad-based constraints, such as cutting funds for R & D. But, as has already been suggested, budgetary constraints are hard to monitor. Moreover, there is no essential correlation between cuts in funds and the development of particular weapons; a country may simply eliminate lower priority projects or concentrate on those where the research is nearer completion and the prospects for success appear more certain. On the other hand, it may make fewer tests before procurement, with consequent effects on knowledge about the reliability of the weapon but with no hindrance to the design, which could, if required, be modified in the light of operational experience.

Probably the best that could be done (aside from limiting the numbers of weapons produced or prohibiting their deployment to particular

[24] 'Controlling the Qualitative Arms Race', in *Bulletin of the Atomic Scientists*, vol. XXIX, no. 3 (March 1973), p. 8.

[25] These could include limitations on numbers of flight tests, which would slow the development of MIRV; restrictions on the missiles which could be equipped with MIRV, with test flights of these missiles monitored to ensure compliance; a requirement that all tests of missiles be conducted over prescribed (and easily monitored) ranges, thereby easing fears of technological surprises, and so on.
[26] Agreed Interpretations concerning the ABM Treaty, *The New York Times* and *Survival, op. cit.* in note II.

areas) would be to adopt a combination of measures which would inhibit the production of new weapons. These might include freer exchanges of information and more extensive discussions of fears arising from technological innovations (it is possible to discuss the potentially undesirable implications of 'mini-nukes' without knowing, or saying, anything about their design). They might encompass limitations on weapons systems based on certain physical principles, as with laser anti-missile systems; even though this stimulated research into ABM based on other principles, the resultant weapons might be less efficient and hence less destabilizing. They could also include a possibly very effective constraint: the provision of advance information concerning tests of agreed types of weapons, coupled with authorization to observe and record such tests. Finally, they could, of course, include bargaining over the construction of such weapons. To a certain extent the United States and the Soviet Union are moving in this direction, but they still have a long way to go, even in the area of strategic weapons systems, and no other country has taken the first step.

Obviously, such measures would have but little effect upon the R & D programmes of the two super-powers: their funds would remain untouched, most of their progress would continue untrammelled, and only a few weapons would meet the criteria of importance and visibility which would warrant (and make possible) the monitoring of test firings. The impact upon military R & D in the countries of Europe would be even smaller, since none of these countries, with the possible exception of France, are building new weapons which might be called 'threatening'. In fact even more stringent controls over European R & D would have but little effect, since these countries depend heavily on both super-powers for advanced weapons and new technology.

This means that the United States and the Soviet Union have it in their power to inhibit weapons development by other countries with fewer resources and smaller research programmes. They could do this first of all by withholding information about technological innovations in weaponry – especially nuclear warheads, 'smart bombs', and active sonar, where R & D might be both costly and difficult.

They could inhibit improvements in the military capabilities of other countries to an even greater extent by limiting the sales or grants to them of advanced equipment. Britain's nuclear force, for example, might be less effective if the United States refused to sell her *Poseidon* SLBM, and the air defences of Czechoslovakia and East Germany might be less efficient if the Soviet Union denied them SA-3 surface-to-air missiles. If, however, such restrictions are to be constructive rather than destructive, they would require a definition of areas where shifts in military capabilities presented a threat to European peace and security. More importantly, they would require a common awareness of this threat, sufficient to overcome all the influences working for the sale or transfer of military equipment. And they would require a system of monitoring which would comprehend not only weapons sales but also transfers of information – something much easier to conceal.

It is, therefore, difficult to imagine that the super-powers would apply such limitations to any extent. For one thing, their refusal to sell advanced weapons to their allies could have serious military – and political – consequences. Furthermore, such sales are sources of revenue for both the United States and the Soviet Union, help to keep their own production lines going, and are, in Eastern Europe at least, a major contribution towards the standardization of equipment. Moreover, there is a tendency among the advanced countries to co-operate in research, development and procurement projects, something which restrictions on the transfer of technology could curtail. Lastly, countries providing weapons and information gain some influence over countries acquiring them, and a certain control over the ways in which they may be used – advantages they might well be reluctant to forego.

## Evaluation

It would, therefore, seem that most of the measures intended to constrain armed forces and their capabilities bear more thorns than fruit, in the sense that their potential advantages are more than offset by the undoubted difficulties of implementing them, and by their asymmetrical effects upon the states which might be involved. Moreover, the interests of these states differ; the United States and the Soviet Union are seeking maximum flexibility in their defence establishments and are primarily concerned in bargaining with one another, while the lesser powers are uncomfortable about super-power 'decisions' and would like to impose constraints on the super-powers to match or offset any that they may accept in the course of mutual force reductions.

This means that there may be some pressure towards the establishment of force ceilings, with all their imperfections. The Warsaw Pact is certainly interested in setting overall ceilings which would help to equalize the numbers of men in the armed forces, where NATO still has a numerical edge of about 550,000 men[27] despite major cuts in American strength following the end of the Vietnam war. At the same time, certain of the Western Allies recognize that force ceilings afford one way of imposing constraints on the Soviet Union, and also that the ability of NATO to bargain over such force ceilings might diminish if and when changes in force structures like those proposed for West Germany come into effect.[28]

NATO is, however, likely to resist efforts to establish over-all force ceilings which would erode its advantage in numbers, for three reasons. The first is that some of the men in these NATO totals are largely irrelevant to any conflict in Europe (for example, the bulk of the Portuguese troops have been deployed in Africa, armed and organized for anti-guerrilla operations: they would not be effective in Europe unless re-equipped with heavy weapons and re-trained). The second is the belief that the present imbalances are needed to rectify geographical differences between the alliances, differences which require some NATO member countries to keep troops in distant areas and all of them to maintain much

larger navies than the contiguous and largely land-locked countries of the Warsaw Pact need. The third reason is, of course, that it is impossible to verify such force ceilings, even if one is talking only about counting men in uniform.

Conversely, there is no good reason for the members of the Warsaw Pact to accept force ceilings which would perpetuate such disparities, especially since they are being asked to cut back their troops in Europe disproportionately under mutual force reductions.[29] As the Soviet Union has noted, geography also imposes hardships on her, and she also must keep large numbers of troops in distant areas, notably along the frontier with China.[30] Thus the best one can hope for in the near future is force ceilings which would apply to specific regions, such as Central Europe, or perhaps to larger areas where the forces of the two alliances are in reasonable balance, as might be the case if the example of Charles de Gaulle was followed and one looked at the territory stretching 'from the Atlantic to the Urals'.[31]

Whether or not regional force ceilings are established, the super-powers (and especially the United States) would find it difficult to argue that their forces should remain intact while those of other countries are reduced. Moreover, there are economic reasons why each super-power might like to cut its own forces, and there are psychological, as well as military, incentives to seek reductions in the troop strength of the other. It is, therefore, conceivable that the United States and the Soviet Union might be willing to

[27] According to *The Military Balance 1974–1975*, table 6, p. 82. NATO has 5,150,000 men under arms (including those of Portugal), and the Warsaw Pact 4,600,000 – exclusive, in both cases, of border guards and other para-military forces.
[28] These would expand the Army from 33 to 36 brigades but would simultaneously reduce manning levels in the companies and battalions comprising twelve of these brigades. The net result would be to cut active duty personnel by 30,000 men (about 6 per cent), this phase-down being accompanied by a corresponding increase in the number of trained reservists available for immediate recall. See *The Bulletin* [of the Press and Information Office of the Federal Republic of Germany], vol. 21, no. 43 (4 December 1973), p. 332.

[29] According to press reports NATO has proposed reductions intended to achieve balanced (i.e., equal) ground forces in Central Europe. These would involve cuts of approximately 75,000 in NATO troop strength compared to almost 180,000 for the Warsaw Pact. See *The New York Times*, 16 September 1973, p. 4, and 31 October 1973, p. 12.
[30] Y. Kostko, 'Mutual Force Reductions in Europe', *Mirovaya Ekonomika I Mezhdunarodniye Otnosheniya*, June 1972, translated and reprinted in *Survival*, vol. XIV, no. 5 (September/October 1972), pp. 236–38.
[31] NATO forces in Europe – excluding the 83,000 Portuguese troops not deployed overseas – total approximately 2·9 million men, compared to about 1·7 million for the Warsaw Pact. Although the Soviet Union probably has more than half of the remaining 2·9 million men in her armed forces deployed west of the Urals, the difference in total strengths within the area is not so great as to rule out a possible decrease in Soviet force levels or some form of accommodation, such as the transfer to Central Siberia of a dozen Soviet divisions.

make phased cuts in their own military establishments, perhaps in the following manner:

(1) the demobilization of any units or men withdrawn from Europe pursuant to agreements on force reductions;
(2) small annual cuts for a prescribed period of years.

The net result of (1) under any of the proposals for MFR advanced so far would be to diminish the Soviet advantage in numbers of men under arms, presently of the order of 3 : 2 over the United States. The net result of (2) would be to establish *de facto* ceilings on an asymmetrical basis, the degree of asymmetry depending both on the magnitude of the cuts, and on whether they were made on a proportional or an equal basis. Although NATO might prefer the former, it should, given the overall balance in its favour and the desirability of placing some constraints on Soviet military manpower, settle for the latter – especially since the United States may continue to cut her troop strength anyway.[32]

As mentioned above, overall force ceilings, or those covering very large areas and forces, will be more important psychologically than militarily, since there are many ways of offsetting the effects of constraints on the number of men under active service and also serious difficulties in monitoring the effectiveness (and effects) of these constraints. To some extent, the military impact of any force ceilings could be enhanced by agreement on ancillary measures, such as the provision of information concerning the induction and release of conscripts, or the imposition of limits on the call-up of reservists. By and large, however, the problems of establishing and verifying limitations on numbers of men under arms are so enormous that such value as they may have is very limited.

Ceilings on classes of weapons are a more promising approach, partly because these are easier to implement technically, and partly because of the precedent set by SALT. With weapons ceilings, however, one comes up against the problem that the interests of the two alliances are very different. Above all, the Warsaw Pact would presumably like ceilings on, or cuts in, NATO tactical nuclear delivery vehicles, especially strike aircraft. In addition, the Soviet Union has indicated some desire to safeguard her missile-submarines, whose vulnerability could be decreased if NATO anti-submarine warfare (ASW) forces were constrained.[33] Moreover, the Soviet Union may have a special interest in restricting the number of American aircraft-carriers, which give the United States an advantage in any naval conflict and enable her to support military operations in distant areas.

Obviously, NATO would prefer to keep these weapons intact, since the land-based and carrier-borne aircraft outside Europe can quickly be redeployed to that area, should the need arise, and the ASW forces are considered essential to keep the sea lanes open. If weapons ceilings are to be imposed, NATO would presumably like them to cover tanks, guns and attack submarines, and not fighter-bombers, escort vessels and other categories of weapons in which it has both an advantage and a military reason for maintaining such advantage.

At first sight, this would seem to render unlikely the imposition of a ceiling on weapons, even if the problem of ascertaining the number of tanks and guns in the possession of an adversary could be solved. There may, however, be some overlapping interests which could lead to the establishment of a ceiling on selected classes of weapons which are more easily verifiable. Among these might be:

(1) Asymmetrical ceilings on submarine-launched cruise missiles (SLCM), with the United States allowed perhaps half as many as the Soviet Union[34] and with the understanding that if the Soviet Union scrapped some of her submarines the United States would refrain from building an equal number of those she could otherwise construct. At the very least,

[32] The strength of the American armed forces went down by 140,000 in FY 1973. It is scheduled to drop by another 78,000 in FY 1974 and by 22,000 more in FY 1975, i.e., by 30 June 1975. *Report of Secretary of Defense James R. Schlesinger to the Congress on the FY 1975 Defense Budget and FY 1975–1979 Defense Program*, 4 March 1974, mimeograph (hereafter cited as *Schlesinger Statement, 1974*), table 3, p. 237.

[33] *The Washington Post*, 19 November 1972, p. A-26. According to Joseph Kruzel, they also introduced during SALT I the idea of establishing sanctuaries for missile submarines. See 'SALT II: The Search for a Follow-on Agreement', *Orbis*, vol. XVII, no. 2 (Summer 1973), p. 353.

[34] As of mid-1973 the Soviet Union had 314 SLCM, carried on 40 nuclear-powered and 25 diesel-engined submarines (*The Military Balance 1974–1975*, pp. 9 and 73).

this would set limits to any American programme for the deployment of SLCM, while if the Soviet Union chose to take out of service any of her missile-carrying submarines it would also reduce her capability for attacking both civilian ships and naval vessels, including submarines.[35]

(2) An upper limit on the number of aircraft carriers the Soviet Union might construct, in return for which the United States would continue her temporarily deferred phase-down from fifteen attack carriers to twelve and would observe the same limitation on the number of 'sea control carriers'[36] she would build as the Soviet Union did with her somewhat larger Moskva-class ships. Although this would leave the United States with an advantage (and NATO in general with an even greater one), it would restrain the West from acquiring still sharper teeth, since the United States plans to construct eight 'sea control carriers' and the Soviet Union has only two such ships afloat.[37] In any case, some ceiling on the number of Soviet carriers would seem a fair exchange for a ceiling on American submarines with SLCM which, like their Soviet counterparts, could presumably double as 'hunter-killers', if required to fulfil that function.

(3) Rather tight ceilings on the numbers of attack submarines, this time on a NATO–Warsaw Pact basis. At this moment, the two alliances have almost equal numbers of attack submarines, with the advantage on the side of the Warsaw Pact when submarines carrying SLCM are also included.[38] If these fleets could be kept at present levels (plus that augmentation needed to cover the American SLCM already mentioned), and old submarines could be scrapped as new ones were built, the Soviet Union would benefit in terms of the survivability of her missile submarines, while the Western Alliance would benefit in terms of reduced vulnerability of surface ships and convoys. Given this, it is conceivable that ceilings on the numbers of attack submarines could have a 'ripple' effect, with NATO reducing or freezing its ASW forces, rather than further expanding them,[39] and the Warsaw Pact continuing to reduce its submarine fleet, the consequence being a heading-off of the deployment of American SLCM. (Indeed, this area is so promising for a multitude of reasons that it might well be the subject of special negotiation leading to reductions in present forces rather than restraints on the increase in numbers.)

All this is, of course, highly problematical. Moreover, even if it came to pass, it would at best freeze certain types of ships, and might do no more than limit increases in these categories. Given, however, the asymmetrical interests of the two alliances and their differing perceptions of threat, a limited freeze to the number of warships is about as much as can be expected – or even desired – at the first stage of an attempt to impose ceilings on classes of weapons.

Greater pressure for constraints on budgets than for ceilings on weapons might be expected; some of this pressure will come from countries which can control their own price structures, and hence manipulate their defence costs, like the member countries of the Warsaw Pact – in 1973 the Soviet Foreign Minister, Mr Gromyko,

---

[35] According to the Chairman of the United States Joint Chiefs of Staff, Soviet submarines carrying SLCM can employ torpedoes and mines against other submarines (Moorer Statement 1973, p. 39).

[36] These are planned to be comparatively small carriers of about 14,000 tons, equipped with ASW helicopters and V/STOL (vertical or short take-off and landing) aircraft. Their primary mission would be to escort convoys unprotected by attack carriers, their secondary missions fleet protection and support of landing operations on lightly-defended coasts. See the article in the Washington Post, 7 January 1974, p. 1, which outlines the programme and refers to its advocacy by the US Chief of Naval Operations, Admiral Elmo R. Zumwalt, Jr.

[37] The projected size and composition of the United States carrier forces is detailed in the Schlesinger Statement 1974, pp. 118–22. The Soviet Union has, as noted above, two ASW helicopter cruisers (the Moskva and the Leningrad) and has under construction two true carriers of about 40,000 tons each (ibid., p. 94).

[38] As of mid-1973, NATO had 67 nuclear-powered attack submarines and 139 diesel-engined ones and the Warsaw Pact 35 nuclear-powered and 202 diesel-engined attack submarines (exclusive of the 55 submarines armed with SLCM which, as indicated earlier, could function in a dual capacity). Not all of these on either side are ocean-going, and, of course, not all of them would be available for operations in European waters.

[39] Anti-submarine warfare was one of the areas singled out under the European Defence Improvement Programme (EDIP), on which the West Europeans are spending approximately $1·5 billion annually. It is also an area wherein the United States is preparing to expand her efforts, at an increase in costs from $2·6 billion to $3·6 billion per year (The New York Times, 17 January 1974, p. 12).

proposed to the United Nations a 10 per cent reduction in all defence expenditure.[40] More pressure will come from Third World countries, which see such constraints as both curbing the growth of super-power military capabilities and making resources available for foreign aid and investment to their advantage. Most of the pressure will come from the ordinary public, which may see budgetary constraints as acting as a curb to the military both in its domestic context and in its role as an arm of foreign policy, thus enabling a greater allocation of resources to be made for non-defence programmes – an attitude particularly strong in Western countries.

A probable reaction might be a series of pledges by various NATO or Warsaw Pact countries to freeze their budgets as percentages of GNP or in terms of constant dollars. Strenuous efforts might be made to hold down increases in costs, perhaps through tacit bargaining; to take one instance, the United States might announce that, all else being equal, she would have had to increase next year's defence budget by 5 billion dollars but that, thanks to self-imposed limitations on the Soviet defence budget, she will only require an additional 2 billion dollars. There might also be token reductions in defence budgets (although the trend in many countries is away from this)[41] or diversions of resources from them in the form of payments to the United Nations, as suggested earlier. However, in view of the unworkability of budgetary constraints and of their markedly unequal effects on different countries, little progress can be expected here.

The same could be said of controls on research and development, not because these are in themselves undesirable but because they are highly unlikely. Moreover, the individual interests of countries tend to move them in markedly different directions. Most of the Western Allies would like to modernize their armed forces but to inhibit the Warsaw Pact countries from doing likewise – probably the reverse is also true. Nor are the European members of NATO likely to accept restrictions either on their own research or on the transfer of technology, resulting in their falling further behind in military capacity or in handicapping the establishment of a European Nuclear Force. The United States may wish to maintain disparities in certain fields, like nuclear weapons technology, but not in, say, air-defence radar.

Given both the technical and the political obstacles to the imposition of realistic constraints on research and development, one might have to settle for something less. This 'something less' should at the very least consist of arrangements to define those categories, or types of weapons, which could have a destabilizing effect, either because they could alter the military balance significantly or because of their psychological impact. This process could be undertaken by a Committee on European Security, if one were established, by the Twenty-Five Nation Disarmament Committee or by *ad hoc* groups including the five nuclear powers – though not, at any rate for the present, all in the same group! The participant countries should also make provision for the monitoring of weapons tests which fall into the designated categories, perhaps by the super-powers themselves, with the results being made available to each country, or by relatively small teams with the super-powers contributing personnel and equipment. They should also try to develop an understanding that, should weapons falling into the dangerous categories be tested, negotiations in an appropriate forum would be opened immediately on measures to preclude their production or deployment.

Although other restrictions might be imposed, they do not seem very probable – nor really at all rewarding. Whether we like it or not, we must look to internal economic, political and bureaucratic pressures, and to interactions between East and West to set limits on the sizes and the capabilities of the armed forces of the two alliances. In this case, at least, arms control will follow *détente*, not precede it.

---

[40] *The New York Times*, 26 September 1973, p. 2.
[41] For example, the United States Department of Defense is requesting for FY 1975 $92·6 billion in obligational authority and $85·8 billion in projected expenditures, an increase of $6·3 billion over FY 1974. In addition it will seek a supplemental appropriation for FY 1974 of $6·2 billion (*Schlesinger Statement, 1974*, pp. 16–19). About half of these amounts will go simply for pay increases, which illustrates the difficulty of controlling military expenditures, let alone curtailing them.

Limiting the size and the capabilities of armed forces is admittedly the most permanent way of reducing their utility, but not the only one. It can also be achieved by precluding the establishment of new bases, by imposing restrictions on deployment and by requiring advance notice of major troop movements, of the conduct of manoeuvres and so forth. As I suggested earlier, such measures can inhibit the application of force, an achievement which may be all the more significant in view of the difficulty of constraining military capabilities. More importantly, they might increase confidence in the intent of an adversary, and hence enhance a country's sense of security – as most recently shown by the restrictions on the deployment of Egyptian and Israeli troops and weapons in the area east of the Suez Canal. In this section, therefore, I will look at the attractions and the disadvantages of these kinds of measures, with particular reference to their possible application in Europe and to the forces of the two super-powers in other parts of the world.

## Precluding the Establishment of New Bases

Bases in other countries can obviously serve a variety of purposes. They can provide facilities for overhauling ships and other major items of equipment, obviating the need for returning them home for rehabilitation. They can provide for the storage of arms and equipment which might be urgently required in areas far from the source of supply. They can house troops which might be needed to defend an ally, or can service aircraft shadowing the movement of naval vessels. They can serve as communications centres, as places from which to monitor test firings of missiles, or as sites for carrying out these and similar tests. In a variety of ways, then, bases overseas both extend and multiply military capabilities.

They may also extend and multiply political influence. This follows in part from the common interests and the shared perceptions of threat which led initially to the establishment of such bases. It reflects the fact that the mere presence of foreign troops enables the state providing them to limit the options open to the host country. It stems also from the money spent and the opportunities for employment offered at

these bases, and from the economic and military aid which almost invariably accompanies their establishment. And, while this influence is by no means one-sided, it may be important enough to justify the retention of bases long after their military usefulness has declined.

In the post-war period it was the Western Allies – and in particular the United States – who built and manned such bases, and the Soviet Union who protested at this activity. She tended to see these bases as being directed against herself (as in some sense they were, particularly during the early 1950s) and to inveigh against the 'ring of steel' which the 'imperialists' were attempting to forge around her. Partly for military reasons, therefore, and partly for political and psychological ones, she has called over the years for the withdrawal of all foreign troops and for the abolition or curtailment of bases on foreign soil. The Soviet Union, moreover, put pressure on different countries to revoke the base rights granted to the Western Allies or to restrict their use, as did Mr Khrushchev when he threatened to bomb the Pakistani airfield from which U-2 reconnaissance planes took off for their flights over the Soviet Union.

In the past, the members of the Western Alliance have rebuffed or turned a deaf ear to these threats and have encouraged their supporters in the Third World to resist Soviet pressures. The situation has, however, changed. With the granting of independence to most colonial areas, and with the accession to power there of nationalist governments, Western base rights have been cancelled or curtailed, as in the case of Algeria, Libya, and Kenya. The facilities which the Western Allies are now building are on a relatively small scale and for specialized purposes. Furthermore, the United States, which has easily the most, and the most widely scattered, of these bases, has been voluntarily relinquishing or reducing some of them in accordance with the 'Nixon Doctrine' for the Pacific. At present it is the Soviet Union which is probably interested in finding air and naval bases, to replace those lost in Egypt, to substitute for the open anchorages occupied by her Mediterranean flotilla, and the better to enable her to maintain a sizeable naval presence in the Persian Gulf and the Indian

Ocean. Should she significantly extend her system of bases, this might induce intensified counter-action by the West and could lead to political confrontations (if not military ones) east of Suez, where the Soviet Union is already diplomatically and economically active.

It is obviously too much to expect that the Soviet Union will give up her efforts to penetrate this or other areas, but the undesirable consequences of emphasizing the military aspects of Soviet foreign policy and the difficulty of maintaining an effective military presence in the face of Western opposition may incline her to proceed cautiously. Equally, it is perhaps too much to expect the members of the Western Alliance to abandon their bases, a measure which, if taken literally, could mean the end for American troop deployments in Europe. However, the problems confronting the West, in the Mediterranean and elsewhere, are so severe that some members of the Alliance might be willing to strike a bargain with the Soviet Union over bases. In this way both sides could proceed, tacitly if not formally, to alter the nature of any competition for influence and to minimize the possibilities of confrontations which would extend back into Europe itself.

Although any such bargains can only be in the realm of hypothesis, it would seem that it might be in the interests of both sides:

(1) to recognize the existence of areas considered vital to each, where they would not establish new bases, as distinct from naval forces on more or less permanent station;

(2) to refrain from deploying to these areas selected weapons which might be considered particularly threatening by the other side: a move which could preclude the reappearance of Soviet missile submarines off Cuba, the basing of American A-7D strike aircraft in Greece or Turkey, and the stockpiling of nuclear warheads in any additional countries;

(3) to give notice of changes in deployment patterns at existing bases, where these would involve major shifts in the numbers of men and arms there;

(4) to discuss in advance the establishment of any new bases, explaining their nature, their purpose and the duration of the period for which they would be active.

This could conceivably lead ultimately to a ban

on all new bases (at least where these are to house combat elements, as distinct from units concerned with communications and supply) and to a phase-down of selected Western bases in areas close to the Soviet Union.

If such a bargain were struck it could markedly alleviate Western concerns at the establishment of Soviet bases in such key places as Mers-el-Kebir and Aden, and could reduce worries about possible Soviet naval operations in the Persian Gulf. It could head off tests of determination such as occurred in 1971, with the 'on-off' construction of shore facilities in Cuba for Soviet submarines. On the other hand, it could enable the Soviet Union to preclude any build-up of American strike-aircraft in the Eastern Mediterranean, or any establishment of a base for American missile submarines in the Indian Ocean, so lessening her perception of threat.

Admittedly, both sides would have problems with such a bargain – one being the difficulty of reaching agreement on those areas designated as vital. More specifically, the Soviet Union might have to sacrifice not only some of her ability to exercise political influence, but also something of her capability for counter-intervention or for operations against American missile submarines. Moreover, she would, virtually of necessity, have to accept asymmetries in base structures, since she is a late-comer in establishing overseas bases. As for the United States, on whom the brunt of the constraints would fall, she might have to resort to more expensive and time-consuming measures for the maintenance of naval forces in distant waters, and would certainly lose some of her capacity for reassuring anxious allies or influencing doubtful neutrals. And those allies who are already anxious might become more so, even if the restrictions on the redeployment of American forces were not so tight as to prevent demonstrations of support in the event of a new crisis in the area.

It may be hoped, however, that the measures I have outlined could serve to avoid confrontation and to induce restraint in the exercise of force, thus obviating the likelihood of the agreement restricting the establishment and use of bases – and other agreements as well – being denounced. Furthermore, one may hope that such measures might establish a pattern of co-operation having implications far beyond the geographical and technical areas initially covered. For example, restrictions on a permanent military presence in 'vital' areas could be extended to elements not covered in the initial agreement, for example naval forces. Inhibitions on the deployment of 'threatening' weapons to new areas considered vital could be applied to old areas like Central Europe. Additionally, notification of changes in deployment patterns at existing bases outside Europe could also extend to those countries in Europe where troops are currently stationed.

## Setting up Restricted Areas

As I suggested above, there are undoubtedly geographical areas which may be vital for the security of NATO and the Warsaw Pact, either because denial of access would cripple members economically – as in the case of a Soviet blockade of the Persian Gulf – or because an enemy presence in the area would constitute a clear and present danger – as would stationing American air and naval forces in northern Norway. The establishment of even narrow zones from which particular forces would be barred, or within which particular types of weapons could not be deployed, could provide reassurance as to enemy capabilities – and hence, in this suspicious world, as to enemy intentions. Broader restrictions, either on a unilateral or an agreed basis, could have even more important effects on capabilities and more favourable ones on perceptions of intentions.

One measure which could have these effects would be the imposition of restrictions on the deployment of offensive ground force units along the borders between two countries. As an illustration, the deployment of tank divisions well to the rear means that they are both less menacing to an opponent and better positioned for a defensive role, which might involve their moving to threatened parts of the front once fighting began. To a lesser extent this is also true of self-propelled artillery, units transporting mobile bridges and all those other elements essential for the support and maintenance of offensive operations; in fact, their concentration in forward areas is generally considered as an indication that an attack is imminent, and consequently as a cause for concern. Similarly, landing craft which are only four to eight hours away from prospective target areas are more

of a threat than those at a greater distance, and amphibious troops kept close to these landing craft (and hence ready for action) may appear more threatening than those which are dispersed. Again, short-range nuclear-capable delivery vehicles deployed at some distance from frontiers are less able to shatter enemy strong points and pave the way for assaults by mobile forces, and may therefore seem less of a danger.

To some extent, restrictions on the forward deployment of aircraft can have a similar effect. If strike aircraft are based far to the rear, this means that they cannot reach certain targets without redeploying, a factor which reduces both military utility and psychological visibility. Furthermore, even if they attack without redeploying, an adversary will have longer warning of their employment than he would if they were stationed well forward, and can conceivably prevent their penetrating deeply into his air space, with or without nuclear weapons. On both these counts, rearward basing has a more reassuring aspect. As an illustration, the hundred-odd Soviet light bombers stationed in the western Soviet Union are less of a threat to NATO than are their counterparts in central and southern Europe. Similarly, the aircraft aboard an American aircraft carrier deployed in the western Mediterranean are less of a threat to the Soviet Union than those on one in the Aegean Sea. (Admittedly, the carrier in the western Mediterranean is less reassuring to the allies in the eastern Mediterranean and less able to enter into action quickly, should this be required; however, it may be possible to give reassurances, without losing all the advantages of carrier-borne aircraft, by reducing the complement of planes when the ship sails into certain restricted waters.)

However, given the mobility of aircraft (and, to a lesser extent, of ships which carry them), restrictions on forward deployment may have to be complemented by limitations on military aircraft stationed in a particular theatre. The observance of ceilings on numbers of aircraft in a region, and the avoidance of unexplained fluctuations in numbers (such as precede an attack or go with an attempt to overawe an opponent) may both be helpful in reassuring that opponent. And even those who take little comfort from these efforts to be reassuring may find this disadvantage offset by the ability to communicate intent and to signal resolve in time of crisis by the redeployment of aircraft.

Restrictions on the deployment of naval forces could present more considerable difficulties. For one thing, these forces are to some extent tied to bases, which means that they cannot be denied access to, or passage through, the seas adjacent to those bases. Another reason is that they must in some instances be kept in waters distant from their homelands if they are to protect these from attack, as is the case with the Soviet Northern Fleet, which has a mission of precluding strikes by American, British and French missile-submarines. A third reason is that the political utility and visibility of warships is so high that even minor changes in deployments tend to be viewed as important.

This gives all the more support for avoiding movements which could have disruptive effects, such as the entry of Soviet submarines into Norwegian fjords. It points towards the establishment of both 'sanctuaries' (where only certain types of warship would be permitted) and restricted areas, from which particular types of ships would be barred, except for the right of innocent passage after advance notice has been given. And it suggests that these restricted areas be set up in such a manner as to minimize possible confrontations between opposing navies: for example, by establishing parallel but distant east–west channels through the Mediterranean for the use of the Soviet and American squadrons there.

Restrictions on deployments should apply particularly to any troops, planes or other weapons removed from Europe. Certainly the Soviet Union would not be happy if American fighter-bombers taken from Western Europe were transferred to Japan, any more than Norway would be if two Soviet divisions withdrawn from West Germany ended up on the Kola Peninsula. In the case of the Soviet Union one might go further and say that the stationing of these divisions deep inside the country would have favourable psychological consequences, even though, given the size of the forces already garrisoned in the western Soviet Union, this might not significantly affect Soviet military capabilities. In short, restrictions on the redeployment of units involved in force reductions might be even more significant than restraints on elements not so involved.

Of similar consequence would be measures for restricting military and naval exercises. Prohibiting manoeuvres in border areas could diminish fears that these manoeuvres could cloak a surprise attack; even if such restrictions inconvenienced military commanders (as the loss of tank ranges in West Germany near the zonal boundary might do), such inconvenience might be overshadowed by their reassuring effect. Setting ceilings on the sizes of manoeuvre forces in forward areas could also help, as those involving 40,000 men may not seem nearly as threatening as those involving 200,000. So could limiting the time span within which manoeuvres are carried out, in order that such manoeuvres could not be used to justify a semi-permanent troop build-up, or to buttress political pressures against another state, as in the summer before the Soviet occupation of Czechoslovakia. And so, of course, could restrictions on the types of forces engaged in manoeuvres – those bringing offensive weapons and elements near the frontiers of another country being obviously more of a threat, as would be the case in the off-loading of Soviet naval infantry near the Norwegian coast, or the movement of American aircraft carriers into the Sea of Okhotsk.

All this is not to say that restrictions on the deployment of forces and constraints on the introduction of weapons have no drawbacks. The partial demilitarization of border areas, or limitations on the size and number of weapons therein, may weaken defences against probes or incursions. Restrictions on the forward deployment of aircraft and naval vessels could reduce the ability to cope with a surprise attack, as well as the ability to launch one. Inhibitions on the redeployment of units may preclude moves which could be reassuring to an ally in a crisis not caused or marked by a military build-up on the part of the adversary (in other words a crisis similar to those which have frequently occurred at Berlin). Furthermore, all these types of constraint may operate unevenly because of military and geographic asymmetries between the two alliances. More importantly, they may have different political and psychological consequences, since each alliance has perceptions of the other which will influence its reactions. It may, however, be possible to test such restrictions in a limited area, extending them if they prove fruitful, halting them if not.

## Monitoring Deployment Restrictions

Along with the imposition of restrictions on deployment should go measures to monitor them. In view of the depth of fears and suspicions in Europe, no country is likely to rely on the word of another that it is faithfully observing all limitations on the deployment of forces. Moreover, given the fact that many of these limitations may be self-imposed, or may be the result of tacit bargaining rather than formal agreement, their implementation may be imprecise and their application misunderstood. It would therefore seem useful to arrange for a flow of information and communication which could minimize uncertainties and allay fears.

Perhaps the easiest way of doing this would be by providing reassuring information. If, for example, country X questioned whether country Y had really withdrawn all tanks from a prescribed border zone, Y could transmit to X aerial photographs of the zone, the validity and timing of which could readily be verified. If the photographs showed no tanks, X would know either that they had not been there at all or that they had been removed before the photographs were taken – which would be a gain of sorts. Alternatively, Y could announce the location of the units suspected of being in the border area, inviting observers from X (or Z) to verify that they were in fact elsewhere. In these and other ways, one state could put to rest the doubts of another without establishing extensive and extra-national inspection systems.

Such reassurance could be more meaningful, and restrictions on deployment more effective, if manoeuvres were announced well in advance (so that they could not be associated with particular crises) and if notice were given of major changes in troop levels in a given area. The movement of two or three Soviet divisions from the Oder to the lower Elbe might not be important to the Russians but would be to the Danes, just as the dispatch of two additional wings of American fighter-bombers to Western Europe would be important to the members of the Warsaw Pact. Where these movements are routine, nothing will be lost by informing the world of what will happen; where they are deliberately designed to indicate determination, something may well be gained. And, while notices of troop movements can be used to influence crisis outcomes (as was the American announcement of the dispatch of reinforcements to the Seventh Fleet in 1958 during the Quemoy crisis), the fact that they can be used to unnerve an adversary argues all the more strongly for not doing so inadvertently.

Additionally, confidence in the effectiveness of restrictions would be increased if the manoeuvres themselves were monitored by observers, or the larger areas covered by deployment restrictions were open to inspection by liaison missions. While in either case these measures could help in the gathering of intelligence – which all military commanders want for themselves but wish to deny to their adversaries – they could also serve to verify troop and weapons levels and to insure compliance with either agreed or self-imposed constraints on deployments. They could provide information independent of that gathered by national intelligence agencies, which would possibly be more meaningful politically. In time, as these observation teams increased in status (and perhaps took on a multi-national character), they could increase the political obstacles to employment of force by giving clear evidence of the responsibility for violations of deployment restrictions.

Finally – and the sequence is deliberate – provision could be made for verification by national means, such as aerial observation. To a certain extent this could be accomplished by agreement not to interfere with aircraft with side-looking radar flying along (but not over) borders, and three (or twelve) miles from coastal frontiers. It could also be done by allowing either periodic overflights of given areas (such as border zones) or a small number of 'on call' flights through these zones, along main lines of communication or over certain prescribed areas which might serve as jump-off points for attacks or sites for the build-up of supplies and equipment. The aim here would be to complement other national means of verification (such as the establishment of observation posts and the use of reconnaissance satellites) in ways which would provide the maximum of reassurance against gross violations of restrictions on deployments without at the same time acquiring the sort of detailed information about weapons systems and military installations which has, quite understandably, been regarded as unacceptable.

25

Aside from this last possibility, it is hard to see drawbacks to the measures proposed, which are both modest and non-intrusive. This judgement is, however, based on another: that both the countries of Europe and the super-powers are willing to give up certain uses of force in the interest of enhancing security. This may be so in principle, but in practice it may not hold, since definitions of security may differ and beliefs in the utility of force persist.[42] Thus, the major question concerning both the monitoring of deployment restrictions and the restrictions themselves is how acceptable they might be.

### Acceptability of Restrictions
In the past the Soviet Union and her allies have made strenuous efforts to create nuclear-free zones, to preclude the movement of Western naval vessels through contiguous waters, such as the Black Sea, to bring about the dismantling of bases and to arrange for the withdrawal of all foreign troops to their respective homelands. It is unlikely that this latter proposal will be pushed as hard in the future as it was in the past, since this is happening anyway (at least outside Europe) and since the Soviet Union may not be as ready to reciprocate as she was ten or fifteen years ago. She may, in fact, be less anxious now to see a complete withdrawal of American forces from Europe, partly because they may exert a stabilizing influence and partly because their presence may be reassuring to the other members of NATO – contributing in both ways to the security of the Soviet Union and her allies in Eastern Europe. The Warsaw Pact may still, however, be interested in preventing the establishment of new Western bases and reducing the number of old ones, for which reasons it may espouse arrangements like those suggested earlier, which could speed up the process of withdrawal and would at least limit the uses to which remaining bases could be put.

---

[42] They seem to have persisted in the American–Soviet crisis of 24–25 October 1973, which arose out of an apparent threat by the Soviet Union to intervene unilaterally in the Egyptian–Israeli conflict if the United States did not preclude Israel from exploiting further the military successes gained after the initial (and abortive) armistice of 22 October, leading the United States to place all her forces, including the Strategic Air Command and the *Polaris/Poseidon* fleet, on a state of alert. See the articles by Bernard Gwertzman and Hedrick Smith in *The New York Times*, 31 October 1973, p. 17.

Presumably the members of the Warsaw Pact would still wish to impose restrictions on the NATO forces remaining in Europe or abutting on their frontiers elsewhere, and on the weapons with which these are armed. If they cannot get agreement on the establishment of broad nuclear-free zones (or weapons-free zones) they might accept narrow ones. They may be willing to engage in tacit bargaining about the deployment of troops and weapons within their own territories and those of NATO countries. Furthermore, the Soviet Union has already indicated that she is willing to give advance notice of manoeuvres (if not of troop movements) and that she will allow 'observers from other states to attend military manoeuvres under mutually acceptable conditions'.[43] It is perhaps not too far from this to agreements to instal observation posts (another long-standing Soviet proposal) and to the acceptance of other means of verifying restrictions on deployment – at least so long as these are small-scale, unobtrusive and not sponsored by the United Nations or some international disarmament organization.

In the past the West has been cool to demilitarized zones, nuclear-free zones, 'seas of peace', and other deployment restrictions – all of which it saw as efforts to reduce Western military power, to inhibit freedom of movement, and to expose some of the Allies to new threats and pressures. It will probably continue to oppose large-scale arrangements such as a Scandinavian Nuclear-Free Zone, but it may be willing to readjust its own ground and air force deployments within the European region in return for similar adjustments by the Warsaw Pact – at any rate so long as these do not rule out a more integrated defence of Western Europe. It may also be willing to experiment with narrow weapons-free zones – if not along the boundary between East and West Germany, then along other frontiers, such as those between West Germany and Czechoslovakia or Norway and the Soviet Union. Restraints on the deployment of naval forces may be less acceptable, partly because of traditional attitudes towards the freedom of the seas, partly because of concern over establishing a precedent, as in the British–Icelandic dispute over the unilateral extension

---

[43] Speech of Soviet Foreign Minister Andrei Gromyko at Helsinki, 3 July 1973 (*The Guardian*, 4 July 1973, p. 2).

of fishing rights. It is, however, possible that the West would agree to an interpretation of the rules of the sea along the lines of the American–Soviet agreement of 1972, which would minimize the chance of inadvertent confrontations between NATO and Warsaw Pact naval forces.

It is also possible that the allies would be willing to give advance notice of troop movements on a reciprocal basis. However, a favourable response apparently hinges on the resolution of other issues, such as the area to be included. There would seem to be no problems in giving notification of manoeuvres, in holding them in areas away from frontiers and in inviting observers to attend them, since all of these ideas have been advanced in previous Western proposals. Nor would the Allies find it difficult to adopt reasonable measures to monitor any weapons-free zones that might be established, including installing observers, establishing over-flying rights, and so on – all of which they have endorsed in times past.

The Western attitude towards bases may be somewhat different. Whatever the desirability of precluding any additional Soviet bases in the Near and Middle East, or any new ones on the North African littoral, there is no sign that the West is willing to limit its own establishments in order to achieve this. It is conceivable that it would be willing to withhold counter-deployments on the ground that these are not needed militarily or that they would be unduly disturbing politically. At the moment, however, there are no indications that the West would do this much on a unified basis, much less that it would forgo its own freedom to redeploy forces, which is viewed both as valuable in the management of crises and as essential to the operation of a European Defence Force, should one ever be formed.

It may be that the United States, the Soviet Union and their more reluctant allies will be forced into more responsive attitudes by pressures from other countries. There is some interest on the part of the smaller European states in reductions of forces, withdrawals of weapons and the dismantling of bases. There is a strong desire to restrain any build-up of troops and the conduct of manoeuvres, and to inhibit further their use for political purposes by requiring advance notice, by exchanging observers, and so on. Some Europeans, notably in the non-aligned countries, may wish to extend these ·inhibitions by setting up demilitarized zones, by introducing neutral monitors into them, etc., since these are the best – and perhaps the only – ways in which they can enhance their own security when confronted by more powerful nations. How hard they will push one cannot say, but they will certainly try to move in this direction – which is one reason for their interest in establishing a permanent Committee on European Security.

How far these various pressures will move the major powers, and to what extent the latter will reconcile their divergent interests, are difficult to forecast; the outcomes are both speculative and uncertain. An optimistic estimate would be that within the next two or three years one might expect acceptance of limitations on the utilization of present bases, like those outlined earlier, and possibly some unilateral restraint on the establishment of new bases and/or on the kinds of forces stationed there. One could also expect to see within this period some relocation of forces and weapons on both sides which would make them appear less threatening, and perhaps the establishment in Europe of narrow denuclearized or partially demilitarized zones. It is virtually certain that all countries will agree to give advance notice of manoeuvres, and it is possible that they will inform each other in advance about major troop movements, such as the transfer of a division, the displacement of an air wing or the dispatch of a major combat surface ship.[44] Undoubtedly observers will be admitted to manoeuvres and, if any demilitarized zones are established, probably to those also. Finally, it is possible that other means of verification will be permitted, both for their contribution to reassurance and because they may help to preclude the use of force by or against the nations of Europe – an objective common to all those nations and the super-powers.[45]

---

[44] As of April 1974, both the United States and the Soviet Union were balking at giving advance notice of troop movements, but it is conceivable that their objections could be overcome by excluding troop movements on their own territories, by shortening the notice required, or by increasing the size of the unit(s) concerned.

[45] The exact words of President Nixon and Mr Brezhnev, on behalf of their respective countries, were that 'ensuring a lasting peace in Europe is a paramount goal of their policies' (Nixon–Brezhnev Communiqué, *The Times*, 26 June 1973, p. 6).

This look at global restrictions on forces and weapons was prompted in part by awareness that measures which affected only the countries of Europe, and not the super-powers, could lead to greater military imbalances than now exist, especially between the Soviet Union and the countries on her western borders. It was also prompted by recognition that some arms-control measures, like restrictions on the deployment of naval forces, have to apply on a global basis if they are to be meaningful. And it derived from the knowledge that actions outside Europe could threaten European security either directly, by the interdiction of sea lines of communication, for example, or indirectly, by starting conflicts which might ultimately extend to the continent of Europe. The question which still has to be answered is: What effect will those global restrictions which seem both workable and acceptable have on these problems?

The first answer is that measures affecting the size of armed forces which are both workable and acceptable are unlikely to close the gap between the military capabilities of the super-powers and those of their allies. Indeed, this gap may in some instances increase, because reductions likely to be made in the armed forces of the super-powers will not approach the cuts in the indigenous forces of some European countries now under consideration at the Vienna Conference on Mutual Force Reductions. Even if the United States and the Soviet Union demobilized any units withdrawn from Europe, this would only marginally diminish the number of men the two countries have under arms. And even if tacit ceilings on their armed forces were set, these are not likely to be so low as to require drastic reductions by either super-power.

Furthermore, ceilings on classes of weapons cannot readily be applied to tanks, planes and guns. Hence, it is not possible to eliminate by this means current imbalances in these categories, which derive from differences in the organization and equipment of the forces of the two alliances. Ceilings on naval forces are easier to verify but so difficult to devise and so uneven in their impact that they have been considered feasible in only a few instances. The proposed asymmetrical ceiling on SLCM, limitations on the number of aircraft carriers and constraints on

attack submarines could curb future threats to European security; however, it must be admitted that they would not markedly affect the current ability of either side to wage war at sea. And, while this may accord with the principle of 'undiminished security', it is scarcely a step towards the goal of achieving it with smaller forces and at lesser cost.

As for budgetary restrictions, those likely to be acceptable will not have much impact, while those with great impact are not likely to be acceptable. This is equally true of controls on research and development, which can only affect most weapons programmes marginally, if at all. Furthermore, some kinds of controls, such as those on the sale of advanced weapons, would adversely alter European military capabilities and hence may not be deemed desirable. The measures which were judged potentially acceptable focus on determining which weapons could be destabilizing militarily or unsettling psychologically, on the monitoring of tests of such weapons and on the conduct of negotiations to preclude their deployment. While these measures could alleviate concern about the introduction of new weapons, they would do little to redress existing disparities in research capacities or to slow programmes for modernization (which may now be being implemented more rapidly by the East than by the West, and by the two super-powers than by their allies).

However, even partial measures such as these can have some impact on perceptions of security. The acceptance of lower force levels by the super-powers, whatever their effect militarily, would affirm the peaceful intentions of these two states. The adoption of ceilings on even a few classes of weapons would be reassuring, and reductions in armaments would be even more so; similarly, constraints on budgets and agreements to discuss limitations on 'destabilizing' weapons would reduce anxieties, particularly if they applied mainly to the United States and to the Soviet Union.

If, however, arms-control measures are to have maximum psychological impact, they must be given great publicity. Unilateral constraints of the past, such as the recent decline in the Soviet defence budget (in rouble terms), have not penetrated the consciousness of many officials and analysts; those who are fearful tend to select information which supports their fears, not information which challenges them. This argues for measures which would create their own sound effects, as would the scrapping of the 1,000-odd T-55 tanks in East Germany replaced recently by more modern T-62, and the destruction of those *Honest John* rockets and *Sergeant* SRBM in West Germany scheduled to be replaced by fewer *Lance* missiles. The danger of overstating the military consequences of such actions is slight by comparison with the danger of letting each side continue believing that the other is hell-bent on improving its defence posture, which seems to be the case at present.

The proposed restrictions on deployments may well have more effect militarily than will limitations on the size and capabilities of armed forces. Even partial curbs on the establishment of new bases and the deployment of 'threatening' weapons to vital areas could alter Warsaw Pact capabilities to conduct military operations in distant waters and NATO capabilities to launch nuclear strikes against targets in Eastern Europe and the Soviet Union. The redeployment of forces and weapons to rear areas would diminish the ability of both sides to launch surprise attacks, and their capacity to defend against such attacks would be further enhanced if restrictions on deployment were formalized by the establishment of narrow zones in which all nuclear warheads and all offensive weapons were banned. Although the effect of such measures would be greatest if they were applied in Europe, their implementation elsewhere could also be valuable. If extended to the Middle East, the Indian Ocean and other areas where the superpowers now maintain forces, they could inhibit these forces from increasing to a level where they could interdict European sea lines of communication or preclude European access to Middle East oil. They could also minimize the chances of a confrontation or conflict between the super-powers which could involve their allies in Europe. In both these ways, therefore, they could enhance European security.

Restrictions on deployment would have even more effect on perceptions of security because of what they would communicate concerning the intentions of the two alliances. These beneficial effects could be further increased by giving advance notice of large-scale manoeuvres and

(better still) major troop movements, by allowing greater freedom and scope for action to present liaison missions, by admitting observers to manoeuvres and (possibly on a permanent basis) to border areas, and so on. Their effects would be still more beneficial if the restrictions on deployment were supplemented by the provision, on request, of reassuring information, by the authorization of overflights in border zones and by the other measures for verification recommended earlier, all of which have been accepted in principle by both sides at one time or another – some of them, like the pledge not to interfere with national means of verification which is contained in the SALT agreement, very recently.

Although these judgments may be disappointing to those seeking drastic alterations in the global balance of power, the combined effect of overall limitations on NATO and Warsaw Pact forces and of restrictions on their deployment will not be negligible. Moreover, these will not be the only measures affecting the military capabilities of the two alliances, for these may be altered not only by unilateral decisions but also by bilateral or multilateral arms control agreements – some of which, like SALT II, could diminish the relative advantages the two superpowers currently enjoy over other nuclear powers. Even more importantly, other kinds of agreements, which could strengthen legal, institutional and political inhibitions on the use of force, may be reached at the Conference on Security and Co-operation in Europe or may be adopted as part of any arrangements for Mutual Force Reductions in Europe.[46]

Inhibitions on the use of force will obviously not affect military capabilities directly: this is not their intent. They are designed to strengthen existing obstacles to the use of those capabilities for either military or political purposes by increasing the costs attendant on their employment. This also involves enlarging the rewards of not using them: better relations among states, expanded trade, increased co-operation and the development of alternative means of preserving vital interests – if not of achieving all national objectives.

---

[46] For a discussion of the probable nature and the possible effects of such inhibitions, see Coffey, *Arms Control and European Security, op. cit.* in note 6, Chapter V.

This emphasizes a point made previously: that improved relations among states may both facilitate arms control and enhance national security. They can do the former by making it easier for states to reduce defence budgets, cancel or defer weapons programmes and practise restraint in the deployment of their armed forces, whether by agreement or as part of tacit bargaining. However, given the impossibility of eliminating weapons which could literally destroy nations, there are limits to what arms control can accomplish, either in reducing military capabilities or in relieving anxieties about the possibility of their use. In these circumstances, patterns of behaviour may have more influence on perceptions of threat than measures to reduce (or to produce) armaments.[47] If this lesson is learned, we can afford to worry less about the difficulty of devising and implementing measures for the control of armaments, on either an over-all or a limited basis.

[47] A clear illustration of this (and of the fact that capabilities are not the only things taken into account in devising defence programmes) is given by Dr Kissinger's remark that the United States could afford to limit ballistic missile defences under the SALT agreements because the American *rapprochement* with the People's Republic of China drastically reduced the likelihood of a Chinese nuclear strike against American cities (Congressional Briefing by Dr Henry A. Kissinger, *Congressional Record – Senate*, 19 June 1972, p. S9604).

# 2 NUCLEAR WEAPONS AND EAST-WEST NEGOTIATION

UWE NERLICH

## INTRODUCTION

When the Soviet Union insisted, very early in the Strategic Arms Limitation Talks (SALT), that FBS (Forward-Based Systems: i.e. American nuclear-strike forces based in Europe and Asia with a capacity to strike the Soviet homeland) ought to be accepted as an element in any negotiable SALT proposal, it took the American side completely by surprise. But what looked like, and indeed was, a brilliant diplomatic coup was in fact little more than the persistent pursuit of a policy the Soviet Union had embarked upon in the mid-1950s. In retrospect, it would have been a major surprise if Moscow had missed the opportunity.

In December 1956 the NATO Council finally decided to adopt the Eisenhower Administration's policy of equipping theatre forces with nuclear weapons. In the United States the new policy had emerged not exactly from strategic analysis but rather from the Administration's hope of saving money and manpower and from the Services' fear that unless they had a nuclear role the dominance of the Strategic Air Command would threaten their endowments, if not their rationales. For Washington's West European allies the decision was much more complex. Firstly it had an impact on Alliance structures. Though in peacetime these would appear cohesive, in the event of an East–West military conflict the stability of the Alliance might be threatened by the excessive European dependence on political decisions in Washington as well as by the uncertainties of escalation. Secondly, this NATO nuclear posture was found to reinforce differences of interest among Alliance members, making the Alliance structure more vulnerable to potential combinations of diplomatic pressure from the Soviet Union and domestic political pressures.

Given West Germany's crucial importance as the major deployment area, as well as the constraints imposed upon her by recent history, Konrad Adenauer seemed to have been fully aware of these implications of NATO's decision. The decision to equip NATO with nuclear weapons occurred before West Germany, the country most likely to be affected by its consequences, had begun to be integrated into the Alliance and at a time when Bonn did not even have a minimum capacity for defence policy-making. For Moscow, therefore, opposing NATO nuclearization looked like a promising opportunity to block West Germany's integration into the Alliance altogether. It was the stalemating effect of the unresolved German issue that kept European security negotiations and NATO defence policies apart. When the German issue began to ease, the building of basic Alliance structures had long been completed.

SALT provided the first opportunity for the Soviet Union to apply direct diplomatic leverage to NATO's nuclear posture. This leverage was directed at a single element of the posture – American nuclear-strike aircraft (and, potentially, *Pershing* missiles) – and came at a time when all the more powerful American nuclear-strike forces had long been withdrawn from Western Europe. In fact, even the number of NATO nuclear-strike aircraft, both American and Allied, had already decreased considerably before negotiations with the Soviet Union began. However, since the Soviet Union had long realized that all-out proposals (e.g. for a European nuclear-free zone) were non-negotiable in the foreseeable future, limited diplomatic access might well have seemed to her to be advantageous. Given the realities of NATO's nuclear posture and its importance for the political fabric of the Alliance, a concerted Soviet effort, focusing on different components of the NATO posture on different negotiating levels and with different NATO negotiators, looked most promising. There was the promise of spill-over and gradual fragmentation of the Alliance through multiple negotiations. The way the Alliance reacted to the FBS issue cannot possibly have been a disappointment for Soviet diplomacy.

Soviet FBS proposals in SALT had been persistently vague, and in the context of negotiations over limitations, rather than reductions, they could only have had marginal impacts. After all, major unilateral reductions had preceded the negotiations anyway, and nobody was expecting peacetime increases in the foreseeable future. Nevertheless, the FBS issue became a major concern within the Alliance. Two general observations are relevant: Soviet diplomacy cannot apply direct diplomatic leverage to NATO's nuclear posture except as a result of Western policy decisions; and it is likely to be successful only to the extent it can cause political over-reaction in the West, where, it seems, responses are shaped by structural conditions rather than simply by individual failure or mishap.

The very process of the negotiations is one such structural condition. It singles out an individual force relationship. However, force relationships are considered in NATO to be all intricately related, whereas in the early rounds of SALT separating force relationships was in fact a prime objective of Soviet diplomacy. SALT focuses on the most static measurements, which are least important in strategic analysis and are likely to distort the definition of desirable outcomes. It gives inappropriate prominence to nuclear issues in a situation where negotiations had become possible as a result of de-emphasis of nuclear matters. It casts light on political stakes and arouses concerns over political objectives, whereas force relationships are normally considered rather abstractly in a political vacuum. It tends to affect old and even create new priorities, so as to narrow the scope for future defence policies. It often shapes frames of reference for changes in the existing posture

which not only look quite artificial – e.g., the reduction area in the Mutual Force Reduction (MFR) talks – but tend to ignore alternatives that are emerging within the Alliance (for example, as a result of new weapons technologies).

This is not to say that East–West negotiations are *a priori* undesirable. However, they do tend to generate dynamics of policy-making on the Western side that clearly favour Soviet diplomacy, and the negative results of this can only be minimized or avoided if Western policy and opinion-makers have a better understanding of the nature of the processes such negotiations involve. However clumsy Soviet diplomacy may be, it seldom misses an opportunity to exploit these kinds of processes. A study of the FBS case is therefore useful not only because FBS have been a major concern of the Alliance for a number of years, but because such a study may reveal characteristics that are common to Western policy-making on a certain kind of East–West security negotiation. Moreover, some lessons ought to be learned in order to cope with the likely re-emergence of the FBS issue in subsequent SALT negotiations.

The Vladivostok agreement resulting from the meeting of Mr Brezhnev and President Ford in November 1974 eliminated only one aspect of FBS; they are not going to be included in the aggregates of strategic weapons that the two super-powers are expected to agree upon in a limitation treaty. But some elements of the old FBS issue are going to be revived on the road to that limitation treaty. There will be some kind of non-circumvention clause that applies to FBS, and there may be a non-transfer clause that could affect FBS much more severely. There may also be some thorny new elements: since counting rules for determining the aggregates are one of the key issues in remaining negotiations on the limitation treaty, the status of new forward-based systems (like cruise missiles which are nuclear-capable, though not necessarily nuclear-armed) is almost bound to be a major issue. In any case, nothing in either the Vladivostok agreement or the final limitation treaty will explicitly rule out FBS from the agenda for later negotiations on reductions. So the FBS issue is likely to stay with us, and it would not be surprising if future negotiations affected NATO's nuclear strike posture much more directly than did the first and second rounds of SALT (SALT I and II), while at the same time that posture becomes ever less important – as a result of negligence, not of increased understanding of the dynamics of Western policy formation. If in the near future the increasing availability of new technologies is not matched by a framework for a common reappraisal of defence policies within the Alliance, especially in its major capitals, Soviet diplomacy is likely to retain its position of direct leverage.

## I. THE POLITICAL SETTING
### CO-ORDINATING NEGOTIATING POLICIES

The co-ordination of negotiating policies within the Alliance tends to complicate the perennial existing efforts to reconcile defence policies of the major members of the Alliance. To some extent this is avoidable, since misgivings often arise over diplomatic style and patterns of consultative behaviour, rather than over substantive issues. Such shortcomings, in turn, tend to reinforce the kind of 'Neustadt mechanisms' of mutual mis-perceptions and missed initiatives within the Alliance[1] which more often than not profoundly influence the definition of substantive issues, thereby diminishing the already modest chances for adequate policy co-ordination.

The FBS issue is a crucial case of this kind. It was widely taken for granted that forward-based systems in Europe would somehow be included in the agenda of forthcoming East–West negotiations, most probably in SALT II. But obviously there was a wide gap between the American and most West European governments as to what this implied, both in terms of perceived risks and preferred options. The following are just some elements of a puzzle which contains the ingredients for conflict and potentially disruptive developments.

### American and West European Attitudes

Compared with the inadequate consultations over the Non-Proliferation Treaty (NPT), there seemed to American officials to be a considerable improvement in NATO consultations during SALT I, although with few exceptions these never went beyond mere information (more often than not after, rather than before, negotiating rounds).

On the other hand, West Europeans had to take the blame from Americans like Senator Jackson, who are concerned both about central agreements and about prospects for NATO, for providing 'little solid advice on strategic arms limitation matters'.[2] Quite contrary to their earlier sensitivity, West Europeans more or less failed to react on numerous aspects of SALT I where European interests were genuinely at stake. The one exception was the FBS issue.[3] However, once the Europeans had come round to agreeing on a suitable negotiating formula for this the White House appeared to be even more cautious than West European governments. It thought it necessary not to disregard critical West European public attitudes on the FBS issue, which to a considerable extent resulted from high-level secrecy in SALT. Therefore, as can be seen from the joint US–Soviet declaration of 20 May 1971, the United States eliminated the FBS issue from the SALT I agenda.

When SALT I began, there was a prevailing expectation within the American Administration that it would provide an opportunity for a comprehensive joint review of NATO strategy. But while within the Administration it led to the most intensive review of American strategic policy since the 1950s, NATO consultations on nuclear strategic matters were confined to (admittedly not unimportant) Nuclear Planning Group routine business, such as the guidelines on the initial tactical and subsequent follow-on use of nuclear weapons.

---

[1] The kind of interactions which Richard Neustadt has described with respect to several crises within the Alliance, such as the Multilateral Nuclear Force and the *Skybolt* affair. See R. Neustadt, *Alliance Politics* (New York: Columbia University Press, 1970).

[2] Speech by Senator Jackson before the Military Committee of the North Atlantic Assembly in Bonn. Reprinted in *Aviation Week and Space Technology*, 11 December 1972, p. 54.

[3] A similar pattern of reacting to the relatively less important issues prevailed during Mr Brezhnev's visit to the United States in June 1973, when it was the San Clemente agreement on the prevention of nuclear war which became the focus of West European obsessions.

33

West European reactions were somewhat surprising. In spite of impressive American reports on the changing central balance, growing uncertainties about American strategic policy, the practically closed game of the SALT negotiations and existing concerns about a decoupling of American strategic power from the European theatre, most West European governments and observers focused their concerns on the one element which 'from a strictly strategic point of view is of least significance in determining the balance between the United States and the Soviet Union':[4] the European-based deployment of American nuclear strike forces. To some West Europeans FBS had taken on symbolic functions, and American handling of the FBS issue was seen as the one indicator of future accountability to European interests of American strategic power in Europe. To some a decoupling of American strategic power from Europe seemed more or less unavoidable, with forward-based systems being the only essential element of nuclear deterrence left for NATO purposes. The fact that these two views often went together simply signals the absence of a commonly accepted strategic doctrine applicable to forward-based strike forces.

While the Americans were prepared to review current strategic doctrines, West Europeans tended to adapt themselves to changes in the strategic environment by putting a conservative emphasis on the one European-based element of the nuclear strike posture – thereby reinforcing the very process of decoupling which they are anxious above all to arrest.

**Divergent Perceptions of the FBS Problem**

At the same time perceptions of what systems are really at stake in SALT negotiations, and what kinds of agreement are likely to evolve concerning these systems, differed widely within the Alliance. These divergences were reinforced by Soviet attempts to blur distinctions and also by the high-level secrecy surrounding SALT, which gave little chance for informed public debate.

For FBS, what is technically at stake in SALT is forward deployment of American nuclear deep-interdiction forces in Europe. This essentially concerns the successor systems of American F-100s – i.e., the F-111s based in Britain and

those F-4s possessing nuclear-mission capability.[5] It could also concern carrier-based A-6s and A-7s in the Eastern Mediterranean[6] and (under rather theoretical assumptions) even *Pershing* missiles. American Secretary of State Henry Kissinger put the total of these forward-deployed nuclear-strike aircraft at about 340.[7] The majority of them is European-based, including the F-111 wing in Britain, but this figure does not include the NATO-committed F-4 wing dual-based in the Continental United States (CONUS) and Europe, and, by implication, any other CONUS-based non-strategic aircraft are also excluded.

From an American point of view, even the strategic value of the FB-111 is considered fairly low, because of the adverse effect upon its range of carrying a significant payload.[8] This understandably implies an American yardstick for the strategic value of tactical strike aircraft, according to which F-111s and F-4s only marginally affect the central balance. Moreover, deployment of these forces in Europe is hardly considered a strategic requirement of overriding importance: 'Tactical air forces are less dependent on forward deployments for immediate employment, because additional planes can quickly be flown in during a period of crisis'.[9]

---

[4] Speech by Senator Jackson, *op. cit.* in note 2.

[5] If the two-way-mission criterion is accepted, the majority of these F-4s could be involved (e.g. those in Greece, Turkey and Italy; not, however, those in Central Europe). See below note 12 and pp. 19 ff.

[6] These aircraft lose their FBS quality (i.e. their capability to reach Soviet territory) if the carriers operate in the more westerly parts of the Mediterranean. In Central Europe *Pershing* missiles could be based close enough to Soviet territory to acquire FBS quality, but in fact are not. Deployment of *Pershing*, e.g. to Turkey, would raise different kinds of problems.

[7] This figure is the rough difference between the totals of Soviet and American strategic bombers and missiles at the time of the conclusion of SALT I agreements (SALT briefing in Moscow, 27 May 1972). However, the number of aircraft with FBS quality varies according to the criteria chosen.

[8] See General Holloway's statement before the House Armed Services Committee, 92nd Congress, *Hearings on Military Posture*, Part I, p. 2922. See also General Ryan's statement: 'The FB-111 just doesn't have long enough legs after the end of the refueling point. You just can't cover the deep targets in Russia with an FB-111' (p. 3537).

[9] *Military Manpower Requirements Report for 1973*, US Department of Defense, February 1972, p. 105. See also the Statement by the Department of the Air Force:

The number of American Air Force tactical fighter/attack aircraft is 21 wings, made up of 64 squadrons – a figure which, in spite of minor changes, does seem to constitute a ceiling for the foreseeable future.[10] The force structure for 1976 essentially results from several current conversion programmes: 12 squadrons of F-111s, 9 squadrons of A-7s, 43 squadrons of F-4s and 1 squadron of F-15s, all of which aircraft are capable of being deployed world-wide.[11] Given a post-Southeast Asia deployment posture, these 21 wings will be CONUS wings, Pacific Air Forces (PACAF) wings or US Air Force, Europe (USAFE) wings. Some of these roughly 1,530 tactical aircraft have a nuclear mission capability and some are forward-deployed under USAFE or PACAF. Theoretically they could all be CONUS-based but committed to NATO or PACAF without any of the regional programmes being substantially changed. In practical terms, however, the American side does also seem to be aware of some of the insurmountable difficulties this would bring about. Therefore it seems reasonable to assume that the United States has a genuine interest in retaining European basing for at least some of these aircraft. There is, however, no intention to increase the number of these aircraft, although such shifts in the world-wide American deployment structure are possible. In particular, any increase in the number of European-based F-111s has been explicitly ruled out.

Nevertheless, there is strong concern among West European analysts about the prospect of future negotiations on FBS. Some West Europeans simply react out of ignorance. They take it for granted that FBS stands both for American and Allied strike aircraft; in fact, some even

'Our NATO committed squadrons [i.e. four F-4 squadrons] . . . can be deployed to Europe in a matter of hours'. (*Hearings before the Senate Armed Services Committee*, 92nd Congress, Fiscal Year 1973 Authorization, Part 2, p. 1193.)

[10] Neither the number of aircraft in a squadron nor the number of squadrons in a wing is consistent within the Air Force. Most tactical fighter wings are authorized to contain 72 aircraft, organized into three squadrons of 24 aircraft apiece. William White, *US Tactical Air Power* (Washington, D.C.: Brookings Institution, 1974), pp. 14–15.

[11] The F-15, which entered service in 1975, was designed specifically as an air superiority aircraft but has proved equally suitable for air-to-ground missions without detriment to its primary role.

assume that not only programmed nuclear-strike forces but also army weaponry is involved, which adds up to the celebrated number of 7,000 warheads on West European soil. To some extent this ignorance grows out of the kind of secrecy surrounding SALT, and should be a matter of concern because political attitudes in Western Europe may be based on such inadequate information.

Some West Europeans doubt that a limitation of American forward-based strike aircraft in Europe and Asia could come close to what the Soviet Union wants to achieve, especially if a SALT agreement only provides further incentives for retaining the existing forward-basing structure in Europe and if fast deployment of CONUS-based (and theoretically even PACAF) forces in a crisis remains unrestricted. The only conceivable reason for the Soviet Union to agree to the inclusion of FBS in a permanent treaty on such a basis would be as a means to buy a higher ceiling for her own strategic forces – much as she did when claiming the inclusion of British and French submarine-launched ballistic missiles (SLBM) in the interim agreement on offensive weapons. On balance, however, this seems very unlikely.

Many West European observers therefore believe that what the Soviet Union is really driving at is a substantial reduction of FBS, or preferably their complete removal from European soil. Moreover, the very fact that these forces could be redeployed 'within hours' indicates to them that the Soviet Union is essentially anxious to use negotiations and agreements on FBS as a 'can-opener' in order to start a process of dismantling the nuclear strike posture of Supreme Allied Commander, Europe (SACEUR). In fact, FBS are well suited for this purpose:

1. They constitute by themselves an important element of SACEUR's nuclear-strike posture.
2. Any major change in the American deployment structure is likely to affect severely the structure and feasibility of existing programmes for operations of SACEUR's nuclear-strike aircraft (i.e., the strength and availability of forces and the ability to launch them on a nuclear-strike mission when necessary).
3. It seems unlikely that a reduction in American strike aircraft or their removal from Euro-

pean soil would leave other allied (i.e., non-American) strike forces unaffected, irrespective of whether these were included in East–West negotiations or not.

From a Soviet perspective FBS can be singled out as a special category.[12] But from a NATO point of view these systems are intimately related to the whole political and military fabric of the Alliance. However, it is not solely Soviet intentions that affect the reaching of an agreement on reductions of FBS. And, even if the Soviet Union had her way, the extent to which the NATO fabric would really be affected would depend on the specifics of any agreement reached (concerning redeployments, etc.).

The question for those West Europeans, then, is whether and in what ways the American side will resist Soviet pressures. The answer, again from a West European point of view is a matter of beliefs: while some observers think that SALT negotiations on FBS will not go beyond

mere limitations, despite Soviet pressures, there are others who are either impressed with Soviet bargaining potential or else assume strong internal tendencies in Washington to change the structure of SACEUR's nuclear posture. The combination of obvious Soviet intentions with uncertainties about American negotiating policies leads these West Europeans to believe that, in terms of possible agreements and as well as of the systems concerned, the most likely outcome of future SALT negotiations on FBS will not represent the kind of consensus on a limitation formula which has been reached within NATO.

Some are concerned about the possible implications of a limitation agreement:

Limitation of forward-based American strike aircraft as part of a SALT agreement on the limitation of offensive weapons could prejudge subsequent negotiations on reductions.

Even a limitation agreement could involve reductions of FBS. One expressed in terms of 'effective equality' would require reductions in specific categories, while one expressed terms of a free mix under a general ceiling for offensive weapons would mean that FBS would be more likely to be reduced than other systems.

Limitation of European-based American strike aircraft could be accompanied by constraints on additional deployment of CONUS-based aircraft in periods of crisis, thereby denying NATO the kind of flexibility it possesses so far in the one area where geographic asymmetries can be most easily compensated for. By implication, such restrictive reinforcement bans would practically destroy dual-basing arrangements for CONUS-based aircraft committed to NATO (currently one wing of F-4s).

A limitation agreement could by implication, or even explicitly, rule out the modernization of SACEUR's nuclear-strike forces. This could become a real problem with respect to F-104 successor systems in Europe. A portion of new tactical aircraft in Europe are designed for nuclear-strike missions,[13] and new sharing arrangements are necessary for these. It would

---

[12] The Soviet criterion for non-central systems in SALT, however, involves any land-based systems which, because of their geographical deployment, can reach the United States and the Soviet Union. Thus the Soviet proposal could apply to home-based systems as well as to forward-based systems unless, in practical terms, the demands are based on a two-way-mission criterion. (Given that neither the United States nor the Soviet Union is on record as having adopted tactics in the Kamikaze tradition, such a criterion may appear to be self-evident.) A one-way-mission criterion would include most forward-based systems as well as home-based medium bombers (including Soviet bombers). A two-way-mission criterion, on the other hand, would exclude all home-based bombers and also most forward-based systems in Western Europe (see below, p. 19). It was clearly in the Soviet Union's interest to keep her medium bombers out of the calculations, and she had no difficulty in achieving this in SALT I: it was agreed not to include medium bombers, and there was even agreement on a classification of existing and future aircraft on a case-by-case basis (see Joseph Kruzel, 'SALT II: The Search for a Follow-on Agreement', *Orbis*, Vol. XVII, Summer 1972/3, p. 347). The Soviet demand was thus limited to forward-based systems but without explicit recognition of the two-way-mission criterion (which would have excluded most of these systems from the discussions). It was only in SALT II, with the Soviet Union apparently realizing that the issue of medium bombers might be reconsidered in SALT, that Moscow explicitly introduced the two-way-mission criterion. At this stage, however, most Western observers tended to understand the FBS category in SALT as including all or most forward-based aircraft. That perception obviously meets neither Soviet nor American criteria in SALT, but, without major educational efforts in the West, it is likely to affect future negotiations.

[13] According to Trevor Cliffe some of the new European-built multi-role combat aircraft (MRCA) will be designed for nuclear strike roles (*Military Technology and the European Balance*, Adelphi Paper No. 89 (London: IISS, 1972), p. 45).

be surprising if the Soviet Union missed her chance of trying to impose appropriate restrictions (e.g., non-transfer clauses).

A limitation agreement could be designed so as to govern also the marriage of nuclear warheads to allied strike aircraft, for example, by non-transfer clauses. This would not yet necessarily mean dismantling existing sharing arrangements (release procedures, etc.) but would impose severe constraints on operating them (especially with regard to training and exercises).

A permanent limitation agreement including FBS is likely to lead on to negotiations on FBS reductions. Most probably a follow-on reduction agreement would not be a comprehensive one: i.e., one that included intercontinental ballistic missiles (ICBM), SLBM, strategic bombers and FBS. FBS would then lend themselves to becoming a preferred American option for reduction, since sacrificing some FBS for these 'central systems' could look attractive and, moreover, mere withdrawal of FBS (rather than disarmament by phasing-out or destruction) could already meet the reduction requirements of a SALT agreement. Given the political implications of a selective reduction agreement, the Soviet Union, too, might favour inclusion of FBS at the expense of other categories. The established principles of selecting according to 'perceived threats' provides ample opportunities for such a course of action. Soviet pressure would thus combine with American incentives to reduce strategically less important (and reinforceable) systems. While the other possibilities mentioned could arise during SALT II, this is more likely to fit into a SALT III context.

Admittedly, the more dramatic concerns are related to the less likely contingencies: substantial reductions of FBS and restrictions on the nuclear arming of all non-American strike aircraft. While it may not be prudent to overemphasize these concerns, they should not simply be ignored either, if only because political attitudes of influential groups tend to create facts.

To sum up, if what is at stake is simply the existing deployment structure of American forward-deployed nuclear-strike aircraft in the context of a quantitative limitation agreement, there is little reason for the West Europeans to be concerned. However, Soviet intentions and uncertainties about the underlying American policy both give reason to doubt the likelihood of SALT being confined within this framework. A limitation agreement could entail precarious elements which might trigger off more radical changes in SACEUR's nuclear-strike posture. But, even if it did not, the dynamics of East–West negotiations are likely to produce follow-on agreements which could endanger NATO's complete system for operating nuclear strike forces.

## Strategic Doctrine versus Procedural Alternatives

The divergent views within the Alliance suggest that current policy problems result from a combination of bureaucratic deadlock and analytical deficiencies. Obviously the problems require comprehensive and thoroughgoing exchanges between the principal partners of the Alliance before the American Administration agrees internally on its negotiating position. However, the current structure of bureaucratic policy formation within the Alliance more or less excludes early 'committal' consultations. As Henry Kissinger put it, the American side tends to present its view 'in a bland relaxed fashion to the ally whose interests are involved but who is not present at the negotiations. The ally responds equally vaguely for three reasons: (a) he may be misled into believing that no decision is imminent and therefore sees no purpose in making an issue; (b) he is afraid that if he forces the issue the decision will go against him; (c) he hopes the problem will go away because agreement will prove impossible. When agreement seems imminent, American diplomats suddenly go into high gear to gain the acquiescence of the ally. He in turn feels tricked by the very intensity and suddenness of the pressure while we are outraged to learn of objections heretofore not made explicit. This almost guarantees that the ensuing controversy will take place under the most difficult conditions.'[14] There is every reason to agree that these kinds of processes 'in which both sides claim to have been deceived . . . suggest structural causes'.[15] The evolving FBS issue

---

[14] Henry A. Kissinger, 'The Viet Nam Negotiations', *Foreign Affairs*, Vol. 47, January 1969, p. 225.
[15] *Ibid.*

37

obviously carries with it all the characteristics of that pattern. But while it is likely to become more complex than the debates in the 1960s over an Alliance-wide multilateral nuclear force and British and American differences over the *Skybolt*, it is still in its 'non-committal' phase, and therefore the process is not inevitable. In fact, Vladivostok may have provided a breathing space.

From an American point of view, Western Europe is concerned with negotiating concepts that are hypothetical and exaggerated. But, while tending to expect a negotiating process which could eventually produce a dismantling of SACEUR's nuclear strike posture, West European countries seem to refrain from comprehensive strategic reappraisals. They combine alarmist attitudes about forthcoming negotiations with conservative strategic arguments which are supposed to be suited to preventing negotiations ending in undesirable outcomes. In fact, rather than reconsidering strategic rationales, West European governments appear to be prepared to consider alternatives at the negotiating level which are different in procedure and concept and which, while they may look less threatening to West Europeans, may well turn out to reinforce and broaden the American–Soviet understandings on FBS, if only because they reinforce existing positions. Thus, substantial divergences of policy may arise between the United States and West Europeans, which could be settled only in terms of a basic strategic consensus.

In these circumstances, West European concerns about an FBS agreement which involved Allied strike aircraft somehow get translated into concerns about excessive American–Soviet bilateralism. Rather than entrusting the United States with the job of confining negotiations to limitations on American forward-based strike aircraft, European governments turn things upside down by suggesting alternatives, in terms of trade-offs and/or procedures, which they hope will allow them to participate in negotiations about issues which they had originally been anxious to exclude. Concerns about amplified agendas are thus gradually accompanied, and indeed replaced, by concerns about closed games between the United States and the Soviet Union. In order to prevent this kind of Big Two-ism, West European governments talk themselves into suggesting European elements as possible items on the agenda, which would require multilateralization of the negotiations.[16]

Two schools of thought have emerged in Europe, both striving to preclude specific developments. One continues to favour preventing negotiations on FBS for essentially strategic reasons, but it lacks sufficient strategic consensus among the major parties concerned. The other, which may very well outweigh the first, wants to shift the level of analysis (and indeed policy-making) from strategic policy, which constrains negotiating policies by focusing on possible strategic interactions between NATO and the Warsaw Pact, towards negotiating policies, which focus on the range of participants and on conceivable trade-offs.

The various views held in the American Administration seem to represent three schools of thought. While the closest approximation to a declared American policy is that the negotiations should be confined to a numerical limitation of FBS which will take place bilaterally in SALT (accompanied by thorough-going NATO consultations), a number of more far-reaching schemes exist. Some are expected to complicate the FBS issue in order to prevent any outcome resulting, whereas others are designed to allow for meaningful trade-offs.

On the bilateral SALT level, as well as trying to trade a reduction in FBS for a reduction in Soviet strategic weapons, one could relate FBS to Soviet medium-range systems (notably medium-range bombers) and/or air defence – if only in order to complicate the issue. In a multilateral framework one could try to achieve limitations on the non-central systems of both sides (i.e., not only FBS) so as to improve European security, and one might also attempt to complicate the issue by interrelating some or all non-central strategic systems in Europe (possibly including Soviet as well as British and French systems) within one procedural framework.[17]

The former possibility has more or less been given up by West European governments because there is no way of persuading the Soviet Union

---

[16] Though MFR was a multilateral undertaking from the outset, some West European governments concluded that indigenous forces should be included in the negotiations if only in order to prevent excessive bilateralism.
[17] Both multilateral schemes seem to have some support inside the American Administration.

to give up her medium-range strategic options.[18] Even a reduction of more than 50 per cent in Soviet intermediate-range/medium-range ballistic missiles (IR/MRBM) would not deny the Soviet Union any options, because she would still have so many of these missiles left. The same holds true for an equivalent reduction of ballistic missiles and bombers.[19] Oddly enough, where medium-range missiles are concerned, a qualitative limitation which prevented further dispersal would be much more interesting for West European governments than a reduction in existing systems, whereas a reduction in Soviet medium-range bombers could be more interesting to the United States. The bombers could be taken as posing an additional threat to the American homeland which would have to be taken into account in central balance dealings, whereas the size and diversity of Soviet medium-range forces means that there are no meaningful negotiating possibilities open to the West Europeans.

There are two conceivable versions of the multilateral trade-off approach: one would utilize the MFR context, the other would call for some kind of 'third level'. The former could involve, for example, the mixed-package approach, of which the usual illustration given is a trade-off between Western aircraft (possibly including nuclear-strike aircraft) and Soviet tank forces.[20] This mixed-package concept is often used in a mechanistic way, as if there were an obvious functional rationality in combining certain elements; in fact, such packages are relevant only as a result of a political decision to combine certain different elements. One should not rule out this approach, but, like any other, it does not offer an easy way out. Even if a trade-off between strike aircraft and tanks could be agreed in principle, there would still remain all the arguments in favour of confining MFR to land forces and against a widening of the

reduction area which would allow the inclusion of more than just aircraft based in Central Europe. (In terms of actual deployment structures and of possible redeployments outside the reduction area an MFR agreement on aircraft which was confined to the MFR NATO Guideline Area[21] would be of little use.)

It remains to be seen whether Soviet tanks are a useful bargaining counter. Given current technological developments in the field of anti-tank weapons, it may be much more promising to neutralize Soviet tank capabilities on a large scale by introducing new anti-tank weaponry than to buy a certain portion of Soviet tanks out of Eastern Europe through mixed-package deals.[22] The worst possible outcomes would be either if procurement options in the anti-tank category turned out to be highly promising but were ruled out in a negotiating framework, or if strike aircraft were given up in exchange for Soviet tanks which are likely to be neutralized through new weapons anyway. If any evidence is needed to demonstrate the need for harmonizing defence and negotiating policies, this certainly is a telling example.

A most complex mixed-package approach could also conceivably be chosen: a two-level approach with a vague kind of limitation proposal for FBS on the SALT level (e.g., non-circumvention) and a reduction offer in the MFR context. The latter could itself be a mixed-package proposal of the type mentioned above (i.e., confined to the MFR reduction area). This approach would leave most aircraft with FBS quality unaffected, because they are deployed outside the reduction area, but would go much further than any SALT formula hitherto considered on the American side, because it would involve reductions and not just limitations. The approach could conceivably be extended to *Pershing* also. (For a more detailed discussion of the criteria involved see pp. 49 ff.)

Whatever the value of such a proposal may be in terms of possible negotiated trade-offs and strategic requirements, the Soviet Union is likely to consider it a precedent for follow-on agreements on geographically and numerically

---

[18] As has been pointed out, however, emphasis on Soviet medium bombers provides some leverage.

[19] This is far from saying that these forces are meaningless or outdated: in fact they constitute a decisive element in the current military situation in Europe. The point is that redundancy tends to rule out negotiability.

[20] Theoretically, trade-offs could be conceived in two ways: by relating nuclear strike aircraft to Soviet nuclear strike systems in terms of balancing deterrent forces, or by relating them to theatre land forces in terms of war-fighting capabilities.

[21] See *The Military Balance 1975–1976* (London: IISS, 1974), pp. 101–2.

[22] This is not to say that mixed packages of this kind are undesirable. In fact, they correspond more obviously to a military rationale than straight symmetrical reductions.

much larger scales; at the same time the package proposal would give her a modest SALT limitation of FBS plus a reduction of F-4s and possibly *Pershings* – which quite conceivably would not be governed by a SALT clause anyway. (Since the Soviet definition seems to have confined the FBS concept to aircraft which can reach the Soviet Union on two-way missions, F-4s in Central Europe would be excluded from a SALT understanding, and it has long been understood in the Soviet Union that *Pershings* in Central Europe cannot be considered as FBS.)

In the circumstances the American Administration seems to take a reluctant stand on schemes for multilateral trade-off approaches which might involve strike aircraft in Europe. While in earlier rounds of SALT I, MFR was occasionally used as a device for delaying the FBS issue, this has changed since MFR has gained momentum. Mixed packages are not ruled out but, pending Soviet initiatives, are not likely to become a preferred American option during MFR I either. Of course, the fact that the United States tends to consider mixed packages involving strike aircraft as a conceivable option for a later stage of MFR talks (possibly MFR II) does not preclude SALT II affecting FBS directly and SACEUR's strike posture at large indirectly.[23]

For West European governments which are worried about the inclusion of FBS in SALT II, there are two ways of assessing the situation: their concerns may be reinforced by the lack of opportunity in the near future to make FBS a multilateral issue in MFR,[24] or they may find some comfort in the fact that on the MFR level the United States is behaving cautiously on FBS, whatever her reasons.

While this multilateral trade-off approach does not offer early options for West European governments (except in case of naturally less desirable Soviet initiatives), the 'third-level'

[23] The mixed-package option was never considered feasible in early phases of MFR negotiations. In fact, it took the Soviet negotiators only a few days in Vienna to table a proposal which envisaged symmetrical reductions also in the categories which NATO was prepared to discuss only in terms of mixed packages, namely nuclear weapons and aircraft. Combining these two elements of the original Soviet proposal in MFR would potentially also include FBS and other NATO strike aircraft.

[24] This could lead to absurd escalation in the form of demands for negotiations about subjects which they were most anxious to keep out and pressing for the early inclusion of strike aircraft in MFR.

approach, which would aim at interrelating all or some European strategic components in a specific multilateral framework ('European SALT', as some have begun to call it), looks even less suited to providing useful options for those who are anxious to pre-empt anticipated SALT agreements by making the FBS issue multilateral. On the one hand, the prospects of meaningful trade-offs are hardly any brighter than they are in the MFR context. On the other hand, it would be a long time before a third negotiating level could possibly be established, especially if it were to include France. Moreover, a broad negotiating framework of the European SALT variety would give countries which are primarily concerned about SACEUR's strike aircraft less influence than countries like France which, because of their indigenous nuclear capability could speak in their own right.

The Soviet proposal was an opening move. It is no longer a serious basis for negotiations. It demonstrated, though, the Soviet ability to combine the losing arguments of internal NATO debates into proposals which are likely to have divisive effects on the Alliance and to pre-empt forthcoming NATO proposals which may increase Western bargaining power. It would be surprising if the Soviet Union emphasized trade-offs instead of nuclear weapons in Europe as a distinctive negotiating category.

On balance, therefore, both approaches towards making negotiations multilateral are unlikely to produce meaningful procedural alternatives while SALT II is going on. There appears to be a shift from a strategic approach towards an increasing emphasis on negotiating schemes which provide better opportunities for West European governments to influence the course of events. Perhaps this could mean that renewed efforts to reach consensus on underlying strategic issues as a basis for agreed negotiating positions will again seem necessary, even though in much more difficult conditions: as negotiations go on, they are likely to eat up more and more options which could matter in future strategic policy.

These are some elements of what might well become a major crisis within the Alliance. Obviously, a point of no return has not yet been reached. But there are those in the political and military élites in NATO Europe who take the FBS issue as something fundamental. There are, indeed, prominent politicians and military leaders who claim that the very *raison d'être* of NATO is at stake if the FBS issue is settled the way they fear it might be. On the other hand, this analysis suggests that, up to now, the elements of potential crisis result primarily from the lack of commitment in bureaucratic interaction and from the lack of precision in defining the issue. Negative outcomes could be prevented, but this would require changing the current *modus operandi*.

Rather than looking simply for procedural alternatives (like negotiating about FBS 'in Vienna rather than in Geneva'), it seems essential to reconsider the whole issue in the context of NATO's nuclear requirements, which have not been static in the past and are quite unlikely to remain unaffected by future developments not only in arms technology but also in international

politics. The United States should understand why West European governments expect the outcome of such reappraisals to affect NATO's very rationale, but the West Europeans on their side should not remain in entrenched doctrinal positions. They should realize that in the longer run functionally sound solutions, provided they can be found, are the most promising way of arresting disruptive change.

While these are requirements for future action, a more general understanding of what has happened during SALT I also seems necessary. An understanding of the historical background may help to reconcile conceptions of Atlantic relationships with the facts of super-power negotiations. It may also help towards more general understanding of the nature of processes during which 'we deprive ourselves of criteria by which to judge progress'.[25]

## II. OUTCOMES OF BARGAINING PROCESSES DURING SALT I

In retrospect, there are three observations to make concerning the FBS issue in SALT I.

First, the Soviet Union had little direct leverage; secondly, Western bargaining positions did change considerably; and, thirdly, internal political pressures had only marginal impact on the bargaining position of the American Administrations. The changes that came about therefore have to be seen in terms of incremental processes with subtly shifting priorities, short-range tactical objectives and little-understood longer-range implications of Soviet moves. Incremental processes of this kind occurred on a variety of bargaining levels: inside the American Administration (as indeed in some West European capitals), in bargaining with Congress, in negotiations with the Soviet Union and in consultations within NATO.

**Soviet Interests and Leverage**

Some Western schools of thought tend to assume that the existence of American, and indeed Allied, strike aircraft constitutes a genuine threat to the Soviet Union. Tactical Soviet moves during bargaining processes are thus taken at face value, or at any rate as legitimate. By implication these schools of thought assume that nothing short of the complete abolition, or at least a massive reduction, of these forces would

meet Soviet requirements for substantial SALT agreements.

There are also the opposite schools of thought which adhere to the opposite simplification: that nuclear strike forces are strategically irrelevant from a Soviet point of view because they are completely neutralized by Soviet forces. Consequently, any inclusion in SALT agreements of strike forces in Europe should be avoided, because of political advantage to the Soviet Union, strategic irrelevance to the United States, and, in addition, because it is a particular obsession of NATO's European members.

Whereas the first generalization assumes a general nuclear response by NATO in a strategic vacuum (i.e., outside any conceivable scenarios for strategic exchange which take into account Soviet first- and second-strike capabilities), the second either is based on abstract notions of force relationships ('imbalance') or else considers Soviet disarming strikes as the only relevant contingency.

A more moderate second version of the 'genuine concern' philosophy is also widespread. This claims that the Soviet Union feels genuinely threatened by European-based nuclear strike forces, but as a consequence of wrong perceptions rather than existing Western capabilities.

[25] Henry A. Kissinger, *op. cit.* in note 14, p. 28.

41

Whereas some people argue that these perceptions are the essential element of deterrence in Europe by virtue of creating Soviet uncertainty over possible NATO responses, there are others who would be prepared to meet the Soviet Union half-way, so as to achieve better reconciliatory results; they suggest a combination of strategic persuasion with some concessions at the conference table which are designed to reassure the Soviet Union.

There is also a third conciliatory approach, which, while not necessarily assuming that the Soviet Union feels genuinely threatened, does concede some logic in Soviet demands for inclusion of European-based strike aircraft in central agreements because the criterion that they can be targeted on the opponent's homeland cannot be easily refuted. Since this approach, too, tends to take Soviet moves at face value, rather than as political gambling, it often leads to the contention that some sort of solution to the 'FBS issue' ought to be found.

It is probably correct to assume, as all three conciliatory approaches apparently do, that strategic interests play a certain role in Soviet policies on the FBS issue, although Soviet priorities are likely to be defined in broader political terms. One may question, though, whether Soviet strategic concerns are properly described in terms of 'threat perception'. This may be an approach which dominates Western strategic thinking much more than Soviet analysis, and it seems reasonable to assume that in Soviet assessments offensive political denial strategies are much more important than defensive military deterrence strategies. One might argue that the Soviet Union is concerned about peripheral weapons precisely because they are non-central systems. In the case of a general nuclear response by NATO, these forces which belong to SACEUR's strike programmes could conceivably be employed without simultaneous (or even subsequent) involvement of external Single Integrated Operations Plan (SIOP) forces; SACEUR's nuclear-strike forces, therefore, constitute a kind of intermediate deterrent. By the same token, however, these weapons, if deployed, would increase the risk of escalation into a central war. However, from a Soviet point of view the escalatory risk would exist even without them – though possibly in a different degree.

Obviously these weapons would be used only in response to massive Soviet aggression involving nuclear weapons.[26] In Soviet crisis calculations the weapons would have to be considered as an intra-war deterrent, in the case of a major aggression forcing the Soviet Union to choose between de-escalation or escalation. However, escalation through pre-emptive strikes against SACEUR's nuclear potential would result in large-scale destruction of Western Europe, which the Soviet Union would prefer to take over in a non-destructive manner. Further escalation would even invite the strategic repercussions of a central war on the Soviet homeland.

It is this cost/objective ratio, rather than the physical capabilities of SACEUR's strike forces, which will matter in Soviet calculations for the remote contingency of a massive Soviet aggression. This argument is reinforced by two facts. First, the penetration ability of deep-interdiction strike aircraft is extremely low, especially through Central Europe. Secondly, the Soviet Union has a capability for disarming as well as retaliatory strikes against Western Europe. In fact, 'neither the current total of NATO fighter-bombers based in Europe, nor double their number, nor triple their number, even if all devoted to attacks on the MRBM, or on MRBM and medium bombers, would be able to avoid the assured destruction capability of the total Soviet threat system against Europe'.[27]

On balance, one might assume that from a Soviet point of view SACEUR's strike forces have a particular strategic relevance as compared with the technically more impressive central systems, because European conflict scenarios seem more realistic than central war scenarios. But even the realism of European scenarios

[26] Nuclear strike programmes are normally designed for a general nuclear response (which is the third level of strategic operations envisaged in the NATO policy document MC 14/3). Under exceptional circumstances some of the programmed aircraft may be used according to regional priorities prior to a general nuclear response. These forces, however, are not considered for the initial tactical use of nuclear weapons.

[27] Frederick S. Wyle, *U.S., Europe, SALT and Strategy* (Chicago: Chicago University, Center for Policy Study, 1971), pp. 15ff. While this assessment seems to be unquestionable, I would disagree, for reasons outlined above, with Wyle's conclusion that 'thus a change of numbers or missions, or ranges, of NATO fighter bombers would not affect European interests from a strategic point of view' (*ibid.*, p. 16).

appears to be quite modest. It thus remains doubtful whether the Soviet Union is genuinely concerned about these non-central systems, so long as they pursue nothing but deterrence, though she would obviously prefer to dismantle them by diplomatic means. However, this aim would have to be seen in terms of the same political denial strategy which creates strong interests on the West European side to retain them: their removal would improve the cost/objective ratio from a Soviet point of view, and West Europeans would feel more susceptible to possible Soviet military pressure or blackmail without them.

There is a striking discrepancy between the Western obsession with the FBS issue and the fact that during SALT I the Soviet Union never came close to specifying her demands. In fact, there is also a striking similarity between this discrepancy and the action–reaction pattern displayed during the preparations for the Conference on Security and Co-operation in Europe ever since 1966, when the Soviet Union used as a sort of negative bait a vague suggestion of organizing a European security conference and then waited until a mix of Western anxieties, internal pressures, pre-emptive moves and compromises had reached a point of no return.

Early in SALT I the Soviet Union made it clear that she would not accept the American definition of the scope of the conference but introduced a variety of notions which were related in one way or another to regional problems, notably West European ones. Among the subjects included was that of nuclear weapons which are targetable on the Soviet Union by reason of their location. The Soviet Union then went on to suggest that the United States should pull back all these American strike forces (which then came to be called FBS) from Europe and destroy all bases to prevent their possible return.[28]

When SALT I was moving closer to possible agreements, Soviet officials adapted their formula so as to allow for continued American forward basing if the United States would make concessions in a forthcoming central agreement – though they never specified the kind of compensation they were driving at. If they were serious about achieving numerical advantages in the way

they capitalized upon American SLBM bases in Europe to obtain a larger SLBM ceiling in the Interim Agreement, they did not succeed, because the United States refused to talk about compensations. When the United States, in her turn, conveyed a certain willingness to agree on some sort of non-circumvention clause, the Soviet Union remained indifferent, as one might have anticipated.[29]

In the American–Soviet basic understanding of 20 May 1971, which broke the SALT deadlock, the Soviet Union is on record as having dropped her precondition concerning FBS in return for some American concessions. Given Soviet priorities at that time, however, it seems doubtful to what extent this really was a precondition; after all, prior to the basic understanding of 20 May 1971, the prevailing view within the American Administration seems to have been that in a more comprehensive agreement the FBS issue could be satisfactorily settled by a non-circumvention clause which might have been acceptable to both the Soviet Union and the major European allies in NATO. In this context it is not easy to understand precisely what the Soviet Union gave up at that time. For obvious tactical reasons the Soviet demand had been made to appear as a precondition, but both the more likely attitude towards a comprehensive agreement at that time and the subsequent public attempts to blur the FBS category have cast some doubt on the Soviet Union's seriousness about this issue.[30]

As a result of the American–Soviet basic understanding and subsequent negotiations, the FBS issue disappeared from the agenda of SALT I; however, the very outcome of SALT I was bound to determine the context in which the issue could be revived in SALT II. Had SLBM not been included in SALT I, the Soviet Union could quite plausibly have tried to counter subsequent

---

[28] At this time the suggestion also included carrier-based aircraft and *Pershings*.

[29] In either case an unresolved FBS issue was likely to be the preferred outcome. If the United States had agreed to compensations or if the Soviet Union had agreed to non-circumvention, the FBS issue could be considered a closed one for the time being, taking pressure off the dynamics of Western policy-formation processes by reducing uncertainties. It so happened that the Soviet side preferred to remove FBS from the SALT I agenda.

[30] To the extent that the Soviet Union was still interested in the inclusion of the Sixth Fleet, it is worth noting that Brezhnev made his proposal for banning fleets from distant seas at about the same time the FBS issue was being dropped from the SALT I agenda.

American attempts to achieve a follow-on agreement on SLBM by broadening the subject; land-based strategic missiles having been agreed upon, it would then have appeared 'logical' to confine subsequent negotiations to 'non-home-based systems', comprising both SLBM and FBS. This would have made the Soviet position on FBS rather strong; fortunately, however, it was avoided through the SLBM protocol. But this avoidance may be regarded as additional implicit evidence that the FBS issue was not of primary importance for Moscow – if only because of foreseeable opportunities to bring it up again.

On balance, therefore, one would have thought that, because of the outcome of the 1972 Moscow summit, there was no imminent diplomatic threat to SACEUR's nuclear strike forces and that if it were to arise it would be in the context of American negotiating proposals, which should therefore be subjected to Alliance consultations in due course. But, paradoxically, since that summit it has increasingly been taken for granted within the Alliance that SALT II will somehow seriously affect SACEUR's strike forces. In spite of new Soviet moves in the early rounds of SALT II, this probably has to be explained essentially in terms of the inner dynamics of Western policy-formation processes.

**Changes in the American Position**

What seems to have evolved as the American Administration's position on the FBS/SALT issue is the outcome of several bargaining processes: within the Administration, with Congress, with the Alliance and with the Soviet Union. To some extent this can be regarded as a sequence which is likely to be repeated in forthcoming rounds. Highlighting a few crucial elements and decisions may help to understand where options have been precluded already and what the present negotiating commitments seem to be.

During SALT I the Administration was faced with three crucial decisions which in one way or another were related to SACEUR's nuclear-strike forces. First, it had to consider the problem for both sides of how to safeguard a comprehensive limitation of central systems against violations and/or circumventions. Secondly, it had then to set the stage for negotiations on an agreement which would limit selected categories of offensive systems. Thirdly, it had to interpret the Interim Agreement so as to avoid a weak bargaining position for forthcoming negotiations on a permanent treaty.

In all three cases the implications for American bargaining commitments were quite different. The comprehensive proposal (originally labelled 'limited agreement', to distinguish it from comprehensive reduction agreements) was suggested in rather tentative form in an open-ended trial-and-error phase.[31] The selective Interim Agreement which was finally envisaged in the joint declaration of intent of 20 May 1971 was the only possible escape for the Administration from a choice between no agreement (which would have meant no summit) and an agreement on anti-ballistic missiles (ABM) only (at that time a clear Soviet preference). Subsequently both sides have repeatedly committed themselves to a (selective or comprehensive) permanent treaty,[32] but while the American Administration was conceivably under stronger pressure to achieve a successful outcome in the negotiations than the Soviet Union, at the same time it had to try to avoid the imbalances allegedly inherent in the Interim Agreement.

In all three situations the American side came to see itself as a *demandeur*. Therefore, whatever the American second thoughts on European-based nuclear forces and the Soviet basic negotiating objectives may initially have been, the American side found that it had to respond somehow to Soviet demands on FBS.

*The Exploratory Phase: the Comprehensive Limitation Proposal*

Given the complexities of the strategic balance, an agreement on the limitation of offensive central systems raises two kinds of problems: possible clandestine changes in categories which are governed by the agreement (violation) and possible overt changes in categories not governed by the agreement which might upset the balance (circumvention). Safeguards against violations are often felt to be necessary for both selective and comprehensive limitation agreements, and must be designed so as to match specified veri-

[31] I.e. the 4 August proposal, the so-called Option E – see John Newhouse, *Cold Dawn* (New York: Holt, Rinehart and Winston, 1973), pp. 186–90.

[32] Given the Vladivostok agreement, the most likely outcome will be a long-term comprehensive treaty which will provide a framework for subsequent selective agreements governing strategic weapons procurements so as to satisfy mutually accepted criteria.

fication requirements; these can be expressed in terms of means of verification and of conditions for verification (as in Article VIII of the ABM Treaty and Article V of the Interim Agreement).[33] Circumventions are, by definition, possible and legal in the case of selective limitation agreements, although additional informal or tacit understandings are conceivable (see some of the interpretations and declarations which have been attached to the Interim Agreement).

In the case of a negotiated comprehensive agreement, the parties may wish to exclude weapons which are not yet deployed in large numbers but have characteristics comparable to those governed by the expected agreement (mobile land-based ICBM, cruise missiles) or to include weapons which differ technically or politically in some respects from those governed by the agreement but which may nonetheless have comparable effects in a central war. There are three categories of the latter type:

1. Weapons with a dual capability (as was widely assumed in the case of those SS-11 which have been put into SS-5 silos).
2. Weapons which can be transferred to a third party, either strategic delivery systems (e.g., to the United Kingdom) or warheads (e.g., under NATO's sharing arrangements).
3. Tactical delivery systems which can reach the opponent's homeland either because of forward deployment (land-based or carrier-based) or by flying one-way-missions (as in the case of the 700 Soviet medium bombers and some of the CONUS-based tactical F-111s or most of the F-4s in Western Europe).

During the spring and summer of 1970 SALT began to focus for a while on the possibility of a comprehensive agreement. The American side, according to what seems to have been the overriding concern of the Verification Panel in the earlier rounds, was then concentrating on the verification requirements of such an agreement: more specifically on the conditions for verification in view of the difficulty of distinguishing mobile land-based ICBM from IR/MRBM on the one hand and of distinguishing new silo construction for ICBM from that for IRBM on the other. The need for verifiability and the apparent

difficulty of separating the two pairs of systems led to the idea of additional bans on silo construction for IR/MRBM and on mobile land-based IR/MRBM, although these obviously were not considered to be central systems. The American side, however, did not seem to dramatize possibilities for Soviet circumvention of the agreement.[34]

The Soviet Union, on the other hand, was apparently less concerned over the verification issue but did emphasize two possible circumventions: by forward deployment and by transfer to third parties. At the same time she was somewhat flexible in her view of what precisely should be included in an agreement, and it remained uncertain (at least to observers) whether she stressed these circumventions because she really wanted an agreement to include them or, as has been suggested above, because she preferred to delay agreements on offensive weapons altogether.

The American and Soviet demands for additional limitations were therefore asymmetrical, in that they stemmed from different requirements, and there was no direct connection. The United States was tentatively suggesting her solution to the verification issue, but was unwilling to include non-central systems except in terms of some kind of non-circumvention understanding. The Soviet Union, on the other hand, was demanding the inclusion of FBS in a comprehensive agreement (if only as a joker), but was unwilling to accept limitations on IR/MRBM on the basis of physical verification requirements; however, she seems ultimately to have accepted the principle of adequate verification by means of satellite reconnaissance, as reflected in the verification provisions of the SALT I agreements.

Though there was no logical connection between these additional demands of the two sides, there was a potential diplomatic link. This seemed important, especially with regard to more simplistic West European wishes to

---

[33] See *The Military Balance 1972–1973* (London: IISS, 1972), pp. 83–6 and *Survival*, July/August 1972, pp. 193, 195.

[34] This may be so because the replacement of SS-5 by SS-11 (possibly with a dual capability) occurred a few months later. As for the tactical systems, it has been recognized that although the Soviet medium-bomber force 'is targeted primarily against the Eurasian area, we cannot ignore the fact that these aircraft do have a one-way-mission capability against the United States'. (*Military Manpower Requirements Report for FY 1972*, US Department of Defense, February 1972, p. 14.)

include Soviet IR/MRBM in a SALT agreement and/or American assumptions about European expectations of this kind. There was, in fact, a well-understood, though modest, West European interest in additional restrictions on mobile IR/MRBM and silo construction for IR/MRBM, but from a West European point of view this was little more than a bonus. Undoubtedly it could not satisfy those who favoured a more straight-forward inclusion of these weapons, and, since it was obvious to most West European observers that this demand inescapably implied the straightforward inclusion of FBS, it never became a prevailing view anyway. Most West European observers recognized that even a drastic reduction of Soviet IR/MRBM would scarcely deny the Soviet Union the strategic options she now has, whereas there was overwhelming agreement that a corresponding reduction of FBS would danger-ously affect NATO's posture.[35]

From the American Administration's point of view, a satisfactory and preferable formula could have been the insistence on corollary measures, in order to meet verification require-ments and to recognize West European interests, in combination with some sort of unspecified non-circumvention understanding, in order to take account of Soviet concerns. As time went on, however, the verification requirements ceased to be of overriding importance, while the American side seemed to develop some second thoughts on corollary measures (possibly because of growing interests in renewed schemes for mobile land-based missiles of a kind which could have been affected by both types of additional limitations).

When the proposal for a comprehensive limitation agreement was finally withdrawn, the American side had not gone on record as demanding any safeguards against possible Soviet circumventions and had dropped its requests for corollary restrictions on the up-grading of IR/MRBM by which it had originally sought to meet its verification requirements. It had given up the only currently conceivable formula for including Soviet IR/MRBM in a central

agreement.[36] However, it had apparently ac-cepted the principle of a non-circumvention understanding as part of a comprehensive agreement, though it still rejected Soviet demands for inclusion of non-central systems. Apart from political and military implications for the NATO Alliance, the inclusion of FBS as part of agreed force levels was then considered to be dis-advantageous for the central balance.

*The Negotiations: the Selective Interim Agreement*
By the end of 1970 it had become clear that the Soviet Union was temporarily driving at an agreement on ABM only, and in the spring of 1971 the Soviet proposal was specified. By implication, this postponed the FBS issue as far as declared Soviet priorities were concerned. The American Administration, on the other hand, was anxious to retain in one way or another a linkage between an ABM agreement and a ceiling for heavy missiles, though a treaty-like comprehensive agreement could no longer be expected to be coupled with an ABM agreement. At the same time, the President linked a success-ful outcome of these negotiations to higher stakes: a summit meeting with a broad prospect for the future development of American–Soviet relationships.

The American side therefore was anxious to include as many categories as possible in as formal an agreement as could be achieved under tolerable conditions. It tried to spell out formulae to remove what again could have turned out to be an obstacle: the FBS issue. Although the 'logic' of an agreement which was less than comprehensive and not treaty-like did not require the inclusion of FBS, the American side was anxious to develop a formula covering the issue which could be acceptable to both NATO and the Soviet Union. Apparently there was still a tendency to link this issue to Soviet IR/MRBM, but in the given situation this could no longer be considered as a serious precondition. On the other hand, a numerical inclusion of FBS was still being rejected.

There were three possible ways of designing an FBS formula: first, an accompanying tacit or informal agreement which would freeze FBS

[35] In fact, from a strategic point of view, a substantial reduction of presently deployed IR/MRBM would be less important than preventing the large-scale replacement of these systems by mobile IR/MRBM. Substitution of mobile IR/MRBM would multiply the targets on SACEUR's threat list three or four times, because, unlike fixed IR/MRBM, they would not be clustered.

[36] However, one should add that, from an American point of view, the Interim Agreement of 26 May 1972 is supposed to govern the construction of new IR/MRBM silos.

quantitatively; secondly, the inclusion of a non-circumvention clause which could be specified in terms of non-central systems; and thirdly, a transfer of this issue to a different negotiation level (e.g., MFR) with a declared negotiating commitment for such a contingency.

From a West European point of view, there would have been a perceptible difference between the first and second of these formulae. The first would probably have been more limited in scope, because it would have applied to American strike forces only, but would have been more disadvantageous by virtue of being a bilateral limitation agreement on FBS. The second, by contrast, might have applied to non-American strike forces in Europe as well – and hence might have been wider in scope – but would not expressly have been a limitation agreement, nor would it necessarily have precluded a future multilateral limitation agreement on FBS. Both formulae, after all, might have turned out to be acceptable to West Europeans, although the implications for future negotiations both on the SALT level and on a European level (possibly MFR) would have to have been specified. NATO did, in fact, agree on the second formula at that time.

In this situation, the Soviet side might have achieved a treaty on ABM only, along with a less binding agreement on offensive weapons, which need not have been strictly comprehensive. They would have got a non-circumvention clause on FBS, and such a solution would no longer have been confined to a comprehensive agreement. However, the White House finally decided to drive for a more selective and transitional limitation agreement without reference to FBS,[37] and the Soviet Union agreed, as reflected in the joint declaration of 20 May 1971.

Given her stand on the FBS issue, four possible explanations (or any combination of them) are available. The Soviet Union may have been attracted by the broader political implications of the American offer (summit diplomacy, etc.). She may have seen some sort of American commitment to include FBS in SALT at a later stage and may have considered this a part of the basic understanding. She may have relied

simply on the chance of achieving a favourably balanced force-level agreement (due to the time factor involved), thereby creating an American incentive to rebalance this in subsequent negotiations by including FBS. Or she may have been interested above all in buying the time her construction programmes needed before agreeing on a limitation of offensive weapons. In any event, the joint declaration of 20 May 1971 removed the need to insist on the FBS issue.

Even in retrospect some argue that the United States might have achieved a more comprehensive and balanced agreement at an earlier date (i.e., before the Soviet Union had completed her land-based missile construction programmes) if Washington had introduced its non-circumvention formula. But if the argument is correct that the Soviet Union above all wanted to buy time for these programmes, she could hardly have been expected to be satisfied with this approach, and Washington would have been faced with more far-reaching Soviet demands on FBS. The United States would have been confronted with a hard choice between more substantial concessions on FBS (which she was not prepared to make) and postponement of an offensive agreement granted under much less favourable conditions (i.e., without guidelines for subsequent negotiations and yet with the FBS issue still pending in a slightly dramatized form). On balance, therefore, the White House decisions at that time appear to have been the most favourable for FBS.

### The Ratification Process: Towards a Permanent Treaty

It was the very nature of the Interim Agreement, and especially the protocol on SLBM, which tended to produce changes in the American Administration's position on the FBS issue. Indeed, first evidence became available literally just a few minutes after the signing of the agreements. In negotiating terms any immediate pressure on the FBS issue appeared to be unlikely, because the five years' duration of the Interim Agreement bought plenty of time, and the agreement on SLBM removed the immediate likelihood of Soviet pressure for an early SALT II agreement on non-home-based systems, linking the Soviet interest in an agreement on FBS to the American interest in an agreement on SLBM. But the numerical imbalances inherent in the

[37] In spring 1971 parts of the bureaucracy in Washington (notably the State Department) considered various solutions for the FBS issue; they seemed to prefer a non-circumvention approach which they submitted to NATO.

agreements (particularly in the SLBM protocol) were felt to require an effort by the Administration to ensure favourable domestic consumption of the agreements and of summitry at large – of which these agreements were seen as the most important expression. With elections due in fall 1972, Congressional approval was the obvious short-term target. Consequently, Henry Kissinger stressed that, in the current situation, the numerical imbalances largely disappeared if one took into consideration additional weapons categories, such as strategic bombers and forward-deployed strike aircraft, not governed by the agreements.

Thus the FBS issue was back again as a crucial element of domestic controversy; moreover, for the first time it was stated in terms of numerical inclusion – although admittedly inclusion in the central balance rather than in forthcoming agreements. Given the fact that both American allies and the Soviet Union listen carefully to what comes out of American domestic debates, this selling effort was bound to alarm West European governments (possibly unduly) and to encourage the Soviet Union to jump back on the FBS issue early during SALT II (as indeed she did). It did not seem to satisfy conservative opponents of the agreements either.

Effectively, the American Administration claimed in a domestic context what it had denied to the Soviet Union all the way through: FBS were now offered as an element in the central balance. Whatever may have been the Soviet motivation for driving at inherent numerical imbalances in the Interim Agreement, it generated an interest on the American side in using FBS to re-establish an apparent balance in central force relationships. This may have been done only for temporary tactical purposes during the continuing domestic debates – indeed the Administration was anxious not to enter into subsequent negotiating commitments (although it did not rule them out either) – but it triggered off a Congressional debate (to some extent echoed by the press) that in future negotiations are likely to affect political assessments of FBS. The strategic value of FBS became the key issue of this debate.[38]

The liberal forces which had generally tended to downgrade, ignore or even criticize the strategic role of FBS in the European theatre were quite prepared to attribute a significant central-war role to these forces – at least in terms of Soviet perceptions, which allegedly should be recognized. In fact, some even went so far as to include many more or all of the 7,000 nuclear warheads in Europe in such considerations. The conservative forces were in a more difficult position. While they were anxious to exclude any European-based nuclear forces from future central agreements, they had to apply double standards, i.e., they had to argue that FBS must not be included in central agreements because of their strategic irrelevance in the central balance and because of their overriding strategic importance in the European theatre. That came close to squaring the circle.

There were four principle arguments to disprove significant central-war capabilities of FBS. First, their very mobility rules out clear-cut definitions of FBS in a central balance; e.g., carrier-based aircraft in the Mediterranean possess or lack FBS characteristics according to the position of the carriers at any given time. Secondly, FBS are not exclusively designed for a nuclear-delivery role; the very fact that they have multi-purpose roles renders their central strategic role 'almost negligible'. Thirdly, in a central war FBS could be completely neutralized: their dispersal on roughly 40 bases renders them fatally vulnerable to Soviet pre-emption – 100 of the existing 500 IR/MRBM could knock out even SACEUR's complete nuclear arsenal. Fourthly, forward basing involves serious political uncertainties, as the cases of France, Libya and Okinawa have suggested. Thus the deep nuclear interdiction role of FBS, which most West European analysts still consider as their decisive purpose, has been deliberately downgraded.

But American Administrations will continue to live with three very different audiences: those in Washington, in West European capitals and in Moscow. It is likely, therefore, that the politics of SALT will affect the FBS issue in the future as they did in the past. In addition, this account of SALT I may suggest that not only the politics of SALT but also the processes of bureaucratic decision-making are prone to the danger of depriving 'ourselves of criteria by which to judge the process'.[39]

---

[38] See 'Strategic Arms Limitation Talks (SALT): Legislative History of the Jackson Amendment', 1972 (from the office of Senator Henry M. Jackson), particularly pages 61, 62, 65, 74, 104, 209, 211.

[39] Henry A. Kissinger, *op. cit.* in note 14, p. 221.

## III. DIMENSIONS OF CHANGE: POSSIBLE NEGOTIATING OUTCOMES

The lessons of SALT I result from concerns and perceptions which by far outgrew real possibilities and from incremental changes that more often than not went almost unnoticed. SALT II, and possibly MFR, may well produce changes in the existing nuclear strike posture of NATO that go far beyond SALT I. Yet it will probably be understood that these would be specific changes within a structure which is already undergoing numerous non-negotiated changes anyway – or else, if alarmism developed again, the changes would result from broader policy decisions which are perceived to affect the strike posture of NATO.

In order to identify the likely negotiating issues and to put them into proper perspective, it seems prudent to recognize four difficulties.

1. Given the complex nuclear strike posture in Europe, forthcoming negotiations are unlikely to produce criteria which would single out self-evident categories of weapons systems in terms of strategic missions, deployment or technical characteristics. Any accepted definition would result from political bargaining.

2. In terms of force generation programmes, take-off schedules and strike plans, SACEUR's nuclear strike forces appear to be among the most tightly integrated forces within NATO, although they consist of many more or less heterogenous components. A substantial number of American strike aircraft is based in Britain or Spain or on the Sixth Fleet – i.e., outside the areas with which Allied Forces Central Europe (AFCENT) and Allied Forces Southern Europe (AFSOUTH) are identified.

3. Overall American tactical air forces appear to be coherently structured. This includes the American basing structure in Western Europe. In fact, the 'NATO commitment to the common defence of Western Europe is one of the most significant factors in determining the size of our . . . tactical air forces'.[40] Nevertheless it has been suggested that 'probably no other support area suffers more from piece-meal planning than does base operations,'[41] and American basing policies in Europe usually have a tendency to present multi-dimensional problems.

4. Changes in the existing nuclear strike posture of NATO in Europe can occur in many ways, especially as a result of unilateral constraints, conversion programmes, obsolescence without adequate replacement, and negotiated agreements. Thus the impact of potential agreements could well turn out to be much more modest than other kinds of changes which usually receive no significant public attention.

### The Issue of Criteria in SALT II and MFR

Criteria for defined categories of strike aircraft for potential agreements have become increasingly specific in SALT and may become less specific in MFR. While in SALT the category is defined according to a Soviet criterion, in MFR it will be defined according to a NATO criterion. In SALT only those aircraft which can reach Soviet territory in a two-way mission are now included in the so-called FBS category; this rules out numerous aircraft which, because of their one-way-mission capability, were considered likely candidates in the past.[42] In MFR only strike aircraft in West Germany and the Benelux countries (essentially the Netherlands) could be included on the Western side according to the NATO definition of the reduction area, though, given current uncertainties over the eventual reduction area and possible readiness to compromise in view of the mobility of aircraft, deployments in additional areas could conceivably be affected.

It should be added that there is an important functional difference between SALT and MFR criteria. In SALT the issue for the West is which elements of the NATO posture are to be kept out of these negotiations, whereas in MFR the criterion determines which elements NATO could consider as possible candidates for bargaining offers. In other words, in SALT there is a tendency to deny the Soviet Union certain bargaining advantages with regard to FBS; but in MFR the

---

[40] *Military Manpower Requirements Report, op. cit.,* p. 24.
[41] Martin Binkin, *Support Costs in the Defense Budget. The Submerged One-Third* (Washington, D.C.: The Brookings Institution 1972), p. 26.

[42] Supposedly the Soviet Union chose the two-way-mission criterion in order to pre-empt possible American attempts to counter Soviet FBS demands by bringing in the Soviet medium-bomber capability. Soviet medium bombers are not covered by a two-way-mission criterion.

opposite has been studied, namely the 'selling' of nuclear-strike aircraft. Although this is not necessarily inconsistent, the latter tends to weaken Western arguments for keeping FBS out of SALT. It would make sense if this kind of interdependence between the two approaches had been a deliberate choice on the American side, but it is equally conceivable that it resulted simply from bureaucratic accidents.

In SALT only American aircraft would be included in the FBS category, and non-American aircraft could not be governed by an agreement on FBS. In fact, no Soviet attempt has so far been made to include them indirectly (for example, in a non-transfer clause) and any such attempt is unlikely to be accepted by the United States. In MFR, however, all NATO strike aircraft in a specified area could be affected, though in practical terms only American strike aircraft are likely candidates for inclusion. There is a familiar line of general arguments which emphasizes a fundamental difference between reductions of stationed and indigenous forces, the former requiring simply redeployment, the latter allegedly partial disarmament. Given the variety of conceivable technical possibilities for eliminating the nuclear strike mission of interdiction aircraft, these arguments seem less pertinent to this particular category, but there are, nonetheless, some specific reasons which suggest that only American strike aircraft are likely to be included in any mixed-package agreement which might come out of MFR.

First, East–West negotiations on redeployment of American strike aircraft appear to be diplomatically less risky than negotiations which involve existing sharing arrangements, even though the West German Air Force years ago began to undertake unilateral conversion programmes which do in fact reduce its strike role, and the Netherlands seems to be increasingly prepared to give up her nuclear strike role altogether. Secondly, redeployments of air force units (as in the *Crested Cap* programme in 1968) seem to be somewhat more promising in terms of balance-of-payments savings than redeployments of army units (as in the *Reforger* programme in 1968).[43] An expansion of the

dual-basing system therefore may find considerable support in the United States.[44] Thirdly, in the case of mixed packages which would involve aircraft on the Western side and some sort of ground forces (e.g., tanks) on the Eastern side NATO could benefit from asymmetries as it could not do in the case of mutual reductions of ground forces: American redeployment of aircraft might take less time than redeployment of Soviet tanks.

None of these arguments would provide a sufficient basis for supporting mixed packages of this kind, but they do suggest that, if mixed packages ever become a possibility, then it is stationed aircraft that are the most likely to be involved. Given the British stand, this would essentially involve American aircraft. Thus in both conferences only American aircraft seem to be at stake – in SALT by definition, in MFR due to circumstances.

At the same time, it is worth noting that the criteria governing SALT and MFR are complementary in the sense that a combination of a SALT agreement on FBS and a mixed-package agreement involving nuclear strike aircraft could theoretically affect the bulk of American strike aircraft in Europe (in SALT, F-111s in Great Britain, F-4s in Turkey and northern Italy and carrier-based A-6s and A-7s in the Mediterranean; in MFR, F-4s in West Germany). Some F-4s would be excluded because of their normal deployment (in Britain) and some could be considered to be outside the scope of negotiations if FBS quality were defined by reference to parent bases rather than intra-European rotation patterns (e.g. those based at Torrejón in Spain); Sixth Fleet aircraft would be excluded if the fleet's operational areas were restricted to the Eastern Mediterranean.

If it should ever come to negotiations on mixed packages, MFR would probably affect the NATO posture much more than SALT II. In SALT II only some kind of modestly constraining limitations of strike aircraft is a likely contingency (although some reductions – e.g., adaptations to an 'effective equality' agreement – cannot be

---

43 Under the *Crested Cap* programme 96 nuclear-capable F-4s were practically withdrawn from West Germany although under a dual-basing scheme that provided for regular forward-deployment exercises. Under the *Reforger*

programme army combat units based in America were airlifted to Europe for combat exercises using pre-positioned equipment.
44 Roland A. Paul, *American Military Commitments Abroad* (New Brunswick, N.J.: Rutgers University Press, 1973), p. 137.

ruled out altogether). In MFR a limitation agreement would seem more or less meaningless unless it imposed constraints on dual-basing arrangements, which the United States is not likely to accept. One conceivable possibility is a partial reduction of American aircraft, although with sufficient allowance for redeployment under dual-basing schemes (a mixed package agreement would probably somehow regulate dual-basing schemes on both sides). In other words, a *Crested Cap* type of reduction in the AFCENT area as part of an East–West MFR agreement is conceivable, though not likely.

Whether a limitation agreement on these aircraft would merely rule out certain reinforcements and/or modernizations of these forces or whether it would effectively constrain their operational procedures depends upon what, in the context of SALT is being considered as the forward-basing structure. In the case of the 20th tactical wing of the Third Air Force in Upper Hayford, Britain, (i.e., the F-111s) there are no ambiguities. In the case of carrier-based aircraft it probably boils down to the possibility of certain restricted operational areas in the eastern Adriatic and eastern Aegean.[45] The most crucial element in the American posture are the F-4s in the Mediterranean. The parent or home base of many of these aircraft is Torrejón in Spain,[46] which is well outside the area defined by the Soviet two-way-mission criterion, while some seem to have their home base in Germany or Britain. Many of these aircraft are dispersed from parent wing locations. In the AFSOUTH area they are primarily forward-

deployed to Incirlik (Turkey) and Aviano (northern Italy), where they are on alert, and some (like the F-4s at Incirlik) are supposed to have a nuclear-strike mission.

There are three obvious SALT negotiating options applicable to these American nuclear-capable F-4s. In Option I only parent bases (notably Torrejón) are forward bases in the SALT context, and American forward detachments to Incirlik or Aviano would be left out of the picture. Indeed, land-based F-4s in the Mediterranean would practically cease to be potential candidates for a SALT agreement on FBS, because the ranges involved clearly do not meet the two-way-mission criterion, leaving only the F-111s in Britain as possibles for the FBS category. Option II would refer also to forward deployments on mission airfields like Incirlik or Aviano; given the two-way-mission criterion and the range of forward-deployed F-4s on these mission airfields, they could qualify for the FBS category. But these aircraft are deployed on a rotational basis. If forward-basing in the SALT context were taken to imply temporary dispersals, this might blur distinctions between parent bases and temporary deployment, though on the other hand a limitation agreement based on this interpretation might still leave existing rotation and forward-deployment procedures basically unaffected, simply imposing some kind of ceiling. Option III would presuppose additional Soviet demands; the Soviet Union may accept that rotational forward-deployments do not belong in the FBS category, as she already accepts that parent bases like Torrejón are outside the area defined by the two-way-mission criterion, but she might instead try to impose constraints on rotations and forward deployments ('operational practices'). This would require a different Soviet approach which has apparently not been suggested in the past, but in SALT Soviet officials did in fact move from emphasis on force relationships towards emphasis on operational practices.

Thus, on the basis of currently accepted criteria, the FBS category in SALT comprises three components which differ considerably on most counts: the F-111 wing in Britain (the only unambiguous item in this category), possibly F-4s in the Mediterranean (subject to the three options mentioned above), and carrier-based aircraft, which would be subject to restrictions

---

[45] However, given the fact that carriers would be particularly vulnerable in these areas, where they might well be within range of Soviet aircraft, in effect such restrictions may not be of overriding importance to the Alliance. One might even doubt whether training programmes during recent years still allow for instant nuclear strike missions by carrier-based aircraft in the Mediterranean. It might require several months at least to reactivate this role fully – and the political decision to do so. It is widely assumed that land-based aircraft are in a much better position to carry out nuclear strike missions than carrier-based aircraft.

To the extent that the Soviet Union takes the verification issue seriously she may find an agreement on carrier-based aircraft even harder than one on land-based aircraft. These considerations may well render this contingency fairly insignificant from a Soviet point of view.

[46] Torrejón is also where the Sixteenth Air Force has its headquarters.

on their operational areas (still assuming a nuclear strike mission for carrier-based aircraft in the Mediterranean). The F-111s in Britain and the F-4s covered by the forward-deployment option (Option II above) would be included in the FBS category simply because of their basing characteristics. F-4s covered by the third option and carrier-based aircraft could be included only if additional operational constraints were demanded by the Soviet Union: constraints on rotational procedures in the case of land-based F-4s and restricted operational areas in the case of carrier-based aircraft.

The American non-circumvention clause as it appears to have been proposed to the Soviet Union during SALT II was probably meant as a delaying counter-proposal, but – unlike the non-circumvention clause NATO had agreed upon in 1971 (which emphasized different types of non-central systems including FBS) – this formula could possibly be framed so as to provide the kinds of constraints on operational practices referred to above.[47] In the case of the Sixth Fleet this does not seem to pose major problems, but in the case of dispersals of F-4s negotiated constraints might well cut into the whole fabric of SACEUR's nuclear strike posture. This would involve only a minority of nuclear strike aircraft,[48] but constraints could have operationally significant consequences that could affect major programmes not otherwise covered by possible SALT agreements.

## FBS: Three Categories

In order to assess possible consequences of SALT outcomes for the entire NATO strike posture, it seems appropriate to review briefly those three types of FBS most likely to be affected, in the light of their deployment rationales, their role in NATO integration and the kinds of problems they pose for American basing policy.

### F-111s in Great Britain

At present there is only one unambiguous FBS candidate in Europe: the 20th tactical wing of the Third Air Force, deployed since spring 1970 at Upper Hayford in Britain and equipped with 72 FB-111s. In a SALT context no reduction of these aircraft is currently on the cards, even though some kind of limitation is conceivable. However, given the specific case history of this European-based wing, even an agreement to withdraw it from Europe would hardly allow straightforward conclusions to be drawn concerning NATO's existing nuclear strike posture or the prospects for general American basing policies.

The deployment of an F-111 wing in Britain had three different causes: efforts to prolong the nuclear-strike role of the Royal Air Force, which finally resulted in failure; the need for conversion programmes in order to replace F-100s; and the availability of the F-111 as a plane in search of a mission. The background of the F-111 deployment is relevant to the FBS issue because of the usual tendency for anticipated changes in NATO force structure to be resisted, rightly or wrongly, by generalized doctrinal arguments, without reference to its mostly accidental origins and developments.

In 1965 Britain cancelled her TSR-2 bomber programme, and Strategic Air Command withdrew its remaining bombers from British soil (a number of B-47s). Thus the future of the Royal Air Force (RAF) in a strategic role and Britain's role as a strategic SAC base (begun in 1948) seemed to come to an end at the same time. When in summer 1967 Britain decided to replace her V-bombers by the mid-1970s the choice lay between the F-4 (with possibly insufficient range and payload), additional F-111s (the suitability of which for the European theatre still seemed arguable) and the outcome of a project study which was subsequently to lead to the Multi-Role Combat Aircraft (MRCA). On 29 April 1969 the decision was reached to go ahead with the MRCA, but it was no longer considered in a strategic role. In fact, on 1 July 1969 the RAF

---

[47] It is not known at this stage whether the removal of the FBS issue from the SALT agenda means that FBS will not be included in agreed aggregates (which has been the American position all along), or whether the issue has simply been delegated to MFR without any kind of non-circumvention agreement. The latter remains doubtful with regard to strike aircraft. It seems more likely that the non-circumvention issue will become crucially important again, but in a generalized form, so as to involve precision-guided cruise missiles as possible successors to currently deployed strike aircraft.

[48] Constraints of this kind could, however, involve certain aircraft which would not satisfy the two-way-mission criterion for FBS, e.g., F-4 in Britain with respect to possible detachments to Northern Europe, although in some cases (like Norway) such detachments would occur only in emergency situations which would not be affected by SALT agreements. Such agreements might affect peace-time deployments only.

52

formally gave up its strategic deterrent functions, which were taken over by the Royal Navy. At the same time the United States decided to replace one F-100 wing with an F-111 wing, and in spring 1970 this wing was being deployed in Upper Hayford. However, 'no additional F-111s will be there', i.e., the three other F-111 wings were to remain CONUS-based.[49]

Many American nuclear planners seem to imply that this wing belongs to American-targeted strategic forces rather than to NATO-targeted theatre forces. Thus, despite its NATO assignment, it has a somewhat unique role. The F-111 wing has a mission in NATO programmes but it seems to be much less integrated than, for example, West European F-104 wings; it is a tactical fighter wing with nuclear deep-interdiction missions but, in terms of NATO integration, its status does not seem very different from that of the three CONUS-based F-111 wings.

It is evident that in almost every respect this principal candidate for the FBS category is in a class of its own. It has been deployed in Britain since just before the beginning of the SALT negotiations – and, indeed, without attracting much public attention. In terms of American basing policies there seem to be no plans to increase or reduce the number of these aircraft on British soil. Thus, as long as only the number of aircraft (rather than specific types) matters in SALT, the mere inclusion in the talks of 72 F-111s in Britain in one way or another is what is at stake.

*Nuclear-capable F-4s in the Mediterranean*
As has been pointed out, F-4s in the AFSOUTH area are more controversial candidates for the FBS category. The basing structure for these aircraft appears to be relatively flexible, and yet this very flexibility poses problems for American basing policy which make the case of these F-4s, too, unique and diplomatically sensitive.

This is particularly obvious in the Turkish case. Ever since the Truman Doctrine in 1947 military relations between Turkey and the United States have been of a special kind. Evidence for this can be seen in the deployment of *Jupiter* IRBM on Turkish soil as well as in the way these were subsequently removed. As a response to domestic changes in Turkey, as well as to frictions which resulted over Cyprus, the United States reduced her military presence in Turkey substantially after the mid-1960s, turned a number of installations over to Turkey, accepted a number of legal restrictions on American forces and renegotiated some 55 agreements. After three years of clumsy negotiations these various agreements were consolidated, but, since American base rights had become a delicate issue, in order to pre-empt domestic criticism Prime Minister Demirel insisted that this should involve a more specific base-rights agreement. In so doing he tried to get the best of both worlds by making the American commitments more specific, but on 3 July 1969 the new base-rights agreement was signed without a more specific American commitment.[50] In other words, after difficult negotiations a new base-rights agreement had been reached which was probably an improvement in terms of Turkish sovereignty but reinforced Turkish sensitivities towards American defence commitments.

Obviously, American nuclear strike aircraft are of particular importance in this context. When the FBS issue was being played up in a more dramatic fashion during SALT I the Turkish government expressed concerns similar to her concerns in the early 1960s, when *Jupiters* were being removed from Turkish soil. Thus, after its three years of hard bargaining over American basing rights, the Turkish government felt threatened by the prospects of a SALT agreement on FBS that might affect American deployments on Turkish soil. This appears to be paradoxical unless the complex domestic situation is taken into account. In the light of this situation, however, with the Turkish government trying to balance its handling of domestic anti-Americanism against its anxiety to keep the American defence commitment alive, changes in American basing schemes for F-4s in Turkey (unlikely as they seem to be) are bound to cause problems in Turkish–American relationships.[51] In fact, these

---

[49] Gen. Boylan's testimony in *Hearings before the Senate Committee on Armed Services*, 92nd Congress, Fiscal Year 1973 Authorization, Part 6, p. 3520.

[50] See Roland A. Paul, *op. cit.*, p. 172.
[51] Recent political developments in Turkey and their interactions with Congressional politics in Washington have come close to jeopardizing American bases in Turkey altogether. Similarly, political developments in Greece, as well as the renegotiation of base rights in Spain, underscore the relevant point that specific base

problems appeared to be aggravated when the home-port agreement for the Sixth Fleet was concluded with Greece early in 1972. There may also exist some American misgivings over the 1969 basing-rights agreement, which allows forward deployments in Turkey only for NATO missions and under NATO programmes except for cases where the Turkish government has expressly agreed on a special contingency.[52]

### Carrier-Based Nuclear Strike Aircraft

The Sixth Fleet is yet another case. It was established long before nuclear-capable tactical fighters were deployed anywhere, and in fact existed in its embryonic form long before the NATO machinery had been set up. It always has been a multi-functional force, and for the foreseeable future it will be important to retain the Sixth Fleet for a variety of purposes.

The Sixth Fleet acquired a nuclear-mission capability in the late 1950s, above all as the result of American inter-service rivalries which led to the notion of naval tactical aircraft sharing nuclear-strike programmes in Europe. However, in spite of the advantages of carrier-based aircraft (e.g., independence from bases on foreign soil), it was always widely accepted that they are more vulnerable and less suitable for strike missions than land-based aircraft.[53] Moreover, the operational area for nuclear strike missions against Soviet territory is very limited, which further increases the natural vulnerability of carriers. In addition, the status of the Sixth Fleet was ambiguous from a NATO point of view: although they were supposed to operate in accordance with NATO strike programmes, its ships were just 'committed' forces. The US Navy has apparently realized these disadvantages, since it seems that training programmes, etc., relating

to nuclear-mission capability have been substantially reduced. At the same time, there is no obvious pretext in SALT II to include nuclear-capable aircraft on board the Sixth Fleet.

The Sixth Fleet will remain important in many ways. For political reasons it may turn out to be somewhat more difficult than in the past to retain it in the Mediterranean, and it therefore seems important clearly to distinguish the Fleet's nuclear-mission capability from all its other functions. It would probably be a gross mistake to let the Sixth Fleet become a subject of negotiations like SALT in a way which might also affect its other functions (and units), simply because of a failure to make this distinction.

It would be difficult to define the issue of nuclear-capable carrier-based aircraft in terms of FBS demands in a SALT context. The most far-reaching results of SALT II that might specifically affect these aircraft would be (a) the acceptance of restricted operational areas in the eastern Mediterranean, in case nuclear-capable aircraft happened to be aboard a Sixth Fleet carrier (virtually impossible to verify),[54] or (b) the counting of these aircraft or (c) even the elimination of their nuclear-strike role, no matter where the carrier is at any given time (which not only raises the issue of verifiability again but also would broaden the FBS category considerably beyond the scope implied by the two-way-mission criterion).

Given the low strategic importance of these nuclear strike aircraft, it would be possible to consider specific concessions on the carrier issue (along with potential Western counter-demands) in order to be able to control the negotiations and prevent them from affecting the Sixth Fleet at large. Unlike forward detachments in the Sixteenth Air Force, the nuclear-mission capability of the Sixth Fleet seems to pose no serious problems within the Alliance, even among the southern flank countries; in fact, not even the US Navy seems to be particularly concerned. What matters is the presence of this fleet. In the current context the prospect of East–West agreements which resulted in the reduction or

---

policy issues are vastly more important than any change that could conceivably result from a SALT agreement on FBS. Fortunately, the base issue never became intermeshed with SALT considerations. Once more, bureaucratic compartmentalization proved the virtues of inertia, whatever its shortcomings.

[52] During the 1973 Middle East war the United States was denied the use of facilities in Turkey for supply operations to Israel. Subsequent American criticisms must be understood in the light of Soviet transit flights to supply Syria and Egypt, against which Turkey apparently did not protest.

[53] Indeed in the early 1960s it was widely assumed that carriers would lose their nuclear-mission capability as soon as SLBM became operational.

[54] It seems impossible to verify any agreement on FBS by national means only. Thus the Soviet–American agreed guidelines for SALT II, which provide for national means only, have important implications for the FBS issue.

even removal of this fleet would probably jeopardize the structures of the Alliance in that area – and, in fact, more than Alliance structures.[55]

## The Three Cases Compared

The three case histories display a striking disparity between, on the one hand, the specific issues involved and, on the other, the widely accepted definitions of the FBS problem and the corresponding perceived risks of potential SALT agreements on FBS. The three possible SALT contingencies have, in fact, few characteristics in common. They hardly constitute a self-evident category of strike aircraft. But, while political perceptions tend to create facts, the specific issues involved in any of the three more likely cases are unlikely to gain the kind of political attention they deserve in order to prevent specific crises. Disparities of this kind cannot be explained in terms of bureaucratic accidents or individual failures; they seem to have structural causes.

The role of bureaucracies within the Alliance is of crucial importance in such processes of issue identification, and this is particularly true of NATO's military bureaucracies. Three types of origin of issue-identification processes (in Alliance politics, in military bureaucracies and in East–West negotiations) seem to lead to three kinds of attitudes in bureaucracies. These can be illustrated by pointing to (a) the slow process of introducing some flexibility into strike programmes in accordance with NATO policy document MC 14/3; (b) large-scale conversion programmes (e.g., to dual capability), and (c) the process of vaguely generalizing the so-called FBS problem. Their respective origins are obvious.

A more specific example is the possible role of European-based American nuclear strike aircraft in SALT and MFR respectively. Although MFR could well produce much more substantial agreements on strike aircraft (reduction) than SALT (limitation), the FBS issue in SALT gave rise to major alarmism, whereas mixed packages (possibly including strike aircraft) in MFR are

[55] Another question is whether in the longer run it would be politically feasible to keep both American and Soviet fleets out of the Mediterranean. American analysts seem to have come round to the conclusion that in an emergency situation it would be much easier for the United States to get back into the Mediterranean than for the Soviet Union.

widely considered a conceivable option. The mixed-package proposal originated in NATO and was studied in a routine fashion; the FBS problem was introduced by the Soviet Union.

This divergence looks less paradoxical if account is taken of the fact that ever since 1968 MFR has been a subject of intense consultation in NATO, where it necessitated new machinery, and may well be considered as the focus of multilateral efforts within the Alliance until the negotiations started in 1973. SALT, on the other hand, developed outside the Alliance framework. Occasional consultations were confined to very specific aspects, such as the FBS problem or the non-transfer clause in the ABM Treaty. NATO was fairly regularly informed about the state of progress in SALT, but, given the 'back-channel system' in Washington (private discussions between high-level American and Soviet officials) it occasionally seemed that even the members of the American SALT delegation who briefed NATO did not know at every stage what was going on.

NATO's nuclear strike aircraft lend themselves particularly to these mechanisms for generalizing issues. Since the three major operational programmes – generation of forces, scheduled take-off and programmed strike missions – require a high degree of integration, nuclear strike aircraft can usefully be considered as an operational whole. However, in assessing the need for certain components of NATO's air-strike potential one cannot ignore their case histories: normally American basing or transfer policy and bilateral bargaining determine whether or not certain systems will become integrated in NATO, and this predetermines their future role in NATO. Thus, while integration policy tends to become unitarist, basing policy is complex and multidimensional, involving a variety of issues such as the maintenance of commands and/or manpower and Congressional pressure to reduce both, basing and transition rights, the composition and equipment of forces, requirements for rotation and dispersal, shelter programmes, etc. All decisions affecting outcomes on these issues are more or less being taken outside the NATO framework.

F-111s in Great Britain, nuclear-capable F-4s in the Mediterranean and, potentially, carrier-based nuclear-capable aircraft of the Sixth Fleet get their targets from SACEUR's threat list, and so all three are in a sense tied into NATO's integrated programmes. Obviously, however, their military importance differs enormously. F-111s are modern aircraft allegedly meeting optimum interdiction requirements, but their number is fairly small and their likely missions somewhat outside the main theatre; the F-4s are considerably more numerous, but in terms of mission profiles, penetration ability, etc., constitute only a modest strike potential against the Soviet homeland; carrier-based aircraft (mostly A-7s) are already considered almost obsolescent for nuclear-strike missions. In terms of their home bases and their national command structures, all three components are somewhat outside the NATO structure (unlike American F-4s in the AFCENT area, for example), and are thus, in a sense classes on their own. If they were affected by the results of negotiations, this would be unlikely to cause immediate and unavoidable repercussions on NATO's politico-military fabric[56] – or at any rate much less of an impact than agreements on the reduction of American nuclear-capable F-4s in Central Europe.[57] It could happen, however, that political issues in specific settings could be reactivated or complicated by SALT, though as a results of the negotiating process itself rather than its likely outcome.

## Negotiated Changes in a Changing Strategic Context

One cannot rule out more comprehensive negotiated changes in NATO's nuclear posture, although modest outcomes seem more likely in the near future. In order to put such contingencies into proper perspective, three questions have to be considered. First, how would such negotiated changes compare with the rate of unilateral changes in NATO's strike posture that has occurred since the early 1960s and is likely to continue in the 1970s? Secondly, as a

[56] This is based on the assumption that only a general limitation formula is being considered (most likely a non-circumvention clause). More specific constraints on rotational procedures and/or modernization of equipment (e.g. increased ranges for air-to-ground weapons for F-111s) would pose more complex problems. However, these would require specific agreements, and specific constraints on rotational procedures could well spill over into the larger structure of NATO strike forces, whereas modernization bans could set precarious precedents with respect to future technological options.
[57] Even here, experiences of the Crested Cap variety would tend to minimize the issue.

basis for judging any of these changes, how strong a military consensus currently exists on the strategic rationale for NATO's nuclear strike posture? Thirdly, which possible future changes in the posture would appear to meet military requirements and make use of future technological options?

These broad issues involve three more specific questions. What are the political characteristics of negotiated changes as compared with unilateral changes? Which parts of the existing posture (if any) appear to be particularly vulnerable with regard to East–West agreements? What are the prospects of East–West negotiations forestalling militarily useful modifications of NATO's current posture?

### Agreements versus Unilateralism

Current concerns over the possible results of negotiations affecting NATO nuclear strike forces are often expressed in such a way as to imply that these forces have remained fairly constant in the past. This is, of course, not so. Similarly, criticisms of SALT I agreements tend to argue that the central balance has been changed by negotiations in the 1970s rather than by unilateral American restraints (and unilateral Soviet efforts) in the 1960s and after.

In the early 1960s a strategic potential targeted against the Soviet Union did exist in Western Europe. There were *Thors* in Britain, *Jupiters* in Italy and Turkey, B-47 and some B-57 bombers. These forces were deployed outside the NATO framework, but had no rationale outside a European conflict. At the same time, NATO's strike forces were quite strong in terms of both numbers of possible strikes and Allied participation.

Since then all American strategic forces have been removed from European soil. At the time of their introduction to service American *Polaris* missiles were taken as a substitute, although in the meantime their use in a European conflict has again turned out to be an extremely remote contingency; thus, except for the British and the even more modest French strategic forces, the Soviet Union came very close to becoming a sanctuary free from nuclear strikes in a future European conflict. This intermediate Western strategic potential had had obvious weaknesses. But its removal, along with the Soviet build-up of a first-strike capability against Western Europe in the first place and of a central-war capability which would neutralize American strategic forces in a European conflict in the second, was the essential change in Western Europe's security situation. Since this situation resulted from Soviet efforts, which probably could not be influenced by any Western policy responses and from American restraints which West Europeans at least failed to influence at that time,[58] it now seems to be irreversible. Fortunately, however, the public in West European countries does not feel itself as exposed to possible Soviet blackmail as it might were the strategic situation the sole framework for political action in Europe.

These earlier strategic forces truly were FBS according to the widely-held SALT definition of FBS, and would undoubtedly have to be considered in any SALT agreement on offensive weapons if they were still around. Thus, in a sense, the FBS problem had been unilaterally dealt with almost a decade before it was talked about in the SALT context.

In subsequent years substantial changes occurred also in NATO's nuclear strike forces. The *Mace* tactical missile was phased out, and the *Crested Cap* programme in 1967 led to the withdrawal of a substantial number of American nuclear-capable F-4s from West Germany. Large-scale conversion programmes took place, especially of Allied nuclear-capable aircraft, converting strike aircraft (above all F-104s) into dual-role aircraft – which many observers take as an effective massive reduction of nuclear strike potential in NATO. More recently the partial replacement of West German nuclear-capable F-104s by F-4s took place (the German Air Force does not use the F-4s for nuclear missions). More generally, the number of nuclear strike aircraft seems to have been reduced over the years in favour of battlefield weapons, while the general nuclear response of NATO's nuclear strike forces appears to have been consistently downgraded in military planning.

---

[58] It is puzzling that, whereas the Soviet Union was unwilling to negotiate (let alone agree on) very modest arms control measures, the United States unilaterally gave up a strike potential in Europe which was much bigger in scope than the outcome of any conceivable agreement at that time. Not only was this process of dismantling never reciprocated by the Soviet Union but it was accompanied by a massive Soviet build-up on the same intermediate level of nuclear forces.

(Given present tendencies, one might well argue that some time in the future NATO will have to rely essentially on three air forces: USAFE, the British Air Force and the West German Air Force. However, the limited lifetime of F-104s, continuing conversion programmes and the uncertain prospects of some future F-104 replacements – notably the MRCA – having a nuclear role suggest that West German participation in NATO's nuclear strike programmes may diminish substantially in the future.)

These are obviously massive changes which will hardly ever be matched by the results of possible East–West negotiations. The policy of nuclear constraint, which has always governed the United States' Alliance policy, has affected some of these outcomes. But, on the whole, the changes result from a cumulative process, where constraints, conversion programmes on military and/or technical grounds, obsolescence, domestic pressures and intentions to make gestures to the Soviet Union combined in one way or another. Some of these changes went almost unnoticed by the West European public; some caused considerable concern. None of the steps taken, however, was ever perceived as the kind of risk which so many West European observers see a possible SALT agreement on FBS as posing. This is paradoxical even if one assumes that such an agreement would lead to a substantial reduction of strike aircraft in Western Europe – obviously a rather remote contingency in the foreseeable future.

One reason for this may be that earlier changes may have seemed to occur in an environment of nuclear plenty where there were still sufficient options available or substitutions forthcoming. In the present situation it is often felt that nuclear strike aircraft in Western Europe are all that is left of the backbone of nuclear protection and that SALT could thus lead to a sell-out of West European security. A second reason may be that earlier changes resulted from internal Western processes which would remain controllable at least somewhere within the Alliance, whereas a SALT agreement would establish a Soviet role in future nuclear affairs in Western Europe which might expand to unfavourable proportions.

However, there are also some more specific anxieties which apply to the realities of current negotiations. Unlike unilateral actions, negoti-

57

ated agreements have a binding character. Quantitively they are very unlikely to produce results in any way comparable with those produced by earlier unilateral action.-But they may lead to constraints of two kinds: on operational practices (such as redeployments, rotations etc.) and on modernization. It could happen, in other words, that a network of selective operational constraints and selective modernization bans develops either in the SALT context or in another set of negotiations, such as MFR, which would severely limit the chances of maintaining military options considered essential and of modernizing the NATO posture so as to adapt it to the dramatically changed strategic environment to which Henry Kissinger repeatedly draws the attention of West Europeans.

No such outcome seems inevitable or even very likely in the present SALT context, but at the same time the military requirements on which such concerns are based are themselves in a fluid state – in all major NATO governments the future of nuclear strike aircraft seems to be a subject of reappraisal. It is this very coincidence of East–West negotiations with strategic reappraisal within the Alliance which is at the bottom of so many anxieties: it could well lead to unfavourable interactions between the two processes unless the United States indicates her priorities as clearly as West European governments see them. One should, however, also point to the fact that Alliance consultations on negotiating matters can help to start a process of reappraisal within the Alliance which bureaucratic inertia might otherwise delay for too long. It would seem that the notion of a mixed-package approach in MFR and an American review of the existing nuclear posture of NATO was above all intended as a device to get a nuclear review started within the Alliance – preferably in the Nuclear Planning Group.

## Standard Military Arguments

Within the Alliance, debates over FBS or, more generally, over NATO's nuclear strike forces tend to revolve around two sets of standard military arguments:[59] one in favour of maintaining them, the other in favour of reducing or abolishing

[59] The emphasis given to these arguments and counter-arguments reflects current general debates. Of course derivative arguments are legion.

them. They can be summarized as follows.

There are six standard arguments in favour of maintaining NATO nuclear-strike forces.

1. They are the most tightly integrated of NATO's forces, and dismantling them would most likely tend to disintegrate NATO at large.

   Opponents, however, claim that, precisely because of this tight integration, optimum political timing and co-ordination would be required in order not to render these forces useless. Given the need for American authorization and the clumsy nature of the release procedures, integration seems to be a peacetime virtue only. In addition, giving up the nuclear capability of these aircraft does not necessarily make integration impossible.

2. Their main function is to serve as a link between nuclear battlefield weapons and American strategic forces. They constitute the essential escalatory risk on which NATO strategy appears to be based. Their removal would thus result in a decoupling of American strategic forces.

   Opponents, claim, however, that NATO's general nuclear response is essentially designed to be implemented by these strike aircraft: they would thus themselves be the ultimate weapons, rather than a trigger. On the other hand, any trigger function of these weapons (e.g., in terms of their pre-emptive instability) would in principle, be subject to the same logic that led to the removal of the *Thors* and *Jupiters* from Western Europe.

   As for the decoupling, these forces would not make any difference. In current circumstances American strategic forces appear to be decoupled from Western Europe anyway; the possibility of their use in Europe under extreme crisis conditions is hard to anticipate; and forward-based aircraft would not seem to affect the outcome, very likely because the key issue would be whether or not to risk a Soviet retaliatory strike. Some opponents would even argue that decoupling is desirable and that removal of nuclear strike aircraft from Western Europe would be desirable if it reinforced decoupling.

3. There is also the opposite argument that, because of the decoupling of American strategic forces, it is essential to have nuclear-capable strike aircraft in Western Europe as all that is left to give substance to nuclear

deterrence: they are NATO's ultimate weapons. Supporters of this argument do not, however, assume that present levels of nuclear strike aircraft must not be changed. Indeed, as has been pointed out, these levels have varied considerably in the past, due partly to planning by the military authorities.

Opponents claim, however, that this cannot be considered a minimum deterrence posture. Taking into account both likely American reluctance to authorize the use of these forces and Soviet retaliatory power, any strategy for using them could only result in suicide (or, more likely, failure to commit suicide) and therefore lacks credibility. Moreover, heavy reliance on these forces could preclude efforts to achieve a more credible defence posture.

4. There is the more specific argument that nuclear strike aircraft are indispensable for deep interdiction.

Some opponents claim that interdiction is unnecessary. Others argue that it is close to impossible to reconcile battlefield requirements (to buy time) with interdiction requirements (to act instantly). Yet others argue that though deep interdiction is important there will be other and more appropriate means to carry out at least some types of interdiction mission (e.g., conventional precision-guided munitions).

5. There are also those who argue that nuclear strike aircraft ought to be maintained in Western Europe as a counter to Soviet medium-range systems (IR/MRBM and bombers).

Opponents point out, however, that current mission profiles would not correspond to any such counterforce contingency, and that neither technical characteristics nor the more likely scenarios would suggest any such option as feasible.

6. There is also the opposite argument that, because of these forces' low ability to penetrate Soviet air defences, they can be more realistically considered as theatre forces which do not constitute a direct threat to the Soviet Union.

By the same token, however, opponents would question the general utility of maintaining these forces.

From this list the first, third and fourth arguments appear to deserve more serious consideration, though obviously none is uncontroversial. The same holds true for the second set of four standard arguments for reduction or removal of NATO nuclear forces.

1. One argument says that nuclear strike aircraft ought to be taken out because their Quick Reaction Alert (QRA) status could give rise to all sorts of uncertainties.

Opponents point out, however, that current force generation programmes are based on the fact that only a small fraction of these aircraft (as of *Pershings*) has QRA status. The generation of forces itself could not be considered as an unusual threat by an aggressor, and, moreover, independent decisions are required for force generation and scheduled take-off.

2. A generalized version of this argument is that the combination of the vulnerability of these forces, their considerable striking power and the existence of Soviet missiles ready for instant action produces a pre-emptive instability. The removal of these forces would thus serve NATO's security interests.

Opponents claim, however, that the very uncertainty inherent in this pre-emptive instability is the essential element in NATO's deterrence posture in Europe. They tend to support this point of view by a general belief that deterrence is what NATO's posture is supposed to achieve anyway, and that for various reasons any real war-fighting capability would most likely be counter-productive.

3. A related argument states that the Soviet Union has a first strike capability which she would use on the basis of her doctrine as the need arose. Nuclear-capable strike aircraft in Western Europe would constitute a high-priority target and would invite Soviet strikes with weapons which, due to their high yield, would then account for something like 90 per cent of the total fallout in Europe.

Opponents point out, however, that large-scale destruction of Western Europe would not be consistent with any conceivable Soviet rationale for invading Western Europe. In Soviet military doctrine the primacy of political purpose ranks much more prominently than what could be considered a nuclear counterforce doctrine: thus, the value argument would override the incentives for massive nuclear strikes. IR/MRBM particularly might prove to be a very powerful intra-war deterrent but they are unlikely to be used on a large scale except as a last resort.

4. There is also what is in a sense the opposite argument, that the mission airfields of these strike aircraft could either be destroyed with conventional means or even overrun by land forces.

This argument obviously depends to a particularly high degree on the kind of underlying scenarios. In general terms, however, opponents tend to argue either that this would require a conventional attack of such proportions that a nuclear response by NATO would be necessitated anyway, or else that, since the Soviet Union knows this, she is likely to be deterred from this kind of aggression precisely because NATO has this nuclear strike potential available and ready to hand.

These are the more canonical views for and against maintaining nuclear strike forces in Europe. On balance, none of them appears to be of overriding importance. In fact, this account suggests that the issue of strike aircraft in Western Europe simply cannot be resolved on this level of generalized discussion.[60] There is no answer to the problem, which is both simple and general.

The arguments included in these two catalogues ought to be seen in the light of the political forces that put them forward. This applies to the divergent views of various national governments as well as to inter-service controversies, and a closer look could explain why a certain argument is put forward by a particular political group. More important, though, would be a fuller understanding of what these groups are really aiming at. Weighting these standard arguments to take account of their political background hardly offers a clue to that, but any attempt to speculate about the likely outcomes of future changes in the Alliance would have to rely heavily on assessments of these political forces.

Such an assessment is clearly outside the scope of this study, so I propose to discuss instead some priorities for modifications of the existing nuclear posture of NATO. Whereas current standard arguments seem to be of little use in resolving the FBS issue, a perspective of desirable changes in NATO's nuclear posture may well provide a basis for assessments of negotiating options in SALT as well as in MFR.

### Modifying NATO's Nuclear Posture

In current debates a number of more radical solutions have been put forward which deal with functions rather than means, and which would call for sweeping changes if they were accepted. One school of thought claims that in terms of both doctrine and weaponry there is no nuclear posture in Western Europe, and a purely conventional defence is no longer considered a substitute, as it was in the 1960s. In order to achieve the only conceivable war-fighting capability, a substantial change in the nuclear arsenal of NATO would be necessary: a large-scale replacement of existing weapons by discriminate nuclear capabilities.[61] The second school shares some of the assumptions of the first, but argues that a nuclear war-fighting capability is as undesirable as a conventional defence is unfeasible. It essentially recommends a return to a massive retaliation posture for NATO. There also is a third school of thought, which claims that, though a nuclear war-fighting capability would not necessarily require discriminate nuclear weapons, it would require a more appropriate doctrine for the use of existing army weaponry, as well as the complete abolition of nuclear-strike aircraft.

While the second proposition would call for heavy reliance on existing strike forces in NATO (notably aircraft), the other two would suggest their complete removal. However, none of these more radical proposals seems likely to be accepted within the Alliance.

More moderate proposals deal with means rather than functions. They centre around two basic considerations: intermediate deterrence and interdiction.

According to these proposals some kind of

---

[60] Some of the military aspects have been discussed in earlier sections: the role of strategic analysis, pp. 41-4; the Soviet approach pp. 47-8; the strategic relevance of for the United States, pp. 37-41.

[61] This is basically the same kind of substitution policy which was being adopted in the mid-1950s (given this analogy and the weapons involved, one might label it a 'Mini-New Look').

intermediate deterrent ought to be maintained in Europe, and this would essentially require the maintenance and possibly (with American support) modernization of the British and French strategic forces; it would also appear useful to keep a number of American and Allied strike aircraft and *Pershings* for this intermediate deterrent function. There are two distinct reasons for this. First, a Soviet aggression has to be considered as a Warsaw Pact operation. Existing strike forces in the AFCENT area would undoubtedly deter the Soviet Union's East European allies and thus complicate any decision within the Warsaw Pact to launch a major aggression. A Soviet early disarming strike, on the other hand, would hardly fit into more likely political rationales for Warsaw Pact military aggression, so that one might expect the concerns of other members to have a restraining influence on a Soviet decision to go to war. Secondly, American support for modernizing the British and possibly the French strategic forces would become vastly more complicated if West Germany and other non-nuclear members of the Alliance insisted on meaningful sharing arrangements short of violation of the NPT (i.e., steps towards 'Europeanizing' these forces). Avoiding the politically sensitive area of nuclear proliferation would become more difficult for the non-nuclear members if sharing arrangements for strike aircraft and *Pershings* were being abolished at the same time as participation in the two West European strategic forces were denied to them.

West Germany and possibly other non-nuclear members of the Alliance would probably favour American support for British and French nuclear programmes. They would also agree to a reduction of present levels of nuclear-capable strike aircraft, indeed as they have in the past. However, it would seem important not only to maintain some nuclear strike aircraft for deterrent purposes but also to keep open the option of some kind of follow-on sharing arrangement for the next generation, once aircraft like the F-104 have to be phased out. By then, though, it may be that aircraft will no longer be the appropriate means of delivery (indeed the MRCA may well be obsolescent by the time it is expected to be introduced).

On the other hand, according to these moderate proposals interdiction seems to be indispensable, although existing interdiction programmes may well undergo major changes in the future. Since the interdiction function has to be considered from a military, rather than a mere deterrent, point of view, the fact that interdiction with nuclear weapons depends upon politically sensitive and technically clumsy release procedures is an important factor inhibiting their use. There thus exists an incentive to carry out interdiction missions by less constrained conventional means if that should turn out to become possible. Given present developments in the field of conventional precision-guided munitions (PGM) it does seem possible to use PGM to replace nuclear weapons for a variety of interdiction purposes. There is, however, no evidence so far that future developments will provide conventional means for all the kinds of interdiction missions which are currently to be carried out with nuclear-capable aircraft and *Pershing*.

There are essentially three developments which are likely to shape future efforts to modify the existing nuclear interdiction capability: a review of current plans and operations with a view to possible streamlining and reductions; a study of possible replacements by either conventional means or more appropriate nuclear means; and an increasing dependence on rotational schemes or, more generally, on mobility.

A review of current plans and operations (which, of course, would not be confined only to interdiction forces) would presumably go into questions such as whether all interdiction targets have to be covered instantly or at all, whether the insurance factor could be lowered, whether the yields are appropriate, etc. Unless there are major policy changes, such reviews could be expected to allow considerable reductions in nuclear weapons currently deployed in Western Europe, and their outcomes might well provide a basis for designing negotiating proposals, such as mixed packages. The phasing out of *Sergeant* and *Honest John*, among other things, could be considered as a result of such reviews, and strike aircraft could also conceivably come within their scope.

The study of possible applications of new technologies to the West European theatre, which has just reached its preliminary stage, does not allow for sweeping solutions but rather requires case-by-case assessments. The possible replacement of nuclear weapons by new conventional weaponry is obviously only one aspect of this study, but it is a very important one. The following examples may illustrate why these new technologies could look promising from a West European point of view.

Firstly, communication lines such as bridges are among the major interdiction targets. The replacement of nuclear interdiction aircraft by conventional precision-guided munitions (possibly delivered by means other than aircraft) would avoid a wide range of existing difficulties, especially in the case of Allied aircraft. The kill probability should be at least the same, collateral damage would be virtually avoided, and operations would therefore no longer be complicated under NATO's existing constraints policy, allowing for much greater flexibility in terms of who is doing what. Current release procedures for nuclear weapons would no longer apply to such interdiction forces, so that the time factor involved would be much more favourable (i.e., the 'mission probability' would increase considerably), and therefore military planning would no longer have to rest on uncertain assumptions about the likelihood of American authorization to carry out interdiction missions at the appropriate time. The pre-emptive instability of nuclear-capable interdiction aircraft in Western Europe would be drastically diminished, and, in case of new means of delivery for PGM, the crucial problem of penetrating Warsaw Pact air defences may also look different.

The second example, which applies to nuclear-armed earth-penetration weapons, may look more exotic and, indeed, controversial. If it were possible, for example, to launch a counter air strike with three or four penetration weapons, to tear up the airfield and thus destroy its structure, instead of using a heavy attack and causing heavy collateral damage, this would completely revolutionize this important type of interdiction mission. Currently, one would have to use either a large number of aircraft for a conventional counter-air attack or else a number of nuclear bombs, which would cause great collateral damage. This kind of interdiction is especially important militarily and yet particularly dangerous: in a heavy conventional attack it would be difficult for aircraft to penetrate Warsaw Pact air defences, and a nuclear attack would constitute one of the most risky escalatory measures that could be taken in a European conflict.

Exotic nuclear weapons like penetration weapons would ease the problem of penetrating air defences; one could use nuclear weapons without in a sense passing the nuclear threshold as traditionally understood (at least theoretically there would be no fallout); and the pre-emptive instability inherent in present counter-air interdiction capabilities would appear to be less threatening. The Soviet Union would have to take a much bigger escalatory step in responding to this kind of attack than she would be expected to take in the case of a counter-air strike with currently available means.

Both these examples have been developed for illustrative purposes. They may indicate, though, that a number of nuclear problems at present considered crucial are likely to look quite different in the light of current technological developments. This would have obvious implications for future negotiating strategies both in SALT and MFR.

The area of possibly increasing dependence on higher mobility is even more difficult to assess at this stage. This could imply redeployment programmes of the *Crested Cap* variety, more flexible intra-theatre schemes for rotation and forward detachment, American desire to make more flexible use of USAFE aircraft outside the NATO framework, increase pressures over both specific bases and transit rights, etc. The overriding consideration is that any major changes (unilateral or negotiated) in current levels of strike aircraft or in the present deployment structure would increase NATO's dependence on intra-theatre and transatlantic mobility. This could well be regarded as acceptable in the Alliance context. In East–West negotiations, however, the Soviet Union might well decide to concentrate on operational practices rather than force levels, while operational flexibility would tend to become rather more important for NATO than it has been in the past.

It is not possible to draw any simple conclusion concerning SALT or MFR from this assessment of the more likely modifications of NATO's nuclear strike potential. In some sense, East–West negotiations could help to stimulate reappraisals inside NATO, which one might consider as long overdue; in some sense, internal changes in the NATO posture could be expected to broaden the scope for future East–West negotiations. In some sense, too, such negotiations could become a key factor in preventing useful internal changes in the Alliance posture. Substitutions of modern conventional means for older nuclear delivery as well as results of nuclear reviews may well improve Western bargaining potential. This does not mean, however, that anything NATO could and will dispose of should be offered at the conference table in return for some kind of Soviet trade-off; nor is the Soviet Union likely to consider bargaining offers of this kind as always serving her interest. On the other hand, SALT and/or MFR could well turn out to have prohibitive effects on modernization (especially if it were to involve new nuclear weapons or the extension of existing sharing arrangements to successor aircraft) and paralyse operational flexibility.

## Possible Options for Future Negotiations

By way of summarizing, a number of possible guide lines for future Alliance politics can be formulated.

1. There is no self-evident FBS category in either the SALT or the MFR context. Correspondingly, there is no 'FBS problem' except in terms of Soviet tactics and Western perceptions. No proposal in this area can therefore be based on any kind of self-selecting process, and everything depends on the definitions chosen. (In fact, agreement on definitions is the essential political problem in SALT and/or MFR.) Given the current state of the art, prevailing definitions (especially the Soviet two-way-mission criterion) have only very modest applications.

2. With regard to nuclear strike aircraft the Soviet Union cannot apply direct leverage to NATO unless she can exploit Western misperception, lack of co-ordination or disagreement within the Alliance. The Soviet Union has her demands, and her criteria would apply to only a few systems in NATO. Moreover, there is no rationale in SALT for talking about the reduction or even removal of FBS so long as the limitation rather than the reduction of strategic forces is at stake. Also there is no conceivable logical extension of SALT limitations to FBS so long as limitations are selective in kind, as the Interim Agreement is. Soviet demands for limitations on FBS could appear to be justifiable only in the context of comprehensive limitations on strategic forces, and, similarly, demands for a reduction of FBS would have to occur as a corollary to a proposal for a comprehensive agreement on the reduction of strategic forces. Whether Soviet demands are to be accepted in any such context depends on bargaining inside Washington, inside the Alliance and at the conference table. There are no inevitable outcomes.

It is the contention of this study that the Soviet Union considers FBS proposals above all as bargaining devices and jokers in order to control the pace of negotiations and, as far as possible, to create misperceptions and divisive issues within the Alliance. Up to now the Soviet Union has had her way, and it is up to the Alliance to limit her diplomatic successes.

3. Given the nature of bureaucratic processes within the Alliance, and given the need for a broader American initiative of the kind Dr Kissinger seems to have envisaged in the early 1970s, in order for agreement to be reached on the premises for any change in NATO's nuclear posture, it would be useful for NATO to review the FBS issue in its broader context and to raise the review from the level of bureaucratic routine to that of political consultations. This could be achieved by getting the Nuclear Planning Group involved in such a review – though it should be pointed out that the NPG involves defence ministries only, whereas in West European governments the final responsibility for both MFR and SALT lies with the foreign ministries.

A useful framework would be provided by parallel national study groups in Washington, London and Bonn, involving representatives from the key ministries working on the same set of problems, exchanging information and results during the process (notably at a limited number of trilateral plenary sessions) and finally submitting their results to the NATO bodies.[62]

---

[62] This procedure worked with considerable success in the mid-1960s, when the United States and West Germany each set up four study groups dealing with various nuclear problems which at certain stages held some plenary sessions, chaired by General Lemnitzer and General Trettner respectively. In some sense, Anglo-German co-operation on provisional guidelines for the initial tactical use of nuclear weapons and the subsequent trilateral work with the United States on follow-on cases also displayed a useful pattern.

In all these cases, however, only the defence ministries were involved, which in this case clearly would not be sufficient. Current work in the New Technology Working Group of the Nuclear Planning Group may well point in the right direction, though it is probably too limited in scope.

4. It is likely that only in such a framework could a comprehensive review be achieved which takes account of the requirements for maintaining a viable defence, making use of future technological options, and achieving sufficient bargaining power and flexibility in East–West negotiations.[63]

As for the crucial issue of harmonizing negotiating policies and defence policies, this can refer to two possible outcomes. First, technological change could alter the need for certain agreements: for instance, new anti-tank weaponry might lessen the urgency of a mixed package arrangement that included Soviet tanks. Second, new technologies might enhance the appeal of agreements that otherwise appeared unattractive: for example, cruise missiles might replace certain types of interdiction aircraft, which would make it easier for aircraft to be included in a reduction package.

5. At this stage what is at stake in SALT is just some kind of limitation of certain types of strike aircraft (if anything), a limitation which could even be in the interest of the Alliance. In the long run, however, more specific constraints as well as some reductions are conceivable.[64] While various constraints may be acceptable (e.g., not to deploy *Pershing* in Turkey or not to equip F-111s with longer range air-to-ground weapons), there are others which would have to be weighed most carefully: constraints on operational procedures, for instance, and constraints on certain types of modernization (applying sharing arrangements to successor systems, certain types of new nuclear ordnance, etc.). Some reductions may in fact be less unacceptable than certain types of constraints. The important

proviso, though, is that the decision to consider a system as negotiable has to result from a comprehensive defence review.

6. It may be that NATO could agree on the possible inclusion of a variety of systems in forthcoming negotiation options or on the negotiability of certain constraints. It may also be a wise policy not to avoid issues but rather to make explicit but possibly non-negotiable counter-proposals. It is very important, however, to recognize the difference between diplomatic flexibility and political utility. It is conceivable that NATO could be in a position to include a variety of systems in negotiating proposals but that there was just no trade-off.[65] There is a noticeable tendency in the Western arms-control community to adopt a commercial approach: agreements are considered as an end in themselves provided they produce some kind of trade-off. For example, NATO might wish to trade some strike aircraft, or (in a different context) West European strategic forces, against Soviet medium-range systems, although this would leave Soviet strategic options virtually unchanged. The trade-off would thus be a waste of bargaining power or else a loss of Western strategic options without compensation. In many cases Soviet redundancy would tend to rule out negotiability.

This assessment suggests that the essential problem for the Alliance, and particularly for its principal governments, is to agree on the future strategic role of nuclear strike forces in Europe. This issue is bound to supersede in importance the issue of the modernization of British strategic forces. Diplomatic pressure over the FBS issue appears to be an attempt to pre-empt this reappraisal within the Alliance and to prevent a viable outcome. Already there is a noticeable tendency within the Alliance to consider the future role of nuclear strike forces in NATO essentially in terms of negotiations. There may be some scope for East–West agreements in this field, but the problem is how to

---

[63] For a systematic assessment, see Johan Holst and Uwe Nerlich (eds), *Beyond Nuclear Deterrence: Structures and Options of European Security* (forthcoming).

[64] In this study no consideration has been given to the question of what constitutes a reduction in nuclear strike aircraft, although the definition chosen would be highly relevant to the outcome. It could mean, for example, the mere elimination of the nuclear capability of an aircraft, with everything else left unchanged (which among other things would raise the issue of verification), or it could mean the mere redeployment of an aircraft to backward positions within the theatre or across the Atlantic (which would raise the issue of constraints on redeployment). While the verification issue would seem to pose insoluble problems, constraints on redeployment would appear to be undesirable, at least from a West European point of view.

[65] To link Soviet *Backfire* bombers and American cruise missiles in SALT I, could be a case in point. The Soviet side is not likely to accept the inclusion of *Backfire* in SALT in any case, but, even if it were, such a trade-off would deny NATO such important options as substituting cruise missiles for aircraft in theatre-strike roles.

arrive at such agreements. Clearly, priorities must be firmly established, and it must be recognized that agreements with the Soviet Union, though possibly useful, are not an end in themselves. Above all, however, a balanced approach, comprising both defence and negotiating requirements, would afford a different outlook on the American side. Comprehensive consultations with principal Allied governments are necessary *before* consensus has been achieved within the American administration on what the United States should table in NATO, and account must be taken of long-term implications. Henry Kissinger is on record as being in favour of comprehensive rather than *ad hoc* appraisals, and he has not favoured excessive reliance on routine channels of bureaucracy. Yet it remains to be seen how such an approach will affect crucial issues within the Alliance, such as NATO's strike posture.

Obviously this sort of approach may mean giving up some of the diplomatic and political flexibility the American side appears to enjoy in an essentially bilateralist framework. Even without additional Soviet demands, the number of strike aircraft left in the FBS category (using the two-way mission criterion) would be even fewer than indicated by the American Administration at the time of the conclusion of the SALT I agreements. It may be useful politically to have as many as possible accepted as part of the central balance, in order to make an agreement on strategic forces more acceptable domestically, but it seems equally desirable to keep the number of European based strike aircraft covered by bilateral agreements as low as possible, in order not to jeopardize the basis for Alliance consensus. For some Americans this could look like a hard choice. It could also be considered as a direct consequence of the principles stated in the major documents on foreign policy issued by the Nixon and Ford Administrations.

Undoubtedly the West Europeans, too, are guilty of not fully appreciating the American viewpoint. On this crucial issue, however, there is little West European governments could do by themselves except respond to American gestures and initiatives. There is, of course, the view that West European governments are not prepared to enter into these kinds of consultations because they fear becoming victimized in the process. In present circumstances West European political élites seem to justify such apprehensions, but the potential obviously exists in Western Europe for redefining its requirements when necessary, instead of finding itself forced into mere acceptance of American intra-Administration compromises. It is lack of participation that produces alarmism.

Two factors give rise to scepticism about the Alliance's chances of making a new approach. First, given the nature of bureaucracy as well as the range of challenging issues at any given time, bureaucratic overload is likely to prevent the approach needed within the Alliance. In fact, a comprehensive review was envisaged within the National Security Council as early as 1970, but all that has happened since then is a build-up of further evidence that such a basic approach is needed. Secondly, events during the Middle East crisis of October 1973 may indicate that the confidence of the Alliance can be profoundly affected by unforeseeable events (both external and domestic). Divergences over nuclear strike forces may seem to be of secondary importance in the light of the erratic convulsions the Alliance experienced in October 1973 and since. It is equally true, however, that an Alliance which has re-established its common purpose in terms of principles and in the light of crucial issues such as the one discussed in this essay is less prone to the impact of events that unexpectedly shatter its confidence. The rift during the Middle East crisis was both an unavoidable event and an alarming symptom. So is the FBS issue.

# 3 THE ROLE OF ARMS CONTROL IN THE MIDDLE EAST

YAIR EVRON

## INTRODUCTION

This study deals with past experience, present issues and the future of arms control in the Arab–Israeli region of the Middle East.

Since the early 1950s, large areas of the Middle East have been characterized by the build-up of a high level of arms and armed forces. This process has become one of the principal features of international politics in the Middle East, associated with the several levels of conflict in the 'heart' of the Middle East, namely, the Arab–Israeli conflict, the competition among the Arab states for positions of power, and the competition between the super-powers.[1]

For the purposes of the study of arms races and arms control,[2] the eastern Middle East (as distinct from the Maghreb) may be divided roughly into two areas. The first, the Arab–Israeli region, comprises Egypt, Israel, Syria, Jordan and, to some extent, Iraq and Saudi Arabia. These are the states most involved in the Arab–Israeli conflict (Egypt, Syria and Jordan have also, for the last few years, been referred to as the 'confrontation' countries). The second, the Persian Gulf region, consists of Iran, Kuwait and, again, Iraq and Saudi Arabia. For political reasons Saudi Arabia and Iraq are involved in both regions.

The analytical division of the Middle East into two sub-regions is corroborated by the existence of two arms races. The allocation of resources for defence purposes in the Arab–Israeli region resulted primarily from the dynamics of the conflict there and, secondly, from political competition among the Arab countries.[3] The Persian Gulf states, primarily Saudi Arabia and Iran,[4] were not involved in a significant arms build-up until the late 1960s, and 1973 arms acquisition increased considerably after the tremendous rise in their oil revenues. Although there are some elements of

the 'action-reaction' process in the acquisition of arms by Iran and Saudi Arabia, and hence of an arms race, there are other motivations for their arms build-up. Iran, in particular, has a range of security interests which extends far beyond her relationship with Saudi Arabia.

The arms build-up in Iran[5] and Saudi Arabia (and Kuwait, although the size there is rather limited) may have serious repercussions on the security concerns of Israel and the Arab confrontation states. This is primarily because Saudi Arabia and Kuwait are purchasing weapons systems which they intend quite openly to transfer to the confrontation countries, and they may send troops to the front in the event of another war with Israel.[6] Iraq was involved in acquiring arms earlier than these states because of her participation in the Arab–Israeli conflict and in the intra-Arab competition.

This does not mean that arms-control arrangements in connection with Israel and the Arab confrontation states are not possible unless related measures were taken throughout the Persian Gulf region.[7] It does mean, however, that the arms build-up in the Persian Gulf area, and especially in Saudi Arabia, affects decisions on arms control in the Arab–Israeli region.

### What is Meant by Arms Control?

Arms control is defined here in a conservative–traditional way: that is, as any measure taken in the military security field which increases strategic stability in the relations of states involved in a conflict. Strategic stability is the diminution in the frequency of wars and, once they occur, their limitation. A related objective of arms control is the limitation and reduction of defence expenditure, provided strategic stability is not harmed.[8] Hence arms control is a broader concept than mere limitations to the acquisition of arms.

So much has been written on arms control that to rehearse the basic assumptions would seem superfluous.[9] Yet precisely because the debate is so extensive, and also because discussion about arms-control agreements reached over the last few years has questioned some of the more traditional notions, it is perhaps worthwhile to refer briefly to the underlying notions and ideas of my more conservative approach.

To begin with, the structure of the international system, which is composed of nation states at times in conflict, is taken for granted. International crises, violence and war are accepted as part of the international scene. Arms control is not expected to bring about a fundamental change in this sad state of affairs but is intended only to increase relative stability within this framework. Arms control operates only in the military security areas; its impact on political developments, although sometimes considerable, is indirect. Arms control is achieved only when the contracting partners' defence establishments recognize that arms-control agreements improve their respective countries' security, or at least do not hamper it. Finally, there is recognition that in every international dispute, or certainly in the great majority of them, common and conflicting interests co-exist. All these points are applicable to the current Middle East situation, and will continue to apply even if a political settlement is reached.

The theory of arms control has developed within the framework of the super-powers' relations. It is part of the 'strategic paradigm', which has focused primarily on the bipolar nuclear relationship. There are, of course, important structural differences between the super-power relationship and the one existing in the Arab–Israeli complex, so that we cannot replicate the same model of relations for the Middle East. My contention, however, is that theories of strategy and of arms control, as developed by the modern strategists, transcend that model and are applicable to non-nuclear, non-bipolar strategic relations such as those in the Middle East.

This study combines an analysis of what has happened with ideas about and proposals for future arms-control measures. Chapter I focuses on past attempts at arms control and demonstrates that there are important precedents for explicit and, even more, for tacit arms-control agreements in the Middle East. In Chapter II the various stages of the arms race are discussed, and the relationship between them and war is analysed. An account follows of the arms build-up since 1973 in conjunction with developments in the strategic doctrines of Egypt, Israel and Syria. Chapter III offers ideas for future arms-control measures, delineating five main areas of arms control. Chapter IV discusses the possible contribution of the super-powers to arms control in the Middle East. A concluding chapter looks at the relationship between arms control and political negotiations for a settlement and finally discusses priorities among the measures proposed and the possible stages by which they could be implemented.

# I. PAST ATTEMPTS AT ARMS-CONTROL MEASURES IN THE ARAB–ISRAELI REGION

## United Nations Control of Arms Transfers

It was at an early stage in the Arab–Israeli conflict that certain external powers and the United Nations (UN) first intervened to impose limitations on arms supplies to the combatants. The first such step – taken during the 1948 war – was a UN embargo. This was part of the Security Council cease-fire resolution of 29 May 1948, which stipulated that no 'war material' should be exported to the warring sides.[10] The embargo's objective was to prevent either side from using the cease-fire period to change the balance of power in its favour. The cease-fire resolution was extended on 15 July (after ten days of hostilities), and the embargo remained in effect even after the adoption of a Security Council resolution calling for a truce in November 1948. The embargo was largely ineffective,[11] as was a General Assembly resolution including an arms embargo, adopted on 2 November 1956.

## The Tripartite Declaration

On 4 August 1949 the United States, Britain and France declared that they were opposed to the development of an arms race in the Palestine area. When Israeli and Egyptian requests for arms multiplied in 1949–50, the United States initiated the convening of a meeting with Britain and France which ended with the Tripartite Declaration, signed by the three powers on 25 May 1950.[12] It included the signatories' guarantee of the territorial integrity of the Middle Eastern countries. This was an attempt to stabilize the area following the tribulations of the Arab–Israeli war of 1948–9. Second, the signatories undertook to regulate the flow of arms to the Middle East which, at the time, they monopolized.

Historically, this became the most important formal agreement among external powers governing the transfer of arms to the Middle East. It was, indeed, a major 'arms-control' agreement, and it established a regulatory mechanism, the Near East Arms Co-ordinating Committee. The Committee was quite effective, and, although both Israel and the Arab countries criticized the Declaration and tried at various junctures to circumvent the Committee's control, they did not consider the Declaration a major irritant, and certainly not something which endangered their security.

The Declaration enabled the United States to continue with her own embargo, which had been imposed in 1948. This was in fact directed primarily against Israel and Egypt,[13] and although only partial and selective, it was quite effective in inhibiting American transfers of arms. It did not, however, suppress the transfer of arms when the arms race escalated in the mid-1950s. (In fact, as will be shown below, embargoes imposed by one supplier alone do not, as a rule, halt an arms race; indeed, on occasions they accelerate it.) American concern to keep a certain military balance between Israel and her Arab neighbours was de-emphasized during her efforts in 1953–4 to establish a pro-Western defence organization in the Middle East. The plan was to centre this organization on Egypt or, alternatively, to concentrate on the 'northern tier' countries, namely, Turkey, Iraq and Iran.

Britain, both independently and in concert with the United States, had taken steps from 1951 onwards which led eventually to the creation of the Baghdad Pact in February 1955. Thus two of the signatories to the Declaration

had already begun to undermine it, and the suspicions thereby generated were among the causes of the next round of the arms race in the Middle East. The tension along the Arab–Israeli borders and the eventual Egyptian–Soviet arms deal of 1955 (which came to be known as the Egyptian–Czechoslovak arms deal) led to a major quantitative and qualitative escalation in the arms race; for all practical purposes the Declaration died with the Egyptian deal.

Yet time and again the United States refused large-scale supplies of arms to Egypt. This stance dates back to the late 1940s and has, with some exceptions, continued since then. (One outstanding exception was the supply, during the 1950s, of 150 M-4 *Sherman* tanks.)[14] There have been several occasions when the United States has considered arms deals with Egypt, especially during the first half of the 1950s, but in each case the United States has attached certain political conditions, all of which have been rejected by Egypt.[15] Later, once Egypt had become dependent on Soviet arms, the whole question of American arms supplies became irrelevant. Britain, for her part, had traditionally served as the main supplier of arms to Egypt, but when negotiations on the future of the British military base in Egypt began in earnest in 1953, Britain became reluctant to supply her with large quantities of arms, hoping that this would serve as a bargaining chip. This attitude changed only after the signing in October 1954 of the British–Egyptian Agreement stipulating British withdrawal from the Suez Canal base.

After the 1955 Soviet–Egyptian arms deal, the United States realized that the military balance between Israel and Egypt had tipped in favour of the latter, and, rather than supplying Israel with the necessary arms, she preferred that another arms-producing country should do so. This decision stemmed from American concern about possible adverse Arab reactions. It was with American encouragement, therefore, that France acted as a major supplier of arms to Israel until 1967 – though in 1963 the United States did supply Israel with 288 *HAWK* surface-to-air missiles, and in 1966 an order was confirmed for the supply of 48 A-4H *Skyhawk* fighter-bombers.

In contrast to her reluctance to supply arms to Israel – over a long period of time – and to

Egypt, however, the United States was prepared to transfer arms to other countries in the Middle East and supplied Iraq (in the 1950s), Iran, Saudi Arabia, Jordan, and Lebanon with many of their arms. The deals were accompanied by publicly voiced concern about an arms race in the Middle East and the need to curb it. In his speech on 7 August 1958 before the UN General Assembly Emergency Session, for example, President Eisenhower called for steps to pre-empt a new round of the arms race in the Middle East. President Kennedy pointed out on 8 May 1963 that the United States was searching for ways to 'limit the arms race in the Middle East'.[16] Apart from the *de facto* embargo on supplies of American arms to Israel and Egypt referred to above, however, no other arms-control measures were applied.

## The French Embargo

France imposed a partial embargo during the 1967 war, directed at all the Middle Eastern countries involved in the conflict. Since Israel was the main recipient of French arms in the Middle East, she was most affected by the embargo but, although total at its inception, it very quickly became a very partial embargo, relating only to 50 *Mirage V* fighter-bombers ordered by Israel in 1965, delivery of which was expected by late 1967. Ironically, the volume of French arms transferred to Israel *increased* after the imposition of the partial embargo.[17] In a frantic effort Israel bought as much as she could from France to escape the effects of a possible reimposition of a total embargo. Such an embargo was imposed in January 1969, after the Israeli raid on Beirut. It was again replaced by a 'selective' embargo in July 1969 but, following the smuggling out from Cherbourg of missile boats ordered by Israel and built in France, the French reimposed a total embargo, which, in turn, gradually became partial. By then, however, Israel had come to prefer American arms.

The French embargo was intended to apply pressure on Israel to comply with French political demands, but it also served as a symbolic gesture towards the Arab world, which the French government was trying to woo. As far as arms control was concerned, though, the embargo was counter-productive. It heightened Israel's anxieties and forced her to increase, rather

than decrease, purchases of arms from every possible quarter. It also contributed to the Israeli decision to rely much more on indigenous production of arms and ammunition: the decision to launch the enterprises of an Israeli tank[18] and an Israeli fighter-bomber/interceptor was to a large degree prompted by the lessons Israel had learnt.

## The Soviet Position
### Soviet Arms-control Initiatives

The Soviet position on arms control in the Middle East has in most cases had a negative effect. The Soviet Union succeeded in penetrating the Middle East primarily by means of arms aid and trade, which remains of major importance in her calculations. At the same time, the Soviet Union has shown some interest in arms-control measures when this has served her interests. During the second half of the 1950s, for example, the Soviet Union at least *appeared* to be interested in curtailing arms transfers to Middle Eastern countries and in other arms-control measures. At a meeting in London in spring 1956 the British delegation suggested limitations on deliveries of arms to the Middle East,[19] and on 27 April Mr Khrushchev, the First Secretary of the Soviet Communist Party, responded by suggesting an embargo on the flow of arms into the same region.[20] In a 1957 memorandum, the Soviet Union again urged an agreement between East and West on halting deliveries of arms to the Middle East,[21] insisting that such an agreement should include, among other things, the renunciation of attempts to involve Middle Eastern countries in military blocs, the elimination of foreign military bases and the withdrawal of foreign troops. One of the consequences of such an agreement would have been the dissolution of the Baghdad Pact – later replaced by the Central Treaty Organization (CENTO) – another would have been withdrawal of American military units from Turkey and Iran. The United States State Department, of course, rejected both the 1956 and the 1957 proposals.[22] Two more Soviet initiatives for the control of conventional arms transfers to the Middle East were made in 1958. On 31 January 1958, in an interview with *The Times*, Mr Khrushchev emphasized the need for a moratorium on arms shipments to the area. The second initiative was included in a memorandum to the United States government on 5 May 1958 calling for an agreement to limit the supply of arms to the Middle Eastern countries.

At the time the Soviet position in the Middle East was still very insecure. Against that background the Soviet demands appeared to the West extreme, an attempt to secure for the Soviet Union advantages far beyond what she could gain through continued 'free' competition with the West. The more the Soviet Union's influence increased in the Middle East, the less eager she became to conclude such agreements. She assumed, instead, that massive backing of the 'radical' Arab states – chiefly demonstrated by the transfer of arms, partly as gifts and partly under very generous credit arrangements – would give her the same political and strategic profits she hoped to gain by reaching an arrangement with the United States.

The first Soviet proposals pertained to the whole of the Middle East (and not just the Arab–Israeli area), but other Soviet proposals of the time extended the area under discussion to the whole of the Mediterranean. Moreover, the emphasis had shifted to nuclear weapons and their delivery systems, and several Soviet statements and initiatives referred to this: a statement in Tass on 21 January 1958;[23] the aforementioned memorandum of 5 May 1959 (although in that only the Middle East was mentioned), and a note to the United States government of 20 May 1963 about denuclearization of the Mediterranean.[24] Whereas the United States was seeking to bring about a stable military balance in the Arab–Israeli region, the Soviet Union was trying to extend the area to which arms-control agreements might apply to the whole of the Middle East and the Mediterranean. *Regional* military balances were, at the time, of less concern to the Soviet Union.

*A Conflict of Aims in Soviet Policy*
A shift in this attitude came about only after the 1967 war, when it became clear to the Soviet Union that changes in the Arab–Israeli regional balance were of the utmost importance to Soviet interests.

The Soviet Union had three additional reasons for supplying her Arab clients with arms and, indeed, for increasing the quantity. In the first place, as the patron and informal guarantor of Egypt and Syria she had to prove to these countries (and to other clients and allies) her credibility as a super-power ally. Second, if another outbreak of hostilities occurred between Israel and Egypt and Syria, the extreme weakness of the Arab armies might lead to their immediate collapse.[25] The Soviet Union would then have to face a tortuous dilemma: to honour her informal commitment to come to the aid of these countries, thereby increasing the danger of a direct confrontation with the United States, or to stand aside and thus lose further credibility and substantial tangible stakes. Third, the Soviet Union realized – as did her Arab partners – that in order to secure the return of the territories conquered by Israel in 1967 diplomatic activity had to be combined with the creation of an option for some military action against Israel. Only if this option existed – an option the exercise of which was not necessarily in the Soviet Union's interest – could the Arab countries establish a strong position in any future diplomatic negotiations; but such an option necessitated the rebuilding of the Arab armies and the narrowing of the military gap between Israel and the Arab states.

On the other hand, the Soviet Union probably realized that unlimited and uncontrolled arms transfers to the Arabs might lead the Arab governments to the conclusion that they were capable of launching an offensive against Israel, even if that offensive was not politically convenient for the Soviet Union. Soviet opposition to such a military operation was prompted by two considerations: first, it might end with a major Arab defeat, thus forcing upon the Soviet Union precisely the dilemma she wanted to avoid, and second, but less significant in her calculations, even if she were able to avoid such direct confrontation with the United States, a war might nevertheless endanger the process of detente. This latter consideration was a complex one, since the Soviet Union must have been aware that her ability to control the Arab countries was in any case restricted, and that a limited Arab gain, achieved by a swift military operation, would, in certain circumstances, do only small damage to the process of detente. Indeed, to an extent, the very process of detente was possible only because areas of high tension such as the Middle East were dissociated from the three major issues confronting the super-powers which served as the focus of detente: limitations on strategic arms, the *status quo* in Europe and economic and technological relations. This was not the American concept of detente, but even Washington eventually partly abandoned her insistence on 'coupling' as a main feature of detente.

The Soviet Union did use her power to withhold arms, probably in order to discourage Egypt from pursuing military initiatives. In October 1971 an agreement on arms deliveries to Egypt was concluded, but the Soviet Union did not act on it fully.[26] This Soviet reluctance was motivated either by concern that these deliveries might lead to war, or by Soviet pre-occupation with arms deliveries to India during the Indian–Pakistani war of 1971.[27] The Soviet Union was also careful not to supply some types of arms which could clearly have been used for offensive missions, such as the Tu-22 medium bomber armed with the *Kitchen* stand-off missile. These systems, and surface-to-surface missiles such as the *Scud*, may have been among the 'offensive' weapons included in arms agreements in early 1972, non-delivery of which was among the factors which caused the break in relations in July 1972.* On the other hand, weapons systems such as tanks, artillery and armoured personnel carriers (APC) were delivered in sizeable quantities. Last, the Soviet Union refused to transfer MiG-25 aircraft to Eygptian control. She did deliver some (in spring 1971) but they had Soviet pilots and were under Soviet control.[29]

### The Restoration of the Soviet–Egypt Alliance: Its Effect on Arms Supplies

By February 1973, however, after several months of diplomatic activity, the Egyptian–Soviet semi-alliance was resurrected, and Soviet arms again began pouring into Egypt. They included tanks, *SAM*-6, the *Kelt* stand-off system (to arm the Tu-16 already deployed in Egypt) and *Sagger* anti-tank missiles. Perhaps the most significant weapons system sent to Egypt was the *Scud* surface-to-surface missile, some 30–48 of which were delivered prior to the 1973 war.[30] These missiles deterred Israel from deep-penetration bombing of the heart of Egypt in the 1973

---

* Other reasons, probably as important, were dissatisfaction with the Soviet attitude towards a military operation against Israel, and tension between Egyptian and Soviet officers and officials which led to strong resentment among the Egyptians.

war. Although their destructive potential was limited and the damage they could have inflicted on Israel would have been very small compared with what Israel could have done to the Egyptian infra-structure, Israeli policy-makers preferred to avoid mutual counter-value air strikes and to limit the activities of the Israeli air force on the Egyptian front to attacks on military objectives in the battlefield itself or its environs. It is possible, although by no means certain, that if the Soviet Union had not supplied these missiles to Egypt, Israel would have resorted to a counter-value strategy to 'punish' Egypt by destroying her economic and technological infra-structure. To some extent, therefore, by limiting the destructiveness of the war, the supply of the *Scud* missile by the Soviet Union constituted an arms-control measure. On the other hand, however, it strengthened Egypt's intention to start the war in the first place.

Soviet concern, over the years, about the possibility of a resumption of hostilities between Israel and the Arab States had some paradoxical consequences. The Soviet Union was ready to give arms to Egypt on occasion as a *quid pro quo* for an Egyptian agreement not to begin a war. Soviet deliveries of arms in March and April 1971, for example, were linked to an Egyptian undertaking not to seek a military solution. The Egyptian approach at the time was, in any case, to try to reach a 'political solution', and, during the first half of 1971 (and in varying degrees up to Spring 1973) President Sadat was interested in some kind of an interim agreement or other political move. The Soviet supply of arms at that juncture had the objective of encouraging a political approach as well as the more traditional objectives of gaining influence with the Arab countries and strengthening their capabilities.[31]

### The American Position since 1967 and American–Soviet Contacts

*Attempts to Promote Arms-control Measures*

When the war broke out in June 1967, the United States imposed an embargo on supplies of arms to Israel, Lebanon, Tunisia, Morocco and Saudi Arabia, which was maintained until 24 October. She also took initiatives to reach an agreement with the Soviet Union on the limitation of arms supplies to the Middle East. On 19 June 1967 President Johnson outlined five principles for peace in the Middle East. These included a proposal that the United Nations should 'immediately call upon all its members to report all shipments' of arms into the area and should 'keep those shipments on file for all the peoples of the world to observe'.[32] At a special session of the General Assembly on the following day US Ambassador Goldberg submitted a draft resolution which proposed the achievement of 'a stable and durable peace' in the area 'through negotiated arrangements' on the basis of President Johnson's five principles, including 'registration and limitation of arms shipments into the area'. The Soviet Union opposed the American proposal, and the eventual resolution which was accepted did not refer to the arms-control clause. The Johnson proposal was also raised at the Eighteen-Nation Disarmament Committee in Geneva by the Canadian delegate but it was not followed up.

Another attempt was launched at the highest level at the Glassboro meeting in June 1967 between President Johnson and Premier Kosygin. In the eleven-point proposal which the United States presented to the Soviet Union at this meeting, a special clause called for limitations on the arms race in the Middle East. The Soviet reaction was conditional; the Soviet Union was ready to participate in an arms-control regime, but only if Israel withdrew from the territories conquered in 1967.[33] Then in November 1967 the United States raised in the Security Council the possibility of limiting 'the wasteful and destructive arms race in the area'. The Soviet Union this time responded with a draft resolution urging both sides to limit their 'useless and destructive arms race', but again made her participation conditional on the withdrawal of Israeli forces from the conquered territories. The basic political problems of the Middle East seemed more urgent, however, and neither superpower pressed its position. Instead they agreed to endorse Resolution 242, which did not include any reference to the arms race or to arms control.

American interest in an arms-control regime for the Middle East was probably based on the following considerations. The United States preferred not to become the main supplier of arms to Israel – a position she was likely to assume as a result of the French partial embargo – because that role would adversely affect her relations with the Arab countries. Second, immediately after the war and before the Soviet Union was able to re-equip the Arab armies, Israeli military superiority, which had been demonstrated by the war, was assured. According to American views at the time, this military superiority would have made it easier to try and arrive at a political settlement of the conflict acceptable to both the United States and the Soviet Union. Third, the continuation of uncontrolled arms transfers to the Middle East would have enabled the Soviet Union to resume her influence in that area. Last, an arms race in the Middle East might again lead to instability and possibly to war.

*A Change in American Policy*

American efforts to reach some understanding with the Soviet Union on arms control in the Middle East continued throughout the late 1960s and early 1970s without, however, leading to an agreement. The United States, for her part, imposed at different times some limitations on her supplies of arms to Israel. Initially, as mentioned above, she imposed an arms embargo on all belligerents in the Middle East. Towards the end of 1967, however, American policy changed as a result of the French embargo on the delivery of the *Mirage V* to Israel, the possibility that this embargo might become total, and the massive transfer of arms from the Soviet Union to Egypt and Syria. At the same time the United States employed arms transfers as an instrument to pressurize Israel politically, as well as a tool in the continued bargaining process with the Soviet Union over possible arms control in the area. This strategy was most obvious in the case of the sale of F-4 *Phantom* to Israel. Israel asked to buy the *Phantom* in autumn 1967, but it was not until March 1968 that a tentative decision was taken by the United States to sell the aircraft. The decision was later ratified; the delay was apparently connected with American hopes that the Soviet Union would be ready to limit her own shipments of arms to the Arab countries.[34] Another consideration was probably the possible effects of the *Phantom's* appearance on the military balance in the Middle East. By mid-1969 (the War of Attrition had begun in March) the first batch of *Phantoms* appeared in Israel, and indeed their use – from January 1970 – in the deep-penetration bombing of

Egypt did destabilize the strategic balance between Israel and Egypt and eventually provoked Soviet military intervention in Egypt. These developments led the United States, in March 1970, to halt further supplies of *Phantoms* as a means of political pressure on Israel and also as part of an attempt to reach an arms-control agreement with the Soviet Union. Supplies were resumed after the August 1970 cease-fire.

The discussions between the United States and the Soviet Union concerning arms-control agreements, which formed part of the negotiations for a settlement of the Arab–Israeli conflict, remained unproductive. It appears that these discussions were preliminary, although most of them were held at the highest possible level, that of either the President in his contacts with the Soviet Union or the Kissinger–Dobrynin meetings.[35] The United States raised the problem from time to time and suggested extensive negotiations, while the Soviet Union held to the position she took at the Glassboro meeting and demanded a complete Israeli withdrawal from the occupied territories as a prerequisite to an agreement. The official Soviet position was that, because the military balance in the Middle East was heavily tipped in favour of Israel, a precondition for stability in the region would be further military strengthening of the Arab side. The two super-powers were thus trapped by their commitments to their regional allies and held different views about a possible settlement of the conflict and about the nature of a stable balance of military capabilities in the area.

Following the cease-fire agreement of 1970, two further considerations influenced American policy concerning large-scale arms transfers to Israel. First, Israel was seen not simply as a local client to whom some American commitments had been made, but increasingly as a potential partner in the overall Western strategic posture in the Eastern Mediterranean.[36] The Israeli air force became an instrument which, in case of need, could be used as a local deterrent to limited Soviet involvement in the area. Military aid to Israel thus assumed a further dimension. Second, the United States reaffirmed her conviction that only an Israel that considered herself strong would be ready to make concessions, and thus American transfers of arms to Israel were necessary to stimulate Israeli confidence.[37] Indeed, in the short run, the consider-able strengthening of Israel's capabilities deterred the Arab countries from resumption of military activity and secured some stability. To this extent its function was one of arms control. Yet war was not ultimately prevented, since the Arab states continued to resent Israeli occupation of the territories and they in turn accelerated the build-up of their forces.

## The 1973 War and its Aftermath

The 1973 war further complicated the dilemma facing the super-powers in the field of arms control. During the war the super-powers undertook a massive effort to resupply the belligerents by air and sea. The American airlift began only after the Soviet airlift had started and after attempts to achieve a cease-fire had failed because of Egypt's rejection of the proposals. In their resupply efforts during the war and immediately after it, the super-powers were motivated primarily by their commitments to their local allies, whom they supplied with the weapons systems needed for the continuation of the battle. These included ammunition, spare parts, replacements for lost arms and also – primarily in the Israeli–American case – some new systems. The total tonnage delivered by airlift to Egypt, Syria and Iraq during 10–23 October amounted to approximately 12,500 tons. The sealift to the same countries during 7–20 October amounted to 63,000 tons.[38] Egypt and Syria received chiefly tanks, spare parts for all weapons systems, and SAM-2, -3, -6 and -7 launchers and missiles. Israel received aircraft, tanks (which in fact remained unused), ammunition (especially for artillery and tank guns) and electronic countermeasures which were used by the air force to suppress the Arab air defence systems. The new weapons systems they received were *Maverick* and *Shrike* air-to-surface missiles and *TOW* and *LAW* anti-tank missiles.[39]

Thus, during the war itself, the primary consideration of the super-powers was to aid their allies to achieve a military success. The United States tried by other means, however, to promote a measure of political stability, partly through preventing Israel from imposing total defeat on her adversaries. After the war, transfers of arms from the United States increased considerably, but even then some restrictions were imposed, and now and again the United States delayed the delivery of advanced systems in

73

order to apply political pressure on Israel. The most obvious case was the reluctance of the United States to supply the *Pershing* surface-to-surface missile which was promised to Israel in September 1975 in the document *Assurances from USG to Israel*, which formed part of the package deal concerning the Israeli–Egyptian agreement.[40] Another restriction still applies to transfers of technology for advanced systems which Israel would like to produce herself. Both these restrictions are intended as measures of arms control.

### The Super-powers and Nuclear Proliferation*

Both the United States and the Soviet Union regard nuclear proliferation in the Middle East as a threat to their national interests and this concern has informed their opposition to world-wide proliferation. The efforts of the United States to curb nuclear developments in Israel, which began as early as 1960, increased during the Kennedy and Johnson administrations. (One of the results of her intensified demands was that American inspectors were allowed to visit the Dimona reactor twice a year.) The ratification of the Non-Proliferation Treaty (NPT) in 1970 created the impression that the problem of proliferation had found at least a partial solution, and that the super-powers' task would be to encourage or coerce non-nuclear powers to accede to the NPT. Although the prevention of proliferation remained high on the list of priorities of the super-powers, the level of activity surrounding the issue diminished. In the Middle East itself the tension which followed the 1967 war had almost completely absorbed the attention of both super-powers, although from time to time there were indications that both were worried about the possibility of proliferation in that area and would act to prevent it. The United States government asked Israel repeatedly but unsuccessfully to sign and ratify the NPT. Egypt signed the NPT but made ratification conditional on Israel's accession to it.

Indeed, it seems that Israel's considerations regarding her security needs, coupled with her concern about American political reaction and the possibility that the Soviet Union or another nuclear power would provide nuclear arms to Arab countries in response to Israel's producing such arms, have considerably affected the Israeli decision not to 'go nuclear'. It should, of course, be noted that the actual state of the Israeli nuclear programme is not fully known. Some sources have suggested that Israel has, in fact, already produced nuclear warheads and is adopting a strategy of 'a bomb in the basement'.† Others maintain that Israel has developed a 'high option' with a short lead time to the production of the bomb. Even if the first suggestion is true, Israel has not admitted to it, and a measure of ambiguity surrounds the existence of such a capability. Moreover, the deterrent effect of the 'bomb' on *limited* Arab attacks would be negligible. Indeed, if the Arabs did believe that Israel had nuclear weapons in 1973 – and their strategic planners probably applied a 'worst-case analysis' – the war would have been the first between two regional powers in which the attacker suspected that his opponent might use nuclear weapons. (The Chinese attack on the American forces in Korea was of a different nature, because the United States itself was not attacked.)

The strong political opposition of the super-powers to nuclear proliferation in the past is one of the reasons why it has been averted in Middle East. The nuclear field is thus an area in which some deliberate arms control has been applied by the super-powers. Lately there has been renewed interest in the United States in measures to prevent nuclear proliferation, stimulated partly by the growth in the uses of nuclear energy for energy production. First steps, such as a Suppliers' Conference, have already taken place.[41] It can be assumed that the super-powers, probably with the co-operation of other nuclear powers, will again become more active in taking measures to halt the proliferation of nuclear capabilities and in applying more stringent safeguards to the use of nuclear material.‡

---

* The position of the United States and the Soviet Union on nuclear weapons in the Middle East deserves a separate, extensive discussion. However, since the issue constitutes an important arms-control measure it is discussed briefly here.

† The last and most dramatic serious report, based on a Central Intelligence Agency source, appeared in the *New York Times* on 16 March 1976. A sensational story in *Time* magazine followed. The *Time* story claimed that Israel assembled thirteen nuclear bombs in the early stages of the 1973 war.

‡ The Carter administration has made non-proliferation one of its most important foreign-policy objectives.

## Demilitarized Zones

The armistice agreements signed in 1949 between Israel and Syria and between Israel and Egypt stipulated the creation of very small demilitarized zones. There were several along the Israeli–Egyptian border. The experience with these demilitarized zones, especially the Israeli–Syrian ones, was highly unsatisfactory.[42] They became areas of continuous friction, and they were so small, in military terms, that their relevance and arms-control function was miniscule.

However, another *de facto* demilitarized zone did serve as a major arms-control measure. During the period 1957–67 (from Israel's withdrawal from the Sinai after the 1956 Sinai campaign until President Nasser moved his troops into the Sinai in May 1967), the Sinai was in fact partly demilitarized, though not through a formal agreement;[43] indeed, it was stated quite clearly that no such measure was agreed upon between Israel, the United States and Egypt during the negotiations on Israeli withdrawal from the Sinai in 1956–7.[44] Rather, this limited demilitarization appears to have been the result of a unilateral decision by Egypt, prompted by her own security interests, which included, first and foremost, tacit recognition that a major military build-up, especially in the forward area of the Sinai, might invite a strong reaction from Israel. Although this has never been confirmed as official policy by Israel, two Israeli decision-makers, Yigal Allon and Shimon Peres, indicated in private statements that such Egyptian concentration would constitute a *casus belli*.[45] Moreover, the structure of the Israeli forces and their operational doctrine indicated that Israel would have to react by military means to Egyptian remilitarization of the Sinai. Second, Egypt probably recognized that it was cheaper and more effective to accomplish her military objectives by keeping the majority of Egyptian forces either around the Suez Canal or in the desert to the west. Third, in terms of defending the Egyptian heartland and the Canal area against outside attack, it was faulty strategy to deploy large units in the forward areas of the Sinai.[46] For one of the lessons learned in the 1956 war was that Egypt must be prepared for an attack not only from Israel, but also from other, outside, powers. Once Egyptian involvement in inter-Arab politics became very intense,

there was an additional reason for keeping Egyptian forces close to home: they might be needed for overseas activities. This was fully demonstrated in the Yemen war which began in the second half of 1962.[47]

However, this partial demilitarization of the Sinai was very restricted in its application. In the first place, Egyptian regular troops were deployed throughout the Sinai during this period, although their *numbers* were very limited.[48] Second, and more important, Egypt had built an extensive strategic infra-structure in the Sinai which included airfields, supply depots and a forward system of defensive positions in the more important strategic areas close to the Israeli–Egyptian border.[49] The network of roads and water-pipes covering the Sinai desert made possible the quick build-up of a logistic system essential to large-scale forward deployment of troops. Furthermore, this road network enabled the Egyptian forces to move quickly from their permanent bases into the critical forward area. Third, there was no clear-cut indication of Israel's possible reaction in case of Egyptian violations in the Sinai. This ambiguity considerably reduced the credibility of Israel's deterrent capabilities. When on one occasion, in 1960, Egypt did move some forces into Sinai in order to deter Israel from attacking Syria, Israel partially mobilized her forces but relied on international diplomatic activity to defuse the crisis.[50] In any case, even Allon and Peres, in referring to the possibility of retaliation, mentioned only the concentration of troops along the Israeli–Egyptian border, and not the Egyptian military build-up inside the Sinai.

Another shortcoming of this limited demilitarization was the lack of any accompanying formal recognition. As a result there was no inspection system and, concomitantly, no international guarantees to prevent Egypt from moving large forces into the Sinai, nor was there even international acceptance of the fact that such a move would constitute a legitimate *casus belli* for Israel. Indeed, in 1967 the international community began to regard the situation as critical not when the Egyptian army began to concentrate near Israel's border, but only when the Straits of Tiran were closed.[51] Of course, Israel would almost surely have gone to war even without the closure of the Straits, because the deployment of large numbers of Egyptian forces close to her border over a long period of time placed her in an intolerable position.[52] It is conceivable, however, that the Egyptians could have moved forward as in 1960 (declaring as their motive the need to deter Israel from attacking Syria) but have refrained from closing the Straits; after a short while they could have retreated. In such circumstances Israel might not have gone to war at all, and the ambiguity concerning Israel's response to Egyptian violation of the military situation in the Sinai would have increased considerably.

These limitations on the efficacy of demilitarization notwithstanding, it did serve as a major arms-control measure. It diminished the possibility of direct contact between Israeli and Egyptian forces, thus decreasing the chances of accidental war or of escalation from a local military initiative. It added an important psychological barrier to any Egyptian decision to violate the *status quo* and supplied a crucial warning period.

## The Israeli Counter-force Doctrine

Israel's small territorial base (until after the 1967 war), her reliance on the military reserve system and her need to terminate hostilities as quickly as possible led to the development of a tactically offensive operational doctrine. On the one hand, the small size of the country dictated the transfer of any battle to the enemy's territory. On the other, the need to terminate hostilities quickly was determined, first, by the limited economic resources of the country, and hence the necessity to demobilize the reservists at an early stage, and, second, by the assumption that outside powers would intervene shortly after a war broke out in order to enforce a cease-fire. This offensive operational doctrine was also connected with yet another tenet of Israeli strategy; namely, that the main objective of a war is the destruction of the enemy's forces to prevent the war from deteriorating into a static one of attrition. To achieve a quick, decisive victory, Israel had to concentrate her fire-power on the battlefield itself, and this led to the acquisition of weapons systems destined for a counter-force strategy and the avoidance of a counter-value confrontation. Thus, the Israeli forces developed over the years a strategy which had as one of its consequences an interesting arms-control implication: the avoidance of attacks on civilian populations and on the economic infra-structure of an opponent.

This concentration on the battlefield promoted development of an operational doctrine for the air force which concentrated primarily on attaining air supremacy (whether achieved through interception, dogfighting, or attacks on the airfields of the other side) and providing close support for the ground forces. The Arab side, for its part, made greater efforts to acquire counter-value systems. Egypt, for instance, acquired medium bombers (at a very early stage the Il-28,and later the Tu-16) destined primarily for such missions.

In late 1967 there were signs that Israel was beginning to make hesitant attempts at a counter-value strategy (one instance was the bombardment of the Canal cities in retaliation for the sinking of the Israeli destroyer *Eilat*,) but only in 1970 did she finally abandon her previous doctrine and resort to a combination of counter-force and counter-value strategies with the 'deep-penetration bombing' of Egypt. This was an exercise in coercive diplomacy with rather ambiguous political objectives. It destabilized the regional strategic relationship and, moreover, accelerated Soviet military involvement in the conflict. Israel began to rely more and more on a posture of 'deterrence by punishment', in order to dissuade Egypt and Syria from attempting to change the new *status quo* by force of arms, a policy based on increased general air superiority coupled with demonstrable bombing capability. This deterrence posture did not stabilize the situation or operate as an arms-control measure – as was proved by the outbreak of the October 1973 war. During the war Israel did resort to heavy bombing of the Syrian economic infrastructure. In the case of Egypt, however, a certain balance of mutual deterrence against attacks on civilian targets obtained, due possibly to President Sadat's threat that he would use *Scud* missiles against Israeli cities if Israeli aircraft attacked Egyptian cities and other targets in the heartland of Egypt.

## Limited War in the Middle East as an Arms-control Measure

In differing ways all the wars between Israel and her Arab neighbours involved self-imposed restrictions which constituted arms control in the sense that the destruction caused by the wars and their duration were limited. Even in the 1948–9 war, some constraints existed. One of the more interesting among them was the tacit understanding between Premier Ben-Gurion of Israel and King Abdullah of Trans-Jordan that actual fighting would be limited to the only area over which they had conflicting demands, Jerusalem and the road leading to it, and would not extend to other parts of the long front between the two sides. In 1956 the war was restricted to counter-force attacks, and only one Arab state participated. In the 1967 war the restraints were reduced, but again Israel avoided counter-value strikes. She also limited unilaterally the size of the territories occupied. In the 1969–70 war, the campaign was a static one and limited to the Canal zone. The restraint shown here by Egypt was, however, hardly of the 'arms-control' variety, but was prompted by a sober assessment of the weakness of her forces as compared with those of Israel. In the 1973 war, although they committed all their armed forces, the political, and hence military, objectives of Egypt and Syria were limited. This restraint was dictated primarily by the Arabs' perception of the capabilities of the two sides. As far as Israel and Egypt were concerned, there was a common desire to avoid counter-value strikes.

## II. THE ARMS RACE

**Arms Races and War: A Causal Relationship?**

The relationship between arms races and war is a highly complex one and the following is a very brief treatment of an intricate subject.[53] Observation of arms races in the international system does not lead to the conclusion that there is by necessity a causal relationship between them and war. In theory, however, there are four situations in which arms races *per se* could aggravate conflict to the point of war: first, a build-up of arms by a party to a dispute who is determined to effect change and willing to resort to violent action to achieve his ends; second, an uneven arms race which might arouse suspicions about a possible change in the military balance caused by differing constraints on finance or manpower, and which could provoke a decision to launch a preventive war before the balance changed; third, the introduction of new and destabilizing weapons systems which would give an important advantage to the side which strikes first, and which would consequently motivate each side to be the aggressor;[54] fourth, the development of new-technology weapons systems, the relative performance of which is uncertain.*

In the Middle East, consideration of defence budgets and the actual transfer (and local production) of arms[55] permits the identification of five distinct periods:

(1) In the early 1950s there was some build-up of forces in the area but it was partially constrained by the external powers operating through the Near East Arms Co-ordinating Committee established by the Tripartite Declaration of 25 May 1950. Also, no imminent war was envisaged at that time.

(2) The second period was characterized by a sudden increase in the acquisition of arms. After some limited Israeli–French arms agreements in 1954 and 1955, the major change came in 1955 with the Soviet–Egyptian (officially called the Egyptian–Czechoslovak) arms deal. This acceleration continued during 1956, when both Israel and Egypt received large quantities of new weapons systems.

(3) The period between the end of the 1956 war and the outbreak of the 1967 war began with a significant reduction in defence budgets on both sides, as compared with the years 1955–6, but the arms build-up soon increased substantially. New weapons systems were introduced, and increasingly emphasis was placed on supersonic interceptors and fighter-bombers for the air forces and on more and better tanks for the ground forces. In terms of defence budgets as percentages of GNP, the growth was gradual: from about 8 per cent in Israel and 6 per cent in Egypt in 1957–8, to about 11–12 per cent in both countries in 1965–7. There was some levelling off during 1966–7 and, although there

* For a counter-approach arguing that uncertainty about the performance of new-technology weapons serves deterrence, see S. J. Dudzinsky, Jr., and James F. Digby, 'New Technology and Control of Conventional Arms: Some Common Ground', *International Security*, Spring 1977, pp. 143–59.

77

was an increase in the actual transfer of arms, it was evenly balanced.

(4) During the period between the 1967 and the 1973 wars the quantity of weapons supplied to both sides increased dramatically. Defence budgets increased to about 25 per cent in Israel and 20 per cent in Egypt in 1970. After the end of the War of Attrition (1969–70), there was again some levelling off, but the volume of arms transferred to both Israel and the Arab states continued to increase. A significant increase in supplies of arms to Egypt and Syria occurred during 1973. There were also major changes in the quality of weapons systems. The introduction of the F-4 added a new dimension to the Israeli air force, and Egypt and Syria acquired sophisticated surface-to-air missiles.

(5) The period between the end of the 1973 war and the present has been characterized by yet another significant increase in the quantities and quality of the weapons systems transferred to the local parties. In the first place there was a need to replenish the inventories of both sides after the war. Growth in arms and forces, as compared with pre-1973 levels, took place primarily in Israel and Syria.

Five major wars have been waged between Israel and one or more Arab countries – in 1948–9, 1956, 1967, 1969–70 (the War of Attrition) and 1973. A close examination reveals that only in 1956 were the dynamics of the arms race among the *primary* causes of war.

The 1948–9 war was caused by the direct clash between Jewish and Arab communities in Palestine following the 1947 UN partition vote. The Arab countries bordering on Palestine later joined the war for a variety of political reasons. In 1956 clearly a central cause of war was Israel's fear that the military balance between her and the Arab countries would shift to the advantage of the latter. This fear was kindled by the Soviet–Egyptian (Egyptian–Czechoslovak) arms deal of 1955. The 1956 war was, therefore, a typical preventive war, launched by a state fearful that the evolving arms race would disturb the *status quo*.[56] The war in 1967 had a number of causes, of which the arms race was not one. Once the crisis had begun, the behaviour of the two parties, Israel and Egypt, was determined by the dynamics of the situation itself. The Israeli decision to strike was finally provoked by the closure of the Straits of Tiran and, even more, by the concentration of Egyptian (and other Arab) forces along the Israeli border.[57]

The major Israeli victories over her adversaries in 1967 were followed by a long period of tension in the region. The Israeli military presence in the conquered territories was a source of great grievance to Egypt, Syria and Jordan which was quite separate from the general 'Palestine problem' and the ideological Arab rejection of Israel. The nature of the conflict was thus transformed and became much more critical. The 1969–70 War of Attrition was, therefore, a direct outcome of the 1967 war and its consequences. It was preceded by continuous violence on the 'Eastern front' (the Jordan River) and a short spell of violence along the Suez front. What is important to note, however, is that the direct cause was not a sudden and unexpected crisis, as in 1967, or a suspicion on the part of one side that the balance of power was liable to change, as in 1956, but an immediate and acute conflict of political interests. Again, the dynamics of the preceding arms race (which had escalated from 1967 onwards) were not the cause of the war, although they were a necessary condition for it. Egypt, the weaker side, would not have been able to start the war without massive Soviet arms supplies to help reconstruct her army.[58]

The 1973 war, which was the result of Arab distress at Israel's military presence in the territories,[59] was preceded by a substantial build-up of arms on both sides which had gone on since 1970 (with one exception, during the cooling of Soviet–Egyptian relations during July 1972–early 1973). From early 1973 onwards Egypt and Syria had accelerated their military preparations. Syria had increased her defensive capability, especially in terms of surface-to-air missiles. She relied more than Egypt on armour, however, to achieve her limited objective – regaining the Golan Heights.[60] The interesting feature of this build-up was that both Israel and Egypt accumulated those weapons systems in which they already had a qualitative superiority. Israel continued to acquire offensive systems, while Egypt, although she also accumulated a large inventory of tanks, strengthened her defensive systems (surface-to-air and anti-tank weapons). This imbalance eventually enabled Egypt to launch her 1973 offensive, in which she committed all her forces to achieving very limited geographical objectives while exploiting her local superiority in defensive systems. Thus the arms build-up, though not the primary cause of the war, affected the timing of the offensive, its scope and its type.

A consideration of the arms race over the whole period of the Arab–Israeli conflict shows that, with some variation, the military ratios were maintained throughout, and that Israel usually had some qualitative superiority over the Arab confrontation states. This was evident in some of the Israeli weapons systems, but much more in her individual fighters and her military organization as a whole.

As long as the territories are held by Israel, however, it seems that the political 'grievance' of Egypt, Syria and, to a lesser extent, Jordan, will provide a motive for any renewal of hostilities triggered by the Arab countries. The dynamics of the arms build-up will affect only the timing and scope of war. The Arab nations would probably resort to some type of military action even if the relative military capabilities of the two sides remained at their present levels and Israel continued to enjoy considerable superiority. If, on the other hand, a political solution were found and Israel returned most or all of the territories, it seems reasonable to assume that the probability of war would decrease considerably. The problem will persist, however, of how to increase strategic stability to match the relative political stability which will have been secured.

On the basis of the above brief analysis, it seems, in theory, that a symmetrical quantitative growth in the military capabilities of both sides (and thus the maintenance, more or less, of the existing numerical gap between them) will not of itself constitute an independent cause of war. It may become an important indirect cause if the arms obtained by the Arab countries have the capacity to frustrate vital Israeli weapons systems. The same applies if one of the sides (and especially the Arab countries) acquired a crippling first-strike capability or thought that they had acquired one. Also, the nature of the arms race has changed considerably because of the uncertainties associated with the performance of new weapons systems. The introduction of precision-guided munitions (PGM),* 'area

weapons' and various counter-measures, for instance, have increased doubts about the relative capabilities of the two sides. In such circumstances the likelihood of instability may increase.

With respect to the economic situation of the regional actors, a roughly balanced curtailment of the arms race would certainly be crucial; Israel, Egypt and Syria can ill afford to go on arming at the current pace. It is true that, with the enormous increase in oil revenues, the Arab world as a whole has vastly greater financial resources than ever before, but the oil-rich states are not the confrontation states. The readiness of Saudi Arabia and Kuwait to transfer funds to the confrontation countries is limited and is dependent on political decisions that might alter with a change in circumstances. Thus, it seems that the key adversaries in the conflict have a compelling interest in curtailing the arms race. Moreover, if either side (and especially Israel) perceives that it is 'losing' the race because of financial inferiority it might consider a preventive strike. In this case, the dynamics of the arms race would have served as a major cause of war.

### The Arms Race since 1973
Despite the Israeli military victory in the 1973 war, there was a growing realization in Israel, and to a lesser extent in the United States, that it was necessary to increase Israel's military capability in relation to that of the Arab confrontation states. This was prompted by several considerations. First, it was necessary to augment Israel's military strength in anticipation of the political negotiations which were expected. Second, because of the relative success of the first stage of the Arab surprise attack in 1973, it was accepted by the United States that Israel would have to prepare herself for different types of wars in the future and would need wider margins of security than in the past. Third, the sphere of Israeli security interests was broadening The blockade of the Bab al-Mandeb in 1973 on the one hand, and the potential threats to Israeli sea lanes throughout the Mediterranean, in the Red Sea and possibly even around the Arabian Peninsula on the other, demonstrated the need for capabilities beyond those which were destined for a military campaign with the Arab confrontation countries alone.[61]

* For a definition and an analysis of their impact, see James F. Digby, *Precision-Guided Weapons*, Adelphi Paper No. 118 (London: IISS, 1975).

Fourth, the imbalance between Israel and the Arab countries from the point of view of manpower, economy and size, which became more evident during the 1973 war and its aftermath, dictated that Israel should equip herself with 'fire-intensive' weapons systems. These systems require large stocks of spare parts and ammunition, and the stocks would need to be maintained at a particularly high level, since a major resupply operation during a future war might encounter political difficulties. Last, the notion that only a strong and confident Israel would be ready to make political concessions again became prevalent. These factors seemed to carry more weight than arms-control considerations (even if the Soviet Union had agreed to an arms-control regime, something which was not likely in any case).

Israel's arms build-up after 1973 was marked. According to the former Israeli Defence Minister, Shimon Peres, Israel's overall military strength increased by about 30 per cent. Her tank force increased by 35 per cent, artillery by 25 per cent, the APC inventory by 60 per cent, combat planes by 15 per cent (or 35 per cent according to Yitzak Rabin, the Israeli Prime Minister) and war vessels by 45 per cent.[62] By the summer of 1975 the Israeli air force comprised 200 *Phantom*, 200 *Skyhawk* and a sizeable number of *Mirage* ('*Barak*') and *Kfir* fighter-bombers and interceptors.[63] Israel placed orders for F-15 and F-16 air-superiority fighters (she had already received the first deliveries of the former), various air-to-surface, surface-to-air and anti-tank PGM, and the Grumman EC-2 Airborne Warning and Control System (AWACS). The latter system is likely to increase the capability of the Israeli air force significantly. One of the lessons of the 1973 war was that an exclusive reliance on the tank is ill-conceived. Israel is now, therefore, attempting to implement a combined-arms approach.[64]

The level of arms transfers to both Egypt and Syria also rose considerably after the war. The Soviet Union sought to increase the military capability of her Arab allies in order to enhance their position in any political negotiations, and because there was always the possibility of a renewal of hostilities. Transfers of arms would also facilitate Soviet penetration into those Arab countries. However, the pattern of relations between Egypt and the Soviet Union had

changed. Shortly after the war it became apparent that Egypt had decided to reduce her reliance on the Soviet Union and to improve, instead, her relations with the United States. She quite quickly assumed an independent posture with pro-American undertones (a tendency which became stronger with every passing year). The Soviet Union reacted by slowing down the transfer of arms and eventually by limiting them considerably. To be sure, most of the losses suffered by the Egyptian forces were replaced, and indeed Egypt even received a new and very effective weapons system, the MiG-23 (some 48 of which have been delivered). Yet in other areas her level of arms remained similar to that of before the 1973 war. By 1974 Egypt was already looking for new sources of arms, first in Western Europe and, by 1975, in the United States as well.

The new search for arms indicates, in some respects, continued adherence to the strategy applied in the 1973 war; namely, reliance on elaborate air defence systems, infantry backed by armour, big concentrations of artillery and vast quantities of anti-tank weapons (preferably guided munitions). After replenishing her air defence systems from Soviet sources, Egypt is also building up her fighters-interceptor inventory by adding *Mirage* III (transferred from Saudi Arabia) and *Mirage* F-1 (ordered by Egypt and Kuwait, for transfer to Egypt). A large deal with Dassault for the purchase of *Mirage* F-1, some of them to be assembled in Egypt, is in the process of negotiation.[65] These acquisitions accord with the analysis suggested by General Mohamed Ali Fahmy: (1) increased importance of surface-to-air systems, coupled with intensification of the battle for air superiority; (2) increased importance of infantry; (3) diminished importance of the tank.[66] Other recommendations, which did not indicate a radical change from previous strategy, were improved command and control systems and a more significant role for surface-to-surface missiles. There are, however, some indications that Egypt is also searching for an added strategic option which would emphasize strike and offensive capabilities. A good example is her negotiations for the purchase of the British/French *Jaguar* strike-attack aircraft. It has been estimated that Egypt is aiming at orders in the range of 200 units.[67] Another effort is directed at purchasing from France the *AlphaJet* (a Franco-German coproduction; the French version is of the close-support type, whereas the German one is a trainer).[68] Last, about half the MiG-23 referred to above are the ground-attack version.[69]

The build-up in Syria seems to have surpassed her capacity to absorb and deploy the arms supplied by foreign powers. Apart from replacing all the losses incurred in the war, Syria has also received 45 MiG-23 and has increased her air force and tank inventories considerably. New surface-to-air missiles have also been supplied to her.

Iraq and Libya have also received large quantities of arms. Among the new weapons supplied to Iraq is the Tu-22, which is capable of low penetration into Israeli air space. The deliveries to Libya far exceed Libyan capabilities, and in case of another Arab-Israeli war could be transferred to Egypt.

## III. WHAT FUTURE FOR ARMS CONTROL?

The above account of the historical experience in arms control in the Middle East indicates the broad range of the subject. The following discussion suggests five possible areas for future arms-control measures, describes their main features and examines the variables which could affect them. The arms-control measures to be discussed are: (1) measures against surprise attacks; (2) de-militarization of buffer zones; (3) an agreement banning first use of force; (4) an agreement proscribing counter-city attacks; (5) limitations on the supply of specific weapons systems. Before proceeding, it is worth noting the issues which militate against the future application of arms control and those which may encourage it.

### Factors Affecting Arms-control Measures
No adequate criteria exist for what constitutes a stable balance of deterrence based on conventional arms.[70] Concepts such as 'balance of power', which postulate parity in conventional capabilities, are vague and indeterminate, though the formulation of a definition for a stable 'balance of military power' in the Arab-Israeli region did pre-occupy decision-makers in Washington for quite some time. It has been suggested that an adequate criterion would be a quantitative ratio of hardware of one to three (or one to two, depending on the mix of systems) between Israel and those Arab states which may intervene in the war (Iraq, Libya and Saudi Arabia), allowing for changes in specific weapons systems and for the superior quality of Western aircraft and tanks supplied to Israel compared with Soviet arms supplied to the main Arab parties to the conflict, Egypt and Syria. Without other criteria, this could serve tentatively as a guideline for maintaining if not a balance (a very nebulous concept) at least a symmetrical growth of military capabilities between Israel and her adverseries. The quantitative criterion used until now rested on the assumption that Israel should, on the whole, receive systems which had a technological edge over those held by the Arab states. The difficulty in formulating such a criterion, however, indicates the need for focus both on *qualitative* limitations and on arms-control measures other than restrictions on the flow of armaments.

Hitherto, although the Arab 'forces in being' have been larger in terms of manpower and arms (even with all Israeli forces mobilized), Israel has had the advantage in the quality of some of her weapons systems and in intangibles such as morale, organizational ability, leadership and the capacity to decentralize command (which increases the flexibility of her forces and enables them to operate with much greater success in mobile warfare). These intangible advantages are difficult to quantify and hence to incorporate in an adequate model of stable mutual deterrence, as is the fact that account her geographical size, which has a bearing on her powers of deterrence.

There are, moreover, uncertainties about the future. To what extent would the confrontation states be ready to commit more of their resources of money and manpower to a further military conflict with Israel and, in particular, how far would the oil-rich Arab states (notably Saudi Arabia and Kuwait) be ready to transfer large parts of their vast financial reserves to the confrontation states? Doubt also surrounds the possibility of a more unified Arab command system and of changes in the intangibles on the Arab side. The implication of these uncertainties is primarily that, if there is any major change in these factors, it will probably result in a strengthening of the Arab position, and any formal agreement on limitation of the arms race should therefore anticipate the need for modification in the event of such a change.

Another problem is that the recipients of arms have always been able to exert considerable pressure on arms suppliers. As long as there is no fully co-ordinated joint policy on arms control binding all suppliers (primarily the United States and the Soviet Union, but also France and Britain), the regional powers may persist in applying pressure on each supplier individually. In addition, the supply of arms will continue to be viewed partly as an instrument for 'bribing' the local powers into accepting political conditions within the framework of future peace negotiations. There are two (preferably co-ordinated) ways to limit the effects of this problem: to negotiate a political settlement and to reach a suppliers' agreement on restrictions on arms transfers, which will take into consideration the recipients' strategic concerns. However, due to the sudden and dramatic increase in the financial resources available to the Arab oil-producing countries and the economic crisis in the developed world, which has stimulated efforts to export arms, the arms market has become a buyer's market.

One of the lessons learned from all the Arab–Israeli wars is the importance of surprise, first-strike and pre-emption strategies, particularly in the initial period of the campaign. Precisely this experience should therefore provide a focus for elaborate arms-control efforts. But, since the Arab–Israeli conflict is a many-sided one, the effect of some arms-control measures (for instance, the demilitarization of buffer zones) on Israel's relations with the different confrontation states will probably vary. One of the ways of overcoming this problem is through flexible limitations on deployment of forces beyond demilitarized zones.

Finally, there is an increasing capacity for indigenous arms production, both in Israel and in the Arab countries. Israeli production is the more notable. In 1975–6 she was already producing 30 per cent of her weaponry, and is now said to be self-sufficient in small arms, bombs, explosives, some types of guided missile and ammunition.[71] Guided missiles include the *Shafrir* air-to-air missile, the *Gabriel* sea-launched surface-to-surface missile and a development of the *Luz* air-to-air missile.[72] *Saar*-class missile boats are also in production.[73] In particular Israel is producing the *Kfir* fighter-strike aircraft,[74] of which only the engine (a General Electric J79) is currently produced under licence (about 40 per cent are still imported).[75] The Arabs, too, are attempting to develop an indigenous arms industry. Egypt has been trying various programmes since the early 1950s but with only very limited success. However, with the sudden huge increase in Arab financial resources, various ideas about an inter-Arab arms industry have emerged and, indeed, an Arab Defence Procurement Organization has been founded.[76] Separate negotiations with Britain and France over the creation of a defence industrial complex in Egypt are currently under way.[77]

This short account of the factors which could adversely affect arms-control efforts in the Middle East is disquieting. On the other hand, there are some elements in the situation which favour arms control as an important component in the political and strategic environment. Briefly, these are: (1) the experience with the demilitarization of the Sinai between 1956 and 1967; (2) the few tacit understandings concerning limitations on violence; (3) the recognition that war is of no political or strategic benefit to Israel (nor, probably, to the moderate Arab states either); (4) the obvious economic constraints on the principal participants in the arms race, which should direct them towards some tacit or explicit agreements about its limitation; (5) the acknowledgement that some arms-control agreements are a necessary part of any political settlement. This last has already been recognized by both sides in the three interim agreements of 1974 and 1975, which stipulated the creation of buffer zones, limitations on force deployments in specified areas, limitations on some weapons systems (surface-to-air missiles) beyond these areas and the formal creation of early-warning systems.

## Measures Against Surprise Attacks

The value ascribed to surprise attacks in the Middle East is highly destabilizing.[78] In a crisis, fears on both sides about such attacks grow markedly, increasing the likelihood of their occurrence. Measures taken overtly or covertly to avert the possibility of surprise attacks, which would reduce these fears and make crises more manageable, could be very efficacious. Two basic motives for a surprise attack can be postulated: first, to achieve a pre-emptive or anticipatory strike for narrow military-security purposes (almost invariably in a situation of crisis); second, to launch a premeditated strike out of the blue, the aims of which could embrace a multitude of strategic and political objectives. Whereas the first type would probably be directed primarily at the military forces of the opponent, the second might be a combination of limited or unlimited attacks on either military targets or social and economic targets, or a combination of both counter-force and counter-value attacks.

The objectives of surprise attacks would probably be different for Israel and the Arab confrontation states. Israel would probably be more inclined than the Arab countries to launch pre-emptive or anticipatory strikes; this would be particularly true if both sides' forces had already been mobilized – primarily because Israel relies much more than the Arab states on reserve forces, whose mobilization over a long period of time would create grave problems for her. However, Israel's reserve system would impose constraints on such an attack. As the majority of the Israeli forces are composed of reservists, no *large-scale* military ground operation could be conducted without them. Prior to the initial strike, therefore, Israel would have to mobilize a large part of her reserve forces, and this would serve as a warning to the Arab states. If mobilization took place, all the Arab armies would probably be put on alert, since no Arab state would be sure where the Israeli strike might fall. Thus, the only 'real' surprise attack from Israel could be an air strike, possibly coupled with a limited ground operation.[79] The situation, of course, would be different in times of crisis and when both sides had already mobilized their forces. Under those conditions Israel could launch a full-scale surprise, pre-emptive or anticipatory strike.

The likelihood of an Arab surprise attack would be higher, since the Arab states have standing armies. For sure, even the Arab armies could not launch an attack without extensive preparations, which could be monitored, but the significance of such preparations could be distorted more easily than in case of a large-scale Israeli mobilization.

A strategy aimed at diminishing the likelihood of surprise is required and should incorporate the following elements: the creation of demilitarized buffer zones and possible restrictions on the deployment of forces beyond buffer zones (discussed on pp. 84-6); more efficient intelligence and surveillance systems; the provision of information about the movements of forces, including military exercises;[80] greater invulnerability of essential military components; and a treaty proscribing the first use of force (discussed on pp. 86-7).

The Israeli–Egyptian agreements of January 1974 and September 1975 have already set a precedent in connection with intelligence-gathering and surveillance (to be discussed in p. 86), and these arrangements should serve as a model for future agreements between Israel and all her neighbours. Surveillance flights, conducted by both sides and by third parties which are guarantors of the agreements, should be allowed above both demilitarized zones and areas of restricted deployment. One possible procedure could be that every further agreement on limited Israeli withdrawal, which would (necessarily) stipulate demilitarization of certain areas, should also include clauses allowing for still wider areas in which surveillance flights were permitted. Any agreements about demilitarization of zones and restrictions on deployment of forces, or any independent agreements, could also include requirements for the continuous transfer of information about force deployments and military exercises. Military manoeuvres, for example, could be announced in advance, especially if they were to be carried out in areas adjacent to borders or in areas of restricted deployment. This information could be delivered directly to the other party or indirectly through a third party (such as the United States), and would also serve as a confidence-building measure.

The amount of information collected by Israeli intelligence is already considerable. Similarly, the Egyptians (and, by now, probably the Syrians) have received information about Israeli deployments through the Soviet-manned

MiG-25 reconnaissance flights over Israel. The transfer of information about military exercises need not, therefore, be considered a major innovation, though the sanction, by mutual consent, of some surveillance overflights and the transfer of information about military exercises may act as additional stabilizing measures. To facilitate the gathering of military intelligence, both sides would have to be supplied with the necessary systems, and agreements would have to be concluded about non-interference in intelligence gathering procedures.

Agreements about the issues discussed above – demilitarized zones, restrictions on deployment of forces beyond these zones, non-interference in intelligence-gathering, surveillance by third parties and transfer of information about military exercises – would be more effective if incorporated in formal treaties (as opposed to tacit understandings). Such treaties could define restrictions more clearly and accurately, would bar misunderstandings and would formalize sanctions. Although every agreement is vulnerable to violation, agreements are, nevertheless, important; they make violations somewhat more difficult and, more important, they modify the conduct of the parties as long as they are interested in the maintenance of these agreements. Moreover, if third parties (ideally the United States alone, but in some cases the Soviet Union as well) were to guarantee the system of arms control, formal agreements would become a necessity. Only explicit agreements could define the nature and scope of the guarantee and inhibit violations.

A new context of arms-control agreements and the gradual education of the regional powers in the nature of arms control would alleviate fears on both sides about the purpose of measures such as the hardening of military targets and the strengthening of the intelligence-gathering agencies, which would anyway be the likely results of any further unilateral action on each side.

## Demilitarization of Buffer Zones and Restrictions on Deployment of Forces

The stabilizing role of the tacit and partial demilitarization of the Sinai in the strategic relationship between Israel and Egypt during the period 1957–67 has already been mentioned. The reasons why it was so central then still apply today. First among them is that a demilitarized

Sinai would serve as an excellent buffer zone, providing both sides with an important strategic and tactical warning period after the indications of a surprise attack had been received. Some elaboration is required here. There are three types of indicators for a surprise attack: 'strategic' indicators, which signify intentions primarily, but sometimes also a general trend in the building up of capabilities; 'tactical' indicators, which warn of immediate preparations on the part of a suspected attacker; and 'real-time' indicators, which alert the attacked to an aggressor's violation of clear and pre-arranged lines. One of the lessons of the 1973 war was that both 'strategic' and 'tactical' warnings are potentially open to conflicting interpretations.[81] On the one hand, 'tactical' warnings may be ignored, as happened, for example, at Pearl Harbour and in the 1973 war; on the other, they may stimulate over-reaction on occasions when the preparations are only military exercises. The only adequate warning about an impending attack is the last type of indicator – and a demilitarized Sinai, penetration of which from either side would be unambiguous, would provide this facility, while eliminating the danger of over-reaction based on misunderstanding. (Israeli and Egyptian insistence on having early-warning stations which operate within the buffer zone created by the September 1975 Sinai agreement underlines their concern about surprise attacks.) Demilitarization of the Sinai, by physically separating opposing armies, would also contribute to stability by reducing the danger of accidental war, or of war caused by a series of miscalculations.[82]

Moreover, assuming that the two sides are not planning a military campaign against each other, there are some advantages for both in having the Sinai demilitarized, rather than policed by their own forces. From the Israeli point of view, if Egyptian forces invaded the Sinai with the intention of reaching the Israeli border (presumably the pre-1967 international border), they would have to accept the mode of battle best suited to the Israeli forces – a quick, mobile campaign. Israeli superiority in this type of battle has been proved in all previous Arab-Israeli wars. Further, if the Egyptian air defence system had to move with the attacking forces across the Sinai, the ground forces would be dispersed and fast-moving, and hence would sacrifice integrated command and control as well as the aid of warning systems. In the 1973 war the effectiveness of the air defence systems of Egypt and Syria was partly due to their being concentrated in extremely large numbers in relatively small areas: in Egypt, mostly along the Suez Canal and around several important centres inside Egypt; in Syria, mostly on the Golan Heights and along the routes to Damascus. But if a battle raged throughout the Sinai, the Egyptian army would have to spread its air defence capability over an extensive area and would also have to defend its support columns throughout the area, which would probably reduce the effectiveness of the air defence system considerably. Under such conditions it is likely that the Israeli air force would be able to give efficient close support to their own ground forces and to harass and disrupt the 'tail' of the Egyptian forces.

From the Egyptian point of view, it is also arguable that the demilitarization of the Sinai would be preferable to the deployment of troops in the area. Two Israeli surprise attacks (in 1956 and 1967) have pointed to the vulnerability of an exposed forward Egyptian deployment. So long as there is no political settlement which resolves the problem of the territories, Egypt would like to have a credible military option against Israel and would probably prefer to deploy her troops in the Sinai, but the fear of an Israeli surprise attack on Egyptian forces close to the Israeli border would be increased. Two contingencies could provoke an attack by Israel: first, the concentration of Egyptian forces in the Sinai, an eventuality which Israel could not countenance without retaliation; second, a crisis between Israel and another Arab country (notably Syria), which could arouse Israeli fears that Egypt might decide to participate in a possible war.

The strategic advantages that both sides would gain from the demilitarization of the Sinai could stabilize the situation, since the difficulty and cost of an attack across the desert would act as deterrents, and demilitarization of the area – apart from reducing the threat of surprise attacks – would constitute an arms-control measure. The feasibility of an agreement on the demilitarization of the Sinai is, of course, in doubt. Indeed, Egypt has maintained that she is opposed to such an agreement. At the same time, she has indicated some readiness to accept the demilitarization of part of the Sinai, provided Israel undertook to demilitarize an approximately equal strip of land inside Israel (within the pre-1967 border).[83] This, of course, is unrealistic. Demilitarization would only be effective if it covered the entire Sinai Peninsula, creating a broad buffer zone (possibly with the exception of a narrow strip similar to the one created under the 1975 agreement, in which *limited* Egyptian forces are deployed for the purposes of the immediate defence of the Canal works and cities). Besides, since the Sinai is about three times the size of the whole of Israel, equivalent demilitarization inside Israel would clearly be impossible. From the point of view of arms control, a large buffer zone between the two sides is essential, and the Sinai is eminently suitable for that purpose, being almost uninhabited and having already been partly demilitarized, during the period 1957–67.

The advantages to be gained from the demilitarization of the Sinai have convinced the United States in the past that it would have to be an essential component of any political settlement. It appears that the Egyptian government may become more amenable to such an idea. Indeed, there was some indication of that during the negotiations preceding the September 1975 interim agreement, when Egypt agreed to some demilitarization provided the term used was 'limited zone', 'zone of limited forces' or something similar. The same approach could be employed in any future negotiations. Israel, for her part, considers the demilitarization of Sinai a *sine qua non* in any final settlement with Egypt.

An important model for future agreements concerning the demilitarization of Sinai is the September 1975 interim agreement between Israel and Egypt, which stipulated four central and significant arms-control measures: (1) the creation of a demilitarized buffer zone between Israeli and Egyptian forces; (2) limitations on the deployment of manpower and weapons systems in areas contiguous to the buffer zones on both sides; (3) the creation of early-warning systems controlled by Egypt, Israel and the United States; (4) the introduction of American personnel (the American role will be discussed in Chapter IV).

The first two measures were framed in the Sinai 'disengagement' agreement of 1974. Changes were made in the 1975 agreement only to the location of the buffer zone and the areas of limited deployment. The third component had a limited precedent in the 1974 agreement, but the September 1975 agreement goes much further; in addition to allowing for mutual surveillance overflights, it provided for the establishment of a more elaborate warning system to serve the two sides. According to the agreement, Israel and Egypt were each to control one surveillance and intelligence station inside the buffer zone. Apart from their importance as a further means of surveillance, the new stations inhibited violations of the agreement, since personnel on both sides would be exposed in event of a sudden outburst of hostilities and hence would become *de facto* hostages. The buffer zone created by the agreement is relatively narrow but, considered together with the areas of limited military deployment, its significance in providing for a warning of threatening moves, and therefore its importance as an arms-control measure, increases. The agreement, however, allowed the Egyptian forces to 'tail' withdrawing Israeli forces, a provision which has reduced the efficacy of the buffer zone and created an alarming precedent. Instead of widening the zone defined by the 1974 agreement to cover all the ground evacuated by the withdrawing Israeli forces, Egyptian forces were allowed to enter and occupy part of it. The buffer zone was thus 'moved' and, in the process, somewhat enlarged. Obviously, this provision must not be included in any future agreements, for it would violate the principle of the demilitarization of the Sinai.

Since the West Bank and the Golan Heights are much narrower than the Sinai, the effectiveness of their demilitarization as a measure against surprise attacks is far more limited. In the case of the West Bank, some Israeli forces could be deployed in the Jordan Valley for a period of time. In addition – or alternatively, if the former is not politically feasible – deployment of forces beyond the demilitarized buffer zone should be restricted. As a third measure Jordan should undertake not to allow the presence of Arab forces in Jordan. Since the Israeli army depends primarily on reserves, whereas the Arab forces, although they contain

many reservists,* primarily comprise standing armies, restrictions on deployment would have to be directed principally at the Arab armies. To resolve this dilemma, Israel should undertake not to mobilize significant parts of her reservists. The Golan Heights would pose a particular problem for Israel. Because they are a high plateau with easy access from the Syrian side, Syria is in a much better position to re-occupy them in a surprise move. The need to restrict deployment of forces beyond buffer zones is therefore especially critical in their case. The objective should be to restrict the number of Syrian forces and the kind and number of weapons systems deployed along the demilitarized Golan Heights. Even with such restrictions Syria would still be in a position to move into the area, using forces deployed in other parts of the country; nevertheless, limitation on Syrian deployment would partially reduce Israeli anxieties about a surprise Syrian move into the Heights, while it would not pose serious security risks for Syria. Weapons systems restricted on the Syrian side should be primarily of the offensive type – tanks and self-propelled guns. A major point of debate in future negotiations about such an agreement would probably be restrictions on surface-to-air systems. It is likely that Israel would argue that such systems serve as an umbrella for an attack, while Syria would maintain that such systems are needed for the defence of her normally deployed forces.

## 'No First Use of Force' Treaty (NFUFT)[84]

Such a treaty should essentially be aimed at repudiation by both sides of the use of force and should emphasize other means for the resolution of outstanding contentious issues. It would necessarily ban surprise attacks, and would probably be strengthened by the inclusion of a provision allowing both sides to demand information about threatening concentrations of forces.

What could be the real effect of such an agreement? Three advantages could be gained.

---

* Although Egypt, Syria, Jordan and Iraq between them have as many as 1,000,000 reserve soldiers, these could not be compared with Israeli reservists. There is no mechanism for their periodic training, their mobilization takes a long time and their effectiveness in combat is highly debatable.

First, it would serve to silence Arab calls for a resort to force in order to eliminate Israel. Second, it would raise Israel's costs, in political terms, if she decided to resolve a crisis by force. Third, it would have a stabilizing effect on inter-Arab relations. It is reasonable to assume that if one Arab state decided on war against Israel, it would try to persuade others to join in, since no Arab country could hope, in the foreseeable future, to wage war on Israel by itself. The treaty could inhibit spontaneous alliances of this kind, because only two main strategies would be open to a single belligerent Arab state: to establish the alliance before war was declared, or – if other Arab countries refused – to launch an attack on the assumption that they would find it impossible to stay out of the war once it had started. The latter strategy involves two grave risks. One is that the other Arab countries – or country (Egypt, probably, if Syria were making these calculations) – would not join in the war, which would be conducted without the participation of those Arab states considered essential to its success, and Israel would probably win. The second risk is that, even if the other Arab countries found it difficult to avoid involvement, their moves would be slow – either deliberately or for reasons such as problems with fast mobilization – and, again, an Israeli victory would be likely.

The NFUFT would add an element of uncertainty to the calculations of every Arab state which considered an attack on Israel, and would affect its deliberations about the possible success of the war in terms of relative gains and costs. A decision to abrogate a formal agreement requires some effort, and, as this difficulty is apparent to all the regional powers, they would be forced to conclude that parties to the agreement would find it particularly difficult to abrogate it in the context of the threat of war between an Arab state and Israel. Indeed, this uncertainty is already affecting Syrian policy: the Egyptian undertaking in the 1975 interim agreement not to 'use force' against Israel (an undertaking which is understood to be binding for three years and to be valid – according to certain of President Sadat's speeches and interviews – only in the case that Israel is not the first to use force herself) is a factor which Syria has to take into account when she considers her strategy.

The agreement would also embrace contingencies which are not covered by existing agreements on demilitarization of zones, such as sea and air attacks outside the buffer zones. The NFUFT should not, however, refer to reactions to grave violations of other formal arms-control agreements, such as demilitarization of zones. If one side abrogated an important part of an arms-control agreement, the aggrieved party should have the option of punitive or compensatory military reprisals.[85]

### 'No Counter-city Attacks' Treaty (NCAT)

In the wars of 1956 and 1967 military operations were limited to the battlefield; almost no countervalue strikes were registered, although one major exception was Jerusalem in 1967, when civilian targets (mainly Israeli) were shelled. This limitation on the use of force was primarily the result of a conscious Israeli decision rather than a tacit undertaking by both sides; in fact, since the Arab countries lacked a counter-value military capability (their air forces had been destroyed or lacked penetrability), any decision to rule out attacks on civilians had to be an Israeli one.

The wars of 1969–70 and 1973 followed the same pattern, with two major exceptions: in the first war, Israel began, after a while, her deep-penetration bombing of Egypt, while in the second, the Israeli air force imposed severe punishment on the economic infra-structure of Syria. Almost all the Arab states refrained from counter-city attacks, a decision probably prompted by an acknowledgement of the superiority of the Israeli air defence system (based primarily on interceptors). Shortly after the 1973 war ended there were brief press reports that Israel and Egypt were interested in arriving at some kind of understanding about proscription of counter-city attacks. Israel has always been worried about casualty levels and about attacks on her civilian population. Egypt, for her part, has already experienced harsh treatment at the hands of the Israeli air force, and her capacity to protect her skies effectively and, more important, to penetrate Israeli air defences (without surface-to-surface missiles) is very uncertain. Israel also shares an interest in reaching agreement about counter-city attacks with Syria and Jordan. Syria could possibly be in a position to deploy a large number of

87

surface-to-surface missiles (supplied by the Soviet Union) capable of penetrating Israeli airspace, but such an attack would be followed by terrible punishment of Syrian cities, which could bring about the fall of the regime. On the other hand, while Israel could probably defend herself against penetration attempts by Syrian bombers, it would be impossible for her to deploy an anti-missile system, and the only way to eliminate such a threat would be by a pre-emptive strike at Syrian missile launchers. Moreover, the diversion of military capabilities from the battlefield to either air defence or attacks on civilian targets could be counter-productive. The case of Jordan is different, since she has no capability for attacks on the Israeli civilian population. At the moment she does not have any effective air defence either, but this situation will almost certainly change within the next five years or so with the introduction of an American air defence system. Attacks on Jordanian cities, if they were defended by an elaborate air defence system, could be costly, and the military gains would at best be debatable. Thus, Jordan will eventually be able to count on air defences to provide a basis for her inclusion in an agreement banning counter-city attacks.

Discussion of agreements concerning counter-city attacks raises certain questions. How effective could they be as deterrents? What restrictions should they impose on attacks on different types of target? Would their purpose best be served by the deployment by both sides of offensive weapons systems? What purpose would an agreement serve?

## NCAT as Deterrent

Whether agreement were reached or not, would the threat of counter-city attacks deter either side (especially the Arab countries) from another war? The answer is probably, no. The Israeli threat of punishment prior to the 1973 war did not deter Egypt and Syria from an attack, and such threats will probably be as ineffectual in the future. Indeed, with the increased effectiveness of surface-to-air systems, the cost of counter-city attacks, unless conducted with surface-to-surface missiles, will inexorably rise, and even surface-to-surface missiles are too expensive to be cost effective for massive counter-city offensives. Further, those which are not terminally guided are rather inaccurate, whereas those which are precision-guided are expensive and could more effectively be used against military targets.

The main point, however, must still be that attacks against civilian populations do not seem to have the psychological effect which would justify them. This has been proved in one international war after another, and it does not appear that the experience in the Middle East is any different, in this sense, from those of Europe or Vietnam. It might be argued that Arab societies are more likely to disintegrate in the face of large numbers of casualties and destruction caused by massive air attacks. However, the experience of one Middle Eastern country – Lebanon – has illustrated that factions will continue with bitter and strenuous fighting, without loss of morale, in spite of huge numbers of casualties (official Lebanese estimates put them as high as 60,000 killed in a year and a half, most of them civilians), damage to property and complete dislocation of normal life. Similarly, although Israel is very concerned about casualties, it is unlikely that civilian losses would affect her resolve to go on fighting – indeed, it would probably strengthen it.

It seems reasonable, therefore, to assume that counter-city attacks would only arouse deeper feelings and tougher resolve on both sides. Moreover, since most Arab–Israeli wars are short, given the strong likelihood of super-power intervention, the debilitating effects of a long period of counter-population strikes are unlikely to be experienced by either side. For these reasons it would appear that if a strong political or strategic incentive did exist for starting a war, the threat of severe civilian casualties and damage to property would not act as a deterrent.

## Targets: Some Suggested Restrictions

The second question is whether a NCAT should cover only cities and civilian populations or all social and economic targets. Two kinds of limitation on military strikes could apply. First, a geographical distinction could be made between targets located away from civilian population centres, those near them and those near the front line – although military targets located inside major cities could raise complications in this context. Second, different types of target could be distinguished: for example, purely military targets, such as military airfields, camps and ports, and those targets which serve peaceful or joint military-civilian purposes, such as refineries and transport links.

Because of the ambiguities associated with those targets which have both military and civilian uses, it would seem advisable to treat these as a special category in an agreement. But this would create other problems. For example, one of the main concerns of the combatants in any future war – and especially in a war of attrition – will be to maintain their resupply systems, which will depend on their transportation channels, including airfields, ports, railways and roads. The exclusion of such objectives from military strikes would affect Israel particularly, since she is more vulnerable to high attrition rates and yet has the capability to strike at the transportation system of her opponent.

The other possibility is to limit military strikes to a narrow zone near the front line. In this context it is worth pointing out that the main battlefield of the future would in all probability be the Sinai. Since this barren piece of land is almost uninhabited, it would be easier to leave it completely 'open' to military actions and to prohibit military strikes beyond it. This, again, might raise problems. To begin with, part of the logistic systems of both Israel and Egypt extend beyond the Sinai and could be considered purely military targets. Military ground operations, too, could extend beyond the Sinai. What limitations could be imposed then? What about 'pure' military targets, such as military airfields and harbours?

One possible solution is to combine parts of the two criteria: for example, to ban strikes beyond the Sinai and the Golan Heights, though allowing strikes in a limited zone which 'moves' with the front line, but to exclude from the ban all purely military targets, wherever situated. One of the difficulties raised by this solution is that many military targets are located near or even in the midst of civilian centres. Mistakes in guidance might lead to civilian casualties and frustrate the whole intention of the agreement. One of the technical ways to overcome this is by extensive use of long-range PGM, which can hit military targets without collateral civilian damage, but this option would still leave several problems unsolved. For one thing, some PGM might go astray and hit civilian targets, which could lead to a reaction in kind and the possible collapse of the whole system. For another, long-range PGM could be used for a first strike against military targets and thereby threaten to undermine another important possible arms-control system – measures against surprise attacks.

*Offensive Weapons Systems: An Alternative Strategy?*
A third problem concerns the question of whether the purpose of the agreement could best be served by mutual deployment of offensive weapons systems with a counter-city capability (for instance, long-range surface-to-surface missiles armed with anti-personnel area weapons). Such deployment could act as a deterrent to counter-city attacks by posing a credible threat of retaliation in kind, thus leading to what some would maintain was a stable mutual deterrence system. To the extent that such a capability exists anyway, it is possible to argue that it would be better to increase the scope of such deployments – indeed, to add new systems to each side – so that a counter-city strike launched by one side would lead not just to limited retaliation but to a large-scale – and, measured in military terms, unnecessary – destruction on both sides.

In the nuclear relationship the existence of offensive systems which are capable of penetrating the airspace of the opponent and causing tremendous destruction is essential for the stability of the strategic balance. This is so because in the gains/costs calculations of each side the risk of a global nuclear war would be so much greater than any possible gain from a military attack that neither side would contemplate launching one. In a conventional relationship, however, the certainty of causing damage is much less and the scale in any case infinitely smaller, so that the element of deterrence is much weaker. Moreover, if the systems exist and are deployed, the inclination to use them for counter-city missions would be intensified in the following cases: at times of reversals on the battlefields; if one side assumed that there was just enough time to launch a limited counter-city attack before a cease-fire was imposed; if it was assumed – correctly or incorrectly – that the other side had lost its capability to launch a retaliation in kind, having used up these systems in counter-force missions.

89

At present the Israeli air force is in a much better position to penetrate the airspace of an adversary than are the air forces of the Arab states. However, with the deployment of denser and more sophisticated surface-to-air systems around the Arab centres of population, superiority will be somewhat reduced, and although the Israeli air force could still penetrate these defences, it is questionable whether this would be the most cost-effective use of Israeli aircraft. An increase in air defence systems deployed around civilian population centres would therefore serve the purposes of arms control in the Middle East.

The introduction of long-range surface-to surface missiles, on the other hand, could lead to anxieties about their eventual use in a counter-city role, and limitation on their deployment should therefore be one of the objectives of arms control. Fortunately, if an agreement along these lines were to be reached, it would be relatively easy to monitor compliance. Moreover, since the local powers are still dependent on external suppliers for these systems, control could be exercised over their transfer.

*The Uses of a Formal Agreement*
The last question concerns the utility of a formal agreement. It seems that the most important elements in non-counter-city strategy are the weapons systems deployed and the strategic policies adopted by both sides. If each side planned and prepared for concentration on the battlefield, this would have greater impact than a formal agreement on the conduct of war. An agreement, however, would serve a useful function. To begin with, the negotiations would have an effect on the military bureaucracy of both sides, since an agreement is not usually repudiated immediately after signature, and would have to be taken into consideration by the party. Once some planning based on the probable outcome of the negotiations had taken place, inertia would set in which would be difficult to overcome. A formal agreement would also supply a framework for limitations on the supply of weapons systems to local parties.

### Agreements to Curb the Arms Race: Likelihood and Efficacy

The United States, the Soviet Union, France and Britain – the 'Big Four' – control among them about 90 per cent of the international trade in arms. They are, especially the United States and the Soviet Union, the main suppliers of the Middle Eastern countries. A consideration of the arms race in the Arab–Israeli region and of the various measures applied over the years for its limitation reveals that the recipients of arms – when they have recognized their security to be at stake – have been able to apply considerable pressure on their suppliers to provide many of the weapons needed. The super-powers (primarily the United States) have been ready and able to resist this pressure, but in most cases only for a limited period, occasionally measured in years. Eventually they have acquiesced in many of the recipients' demands, either because they have acknowledged their needs or because of a desire to extend influence. Although the suppliers' resistance to demands for arms has generally contributed to stability in the region, their imbalanced response to these requests have at times aroused anxiety on the part of the recipients, which has led, in turn, to an acceleration of the arms race.

To obviate the uncertainties and possible delays associated with supplies of arms from the super-powers, two expedients are ostensibly available to both sides in the Middle East. One is to develop indigenous production, the other to find alternative sources of arms. Israel is in a better position to rely on an indigenous production base; while the Arab countries are planning to develop production, they nevertheless lag far behind in this field and any such base will probably take a very long time to materialize. On the other hand, the Arab states, because of political factors, are more able to diversify their source of arms. The Arab oil countries are also capable of applying economic pressure on their suppliers, either through threats to link the supply of oil to transfers of arms or by their generally strong economic position. However, while economic considerations have had a powerful influence on arms exports generally in the last few years, particularly in the cases of Britain and France, the new phenomenon of the petro-dollar has encouraged the United States to exchange her relatively restrictive policy of the post-World War II years for a more flexible one, similar to that of the 1930s, which has been most evident in the Persian Gulf. Although other countries are now entering the international arms market, it appears that the Big Four will remain the main sources of arms for the Middle Eastern countries for some time, particularly in the case of the more important weapons systems.

Indeed, with specific regard to some extremely important high-technology weapons systems, such as air-superiority fighters, new-generation tanks and possibly some third- and fourth-generation PGM, only the super-powers will be able to maintain their exclusive position. (For example, evidence suggests that France and Britain are not planning an air-superiority fighter to compare with the F-15, F-16 or F-18, and, although West Germany is developing a new-generation main-battle tank, the *Leopard II* – many of the parts for which will be standardized with the American XM-1 – it seems unlikely that she will become a supplier of arms to the Middle East.) Furthermore, although the technology for the development of PGM is not always highly complex at present, it could be argued that the technological requirements for future generations of some types of PGM would be so demanding that only the super-powers would produce them. Finally, given the high rate of attrition likely in another Middle East war, the regional powers must plan to rely on external suppliers who will be capable of transferring large quantities of arms, ammunition and spare parts quickly. This condition could only be met by the super-powers. A measure of dependence on the super-powers will therefore persist for other weapons systems as well as for high-technology ones. This exclusive position could guarantee that, if some arms-control agreements were concluded between the super-powers, they would be in a position to exert pressure on the recipients of arms and perhaps also to contain the exports of the other two major suppliers. The readiness of the suppliers to agree to such measures is, of course, an open question.

### Arms Limitation: Conditions for Success

Two types of agreement on the limitation of arms transfers can be suggested: (1) agreements among suppliers, initiated and ratified by themselves; (2) agreements among suppliers and recipients, initiated by both parties, which clearly do not adversely affect the security interests of the recipients in their own eyes. International suppliers' agreements concerning the control of the flow of arms, particularly in the context of the Middle East, have seldom been successful unless accompanied by agreements with the recipients.[86] Given the relative power of the recipients in the Middle East and the political gulf which separates their main suppliers, the importance of the recipients' initiatives are more crucial than in other areas of the world. Indeed, one observer, commenting on the problems of regional arms-trade limitation agreements, suggested that four factors were essential to their success: local initiative; a common background and attention to arms control; a community framework and identity; and a conjunction of interests, such as the reduction of arms expenditure.[87]

The acceptance by Middle Eastern countries of agreements constraining the flow of arms will probably come about when: (1) the political climate is considered to have improved, or at least to be unlikely to engender imminent war; (2) the possible limitations suit the strategic doctrines of the recipients; (3) a measure of confidence exists, so that recipients could rest assured that if one supplier abrogated an agreement and sent arms to one side, the other supplier would transfer similar (or cancelling) weapon systems to the other; (4) the system of control provides enough flexibility to allow for periodical reviews of the security needs of the recipients; (5) the limitations harmonize with other arms-control measures; (6) some credible verification is obtainable.

As far as the second type of agreement is concerned, tacit communication between the two sides would be necessary. Indeed, one cannot overstate the importance of this particular condition, since the defence establishments of both sides would only accept limitations if they were convinced that agreements among suppliers would not negatively affect the security interests of their countries. It will take an enormous effort to arrive at agreement between the super-powers on arms control: if an agreement adversely affected the security interests of either side, it is highly doubtful that it could be stable or lasting.

Would a political settlement by itself, without collateral agreements on limitation of arms supplies, bring about some de-escalation of the arms race? It appears likely that if a political settlement were reached, the arms race in the

Arab–Israeli region would slow down, and the main participants would gradually reduce their investment in defence. This reduction, however, would not necessarily be structured according to arms-control reasoning, so qualitative or quantitative limitations, or both, would need to be recognized by both sides. Needless to say, the best solution would be to combine both types of limitation, but if a choice has to be made, the qualitative approach should be preferred.

The most likely candidates for inspection and verification under an arms-limitation agreement would be those weapons systems which do not as yet exist in the inventories of the recipients, or exist only in small numbers, and the producers of which are limited. In this context, it should be noted that although the new air-superiority fighters, which are on order but have not yet been delivered, are not necessarily a threat to stability, the situation is different in the case of such weapons systems as surface-to-surface missiles with ranges which could include population centres, long-range PGM (including cruise missiles) and 'area weapons'. Careful attention should be paid to these systems to find out whether their acquisition would be destabilizing and, if so, to try to limit their introduction into the Middle East, even if they are on order or have already been introduced in small numbers. The criteria for limitations on such systems should be determined by previous decisions on issues such as the demilitarization of buffer zones and the prohibition of counter-city attacks. The availability of long-range PGM, for example, could increase motivation to strike first. Similarly, the transfer of 'area weapons', which could have a high counter-city effect might undermine agreements to ban such attacks.

*Short-Range PGM and the Balance*

There has recently been wide-ranging discussion of the role of short-range PGM (of the anti-tank and anti-air varieties).[88] What has been their impact on the strategic balance in the Middle East and how are they likely to affect stability there in the future?

The answers to these questions are complex and equivocal. The first problem concerns their proven effectiveness. For the purposes of this Paper, the experience of the 1973 Middle East war, when PGM were first introduced on a large

scale, appears not to be conclusive. In the first place, the PGM used belonged, apparently, to two different generations. The *Sagger* and *Snapper* anti-tank weapons used by Egypt and Syria could be defined as primitive, first-generation PGM; the surface-to-air missiles used extensively by the Arab states, the 'stand-off' systems used on a small scale by the Israeli air force and the *TOW* anti-tank missiles used on only a few occasions by Israeli ground forces belonged to a more advanced generation. Second, in the early stages of the war the Israeli air force lacked even the more traditional electronic counter-measures against surface-to-air missiles in any significant quantity, and had only a very limited number of air-defence-suppression missiles. It could, therefore, be argued that had the planes carried these more advanced systems, Arab surface-to-air missiles would have been less effective. Third, Israeli ground forces, in the first stages of the war, did not employ the all-arms tactics necessary for the suppression of the Arab anti-tank systems. The combination, traditional since World War II, of tanks, armoured infantry and artillery was neglected in favour of self-contained tank forces,[89] and it could be argued that many of the tanks hit by PGM need not have been lost. On the other hand, more advanced PGM could have caused more damage to Israeli armour. Although there has, as yet, been no definitive test of PGM, most observers would agree that anti-tank and anti-air PGM could change the face of the battlefield considerably and substantially increase the attrition rate of an enemy's attacking units. What would be the consequence of this higher attrition rate? Again, the majority of observers argue that it would favour the defence as opposed to the offence.[90] There is, however, serious disagreement over the extent of this change in the balance and whether or not it has already taken place. A minority contends that the traditional offensive systems, primarily tanks and fighter-bombers, are still the most important weapons systems and would be able, in conjunction with appropriate counter-measures, to overcome the defensive PGM.[71] But even they agree that offensive missions might become more expensive, and if this were the only outcome of the introduction of precision-guided missiles, considerations of expense would militate against decisions to launch offensive operations.

In the Middle East the introduction of PGM, with their effect on the balance of offence and defence, would not necessarily reduce the risk of war. If, for example, no buffer state existed between Israel and the Arab states, the latter might be encouraged to launch a limited offensive with very limited military objectives (as was the case in the 1973 war). The action would be aimed at gaining a narrow strip of land by a surprise attack, thereby forcing Israel to launch a major offensive operation which the defensive systems of the Arab states would be able to withstand. Thus, some limited offensive military operations would, in fact, be enhanced by a change in the balance between the offence and the defence. However, even in the Middle East, such a change could encourage each side to believe that attack from the other was less likely, and might, under some conditions, diminish the likelihood of war. For example, if a political settlement were reached which included major Israeli withdrawals from the occupied territories and their demilitarization, short-range anti-tank, surface-to-air and 'stand-off' air-to-surface PGM might assist the defensive capabilities of both sides without creating conditions conducive to limited attacks, and offensives on a more ambitious scale would certainly become more difficult. Surprise attacks across a demilitarized Sinai would be hazardous and less likely: if one did occur, an aggressor, having crossed the desert, would find himself facing an opponent who was heavily armed and in an environment favourable for close air support for his forces. The problem of penetrating an elaborate and flexible defence equipped with highly accurate weapons would compound the difficulties of the attacker, who would have had to cross large areas of desert with lengthening communication and supply lines. Furthermore, the attacker's troops would be more vulnerable to his opponent's air force, because the surface-to-air PGM systems are most effective in an operation covering the whole air space at varying heights above the battleground. This can be best achieved when the surface-to-air systems are stationary: when on the move, in battle conditions, their co-ordination is considerably hampered. (This analysis of the relative performance of the surface-to-air and air-to-surface 'stand-off' systems applies primarily to confrontations between the Israeli air force and the Egyptian air defence

system. The advantage to the defender would not be apparent, however, in the case of the demilitarization of the West Bank and the Golan Heights. There the potential contribution of short-range PGM to arms control is not clear.)

Three problems would have to be considered by Israeli strategic planners when contemplating this change in the mix of forces. First, if demilitarization were imposed, Egypt would be the more likely to have some motivation for violating it. The questions confronting Israel would be not only how to defend Israel against an advancing Egyptian force, but also how to deter Egypt from a violation in the first place. After all, Egypt might decide to remilitarize only parts of the Sinai, without even attacking the Israeli defence line. Israel would not be able to contain such a violation through a stationary defence system which relied on PGM along her border (presumably the pre-1967 border or close to it), but would depend on a credible threat to destroy the Egyptian forces while they were deployed in the desert. For that, however, Israeli defence strategy would have to continue to emphasize mobile offensive systems such as tanks. Second, Israel's disadvantage in terms of manpower could best be overcome by the deployment of those weapons in particular which are 'fire-intensive', and this consideration might affect decisions about optimal mixes of PGM and other weapons systems. Third, Israel would have to take into account the existence of several possible opponents besides Egypt–Syria, Jordan and even Iraq. The effect of the demilitarization of the Golan Heights and the West Bank (and, for that matter, parts of southern Lebanon up to the Litani river) and the creation of areas of limited deployment behind them would be more limited than in the case of the Sinai. For one thing, because of the narrow width of these two areas, a surprise attack is more probable. For another, the launching of a static campaign by the Arab states is a possibility. The Israeli response to such a campaign would probably be to transform the nature of the battle by going over to a mobile counter-attack. Because of the limited area for manoeuvre in such a campaign, the need for a large concentration of offensive systems (tanks) in order to break through the enemy's line would be crucial. Furthermore, extensive proliferation of Arab surface-to-air systems might limit Israeli air superiority and, in some circumstances, her deterrence capability – a capability which would become a major stabilizing factor if a political settlement were achieved. Israel might be forced to search for weapons systems which could suppress these air defence systems; these could include long-range PGM (as well as some 'area' weapons, electronic countermeasures, anti-radiation missiles and air-to-surface missiles). This would work to Israel's advantage only if the Arab states did not acquire similar systems, otherwise motivation for a first strike would increase.

Egypt, for her part, would probably face less acute problems if she added tactical PGM to the mix of her forces, since they would fit quite well with her traditional strategy of promoting her infantry, which is equipped with a wide range of anti-tank weapons and backed by armour and big concentrations of artillery. Although there are indications that Egypt is searching for new strategic options, she continues to stress the importance of her infantry and the vulnerability of the tank.

In view of the complexity of the problem, the success of a tacit agreement on a change in the mix of forces of all the regional powers is not very likely. It would perhaps succeed only with respect to limitations on the introduction of long-range PGM, because of a common anxiety about first strikes. Such a change should be discussed, however, as one of the possible avenues towards arms control.

Symmetrical quantitative limitations on transfers of arms should also be a subject for negotiations between recipients and suppliers, among whom the United States is likely to play the central role. Although, again, the chances for success are very limited, the attempt should be made. As suggested above, it is possible that the volume of arms transfers would decline as a consequence of unilateral decisions by the regional adversaries, prompted by a political settlement and the gradual defusing of the conflict. It would be worthwhile, however, to begin negotiations about such limitations even before a final political settlement. Qualitative limitations on arms supplies should have priority, both because it is more likely that effective formal agreements could be reached and because they are at present more critical. Quantitative restrictions imposed from the outside would become more critical only if there were a danger of imbalance in the arms race. A two-tier approach to these negotiations could be useful: first, three sets of simultaneous discussions between the United States and Israel, the United States and Egypt, and the United States, Britain and France. Second, a general conference of all the major suppliers including the Soviet Union and recipients in the Middle East.

## IV. WHAT ROLE FOR THE SUPER-POWERS?

The super-powers could play a central role in future arms-control agreements in the Arab–Israeli region. The United States, which has always been committed to stability in the Middle East, will probably lead the way towards a political settlement coupled with arms-control measures. To what extent is it likely that the Soviet Union will become part of this process? Furthermore, to what extent is Soviet involvement desirable?

The answer to the first question depends on the political position that the Soviet Union adopts in the Arab world. If she maintains a close relationship with Syria, it is unlikely that she could be excluded completely from the bargaining process leading to a political settlement. Soviet participation may also be affected by the form of the negotiations. If a Geneva conference were convened and, more important, if meaningful negotiations were undertaken within the framework of this conference, there is a strong likelihood that the Soviet Union would play an important role in the negotiations. On the other hand, if the negotiations were conducted between Israel and the respective Arab states in separate, bilateral forums (under the umbrella of Geneva or some variant of the 'step-by-step' policy), and if, concomitantly, the ability of the Soviet Union to exert pressure on Syria were further eroded, it is probable that the United States alone would act as intermediary. Naturally this would also affect the respective involvement of the two super-powers in the ultimate arms-control arrangements.

As for the desirability of Soviet participation, future arms-control agreements could be divided into two parts: first, the broader issues of demilitarization of buffer zones, restrictions on deployment of forces, and measures against surprise attacks and counter-city strikes; and, second, restrictions on transfers of arms to the regional powers. It seems likely that the former could be agreed upon with considerable credibility, even if the United States acts alone as guarantor – provided, of course, that all the regional powers agreed to exclude the Soviet Union. To secure agreements relating to the transfer of arms to the regional powers, on the other hand, the participation of the Soviet Union would be essential. After all, the Soviet Union is still a major arms supplier to the region and, on the evidence of past experience, would probably be ready to transfer arms to certain Arab states in order to maintain or renew influence. Unless the Soviet Union became party to a system of controls on the flow of arms – in return for which she would surely demand some political consideration – these controls would not hold. Even those regional countries which agree at present to exclude the Soviet Union from negotiations might find it difficult to resist the temptation of receiving arms from her in the future, if the opportunity presented itself.*

It would be easier for a regional state to succumb to that temptation than to violate one of the arms-control measures in a set of broader agreements (if the Soviet Union were excluded from both), because there are two differences between these sets of arms-control measures. An agreement on restrictions on the flow of arms would probably be primarily a suppliers' agreement, even if it were achieved as a result of negotiations among suppliers and recipients. The regional recipients of arms, therefore, might feel free to purchase arms from a supplier who is not party to the agreement. Agreements about the broader arms-control measures, on the other hand, would be signed by the regional states with, it is hoped, a guarantee by external powers,

and the signatories would be formally bound by them. The second difference is that sanctions to be imposed on violators of these latter agreements would probably be codified in the agreements and may be of both a political and a military nature. The sanctions should include movement of military units, remilitarization of zones and even initiation of armed hostilities. It is not clear how similar sanctions could be codified and subsequently imposed on a regional state which violated a suppliers' agreement on restrictions on transfers of arms by receiving prohibited arms from a supplier not bound by the agreement. The problem is not only to codify the sanctions and make them explicit – which is important in this case – but also to define the nature of the violation. In the case of the broader arms-control agreements, any violation will seem a threat to peace, even if it appears to be minor: remilitarization of small, erstwhile demilitarized areas might indicate the beginning of a 'salami-tactic' operation, and would therefore be met by a deterring reaction which would be different in kind from, and disproportionate to, the offence. On the other hand, the transfer of arms by a country which is not party to a suppliers' agreement could not, in most cases, be construed as a major threat: reactions to it would be unpredictable and the political cost to the recipient might be low. The natural reaction would be an equivalent transfer of arms to the other party. But this, of course, would shatter the whole system of restrictions and escalate the race to acquire precisely those systems which have already been shown to be destabilizing.

In conclusion, if some regional state – and the obvious present candidate is Syria – insisted on Soviet participation in the negotiations and hence in the pattern of inter-state relations which would emerge with a settlement, it is unlikely that the Soviet Union could be excluded from both sets of arms-control measures. If, on the other hand, there is no such insistence by any of the regional parties, then from the point of view of arms control the Soviet Union would have to be included in a suppliers' agreement, but could be excluded from other arms-control arrangements.[92] The political price that the Soviet Union would surely demand for participation in a suppliers' agreement can at present only be conjectured. Her demands would probably focus on legitimizing her position in the Middle

---

* John Barton has argued in a private communication that arms suppliers' agreements might gain local support and be enforceable without Soviet participation, particularly in view of the state of the economies of the main participants in the arms race. Although this may happen as well, the Soviet Union – to judge from past experience – is ready to deliver arms for political purposes without insisting on payment.

East by formal American acceptance of it. This could be done, among other ways, by co-operating with the United States as the joint and equal guarantor of all political and arms-control agreements between Israel and the Arab states. Taking into consideration the current ebb in the Soviet position in the Middle East, it would indeed be a considerable concession by the United States to accept such an arrangement. Furthermore, Israel, and probably Egypt, would prefer not to see Soviet influence return in force to the Middle East. It is conceivable, however, that the Soviet Union might be excluded from Israeli–Egyptian and Israeli–Jordanian (and Palestinian) agreements, but included in those between Israel and Syria.

## Guaranteeing Demilitarization

The 1976 interim agreement between Israel and Egypt set an important precedent in establishing greater American involvement in arms-control measures in the Middle East. Under the agreement, three surveillance stations manned by American personnel were created, the function of which is to monitor the immediate environment of the buffer zone and the Israeli and Egyptian intelligence stations. Both Israel and Egypt desired this American presence, which has introduced a new dimension into the situation in the Middle East.[93] It is not only that the Americans in the Sinai can verify compliance with the agreement, but they could also proffer arbitration in the event of violations and mutual accusation, thus preventing the possible escalation of local confrontations. In the case of surprise attacks, their very presence makes them, to an extent, hostages as well as observers. If they are injured, the likelihood of a strong American political reaction increases, and this may act as a limited deterrent. On the other hand, an American military reaction is unlikely, because the number of personnel is so limited and, furthermore, because it is not covered by a formal commitment. Thus the American personnel do not function as a 'tripwire' element.*

In future agreements about the demilitarization of the Sinai the American role could be much more significant. An American guarantee, written into an agreement, to enforce compliance with demilitarization would have a major

---

* There is also an understanding that the personnel will be withdrawn in case of hostilities.

deterrent effect. As distinct from all other American alliances after World War II, which have been aimed at defending states against Communist encroachment, the purpose of this proposed American guarantee would be to deter two regional states – Israel, a close friend of the United States (and, as proposed below, a formal ally as well), and Egypt, a state which is becoming increasingly friendly to the United States – from violating a regional agreement. This distinction would probably encourage a positive domestic American response and dispel doubts – a product of the post-Vietnam syndrome – about the credibility of this deterrent posture. The danger that Soviet involvement on the side of Egypt would deter the United States from fulfilling her obligations if Egypt were to decide to violate the demilitarization, and thus potentially weaken American resolve, now appears very unlikely. Even in the past, when the Soviet Union was Egypt's benefactor and the Treaty of Friendship and Co-operation operated (signed by both countries in 1972 and dissolved in 1976 by President Sadat), the Soviet Union limited her commitment to military involvement to extreme situations in which the very existence of Egypt's regime (and her army) was threatened; she did not undertake to defend Egyptian forces if they attempted to conquer Sinai. The 'red lines' were clear: the Soviet Union would come to the aid of Egypt only if a major catastrophe was imminent: if Israeli forces crossed the Suez Canal (as in 1973), or if the Israeli air force aimed at the destruction of the regime through deep-penetration bombing (as in 1970). With the present strained relations between the Soviet Union and Egypt, Soviet intervention even in these circumstances is doubtful, let alone if Egyptian forces were in the Sinai in violation of an explicit agreement. Once the United States became the guarantor of an Israeli–Egyptian agreement, the likelihood of Soviet interference on behalf of Egypt would further diminish. Even if good relations between Egypt and the Soviet Union were to be resumed, it is highly unlikely that the Soviet Union would become involved in an Egyptian violation of an agreement which the United States was formally committed to guarantee.

An American guarantee, once extended and implemented over time, would signal that vital American interests were involved in the maintenance of demilitarization. The balance of interest and commitment would favour the United States generally, which would be essential in a crisis in which each super-power was weighing the dangers of escalation, because the power with interests to protect would be the more likely to consider further military involvement, and deterrence would consequently be enhanced. But American underwriting of demilitarization would have further importance. If one side clearly violated the demilitarized zone, the other – with the acquiescence of the United States – might decide to resort immediately to force. American backing of this side would also be significant to the political outcome of the campaign.

Such a guarantee, of course, involves several potential costs for the United States and for the regional powers. The United States would have to take into account the possibility – remote as it may seem – of involvement in a political (if not a military) conflict with one or other of the regional parties in the event of violations. Second, the United States would have to consider the possibility of a confrontation with the Soviet Union if the latter – contrary to the dictates of rational analysis – decided to back an Egyptian violation of the agreement. Third, if the United States did not honour her own obligation to the agreement, she would lose credibility with her other allies. There would also be a dilemma for the regional parties. The guarantee would mean the sacrifice of some freedom of choice; violations or responses to them – for instance as part of a political bargaining process – would be severely constrained, and the United States would become the arbiter of many political and strategic issues between the two regional parties.

A joint American–Soviet guarantee would reduce some of these potential political costs to the United States. The two guarantors acting jointly could deter a violator from abrogating the agreement or compel withdrawal. Against the pressure of both super-powers, the regional power would have no chance of success. There would also be less likelihood of confrontation between the super-powers. The difficulties, however, are palpable. The two guarantors might have completely different interpretations of what was happening or about to take place, and this might paralyse them. If one decided, nevertheless, to deter or support a violation a super-power

crisis could ensue. Thus, not only would the guarantee not operate but the potential for international crisis between the super-powers would increase as well. Secondly, the effectiveness of the joint guarantee would depend to a large extent on the global political relations between the super-powers. Only in a situation of enhanced detente (which is unlikely to obtain for quite some time, if at all) would there be a real chance that the United States and the Soviet Union could maintain a system of political co-operation in the Middle East. Although it is reasonable to assume that they would try to deter major escalation in the area even if their global relationship became strained (because of the tremendous risks involved in war in the Middle East), the joint guarantee would probably come under heavy strain. On balance, therefore, it appears that an exclusive American guarantee of the demilitarization of the Sinai as an arms-control measure would probably be more effective than one which involved the Soviet Union.

An additional way in which the United States could guarantee the demilitarization of Sinai is through direct physical involvement, either through participation in the verification of the agreement by means of intelligence-gathering and surveillance systems or through deployment of forces in the Sinai itself. A system of verification controlled jointly by the United States, Israel and Egypt would be an important instrument in the monitoring of possible violations. The system could comprise separate consoles in each country, on which any violations would be recorded simultaneously. A permanent commission composed of representatives of all three parties could meet regularly, and in times of emergency, to discuss and resolve the problems raised by violations, real or suspected.[94] The same commission could also discuss violations of agreements on deployment of forces and other moves which might indicate preparations for surprise attacks (see below). Thus a permanent crisis-management mechanism would be established, which could handle possible escalations and allow an exchange of views, thereby creating an opportunity for 'diplomatic pauses', all of which would help to defuse potential crises.

The deployment of American forces in the Sinai would serve as an important additional deterrent to violations of demilitarization. It is unlikely that their military strength would be sufficient to change, in any meaningful way, the outcome of a battle once it was joined. However, these troops could be made to serve as a 'trip-wire', and thus increase considerably the likelihood of American intervention against the side which violated the agreement.

What about the West Bank and the Gaza Strip? The political structure that would emerge in the Middle East after a settlement is important in this context. If these areas were returned to Jordon, or to some form of Jordanian–Palestinian federation, effective demilitarization would be possible, and the two regional parties to a demilitarization agreement would probably retain their orientation towards the United States. However, it is difficult to envisage the demilitarization of a completely independent Palestinian state, if one emerged, because no sovereign state is prepared to exist without the protection of armed forces. An independent Palestinian state might look to the Soviet Union and under some conditions develop destabilizing tendencies. Because of this, a 'Jordanian solution' is preferable to a 'Palestinian solution'. Only one advantage could be gained from the creation of a Palestinian state on the West Bank and the Gaza Strip, provided it undertook to sign and maintain a full peace treaty with Israel. It would resolve, at least partially, the ideological conflict and would make it very difficult for any other Arab state to maintain a 'rejectionist' position. One possible solution would be to create a Jordan–Palestine federation. However, from the point of view of arms control and stability it would be important, in such a case, to ensure that the real military power still rested with Jordan and that effective demilitarization would be imposed.

American guarantees for a demilitarized West Bank would act as a deterrent against possible violations. But, in contrast to the situation in the Sinai, the deployment of American forces as an additional deterrent would probably be counter-productive. To begin with, conflict between Israel and Jordan (or a Jordanian–Palestinian federation) is less likely than one between Israel and Egypt. Jordan is much weaker than Egypt and is less likely to become involved in a clash. Once a political settlement had been achieved, Israel would have no motive for an attack on the West Bank. An American guarantee would be required primarily to provide Jordan (or a federation) with a justification for refraining from engagement with Israel, should other Arab states demand military support in a crisis. Similarly, the guarantee would inhibit possible Israeli military operations against Jordan in a conflict involving another Arab state. To fulfil these objectives there would be no need for actual deployment of American forces. Besides, such a deployment in the densely populated West Bank and Gaza Strip areas might only arouse animosity, since the American forces might be considered an 'occupation force'.

One of the threats to stability after a settlement might be a renewal of infiltration from across the border of the new political entity. Extreme groups on the West Bank might hope to shatter the settlement (which they might consider a sell-out) by provoking Israel to retaliate on a grand scale against the new regime. This would probably lead to a major crisis from which the extremists could extract political gain. Should an American guarantee refer to this problem as well? It appears that the best procedure would be to deal with this threat through security arrangements approved by the regional parties to the agreement (e.g. a joint policing policy), rather than through American guarantees. There is no way in which the guarantor could effectively handle small-scale, non-government-sponsored actions, it would be better not to burden the guarantee with impossible tasks.

The demilitarization of the Golan Heights would pose a different set of problems. First, it is highly unlikely that the Soviet Union could be kept out of an agreement concerning this area. Indeed, there are clear advantages to her involvement in the system of guarantees applied there, since the Soviet Union still maintains an important link with Syria, and it is not likely that Syria would be ready to sever this link. Moreover, as has already been noted, participation would probably be the minimum political *quid pro quo* that the Soviet Union would demand in exchange for accession to suppliers' agreements on restrictions on the transfers of arms. Indeed, the Soviet Union would probably demand full and equal participation in the whole system of guarantees; whether she succeeded would depend on the reactions of the local parties and of the

United States. But it would be advisable to meet the Soviet Union half-way by involving her in the Syrian–Israeli agreement. The second problem is that the area for potential demilitarization is small, and hence its utility as a credible buffer zone is limited. Either side (particularly Syria) could storm it in a brisk operation. Deployment of joint American–Soviet forces there as a 'tripwire' would thus be the main, and not an ancillary, deterrent.

**Guaranteeing a 'No First Use of Force' Treaty**
It is doubtful whether a guarantee by the super-powers of the integrity of a NFUFT would enhance stability in the Middle East. The treaty would probably be general and would have, as noted on p. 87, both a symbolic and a specific effect inside the Arab world by increasing the uncertainty of each Arab state about the others' readiness to resort to war. To be sure, the super-powers' guarantees could help to allay this anxiety and would confirm the commitment of the super-powers to peace in the region. On the other hand, however, such a guarantee might create graver dilemmas for the super-powers than would guarantees concerning demilitarized zones. To begin with, there is the famous – and extensively debated – problem of how to define the first use of force and whether the force has been used, justifiably, 'in self-defence' or 'aggressively'. Under other agreements, identification of the violator would be relatively easy because it would be based on clear physical and technical evidence: the violator would be the side which has remilitarized parts of buffer zones, has increased forces in areas where this is restricted, or has interfered with legitimate intelligence-gathering procedures, etc. Second, the first use of force might be prompted by a violation of another arms-control agreement (such as demilitarization of zones). Could this act be construed as 'self-defence', or as a justified reprisal for the first violation? As suggested before, such a resort to force should not be seen as violation of the NFUFT. But the two super-powers might put different interpretations on such a reprisal, and this could paralyse their reactions, leading to a loss of their credibility or, worse, to a direct confrontation between them. Things might become even more complex if the United States were to be joint guarantor

with the Soviet Union of the NFUFT and sole guarantor of other arms-control agreements. In that case, the Soviet Union would probably argue the centrality of the NFUFT and its precedence over those arms-control agreements of which the United States was sole guarantor. This last contingency could be avoided if the two super-powers were the joint guarantors, or the United States the sole guarantor, of *all* arms-control agreements in the Arab–Israeli region. The first solution, although it would have some advantages, could generate major political difficulties and could also, as suggested above (p.95), be counter-productive in arms-control terms as well. The second solution would be more satisfactory, but is unlikely to obtain.

The main point, however, is that if there were a conflict between a general agreement (such as a NFUFT) and a more specific one (such as agreements on demilitarization of zones and restrictions on deployment of forces), the latter should prevail, the guarantees by the super-powers of the former should not interfere with the execution and maintenance of the latter, and precisely because such guarantees might lead to conflict, it would be better, on balance, not to solicit them.

**Guaranteeing a 'No Counter-city Attacks' Treaty**
A NCAT would be aimed at modifying the strategic behaviour of the regional parties. This being the case, it is difficult to see the possible advantages to be gained by the involvement of the super-powers. There is, of course, one important link between such an agreement and the super-powers' interests: it could supply part of the conceptual framework for a suppliers' agreement on restrictions on transfers of systems whose main mission is counter-city strikes. This would not, however, justify the super-powers guaranteeing a NCAT. In any case, it is not at all clear how such a guarantee would operate or what strategic interests would compel the super-powers to intervene with force if a NCAT were violated.

**An American–Israeli Defence Treaty**
All the arms-control agreements suggested in this Paper would involve both regional parties, with one exception. This would be an Israeli–American Defence Treaty, to be signed once a complete political settlement had been reached.[95]

After such a settlement Israel's aims would again (as before 1967) be the prevention of war and the retention of the territorial *status quo*. Some Arab elites, or groups within these elites, would probably still reject Israel's status and the major problem would then be how to increase the constraints on an Arab decision to go to war. An American defence treaty with Israel would act as a major deterrent against such plans. The proposed treaty should be a mutual pact, with the terms including military co-ordination between the two countries and assurances about continued transfers of arms to Israel, subject to any restrictions agreed upon by the suppliers.

A defence treaty would create some problems for the United States and for Israel, but would, on balance, make a significant contribution to stability. To begin with, there is the possibility that such a treaty would complicate the American political position in the Arab world, although Arab leaders have often suggested American guarantees to Israel as a way out of the political impasse in the Middle East. Their idea is that in consideration for Israeli withdrawals they would extend a guarantee of non-belligerency, while the United States proffered guarantees to Israel. From their point of view this solution would presumably extricate them from the dilemma of agreeing to full 'normalization' of political relations with Israel. The major dilemma for the United States concerns the question of whether deterrence would be successful and what would happen if it failed. It is highly probable that deterrence would, indeed, be very effective. Once a settlement were reached, Arab motivation to attack would diminish considerably. Furthermore, the Israeli deterrence posture is very credible, and, with their lower level of motivation, the costs of an attack would appear to Arab leaders even more unpalatable than they have since 1967. Last, but not least, the threat of American political sanctions, and in the last resort of military intervention, would be a powerful deterrent. If deterrence should nevertheless fail, the present military situation in the Middle East suggests that Israel could be in a position to defend herself successfully without America support. An American undertaking to send forces to help Israel would really refer to a last resort, which is unlikely to obtain in the foreseeable future but would have, nevertheless, to be averted.

An American guarantee would have two additional effects, both stabilizing: first, it would alleviate Israel's concern about her long-range security, and hence reduce the possibility of Israel's exercising the nuclear option or launching a pre-emptive or anticipatory strike; second, it would confirm American commitment to maintaining the balance of military power between Israel and the Arab states, which might be threatened in the long run by the continued accumulation of financial resources at the hands of the Arab countries.

The terms of the defence treaty would probably, however, impose some limitations on Israel's freedom of manoeuvre in certain strategic affairs. It seems unlikely that the United States would be prepared to be party to any such agreement without a measure of control over Israel's conduct in crises, and strategic moves that Israel might feel were necessary to her security would probably become subjects for bilateral negotiation before any action could be taken by her. This would certainly pose some problems for Israel but would be more than compensated for by the additional security gained through the treaty. From the American point of view, however, the formulation of constraints on Israel's conduct could raise difficulties. In the North Atlantic Treaty Organization such constraints operate through political co-ordination in the alliance and are a by-product of a unified military command system, which is dictated by the large number of participants in the Alliance and the perennial problem of decisions on the use of nuclear weapons if deterrence fails (and to enhance deterrence). In NATO the role of Supreme Allied Commander, Europe (SACEUR), is always filled by an American. It is unlikely that a similar command system could or should develop under the proposed treaty, but control could be exercised through permanent political-military commissions. Moreover the treaty would only be one part of a comprehensive system of security and arms-control measures in the Middle East, in which Israel would probably have a strong interest. Lack of co-ordination with the United States in decisions about crisis management might bring about the collapse of both the treaty and the security system. It is unlikely that Israel would be prepared to pay this high political and strategic price.

Would the treaty impose political constraints on Israel aside from those concerning crisis behaviour? This is highly unlikely. The confidence that Israel would gain from the treaty would strengthen her hand in political negotiations with the Soviet Union and the Arab states. Moreover, since the treaty is not directed against the Soviet Union (though it would be invoked if there were the threat of a Soviet attack on Israel) but would serve a regional function, there would be no undue Soviet apprehension about it. The treaty would probably arouse radical feelings in the Arab world, but Arab radicals in any case consider Israel a 'stooge of American imperialism', and the treaty would not therefore provoke any new suspicions. Furthermore, several leading Arab countries have become (or have always been) American-oriented. In conclusion, therefore, the treaty could serve to increase Israel's freedom of political manoeuvre.

# V. CONCLUSION

## The Relationship between Politics and Arms Control

Is it possible to achieve arms control in the Middle East in the present political context, or must political change precede arms control? A similar debate within the context of Soviet–American relations has persisted since the early 1960s, and three schools of thought have emerged which should be considered, since they will probably influence debates on arms-control efforts in the Middle East as well. The first school argues that arms control can be decoupled from politics; that arms-control agreements and measures are possible even in situations of severe conflict, without concomitant political relaxation; that arms-control measures and agreements can be achieved in such circumstances because they serve some limited shared interests of the adversaries. The second approach argues that there are links between arms-control agreements and changes in the political relationship between adversaries, but that agreements can be reached first and may even pave the way for political change by creating a new international climate. The third group accepts the existence of links between the realm of arms control and the realm of politics, but argues that political relaxation must precede arms-control agreements.

The historical experience in the Middle East indicates that tacit arms-control measures can be achieved in a situation of severe political conflict. Moreover, because of the role played by external powers, such measures, independent of political relaxation, are perhaps more possible than in the super-power relationship. At the same time those past successes have not contributed to political relaxation, but only to the postponement of wars or limitations on the use of force. Direct, significant, formal agreements between the regional powers did not take place between the signing of the Armistice agreements in 1949 until after the 1973 war.

But what of the future? In theory it seems possible that the same *type* of arms-control measures could be applied again, even without prior formal political agreements. These measures are primarily the tacit full or partial demilitarization of the Sinai (if, for example, Israeli forces withdrew unilaterally from this area without reaching any agreement with Egypt beforehand), and agreements among the suppliers about limitations on the supply of arms. Because Israeli occupation of the territories since 1967 has become the central issue of political aggravation, any Israeli withdrawal from these territories would bring about a considerable political relaxation, since it would diminish Arab motivation for another war and therefore stabilize relations in the region. The stabilizing effect of this proposed 'package' of steps would probably be more considerable than in the past, precisely because of the centrality of the territorial issue and because the wars and violence of the period since 1967 have proved the political unprofitability of war. However, such steps which combine political moves (the Israeli withdrawals) with arms-control measures (tacit demilitarization) would not be able to stave off future crises to the same extent as formal and more elaborate measures.

The linkage between arms control and politics in the Arab–Israeli region has three facets: first, to be stable and enduring, a political settlement would need concomitant arms-control measures; second, a political settlement would depend, to a large extent, on gradual steps, which would themselves require the support of a considerable number of arms-control agreements and measures; third, settlement would demand some political concessions on both sides.

Both the 'step-by-step' and the 'final-settlement' approach (the latter to be implemented by stages) would entail such agreements. Without them mutual suspicions might lead to new explosions, even if political developments were propitious, and in that sense it seems that arms control should precede political negotiation. Indeed, a consideration of the three interim agreements reached between the combatants (the first Israeli–Egyptian agreement of January 1974, the Israeli–Syrian agreement of June 1974, and the Israeli–Egyptian agreement of September 1975) proves that arms-control measures were cardinal. One of the reasons was that the Arab states preferred to focus on arms-control and security aspects in the agreements rather than on political contact with Israel. Another reason was the nature of military relations between the two sides following the 1973 war: anxiety concerning both general surprise attacks and limited attacks had gradually to be allayed. Since such concerns will persist, arms-control agreements will be central to political development.

Israel emphasizes both the political dimension of any future settlement (that is, the 'nature of peace'; for example, issues such as diplomatic relations, economic co-operation, open borders, etc. – all subsumed in the notion of 'normalization') and the security requirements. It does not seem realistic, however, to expect that everyone could be fully secured. Indeed, trade-offs could be envisaged between the political concessions which Israel might demand in return for the occupied territories and the various security measures, primarily arms-control agreements, which the Arab states might appear more willing to undertake. The nature of the settlement might be less formal Arab political concessions and more arms-control measures. Indeed, if Israel were faced with a choice between these trade-offs, she would be advised to opt for the latter, because ultimately they are more stabilizing.* This would allow for gradual change in Arab ideological opposition to Israel – which would probably endure for quite some time – and also for the development of direct contacts between Israel and the Arab states, even without formal acknowledgement of that process. Ultimately this might also bring about further formal political change.

The arms-control measures suggested in this study are important not only because extreme anti-Israeli sentiment will probably persist and must be countered but also because the potential for future political conflict, followed by crisis and war, is high in an area where there are many states with active foreign policies, where power blocs keep changing and shifting and where domestic instability is likely to continue. Indeed, even if the ideological component were to disappear and full peace, endorsed by diplomatic and economic relations, were to be established, other forces might provoke conflict between Israel and one or more Arab states. An arms-control regime could make the eruption of war resulting from such conflict less likely.

The political component, on the other hand, is important not only to the defusion of the conflict, but also in furnishing a broad context for the various steps towards arms control. Herein lies the third link between arms control and the political process. The Israeli occupation of Arab territories since 1967 has so aggravated the conflict that it would be impossible to formulate far-reaching, formal arms-control agreements without linking them with gradual Israeli withdrawals from all the territories conquered in 1967 (possibly with some minor modifications agreed upon between the sides). Similarly, the Arab countries would have to make some important political concessions. Negotiations concerning a final political settlement would, therefore, have to include formal arms-control agreements, to be ratified only if both sides

* President Carter's endorsement of 'normalization' and President Sadat's cautious positive reaction to it during his visit to Washington in spring 1977 may indicate a change in the prospects for achieving normalization'. Even then, the problem of trade-offs will remain.

indicated their readiness eventually to make political concessions.

## How to Reach the Agreements and Their Priorities

Some of the arms-control agreements discussed here could be reached in stages associated with partial political arrangements. The obvious candidates for such an approach are agreements about the demilitarization of zones, restrictions on deployment of forces and various methods of verification. Partial agreements on demilitarization of any area from which Israeli forces withdrew could be coupled with intensified restrictions on deployments of forces or weapons systems beyond these areas. Simultaneously, the role of the United States in the verification system could be increased qualitatively and quantitatively. At the same time, the United States, Israel and Egypt could begin discussions on a wide range of arms-control measures. Syria and Jordan could join these or parallel sets of discussions, which could be handled either under the umbrella of Geneva or in other *ad hoc* forums. One possible forum is the Joint Commission created under the Israeli–Egyptian interim agreement of 1975. Another is the Military Working Group which operated in Geneva. The best approach, however, would be to establish a separate, high-powered forum whose sole responsibility would be planning future arms control. These discussions might serve two purposes simultaneously: they could 'educate' the parties in the concepts of arms control and thus prepare the ground inside the defence establishment of both sides for eventual negotiations on arms-control measures, and they could work out the actual details of new arms-control agreements.

While these meetings were taking place, the United States could be seeking to reach understandings with Britain and France about possible restrictions on transfers of arms to Middle Eastern countries. As things stand at present, it is not very likely that contacts among, or a conference between, these three suppliers would be successful in the near future; nevertheless, they could increase the awareness of all parties of the dangers inherent in the continued arms race and might have some limited results. A treaty banning counter-city attacks could also be signed before a final settlement had been agreed upon. Such a treaty could only be the result of full discussions between the regional parties but the process could begin with a limited agreement between Israel and one Arab country. Partial agreements could also include clauses about the non-use of force (similar to that in the 1975 Israeli–Egyptian interim agreement).

There are, however, several major arms-control agreements which will have to form part of, or be predicated on, a final settlement. These are the final demilitarization of all the occupied territories; a treaty banning first use of force; the involvement of the super-powers as guarantors; the convening of a conference of all arms suppliers (including the Soviet Union); and the creation of a permanent mechanism for the restriction of transfers of arms; a comprehensive treaty prohibiting counter-city attacks; and the signing of an Israeli–American defence treaty. It is doubtful whether all these agreements could be concluded. It may be that in the process of bargaining some of them would have to be abandoned, and the question of their order of priority would then be raised. It is clear that agreements about demilitarization of zones and restrictions on deployment of forces beyond these zones, coupled with appropriate verification procedures, would be the most important; second, a defence treaty between the United States and Israel; third, guarantees by the super-powers (or the United States alone, as the case might be) concerning the demilitarized zone and the deployment of their forces there; fourth, restrictions on transfers of arms; fifth, treaties prohibiting the first use of force and counter-city attacks.

# NOTES

[1] For the concept of the 'heart' of the Middle East (Egypt, Israel, Jordan, Syria, Lebanon and Iraq), see Nadav Safran, *From War to War: The Arab–Israeli Confrontation 1948–1967* (New York: Pegasus, 1969), p. 92.

[2] The following is a selection of works on arms races and arms control in the Middle East: Alan Dowty, 'Israeli Perspectives on Nuclear Proliferation', in Johan J. Holst (ed.), *Security, Order and the Bomb* (Oslo: Universitetsforlaget, 1972), and his 'Israel's Nuclear Policy' (forthcoming); Yair Evron, 'Israel and the Atom: The Uses and Misuses of Ambiguity, 1957–1967', *Orbis*, Winter 1974, *The Demilitarization of Sinai*, Jerusalem Papers on Peace Problems No. 11 (Jerusalem: Davis Institute for International Relations, 1975), and 'Arms Races in the Middle East and some Arms-Control Measures Related to Them' in Gabriel Sheffer (ed.), *Dynamics of a Conflict* (New York: Humanities Press, 1975); Fuad Jabber, *Israel and Nuclear Weapons: Present Options and Future Strategies* (London: Chatto & Windus for the IISS, 1971), and 'Not by War Alone: Curbing the Arab–Israeli Arms Race', *Middle East Journal*, Summer 1974; John C. Lambalet, 'A Dynamic Model of the Arms Race in the Middle East, 1953–1965', *General Systems Yearbook* Vol. XVI (1971); Jeffrey S. Milstein, 'American and Soviet Influence: Balance of Power and Arab–Israeli Violence', in B. M. Russett (ed.), *Peace, War and Numbers* (Beverley Hills, Calif.: Sage Publications, 1972), and 'Soviet and American Influences on the Arab–Israeli Arms Race: A Quantitative Analysis', in Walter Isard and Julian Wolpart (eds), *Papers*, Vol. XV (Philadelphia: Peace Research Society, 1970); Nazli Choucri, 'Defence Budgets and the Middle East Conflict: A Commentary', in Isard, *op. cit.*; Colin Gray, 'Arms Races and their Influences upon International Stability, with special reference to the Middle East', in Sheffer, *op. cit.*; Geoffrey Kemp, *Arms and Security, the Egypt–Israel Case*, Adelphi Paper No. 52 (London: IISS, 1968); Michael Mihalka, 'Understanding Arms Accumulation, The Middle East as an Example', in Joseph Ben-Dak (ed.), *International Conflicts and the Methodology of their Assessments* (New York, 1973), George Quester, 'Israel and the Non-Proliferation Treaty', *Bulletin of the Atomic Scientists*, June 1969; Hans Rattinger, 'From War to War to War: Arms Races in the Middle East', *International Studies Quarterly*, Vol. 20, No. 4 (December 1976); Dina A. Zinnes, John V. Gillespie and Phillip A. Schrodt, 'The Arab–Israeli Arms Race: An Empirical Explanation', *Jerusalem Journal of International Relations*, Vol. 2, No. 1 (Fall 1976); Steven J. Rosen, 'Nuclearization and Stability in the Middle East', in Onkar Marwah and Ann Schulz (eds), *Nuclear Proliferation and the Near-Nuclear Countries* (Cambridge, Mass.: Ballinger, 1975); Safran, *op. cit.* in note 1; Dale R. Tahtinen, *The Arab–Israeli Military Balance Since October 1973* (Washington DC: American Enterprise Institute for Public Policy Research, 1974).

[3] On the complex patterns of competition among the other Arab states there are many works. For one widely quoted work, see Malcolm Kerr, *The Arab Cold War: Gamal Abd al-Nasir and his Rivals, 1958–1970* (London: Oxford UP, 1971). On the shifts of coalitions in the Arab world see Yair Evron and Yaacov Bar Simantov, 'Coalitions in the Arab World', *The Jerusalem Journal of International Relations*, Vol. 1, No. 2 (Winter 1975). On the complex relationship between inter-Arab relations and the Arab–Israeli conflict, see, for example, Gabriel Ben-Dor, 'Inter-Arab Relations and the Arab–Israeli Conflict', *Jerusalem Journal of International Relations*, Vol. 1, No. 4 (Summer 1976).

[4] On Iran's foreign policy see, *inter alia*, Shahram Chubin and Sepehr Zabih, *The Foreign Relations of Iran: A Developing State in a Zone of Great-Power Conflict* (Berkeley: University of California Press, 1974).

[5] On the whole problem of arms deliveries to Iran see *US Military Sales to Iran*, Staff report to Subcommittee on Foreign Assistance, Committee on Foreign Relations, Senate, 94th Congress, 2nd Session, July 1976. See also Shahram Chubin, *Implications of the Military Build-up in Non-industrial States: The Case of Iran* (mimeo), prepared for the Conference on Implications of the Military Build-up in Non-industrial States, Fletcher School of Law and Diplomacy, Tufts University, Medford, Mass., May 1976.

[6] For example, Saudi Arabia ordered 38 *Mirage* V from France by late 1973 for delivery to Egypt (see Stockholm International Peace Research Institute, *SIPRI Yearbook 1975*, Cambridge, MIT Press, 1975, p. 229). These planes might, in fact, have been *Mirage IIIAES* (see *The Military Balance 1975–1976*, London, IISS, 1975, p. 37); *Washington Post*, 5 June 1973; *Congressional Record*, 2 March 1976 (insertion by Rep. Benjamin Rosenthal of article by John K. Cooley in the *Christian Science Monitor*, 12 December 1976); *New York Times*, 21 July 1975.

[7] For an initial discussion of some principles for arms control in the Persian Gulf, see Edward M. Kennedy, 'The Persian Gulf: Arms Race or Arms Control?', *Foreign Affairs*, Vol. 54, No. 1 (October 1975).

[8] Schelling and Halperin defined arms control as 'all the forms of military co-operation between potential enemies in the interests of reducing the likelihood of war, its scope and violence if it occurs, and the political and economic costs of being prepared for it'. See Morton Halperin and Thomas Schelling, *Strategy and Arms Control* (New York; Twentieth Century Fund, 1961), p. 2. Needless to say, there are other definitions and also variations of the Schelling and Halperin definition. For an emphasis on defence expenditure reduction as a main objective of arms control, see Bernard Brodie, 'On the Objectives of Arms Control', *International Security*, Vol. 1, No. 1 (Summer 1976).

[9] Some of the early and widely quoted works on arms control are: Hedley Bull, *The Control of the Arms Race: Disarmament and Arms Control in the Missile Age* (New York, Praeger, 1961); Halperin and Schelling, *op. cit.*; Donald Brennan, *Arms Control, Disarmament and National Security* (New York, Braziller, 1961); for one of several recent attempts to generalize and theorize about arms control, see David V. Edwards, *Arms Control in International Politics* (New York: Holt, Rinehart & Winston, 1969); see also Stanford Arms Control Group, *International Arms Control: Issues and Agreements* (Stanford: Stanford University Press, 1976).

[10] On this see, *inter alia*, United States Arms Control and Disarmament Agency, *The International Transfer of Conventional Arms* (A Report to the Congress, 12 April 1974), pp. C-12, 13.

[11] For an account of the Israeli efforts to circumvent the embargo, see, *inter alia*, Edward Luttwak and Dan Horowitz, *The Israeli Army* (London: Allen Lane, 1975), p. 47. A popularized account of the Israeli covert arms purchases can be found in Leonard Slater, *The Pledge* (New York: Simon and Schuster, 1970).

[12] On the Tripartite Declaration, see Safran, *op. cit.*, in note 1; Fuad Jabber, *The Politics of Arms Transfer and Control: The United States and Egypt's Quest for Arms, 1950–1955* (South California Arms Control and Foreign Policy Seminar, 1972); John C. Campbell, *Defense of the Middle East: Problems of American Policy* (New York: Praeger, 1960); and Kemp, *op. cit.* in note 2.

[13] On American arms supplies policy towards the Middle East in the first half of the 1950s, see Jabber *op. cit.* in note 12, pp. 15–30; Campbell, *op. cit.*, pp. 68–72; and Townsend Hoopes, *The Devil and John Foster Dulles: The Diplomacy of the Eisenhower Era* (Boston: Little, Brown, 1973), pp. 323–4.

[14] See Stockholm International Peace Research Institute, *The Arms Trade Registers* (Cambridge, Mass.: MIT Press, 1974), p. 46.

[15] Egypt attempted to secure American military assistance in early 1950, autumn 1950, autumn 1952, early 1953, and finally in March–July 1955. The early efforts were stymied by strong British pressure. Later on, in 1953, the United States became interested in the supply of arms to Egypt but linked it with the idea of a regional security organization. When this idea failed, the American military aid did not come through. See Jabber, *op. cit.* in note 12, pp. 19–23. For a version which argues that Egypt had, in fact, already reached an arms agreement with the Soviet Union in January 1955, see Uri Ra'anan, *The USSR Arms the Third World* (Cambridge, Mass.: MIT Press, 1969). It is not clear whether Egyptian efforts to secure arms from the United States persisted ʼl July 1955, since Egypt was interested in a major political move to undercut the Baghdad Pact initially formed in February 1955, and arms from the Soviet Union could serve this function.

[16] See *Middle East Record 1967*, p. 43.

[17] See Yair Evron, 'French Arms Policy in the Middle East', *The World Today*, Vol. 26, No. 2 (February 1970), pp. 82–98.

[18] References to the development of the *Chariot* tank were made in numerous publications. See, *inter alia*, *Maarachot* [Hebrew] (Tel Aviv: Israel Defence Forces Publications House, June 1977).

[19] See *New York Times*, 18 September 1954, p. 1.

[20] *Documents in Disarmament 1945–1959*, Vol. 1 (Washington DC: ACDA, 1960), p. 615.

[21] See *The International Transfer of Conventional Arms, op. cit.* in note 10, p. C-11, and *Keesing's Contemporary Archives 1957–1958*, p. 15370, which refers to a speech by Shepilov delivered before the Supreme Soviet on the same issue.

[22] *New York Times*, 28 April 1956, pp. 1, 3.

[23] *Documents on Disarmament*, Vol. II, 1957–9 (Washington DC: ACDA, 1960), p. 943.

[24] *Documents on Disarmament*, 1963 (Washington DC: ACDA), pp. 187–93.

[25] Heikal also argues that in the initial phase after the Arab defeat of 1967, Egypt and the Soviet Union were worried lest Israel should decide to attack again and bring about the collapse of the Egyptian regime. The road to Cairo was, in fact, open before the Israeli forces. The Soviet Union therefore decided, as an ally and friend, to help Egypt. See Mohamad Hassanein Heikal, *The Road to Ramadan* (London: Collins, 1975), pp. 44–6.

[26] See mainly Jon D. Glassman, *Arms for the Arabs* (Baltimore: Johns Hopkins University Press, 1975). William Quandt, on the other hand, maintains that the Soviet Union never imposed such limitations; see his report 'Soviet Policy in the October 1973 War', (Rand Corporation, Santa Monica: May 1976, R-1864-ISA).

[27] For the latter interpretation, see Glassman, *op. cit.*, p. 92.

[28] *Ibid.*, pp. 93–5.

[29] See *Janes' All the World's Aircraft 1976–76* (London: Macdonald and Jane's, 1975), p. 501.

[30] See Alvin Z. Rubenstein, *Red Star on the Nile* (Princeton, N.J.: Princeton University Press, 1977), p. 237, pp. 251–3; Quandt, *op. cit.*; Glassman, *op. cit.*, pp. 112–17.

[31] Quandt, *op. cit.*, p. 5; Rubenstein, *op. cit.*, pp. 139–40, 146–9.

[32] See *Department of State Bulletin*, LVII, 1463 (10 July 1967).

[33] *Middle East Record 1967* (Tel Aviv: Israel Universities Press, 1971), p. 40.

[34] On 23 March Secretary of State Rogers stated clearly that the withholding of the *Phantoms* was linked with American efforts to 'engage the other major suppliers . . . in early arms limitations talks'. See *The International Transfer of Conventional Arms, op. cit.* in note 10, p. C-3.

[35] Based on interviews in Washington.

[36] This approach was formulated primarily by Joseph Sisco. On this, see Edward R. F. Sheehan, *The Arabs, Israelis, and Kissinger* (New York: Readers Digest Press, 1976), p. 21.

[37] See, for example, *New York Times*, 6 February 1972.

[38] Quandt, *op. cit.* in note 26, p. 37.

[39] See, for example, *Congressional Record* (Senate), 28 January 1974, 'Congress Files an Extraordinary Report: The Middle East War'.

[40] The actual wording was: '. . . The United States Government agrees to an early meeting to undertake a joint study of high technology and sophisticated items, including the *Pershing* . . . with conventional warheads, with a view to giving a positive response'. *Hearings before the Committee on Foreign Relations*, United States Senate, 6–7 October 1975, Appendix; *New York Times*, 17 September 1975.

[41] A recent instance of growing co-operation between the nuclear-weapons powers (and other states, which export nuclear technology) has been the London 'Suppliers' Club' meetings, which agreed on some safeguards concerning nuclear technology exports aimed at reaching a comprehensive system of such safeguards.

[42] On this see Nissim Bar Yaacov, *The Israel–Syrian Armistice* (Jerusalem: Magnes Press, 1967).

[43] On that experience see Yair Evron, *The Demilitarization of Sinai, op. cit.* in note 2.

[44] During the negotiations between Israel and the United States about the withdrawal of Israeli forces from the

Sinai after the 1956 Sinai campaign, only the following two issues were raised: Israel's passage through the straits, and the future of the Gaza Strip. Israel demanded that the United Nations should have exclusive control over this strip. In this context see, in particular, Dulles's aide-memoire of 11 March 1957 given to Abba Eban, Eisenhower's reference to the matter on 25 February 1957,and Mrs Meir's speech in the United Nations General Assembly of 1 March 1957. See also Theodore Draper, *Israel and World Politics* (New York: Viking, 1967), pp. 19–21, 137–9. Yigal Allon also refers to the fact that Israel did not even demand the demilitarization of the Sinai in *Masach shel Hol* [Curtain of Sand] (Tel Aviv, 1960), pp. 355–6.

45 Allon, *op. cit.*, pp. 343–5; *idem*, 'Hashlav Ha'aharon Bemilhemet Hashirur', [The Last Phase in the War of Independence], *Ot*, Nos. 3–4 (November 1967), p. 4; *idem*, 'Haganah Pe'ila Aruva Lekiumer [Active Defence as a Guarantee for our Existence], *Molad* (July–August 1967), p. 141; Shimon Peres, *Ma'arachot*, No. 146 (1962), p. 3. For an analysis of Israel's *casus belli*, see Dan Horowitz, *Hatfisah Hayisraelit shel Beitahon Leumi* [Israel's Concept of National Security] (Jerusalem: The Eshkol Institute, The Hebrew University, 1973), p. 25.

46 For an Israeli's appraisal of this Egyptian strategy, see Allon, *op. cit.* in note 44, p. 341.

47 At the peak of Egyptian military involvement in Yemen, some 70,000 Egyptian soldiers were stationed there.

48 Estimates of the overall number of Egyptian forces so deployed are various. Estimates in Israel ranged between one division and two divisions, plus varying numbers of tanks (apparently about 250). Only two squadrons of fighters or fighter-bombers were kept permanently in Sinai, and none of them were MiG-21. See Levi Eshkol's speech in the Knesset, 22 May 1967; Shmuel Segev, *Sadin Adom* [Red Sheet] (Tel Aviv, 1967), p. 22; Michael Bar-Zohar, *Hahodesh Ha'aroch Beyoter* [The Longest Month] (Tel Aviv, 1969), p. 40; interview with Gen. (Res.) Gavish, *Yediot Ahronot*, 3 April 1970. The size of the Egyptian forces, as well as the manner and whereabouts of their deployment, were such that Israel felt secure in positioning only one battalion and no more than a few dozen tanks along the southern border.

49 The Egyptian defensive positions on the eve of the 1967 war were based on strong defensive lines astride the three main routes through which the Israeli forces could break into Sinai. The Palestinian Division took its position in the Gaza Strip, while Division 7 held the northern route leading from Rafiah to al'-Arish; Division 2 was in the centre with Abu-Ageilah as its pivot, and Division 6 was placed on the southern approach. Other Egyptian units were positioned between and behind these divisions. Each defensive area was based on a strong combination of infantry, artillery and armour, arranged in three successive defensive lines. Although the actual deployment of aircraft was minimal, there were five airfields which were ready and could be activated at short notice: al'-Arish, Jebal Livni, Bir-Gifgafah, Bir-Tamdah and Nahal. Sixteen radar stations were spread throughout Sinai. The network of roads had also been considerably developed during the 1957–67 period.

50 See *Middle East Record 1 1960* (London: Weidenfeld and Nicolson, n. d.) pp. 202–4; Ezer Weizman in *Yediot*

*Ahronot*, 4 June 1971; M. A. Gilboa, *Shesh Shanim Shisha Yamim* [Six Years, Six Days] (Tel Aviv, 1967), pp. 21–2.

51 For the closure of the straits as a *casus belli*, see T. Draper, *Israel and World Politics: Roots of the 1967 Arab–Israeli War* (New York: Viking; London: Secker & Warburg, 1968), p. 21, quoting Mrs Meir's speech in the United Nations on 1 March 1957; see also David Ben-Gurion's interview in *Newsweek*, 25 March 1957, p. 46; and Allon and Peres, as cited above.

52 However, in closed meetings with American decision-makers during the last phase of the 1967 crisis, Israeli diplomats increasingly referred to the concentration of Egyptian forces in the Sinai as a threat and a major cause for alarm.

53 The most famous treatment of this subject is Lewis F. Richardson, *Arms and Insecurity* (London: Stevens, 1960). For a comprehensive review and critique of it, see Anatol Rapoport, 'Lewis F. Richardson's Mathematical Theory of War', *Journal of Conflict Resolution*, Nos. 1, 2 (July 1975). The subject has been dealt with in several other works. For a more recent one, arguing a pattern of causal relationships between arms races and wars, see N. Z. Alcock, 'Arms Races and War', in *Scientists and World Affairs* (Proceedings of the 22nd Pugwash Conference, Oxford), pp. 251–8. For a preliminary discussion of this subject in the context of the Middle East see Yair Evron, 'Arms Races in the Middle East . . .', *op. cit.* in note 2.

54 And see *The International Transfer of Conventional Arms, op. cit.* in note 10.

55 For details about the arms race in the Middle East, see some of the works mentioned in note 2. Also International Institute for Strategic Studies, *The Military Balance* (London: IISS, annual); Stockholm International Peace Research Institute (SIPRI) Yearbook, *World Armaments and Disarmament* (Stockholm: Almqvist & Wiksell; Cambridge, Mass., and London: MIT Press, annual); SIPRI, *Arms Trade Registers: The Arms Trade with the Third World* (Stockholm: Almqvist & Wiksell; Cambridge, Mass., and London: MIT Press, 1975).

56 And see Michael Brecher, *Decisions in Israel's Foreign Policy* (London: Oxford UP, 1974), chapter 6, and Yair Evron, 'Arms Races in the Middle East . . .', *op. cit.* in note 2.

57 See Benjamin Geist, *The Six Day War* (Ph.D. Thesis, Hebrew University, Jerusalem, 1974. Unpublished) and Brecher, *op. cit.* in note 56, chapter 7.

58 On Soviet–Egyptian co-operation in rebuilding the Egyptian army see, *inter alia*, Mohamad Hassanein Heikal, *The Road to Ramadan, op. cit.* in note 25.

59 That the question of the occupied territories was the major reason for the war is accepted by the majority of observers. The idea that even a limited Israeli withdrawal from the Sinai would have at least postponed the war was eventually accepted even by some members of the Israeli leadership. See Mati Golan, *The Secret Conversations of Henry Kissinger* (New York: Quadrangle, 1976), pp. 144–6, where he describes a conversation between Mrs Meir and Dr Kissinger in which she admitted as much.

60 See, *inter alia*, Chaim Herzog, *The War of Atonement* (Boston: Little, Brown; London: Weidenfeld and Nicolson, 1975).

[61] The increased 'reach' of Israeli military capabilities was dramatically demonstrated by the Israeli raid on Entebbe.
[62] For Peres' assessment, see *Haaretz*, 16 July 1976. For Rabin's assessment, see *Haaretz*. For the rise in armour, see comparison between issues of *The Military Balance* of 1973-4 and 1975-6; Israel's tank inventory rose by 50 per cent between 1973 and 1975 according to these accounts.
[63] See *The Military Balance 1975-1976*, pp. 34-5.
[64] There have been many references to it in the Israeli press. See, for example, the report on a press conference with Brigadier Dan Shomron, *Haaretz*, 22 September 1975.
[65] See the *New York Times*, 13 January 1977; *Aviation Week*, 17 January 1977.
[66] See *Aviation Week*, 14 July 1975, pp. 14-15.
[67] See *Aviation Week*, 17 November 1975, p. 22. Another report places the size of the proposed deal at 80 units; see *Time* magazine, 22 March 1976, p. 24.
[68] West Germany was reluctant to supply the type but encouraged Egypt to turn to France. An Egyptian evaluation team spent some time in Istres, France, in March 1976 flight-testing the plane. See *Aviation Week*, 17 May 1976, p. 11.
[69] Egypt is now believed to have 48 MiG-23 (*Flogger*). Half are of the type E export air-superiority version, the other half of the type F export ground-attack version. See *International Defense Review*, Vol. 9, No. 6, 1976.
[70] Most of the literature on deterrence focuses on nuclear deterrence. For some works on conventional deterrence, see, *inter alia*, Raul Naroll *et al*, *Military Deterrence in History* (New York: New York UP, 1974); George Quester, *Deterrence Before Hiroshima* (New York and London: John Wiley, 1966); Alan Alexandroff and Richard Rosecrance, 'Deterrence in 1939', *World Politics*, Vol. XXIX, No. 3 (April 1977), pp. 404-24.
[71] See Irvine J. Cohen, 'Israeli Defense Capability', *National Defense* (January/February 1976), pp. 271-4.
[72] *World Armaments and Disarmaments 1975* (see note 55), p. 216.
[73] *Ibid*.
[74] See, *inter alia*, *Aviation Week*, 29 March 1977, pp. 15-17.
[75] *Ibid*, 15 December 1975, p. 11.
[76] *Aviation Week*, 5 April 1976, p. 21.
[77] *Ibid*, pp. 20-21.
[78] The literature on conventional surprise attacks is extensive. For some of the better-known studies combining theoretical insights with case studies, see Roberta Wohlstetter, *Pearl Harbor: Warning and Decision* (Stanford: Stanford University Press, 1962) and A. & R. Wohlstetter, 'Cuba and Pearl Harbor: Hindsight and Foresight', *Foreign Affairs* 43, July 1965, pp. 691-707; Klaus Knorr, 'Failures in National Intelligence Estimates: the Case of the Cuban Missiles', *World Politics*, Vol. 24, No. 3, pp. 455-67; Alexander George and Richard Smoke, *Deterrence in American Foreign Policy: Theory and Practice* (New York and London: Columbia UP, 1974), part III; Barton Whaley, *Codeword Barbarona* (Cambridge, Mass.: MIT Press, 1973). For studies of the 1973 surprise attack, see Michael Handel, *Perception, Deception and Surprise: the Case of the Yom Kippur War*, Jerusalem Papers on Peace Problems, No. 19 (Jerusalem, 1976), and Avi Shlaim, 'Failures in National Intelligence

Estimates: the Case of the Yom Kippur War', *World Politics*, Vol. 28, No. 3, pp. 348-80.
[79] For a discussion of possible Israeli military reactions to an impending Arab attack, see Z. Shiff, *Haaretz*, 29 July 1974. Shiff argues that for political reasons (American reaction), there is a higher likelihood of a limited Israeli pre-emptive strike than a full-scale preventive war.
[80] For some parallel measures – albeit in a completely different context, which therefore imposes a somewhat different approach – see Joseph I. Coffey, *New Approaches to Arms Reduction in Europe*, Adelphi Paper No. 105 (London: International Institute for Strategic Studies, Autumn 1974).
[81] For a discussion of the distinction between strategic and tactical indicators for a surprise attack, see Abraham Ben Zvi, 'Hindsight and Foresight: A Conceptual Framework for the Analysis of Surprise Attacks', *World Politics*, Vol. 28, No. 3, pp. 381-95.
[82] And see Yair Evron, *The Demilitarization of Sinai*, *op. cit.* in note 2.
[83] See, for example, Sadat's statement in Washington, *New York Times*, 5 April 1977, p. 11.
[84] For an interesting debate on a proposal for no first use of nuclear weapons, see Robert Tucker, Klaus Knorr, Richard A. Falk and Hedley Bull, *Proposal for No First Use of Nuclear Weapons: Pros and Cons*, Policy Memorandum No. 28 (Center for International Studies, Princeton University, 1963).
[85] John Barton has pointed out in a private communication that, given Middle East history, such punitive or compensatory military action may be disastrous. There is indeed a dilemma. Should deterrence threats be emphasized so as to make violations less likely, or should more flexibility be introduced into the system? The answer is always uncertain. One possible solution is to devise a list of different sanctions for different violations. The main burden of the arguments remains, however, that the arms-control regime to be created should incorporate as many constraints on violations as possible. The threat of military sanctions would be much more effective than the overall arms-control impact of a NFUFT.
[86] See Anne Cahn, 'Arms Transfers Constraints: Who, What, When, How and Why', (mimeo), 1976, p. 12.
[87] Philip Farley, quoted in *ibid*.
[88] For some of the earlier and better-known works see James F. Dibgy, *Precision-Guided Weapons*, Adelphi Paper No. 118 (London: IISS, 1975); Albert Wohlstetter, 'Threats and Promises of Peace: Europe and America in the New Era', *Orbis* (Winter 1974); Richard Burt, 'New Weapons Technologies and European Security', *Orbis* (Summer 1975), pp. 515-6; Geoffrey Kemp, Robert L. Pfaltzgraff, Jr., and Uri Ra'anan (eds), *The Other Arms Race: New Technologies and Non-nuclear Conflict* (Lexington, Mass.: D. C. Heath, 1975).
[89] See Luttwak and Horowitz, *op. cit.* in note 11, an Herzog, *op. cit.* in note 60.
[90] See especially Digby, *op. cit.* in note 88; Steven L. Canby, *The Alliance and Europe Part IV*, *Military Doctrine and Technology*, Adelphi Paper No. 109 (London: IISS, 1975); Richard Burt, *op. cit.* in note 88; also some of the contributions to Donald Brennan (ed.), *The Implications of Precision Weapons for American Strategic Interests* (Croton on Hudson, N.Y.: The Hudson

Institute, HI-2204, January 1975), and to Kemp, Pfaltz-graff and Ra'anan, *op. cit.* in note 88.

[91] See for example Richard M. Ogorkiewicz, 'The Future of the Battle Tank', and Mike W. Fossier, 'The Role of SAMS in Tactical Warfare', both in Kemp, Pfaltzgraff and Ra'anan, *op. cit.* in note 88. Doubts about the efficacy of PGM in general and also about their debatable contribution to arms control are expressed in James L. Foster, *The Future of Conventional Arms Control* (paper delivered to the American Political Science Association, September 1975).

[92] An argument in favour of full Soviet participation in a joint guarantee of a political settlement is included in Zbigniew Brzezinski, François Duchêne and Kiichi Saeki, 'Peace in an International Framework', *Foreign Policy,* Summer 1975. George Ball also refers to the possibility of joint policies devised by the super-powers to bring about a peace in the Middle East; see his 'Kissinger's Paper Peace: How Not to Handle the Middle East', *The Atlantic Monthly* (February 1976).

[93] See US Senate, Commission on Foreign Relations, *Memorandum of the Agreement between the Governments of Israel and the United States, Hearing,* 94th Cong., 1st sess. (Washington DC: USPGO, 7 October 1975) for an important discussion about the implications of this American undertaking, in particular the statements (and following discussion) of Henry Kissinger and George Ball, and for 'Early-Warning System in Sinai', *Ibid.*, Report No. 94-415.

[94] The experience with the armistice commissions set up according to the 1949 armistice agreements between Israel and Egypt, Jordan, Syria and Lebanon respectively was a mixed one. In times of great tension one or the other of the sides to the Israeli–Egyptian and Israeli–Syrian commissions opted out and paralysed the commission. They were also not very effective in dealing with various complaints raised by one side or the other. Nevertheless, they also served many times as a constructive mechanism for solving outstanding problems. Two factors may contribute to the increased effectiveness of future arms-control regulatory commissions: first, they would be established within the framework of a comprehensive arms-control regime; second, the United States (and possibly, in some cases, the Soviet Union as well) would serve as arbiter and would have much more impact than the UN representative who sat on the armistice commissions.

[95] For an expression of support for the idea of American military guarantee to Israel, see Richard H. Ullman, 'After Rabat: Middle East Risks and American Roles', *Foreign Affairs,* January 1975, and his 'Alliance with Israel?' *Foreign Policy,* No. 19 (Summer 1975), pp. 18–33; Stanley Hoffmann, 'A New Policy for Israel', *Foreign Affairs,* April 1975, mentions it but with reservations. For a criticism of this position, see Robert Tucker, 'Israel and the United States: From Dependence to Nuclear Weapons?', *Commentary,* Vol. 60, No. 5 (November 1975), pp. 29–43.

# 4 BEYOND SALT II

## GLOSSARY

| | | | | |
|---|---|---|---|---|
| ABM | Anti-ballistic missile(s) | | NPT | Non-proliferation Treaty |
| ALCM | Air-launched cruise missile(s) | | NTM | National Technical Means |
| CCD | Conference Committee on Disarmament | | PGM | Precision-guided missile(s) |
| FBS | Forward-based system(s) | | PBV | Post-boost vehicle |
| GLCM | Ground-launched cruise missile(s) | | R&D | Research and Development |
| ICBM | Intercontinental ballistic missile(s) | | RPV | Remotely-piloted vehicle |
| IRBM | Intermediate-range ballistic missile(s) | | RV | Re-entry vehicle(s) |
| LRCM | Long-range cruise missile(s) | | SACEUR | Supreme Allied Command Europe |
| MARV | Manoeuvrable re-entry vehicle(s) | | SALT | Strategic Arms Limitations Talks |
| MBFR | Mutual and Balanced Force Reduction | | SAM | Surface-to-air missile(s) |
| MIRV | Multiple independently-targetable re-entry vehicle(s) | | SCC | Standing Consultative Committee |
| | | | SIOP | Single Integrated Operational Plan |
| MLF | Multi-lateral force | | SLBM | Sea-launched ballistic missile(s) |
| MRBM | Medium-range ballistic missile(s) | | SLCM | Sea-launched cruise missile(s) |
| MRV | Multiple re-entry vehicle(s) | | Sm | Statute mile(s) |
| MT | Megaton (one million tons TNT equivalent) | | SRAM | Short-range attack missile(s) |
| NATO | North Atlantic Treaty Organization | | SRBM | Short-range ballistic missile(s) |
| Nm | Nautical miles | | SSM | Surface-to-surface missile(s) |

# Introduction

## CHRISTOPH BERTRAM

The papers published here were originally presented at an international conference of the IISS in the summer of 1977, at a time when the prospects for a new Soviet–American agreement on the limitation of strategic weapons looked far from promising. They have been amended in the light of the conference discussion as well as subsequent events.

Some of the proposals made in the papers may still seem, at first glance, unduly sceptical given the likelihood that there will be a SALT II agreement before too long. But it remains doubtful whether that agreement, however significant it may be in terms of regulating temporarily the strategic nuclear balance between the two major powers, will have a long-term, lasting effect. Underlying the arguments in these chapters is the concern that the present approach to strategic arms limitation may have come to the end of its usefulness. Verification through national means, that least interfering way of observing compliance with an agreement, is becoming increasingly inadequate since new multi-range and multi-purpose weapons systems of strategic significance are much less observable, and, if observable, do not necessarily indicate their performance characteristics. In future, politicians and parliaments will face the difficult dilemma of either restricting arms limitation agreements to what is verifiable – and that means leaving outside the agreement many of the new systems of strategic potential – or of including these systems, which would result in imperfect verification. Similarly, weapon systems which do not fall naturally under existing definitions of what is, and what is not, a strategic weapon, are acquiring increasing weight in security and arms-control considerations, but there is as yet no satisfactory way of dealing with these 'grey area' systems. Nor do some of the suggested remedies for 'real' arms control – such as major reductions in the strategic arsenals of both sides – offer an answer; major reductions in Soviet–American strategic weapons, as Chapter I argues, may well give greater weight to the weapons and strategic forces outside that equation and highlight even more the asymmetries in existing strategic force postures, to the extent of rendering future agreements even more difficult to conclude.

What these problems and their discussion show is essentially this: the SALT method of arms control is increasingly frustrated by qualitative arms competition, and the attempt made in the past few years to cope with this through specific definitions – what is a strategic weapon, what is strategic range, what is adequate verification – cannot succeed much longer. It has led to the situation in which arms control is separated from military security, which is unfortunate for both. This is particularly well illustrated by the example of strategic cruise missiles, which are regarded by many as the most recent villains of arms control. But are they? There is no disagreement that cruise missiles, in their present and foreseeable performance characteristics, are not suited to a disarming first strike against the fixed ICBM forces of the other side. They are not, in other words, 'destabilizing' weapons. If both the United States and the Soviet Union relied largely on strategic cruise missiles for deterrence, strategic stability would be in a much better state than if deterrence were based on large ICBM forces which are increasingly vulnerable to pre-emptive counter-force attack. Cruise missiles, therefore, are not a threat to strategic stability as such, but they are a threat to the definitions of the SALT negotiations. However, unless we succeed in reconciling again the substantive concern of national security with the procedural concern of arms-control negotiations, the latter are unlikely to produce a stable, durable or reliable agreement.

New approaches to arms control will have to be developed to meet this problem. They will have to address directly the qualitative arms race rather than merely seek to control the quantities of specific weapon systems. As the asymmetries of force postures between East and West become more marked, the new approaches will have to insist less on restraining the numbers of weapons (how many should each side have?), than on restraining the military capabilities they provide (what mission should each side be allowed to perform?). Negotiations will have to be quasi-permanent in order to manage a strategic balance that might be upset by technological change or proliferation; they should, perhaps, even go beyond the present bilateral character of SALT, and must take into account the concerns of countries directly affected by specific Soviet–American agreements.*

To point to the weaknesses inherent in the present approach to SALT does not imply criticism of the new accord which the Soviet Union and the United States are currently seeking. Under the circumstances, SALT II, as it is shaping up in these negotiations, is not a bad agreement; it is certainly better than none at all. But it is an agreement which may raise more hopes than it can satisfy, and absorb more time and energy of negotiators and politicians alike than it can, in the longer run, justify. It is already clear that negotiations for SALT III will start immediately after the completion of SALT II. Moreover, the agreement will constantly be exposed to the strain of new strategic weapon technologies; the fact that a three-year protocol is attached to an eight-year treaty builds these dynamics into SALT II from the start. The effort was necessary but the instrument of a largely numerical SALT has become blunted. SALT II shows little prospect of keeping the dynamics of strategic arms competition in check. No other arms-control method may have succeeded in this either. But some of these recent dynamics are more than just irritants; they are now undermining the basis on which SALT has so far rested: symmetry, verifiability, and relative stability. The process is being over-loaded with tasks that it cannot perform – such as establishing a durable deterrence relationship – and with hopes that it cannot satisfy – such as maintaining the in-

vulnerability of strategic delivery systems, on land now and at sea in the more distant future. This is bound to lead to a high degree of political controversy in the American debate – even greater than that we have witnessed over the past five years. Some controversy is inevitable in discussion of arms control which is, after all, an attempt to reach agreement with a military adversary, and to accept constraints on one's own options for deterrence and defence, in return for similar concessions from him. But to this 'natural' degree of political controversy are added new and disturbing doubts about the utility of the instrument of arms control. They are disturbing because they could jeopardize the support of those whose basic political instincts favour some kind of accommodation with the adversary on weapons competition. The yardsticks for distinguishing good from bad means of arms control have become blurred: was President Carter's March 1977 proposal good? Is the new SALT accord now bad because it is less ambitious?

Increased political controversy will not be limited to SALT alone. Since the prevention of nuclear war is the primary purpose of American detente with the Soviet Union, and SALT its major vehicle, disillusionment with SALT will affect the detente relationship as such. Should the US Senate reject the new agreement, the political impact will go far beyond the arms-control arena: it would shape the views of the departing and, more important, the emerging Soviet leadership; it would cool East–West relations as a whole, not just between the super-powers but also in Europe, and it would influence the balance of domestic power in democratic societies as well as alignments in foreign affairs.

To link SALT to detente makes sense as long as SALT goes well. If it does not go well, detente itself will suffer. The logical remedy would be to separate one from the other in lean times, but it is a remedy that lacks political plausibility at this stage. It might be advantageous to see SALT recede from its position as the most prominent symbol of the super-powers' ability to get along with each other, and for it to become just one complex and important issue among many others, no longer the statutory bell-wether of Soviet–American relations. This would, theoretically, reduce the surrounding political contro-

---

* For a proposal for a new approach to arms control see my 'Arms Control and Technological Change', forthcoming Adelphi Paper.

versy, the often unwarranted sense of urgency with which results are sought, and the strain on bureaucracies, on allies and on the negotiators themselves. But political symbols cannot easily be dismantled when they are becoming politically awkward, for the simple reason that the authority of political leaders in the Soviet Union and the United States is staked to them.

This will be more so in the American than in the Soviet political environment. For the Soviet Union (her specific concern to curb American military potential apart), the purpose of bilateral detente with the United States is political: she wishes to be recognized by the leading world power as the equal co-manager of international affairs. If symbols other than SALT can be found to carry that message, this should, in the Soviet perspective, be acceptable. For the United States, however, SALT is more than a symbol for Soviet–American detente: it *is* Soviet–American detente. Deprived of the purpose of preventing nuclear war through accommodation, there would be little on which American detente with the Soviet Union could be based and little on which popular support in the United States could be generated. That makes the continuation of SALT so important. The reasons go beyond strategic arms control itself. But it also gives major importance to the efficiency of the SALT instrument. A worn-out approach to strategic arms control cannot carry the political significance that will continue to be attached to progress in SALT.

To note the limitations of the existing approach is to suggest not a radical but a gradual departure from the present practices. Especially when there are doubts about the prospects of arms control, one important pre-condition for making the necessary adaptations is to keep the process and the framework of dialogue and negotiation alive. A rupture in this process, while perhaps giving an unambiguous push towards the emergence of more promising methods of arms control, would only jeopardize the political base on which future negotiations depend. Reform will have to be sought within the existing framework.

There are signs that this may already be happening, albeit in a modest and cautious way. The outline of the new SALT II agreement appears to contain a number of features which could become the pattern of future agreements: in particular, these are the declaration of principles and the three-year protocol on new technologies. A joint declaration of the principles which should guide the future strategic relationship between the super-powers and specify the focus of negotiations could give to the SALT process a greater stability and continuity than it has hitherto experienced. It will illustrate that each individual agreement is part of a continuing chain, not the end of the effort. The protocol on specific new weapons technologies may or may not produce effective control on the dynamics of technological innovation but, even if it is likely to have the opposite effect by encouraging both sides to seek a position of superior bargaining power once the three years are up, at least its inclusion in the overall agreement indicates recognition of the problem and it seeks flexible means of dealing with it. The relatively 'free mix' allowed to both sides under the agreed ceiling of MIRV launchers takes account of the asymmetries in force postures. Rather than aiming at the impossible and wanting to iron asymmetries out, the concept of 'free mix' permits each side to decide which launcher technology it regards as the best for its security and deterrence purposes. The fact that negotiations for SALT III will start immediately after completion of SALT II reflects the realization that the process needs constant adjustment so as to permit the maintenance of deterrence stability through negotiation.

If these are elements of a future approach to strategic arms control, the period beyond SALT II will be marked by a much greater fluidity, temporary accords succeeding and overlapping each other. There will be less perfectionism and, as SALT decisions affect an increasing number of other countries, possibly less bilateralism. But this very fluidity will make the need for a recognized framework of principal objectives that much more urgent if the dialogue is not to degenerate into random pragmatism. Besides confronting the major technical, strategic and political issues discussed in the following chapters, the chief task of strategic arms negotiators beyond SALT II is to define afresh for the 1980s the basic objectives that arms control should achieve in the interest of national security. Future agreements can then be assessed against these basic objectives.

# Reducing Strategic Arms at SALT: How Difficult, How Important?

RICHARD BURT

Fashions in arms control change. Only 15 years ago – in the aftermath of the Cuban missile crisis – the prevailing view in Western arms-control circles was that strategic stability could best be assured by the super-powers acquiring large and redundant nuclear inventories. In the United States, the procurement of intercontinental-range bombers and land- and sea-launched ballistic missiles was justified on the grounds that, while each element of this strategic 'triad' possessed certain drawbacks, taken together they provided a secure and responsive system for retaliation. Similarly, in the early 1960s American officials such as Secretary of Defense Robert McNamara expressed the hope that the Soviet Union would emulate the American approach to force design and numbers, so that both sides could have absolute confidence in the ability of their systems to survive attack and effectively threaten retaliation.[1]

The growth of American and Soviet strategic forces was, moreover, viewed as a necessary prerequisite to negotiations on arms limitation. The concept of 'arming to disarm' elaborated during the Kennedy period was more than a cynical effort to muster support for rising defence budgets: it accepted the fact that nuclear weapons were firmly woven into American and Western Alliance defence policies and reflected the belief that efforts to manage Soviet–American strategic competition were more

[1] See William Kaufmann's discussion of McNamara's view of Soviet strategic deficiencies in the early 1960s, *The McNamara Strategy* (New York: Harper and Row, 1964), pp. 147–149. See also McNamara's own comments, in *The Essence of Security: Reflections in Office* (London: Hodder and Stoughton/New York: Harper and Row, 1968).

likely to succeed than were attempts to end the arms race altogether. Thus arms control – as distinct from disarmament – became the order of the day. As a result, the American deployment of a large and diverse arsenal of systems met with little domestic opposition.

. Clearly, an important change has occurred in Western arms-control thinking over the last decade. The substantial reduction of the super-powers' strategic forces has emerged as a major objective of American foreign policy and an item of priority on the Soviet–American agenda at SALT. The interest in reductions has been stimulated partly by growing public concern about nuclear matters in general but, more precisely, it reflects the more widespread disenchantment that has arisen in the West with concepts and approaches to East–West arms control which were developed in the 1960s and applied by the Nixon–Ford Administrations at SALT. It is not the purpose of this essay to explain the causes of this disenchantment nor to determine whether it is justified. Instead, it accepts the fact that reductions in strategic forces have become a prime American objective at SALT and attempts to examine the consequences of this for the negotiations as well as for the wider Soviet–American strategic relationship. This essay is thus concerned with the feasibility of force reductions being agreed at SALT and their impact on a new array of strategic problems that confront the super-powers. In addressing these issues, however, it is hoped that some insight will be gained into the more general problems of determining what objectives should be set for arms control and what priorities they should be given.

113

**The Case for Negotiated Reductions**

The case for mutual reductions made at SALT rests on several arguments: the first and most important is that, under almost any conceivable strategy for deterrence or use, the forces of the two sides are now far larger than is necessary. Legions of writers have pointed out that neither the existing American nor Soviet arsenal is the result of a sustained process through which requirements are determined rationally. Instead, current force levels are said to be the product of imperfect intelligence, frequent miscalculation and bureaucratic momentum. Such concepts as the 'triad' are thus said to provide *ex post facto* rationalization for unco-ordinated decisions on procurement.[2] It is suggested, for instance, that had the United States deployed smaller numbers of *Minuteman* ICBM and *Polaris* submarines during the early 1960s, the Soviet Union would have exercised similar restraint in the latter half of the decade. Nuclear parity, it is argued, would thus have been reached sooner and at lower numbers.

It is indeed difficult to justify, in military terms, the size of current and projected American and Soviet missile and bomber forces. While crude 'overkill' arguments fail to take into account such factors as system reliability, vulnerability and penetrability, the American force of some 2,200 launchers (which, with the introduction of the *Trident* SLBM at the end of the decade, will be equipped with almost 10,000 deliverable warheads) clearly exceeds the number necessary to assure the destruction of Soviet society and to carry out any additional operations. Those capabilities that the American force now lacks, such as that of threatening large numbers of hard targets on a time-urgent basis, require neither additional forces nor even the maintenance of current levels, but improvements in missile software, warhead accuracy and yield. The same is true for the Soviet Union. In fact, given the present size of American and Soviet inventories, the forces of both are increasingly 'target limited', that is, each side is rapidly running out of targets in the homeland of the adversary that can be usefully or efficiently destroyed.

Despite this, proponents of mutual reductions note that neither side is likely to undertake unilateral cuts for fear of adverse consequences. Politically, a decision made by either the Soviet Union or the United States not to match numerically the forces of the other might suggest a lack of political resolve or could lead allies to question the credibility of commitments. Militarily, unilateral reductions might also be undesirable if they resulted in large asymmetries in capabilities under various post-attack or intra-war scenarios. It is for these reasons that mutual reductions are thought to be so attractive: by asking both sides to cut back, the potential risks might be avoided.

While the belief that the strategic forces of the super-powers are unnecessarily large provides the main rationale for negotiated reductions, three subsidiary arguments are sometimes also cited.

The first concerns cost. Although roughly four-fifths of the American defence budget is spent on general-purpose forces, strategic forces are still expensive. If indirect support costs are taken into account, during the early 1970s the average annual cost of the American strategic programme was estimated to cost just under $20 billion.[3] This was during a period when no major weapons system was introduced into the strategic inventory. Obviously, small reductions in launcher numbers (of ten per cent or less) would not yield substantial savings on this amount. However, more substantial cuts in these numbers (of 25 per cent or more) would certainly have some impact on expenditure. Negotiated reductions would have a far greater impact on spending if they served to limit the numbers of new weapons or obviated the need for new weapons altogether. For example, former Secretary of Defense James Schlesinger speculated in 1975 that the cost to the Soviet Union of deploying some 1,400 SS-17, -18 and -19 ICBM might exceed $30 billion. The ten-year procurement and operating costs of ten *Trident* submarines or

---

[2] The literature on American weapons-procurement decisions is replete with studies that come to this conclusion. See especially Morton Halperin, *Bureaucratic Politics* (Washington DC: Brookings Institution, 1974). It is clearly more difficult to make this case for the Soviet Union, but for an intriguing analysis that points in this direction, see Edward L. Warner III, 'Soviet Strategic Force Posture: Some Alternative Explanations', in Horton, Rogerson and Warner (eds), *Comparative Defense Policy* (Baltimore: The Johns Hopkins University Press, 1974), pp. 310–325.

[3] Alton H. Quanbeck and Barry M. Blechman, *Strategic Forces: Issues for the Mid-Seventies* (Washington DC: Brookings Institution, 1973), p. 46.

114

500 new mobile ICBM would both probably exceed $40 billion. Advocates of reductions argue that if these programmes could be cut back significantly, the money saved could be used to maintain or to improve American conventional capabilities.

A second argument concerns the spread of nuclear weapons. The SALT process was essentially born out of Article VI of the 1968 NPT, in which the two super-powers promised to make progress towards 'the effective cessation of the arms race'. The criticism which non-nuclear states directed against the super-powers at the 1975 NPT Review Conference for allegedly failing to satisfy these requirements has led some to conclude that progress at SALT and in non-proliferation are intimately linked. It is unreasonable, they argue, to expect other states to renounce nuclear weapons while the two super-powers continue to arm themselves. Thus these observers hope that substantial reductions at SALT might soften the inherently discriminatory character of the NPT while setting a standard of responsible international behaviour for other states to emulate. Hedley Bull, for example, has argued that were the two super-powers to agree to major reductions, 'these tangible measures of restraint might be heeded by some'.[4]

The third argument concerns the SALT process itself. Despite the agreements in 1972 to limit ballistic missile defences severely and to place ceilings on ICBM and SLBM deployment, much of the criticism of SALT in the United States has, ironically, come from the arms-control community. The limits on launchers established by both the Interim Agreement and the 1974 Vladivostok *aide-memoire* are said to be so high that they essentially 'legitimized' continued arms acquisition and competition.[5] Arms control, according to this argument, has thus been devalued in the eyes of the public and is in danger of losing popular support. Reductions, it is claimed, would rekindle the public's imagination on arms control and would contribute to building strong domestic support for SALT.

[4] Hedley Bull, 'Rethinking Non-Proliferation', *International Affairs* (London), April 1975.
[5] This has been the constant theme, for example, of the year books produced by the Stockholm Institute for Peace Research (SIPRI) (Cambridge, Mass. and London: MIT Press/Stockholm: Almquist and Wiksell International).

## Outlining the Problem: Negotiability versus Desirability

The case, therefore, for seeking reductions at SALT seems to be strong. Yet the centrality of super-power negotiations in East–West relations demands that the concept of reductions be examined closely. A starting point is to specify the size of possible reductions. While it would be interesting to consider the impact of 'huge' reductions in existing force levels – say 50 per cent or more – it is not realistic to expect the two sides seriously to consider such an option in the near future. Much smaller reductions, such as the proposal that emerged from former Secretary of State Kissinger's visit to Moscow in January 1976 that forces be cut to between 2,100 and 2,200 from the Vladivostok ceiling of 2,400, are clearly more feasible, but their impact would be trivial. Thus in this section we will examine the possibility of reducing the ceiling on launcher numbers contained in the Vladivostok accord by 25 per cent or to 1,800 – the lower limit sought by the Carter Administration during Secretary of State Cyrus Vance's discussions in Moscow in March 1977. To do this, both the negotiability and the desirability of reductions of this size will be analysed. Negotiability is obviously an important criterion from the American point of view, for, if the idea of reductions is unacceptable to the Soviet Union, proposals designed to bring them about could further confuse an already complicated set of negotiations. Desirability is an even more important standard for judging reductions proposals, for those proposals that meet with Soviet acceptance could very well be seen to run counter to prevailing Western conceptions of strategic stability. Negotiability, then, is concerned with political perceptions of strategic equivalence, while desirability is related to the technical stability of the balance.

Looking at the negotiability problem first, there are several reasons to suspect that the Soviet Union is not entirely comfortable with the idea of reductions. The Soviet military passion for large numbers is well documented: in high-technology areas like strategic forces, the Soviet planners appear to believe that quantity can to some extent make up for lack of quality.[6] The

[6] See Chapter VIII in Arthur Alexander's *Armor Development in the Soviet Union and the United States* (Santa Monica: Rand, September 1976), R-1860-NA, and Edward Luttwak, 'Perceptions of Military Force and

fact, moreover, that most Soviet strategic weapons are newer than their American counterparts also suggests that it might be difficult for the Soviet Union to adjust quickly to the idea of phasing many of them out. This seems especially true when the perceived political benefits of the Soviet strategic arsenal are taken into account. From the perspective of Moscow, it is the continuing momentum of Soviet strategic procurement that is probably judged to have made the SALT process possible in the first place. As a result, proposals for reductions are likely to be viewed there with scepticism.

However, this does not mean that efforts to get the Soviet Union to agree to mutual reductions will be of no avail. In an effort to break the stalemate in SALT that followed the Vladivostok summit, the Soviet Union herself proposed a complicated arrangement under which the Vladivostok launcher ceiling would have been reduced by ten per cent or so. While the Soviet leadership turned down the Carter Administration's proposal made in March 1977 for 'deep cuts', it is not at all clear that the Soviet Union objected specifically to the idea of large overall reductions in launchers. The general Soviet attitude towards reductions, therefore, may not be so inflexible as some evidence suggests.

This raises a critical question, however: would a reduction proposal that was negotiable from the Soviet point of view at the same time be politically acceptable in the United States? As we have seen, the most important argument for negotiated reductions is that large-scale mutual cuts could be undertaken without doing violence to the existing strategic balance. Is this true? Both super-powers seem to accept the existence, at present, of a situation of 'rough' strategic parity. However, this approximate balance is built upon some important asymmetries. Not only do the two super-powers place different emphases on the separate categories of forces that make up their inventories, but the individual characteristics of systems in these categories differ substantially. For instance, the Soviet Union's new heavy ICBM – the SS-18 – has roughly 15 times the throw-weight of an American *Minuteman* III; the American *Poseidon* SLBM, on the other hand, can attack as many as 14 separate targets, but the Soviet SS-N-6 SLBM

US Defence Policy', *Survival* January/February 1977, pp. 2–7.

can attack only one. These differences – in force composition and individual weapons performance – are reinforced by more durable asymmetries in technology, geography, military doctrine and alliance systems. The result is that the strategic balance has become an increasingly difficult concept to define and measure. This has little impact on the stability of the balance, but it does complicate the negotiating process. At present, both sides deploy large and diverse collections of systems, so the various asymmetries that characterize the existing Soviet–American relationship are to some extent balanced out: American advantages in one area, such as bombers, are offset by Soviet superiority in another, such as missile throw-weight; the Soviet Union can deliver a greater total of megatonnage with her missiles, but American missiles can deliver more warheads, and so on. The problem, of course, is that owing to these differences a balanced reduction in one index of strategic power, launcher numbers, is likely to affect existing imbalances in other measures of strategic capability, such as missile throw-weight, bomber pay-load, deliverable warheads or equivalent megatonnage,[7] disproportionately.

The impact of reductions in *overall* numbers of launchers and launchers equipped with MIRV on American and Soviet strategic forces can be seen by comparing the strategic balance under a Vladivostok-type arms-control regime and a reduced arrangement where both are limited to 1,800 launchers and 1,100 with MIRV. (See Table 1.) Under the Vladivostok guidelines both sides were to be permitted freedom to mix; that is, each side was relatively free to determine how many systems of any given type would be deployed under the overall aggregate ceiling. As shown in column A of the table, this means that while both sides could deploy relatively large numbers of SLBM, the Soviet Union could continue to emphasize ICBM in her inventory and the United States could give greater weight to the bomber component of her forces. As the table reveals, this would result in some significant

[7] This was recognized by presidential National Security Adviser Zbigniew Brzezinski, in remarks made to the press following the Vance mission to Moscow in March 1977: 'If you have fewer total numbers, then any asymmetry becomes increasingly significant'. (Official text of press conference, 1 April 1977, United States Information Agency.)

**Table 1. US–Soviet Strategic Balance under Hypothetical SALT Regimes (early 1980s)**

| | | A<br>Vladivostok<br>Regime<br>*2,400 launchers*<br>*(1,320 MIRV)* | B<br>Aggregate<br>Reductions<br>*1,800 launchers*<br>*(1,100 MIRV)* | C<br>Reductions with<br>Sub-ceilings<br>*1,800 launchers*<br>*(1,100 MIRV)*<br>*150 heavy ICBM*<br>*550 ICBM with MIRV* |
|---|---|---|---|---|
| | ***(i) Delivery Systems*** | | | |
| USA | Heavy ICBM[a] | 54 | — | — |
| | Light ICBM[b] | 1,000 (550 MIRV) | 550 (all MIRV) | 550 (all MIRV) |
| | SLBM[c] | 896 (736 MIRV) | 900 (550 MIRV) | 900 (550 MIRV) |
| | Intercontinental Bombers | 450 | 350 | 350 |
| | *Total* | 2,400 (1,286 MIRV) | 1,800 (1,100 MIRV) | 1,800 (1,100 MIRV) |
| USSR | Heavy ICBM[a] | 310 (all MIRV) | 300 (all MIRV) | 150 (all MIRV) |
| | Light ICBM[b] | 1,100 (1,000 MIRV) | 800 (all MIRV) | 800 (all MIRV) |
| | SLBM[c] | 950 | 700 | 850 (350 MIRV) |
| | Intercontinental Bombers[d] | 40 | — | — |
| | *Total* | 2,400 (1,310 MIRV) | 1,800 (1,100 MIRV) | 1,800 (1,100 MIRV) |
| | ***(ii) Measuring the Balance[e]*** | | | |
| USA | **Warheads** | | | |
| | ICBM | 2,054 | 1,650 | 1,650 |
| | SLBM | 8,520 | 5,850 | 5,850 |
| | Bombers | 1,800 | 1,400 | 1,400 |
| | *Total* | 12,374 | 8,900 | 8,900 |
| | **Equivalent Megatonnage** | | | |
| | ICBM | 1,180 | 420 | 420 |
| | SLBM | 1,260 | 1,380 | 1,380 |
| | *Total* | 2,440 | 1,800 | 1,800 |
| | **Missile Throw-weight** | | | |
| | ICBM | 2·4m lb | 1·1m lb | 1·1m lb |
| | SLBM | 1·2m lb | 1·2m lb | 1·2m lb |
| | *Total* | 3·6m lb | 2·3m lb | 2·3m lb |
| | **Bomber Payload** | 27m lb | 21m lb | 21m lb |
| USSR | **Warheads** | | | |
| | ICBM | 7,980 | 6,500 | 3,500 |
| | SLBM | 950 | 700 | 1,950[f] |
| | Bombers[g] | 80 | — | — |
| | *Total* | 9,010 | 7,200 | 5,450 |

117

Table 1—*continued*

| Equivalent Megatonnage | | | |
|---|---|---|---|
| ICBM | 4,950 | 4,100 | 3,200 |
| SLBM | 950 | 700 | 850 |
| Total | 5,900 | 4,800 | 4,050 |

| Missile Throw-weight | | | |
|---|---|---|---|
| ICBM | 9·5m lb | 7·6m lb | 5·4m lb |
| SLBM | 1·4m lb | 1·0m lb | 1·2m lb |
| Total | 10·9m lb | 8·6m lb | 6·6m lb |

| Bomber Payload | 0·8m lb | — | — |
|---|---|---|---|

a Includes for US: *Titan* II; for USSR: SS-18.

b Includes for US: *Minuteman* II and MIRVed *Minuteman* III; for USSR: SS-11 and SS-13 and MIRVed SS-17 and SS-19.

c Includes for US: *Polaris* A3 and MIRVed *Poseidon* and *Trident* I (not yet deployed); for USSR: SS-N-6 and SS-N-8 and MIRVed SS-N-18 (not yet deployed).

d Includes for US: B-52G/H/F/D and FB-111A; for USSR: Tu-95.

e These are rough approximations, based on weapons characteristics detailed in Table 1 of *The Military Balance 1977–1978* (London: IISS, 1977). For a survey of the strategic significance of the measures depicted here, see the article 'Measuring the Strategic Balance', *The Military Balance 1976–1977* (London: IISS, 1976), pp. 106–108.

f Assumes 3-RV warhead for Soviet MIRV SLBM.

g Assumes gravity weapon deployment only. US total thus does not take into account SRAM or potential ALCM deployment.

differences between the two forces in such measures as missile throw-weight and deliverable warheads. Yet under an aggregate reductions scheme these differences would be far greater. For a start, it is highly likely that the force structures of the two sides would diverge more sharply under a ceiling of 1,800 than under the levels permitted by Vladivostok. As the table implies, if forced to make a choice between land- or sea-based systems, the United States would opt for the latter while the Soviet Union would prefer to concentrate her power in ICBM.

The results of such choices would be the emergence of increasingly large disparities in American and Soviet capabilities: column B shows that, while American SLBM and bomber forces would outmatch their Soviet counterparts in almost every measure, the imbalance in Soviet and American ICBM capabilities would become even more marked. (The ratio of Soviet superiority in ICBM throw-weight, for example, would grow from four-to-one to eight-to-one, while American advantages in bomber pay-load would increase even more.) Superficially, there appears to be nothing wrong with such a development, for the freedom-to-mix approach is specifically designed to permit both sides to respond to their own preferences for deployment. Whether either side is prepared to permit the emergence of asymmetries on this scale is, however, questionable. If under a scheme for aggregate reductions Soviet–American forces do diverge further, then greater attention in both countries will inevitably be focused on the disparities that characterize the balance: measuring super-power strategic capabilities at SALT will increasingly become a process of 'comparing apples and oranges'.

However, a more important question than whether the emergence of disparities of this size would be politically acceptable is whether these asymmetries would affect the stability of the strategic balance. While governments and external observers may attach symbolic importance to growing disparities in static measures such as warhead numbers of missile throw-weight, the strategic significance of such disparities depends on whether they could offer any important military advantages to one side or the other. The most significant asymmetry that is likely to emerge from a 25 per cent aggregate reduction in American and Soviet strategic forces would lie in the area of American and Soviet ICBM capabilities. Under the reductions regime outlined in column B, the Soviet Union would possess some 1,100 ICBM equipped with some 6,500 high-yield warheads. Under the right conditions, a relatively small fraction of this force (some 200

SS-18 with 1,200–1,600 megaton-range warheads) might easily destroy over 90 per cent of an American land-based missile force that consisted only of 550 *Minuteman*.

It is not the purpose of this essay to determine how serious a problem *Minuteman* vulnerability would be. It is sufficient to note, however, that there are many who believe that *Minuteman* vulnerability would weaken the American deterrent and confer upon the Soviet Union some important advantages in fighting a nuclear war. This being the case, the United States might be led inevitably under an aggregate reductions regime to place even greater emphasis on the sea-based and bomber elements of her forces and to phase out the *Minuteman* force altogether. In the short term this would solve the ICBM vulnerability problem, but in the longer term it would pose a host of other political and technical difficulties, not the least being that American and Soviet capabilities would tend to diverge even further. The questions posed by moving towards a strategic 'diad' of aircraft (or air-launched missiles) and SLBM are numerous and cannot be adequately addressed here.[8] One point is clear. An outcome in arms control, such as the reductions proposal outlined above, that increased incentives for adopting a diadic posture should not be an unintended consequence of SALT: a full debate on the strategic costs and benefits of such a move should be undertaken before decisions are taken in negotiations.

An agreement on mutual reductions, however, need not produce large asymmetries: additional deployment constraints can be introduced to ensure that static or operational capabilities do not grow too large. Thus, as the Carter Administration's comprehensive proposal envisaged, sub-ceilings can be applied to certain classes of weapons, such as heavy missiles, and limits on testing and the introduction of new systems can be introduced so that potential imbalances stemming from force modernization are minimized.

The impact of sub-ceilings on disparities in the balance are shown in column C of Table 1. With Soviet heavy ICBM reduced by half and ICBM with MIRV limited to 550, Soviet ICBM throw-weight

and warhead advantages are significantly reduced. The impact of sub-ceilings is further enhanced by restrictions on testing and the introduction of new systems: together, limitations on modernization and launcher sub-ceilings would go a long way to relieve American anxieties about both perceptions of the balance and ICBM survivability. There can be little doubt, therefore, that, compared to the aggregate reduction approach, 'comprehensive' reductions are more desirable. This is especially true if sub-limits and modernization constraints placed on specific categories of weapons are designed, as seems to be the case with the Vance proposals, to rule out the possibility that either side could achieve the ability to threaten significant numbers of the other's forces.

The joker, of course, is that, as theoretically attractive as they are, such arrangements are unlikely to be negotiable. In moving away from the freedom-to-mix principle, reductions with sub-ceilings force one side or the other to make unequal sacrifices. The Carter Administration's comprehensive proposal, for instance, called for an 18–25 per cent reduction in the Vladivostok ceiling for total launcher numbers, but required the Soviet Union to reduce heavy missile deployment by 50 per cent. By placing a sub-limit of 550 on ICBM equipped with MIRV and linking this with a low ceiling (six) on annual missile test launches, the proposal also required the Soviet Union to make disproportionate sacrifices in ICBM modernization, not only in terms of the numbers she might seek to deploy but also in her ability to carry out tests in order to achieve accuracies comparable with American forces. Thus, as was suggested above, it was probably not the general idea of reductions to which the Soviet Union objected in turning down the Administration's reductions proposal, but the additional constraints on Soviet options that the proposal envisaged. A proposal that from the American point of view had the virtue of solving, or at least mitigating, the problem of missile vulnerability was regarded from the Soviet perspective as demanding unequal concessions in the one area of strategic capability where she enjoys a measure of superiority. This tension – between how desirable and how negotiable are proposals for reductions at SALT – constitutes the most important problem connected with the idea of deep cuts: without

[8] For a discussion of the various advantages of a triadic over a diadic strategic posture, see Colin Gray, *The Future of Land-Based Missile Forces*, Adelphi Paper No. 140 (London: IISS, 1978).

launcher sub-limits and modernization constraints, reductions proposals will only widen existing gaps between American and Soviet capabilities and hasten the onset of American land-based missile vulnerability. With these constraints, however, it is difficult to see how any proposal for reductions can meet with Soviet approval.

## Reductions and Peripheral Weapons

Mutual reductions not only threaten to widen asymmetries within the Soviet–American strategic balance, but also those that exist outside it. In addition to ICBM, SLBM and long-range bombers, both super-powers deploy hundreds of systems capable of delivering nuclear weapons on each other's homelands that have not been limited by SALT. The United States, for example, deploys some 400–500 nuclear-capable strike aircraft in Europe or aboard carriers in the Atlantic or the Mediterranean that might be used to deliver strategic strikes against the Soviet Union. For her part, the Soviet Union deploys several hundred medium-range bombers and 300-mile-range cruise missiles (aboard surface ships and submarines) that, under certain circumstances, could be targeted against the United States. Although these systems have not been limited by SALT, they have not escaped the attention of negotiators altogether. The Soviet Union, in particular, has voiced concern about the American nuclear-capable aircraft in Europe, and while she agreed to leave these FBS out of the 1972 Interim Agreement and the 1974 Vladivostok accord, she insists that these systems will sooner or later have to be introduced into negotiations at SALT. The United States, however, is not prepared to let this happen: few, if any, of these aircraft are actually assigned strategic roles (that is, missions against the Soviet homeland) and, more important, their inclusion in the bilateral SALT negotiations would create strains with American allies in Europe.

At Vladivostok, the super-powers were able to finesse the sensitive political and definitional problems which peripheral weapons raised by agreeing on ceilings for 'central' systems (ICBM, SLBM and long-range bombers) that were sufficiently high to allow them essentially to ignore the impact of systems not covered by the accord. Yet disparities in peripheral forces would be of greater significance under a reductions regime.

This is particularly true at a time when the deployment of new weapons such as the American cruise missile and the Soviet *Backfire* bomber seem certain to increase the numbers and strategic significance of non-central systems. Since both systems possess characteristics that could enable them to carry out strategic missions, the incentives to include them in a new agreement are strong. Yet because both the cruise missile and the *Backfire* can clearly be used for other roles, the incentives for leaving them out are equally powerful. This is especially true for the cruise missile, which is likely to be exploited in a wide range of theatre roles, equipped with conventional as well as nuclear munitions.

Thus efforts to reduce central systems will only serve to give greater prominence to the cruise missile and *Backfire* at SALT. At a ceiling of 2,400 launchers the United States might be prepared to countenance the Soviet deployment of an additional 250–300 *Backfire*; at ceilings of 1,800 this becomes more difficult. Reductions to this level will make it even harder for the Soviet Union to leave cruise missiles out of an agreement. With the possible deployment by the West of large numbers of these weapons in the 1980s, even the Vladivostok ceiling would probably be too low for Soviet tastes.

## Reductions and Alliance Cohesion

There are, in theory, a number of ways in which reductions in American strategic forces could disrupt Western alliance relations. An American decision to cut back unilaterally on strategic forces, for example, would lead some Europeans to conclude that the United States was moving towards a minimum deterrent posture that ruled out the use of nuclear weapons for the defence of Europe. Mutual cuts in American and Soviet forces could also increase this concern if the resulting forces reduced the capacity of the United States to react to theatre contingencies. The elaboration of an American nuclear targeting strategy of 'selective options' has bound American strategic systems more closely with the defence of the European theatre, and portions of the *Poseidon* SLBM force have been assigned roles in NATO nuclear strike plans. Thus, American reductions could have a direct impact on Alliance capabilities. However, the military significance of this impact should not be overestimated: the United States is unlikely to undertake large-scale unilateral reductions in strategic forces, and mutual reductions to a level of 1,800 launchers or so would not deprive American forces of any important war-fighting capabilities, in or beyond the European theatre.

This does not mean, however, that reductions to this level will not affect the cohesion of the Alliance. As the cruise-missile problem suggests, it is becoming more difficult to dissociate the Soviet–American strategic relationship from the East–West theatre balance in Europe. To the extent, therefore, that reductions schemes place a new urgency on controlling developments such as cruise missiles at SALT, negotiations between the super-powers will increase anxieties among West European allies. Since forward-based American aircraft (or, in the future, cruise missiles) are assigned an integral role in deterring and defending Western Europe, Europeans have a strong and continuing interest in keeping these systems outside the bilateral SALT framework. Yet it would be difficult, if not impossible, for a reductions agreement not to limit existing or future FBS in some manner, for, as we have seen, a reductions proposal that did not come to grips with these weapons would have little appeal.[9] However, if the United States agreed to include forward-based aircraft or cruise missiles in a reductions arrangement, it would be equally difficult for many Europeans to resist the conclusion that the United States was prepared to sacrifice Alliance interests in order to establish a more stable strategic relationship with the Soviet Union.

This would be particularly true if the agreement in question did little to limit the growth of Soviet medium-range missiles and bombers. At present, the existence of some 600 Soviet IRBM and some 500 medium-range bombers targeted against Western Europe does not constitute an important intra-Alliance irritant. Like American forward-based systems, however, these weapons could be of greater significance were the super-powers to agree to reduce their inter-continental-range forces. However, since Soviet IRBM do not threaten the American homeland, they are unlikely to be limited under a reductions agreement. With Soviet deployment of a new IRBM – the SS-20, fitted with MIRV – this is an anomaly of the existing arms-control framework that will not escape notice in Western Europe. How would NATO governments react to an agreement that reduced American inter-continental-range forces to levels below 2,000 but left the Soviet Union free to deploy 1,000 or more new medium-range missiles and bombers?

**Reductions and Costs**

The argument that large reductions in strategic forces would yield significant savings rests on the assumption that deep cuts would reduce the operating costs for existing systems and the procurement costs for new systems. This may not be the case. While a reduction in launchers of 500–600 would result in a saving of *direct* operating costs, this would have minimal impact on spending for *indirect* support (command and control, communications, training and infrastructure). These activities are relatively insensitive to force size and only dramatic launcher reductions of 50 per cent or more would be likely to yield significant savings. Since indirect operating costs make up roughly half the strategic forces budget, this suggests that a 25 per cent cut in launcher numbers would only result in a cut in costs of approximately 12–13 per cent.

It is even more doubtful whether reductions would result in lower spending on force modernization; they could in fact reinforce pressures for new weapons development and deployment. With high ceilings on forces, military planners might be prepared to make do with existing systems, but as ceilings are lowered, the qualitative advantages of, for example, *Trident* over *Poseidon* or of the MX ICBM over *Minuteman* will assume a new importance. (Indeed, before the Carter Administration's decision to cancel the B-1 bomber programme, the inclusion of long-range bombers in SALT probably strengthened the case for deploying a follow-on aircraft.) If, moreover, reductions result in growing asymmetries in Soviet–American capabilities, the pressure to modernize existing systems will be even more difficult to resist. This is especially true for American land-based missiles: as doubts about *Minuteman* survivability grow, so does the case for deploying a land-mobile ICBM.

[9] In SALT discussions held at Geneva on a new 'framework' for agreement, the Soviet Union is reported to have linked the reduction of central systems with the inclusion of FBS in a new accord. See *Herald Tribune*, 14 June 1977. Zbigniew Brzezinski, in an earlier statement, made a similar point in tying controls on *Backfire* deployment to a reductions regime. (See note 7.)

### Reductions and Nuclear Proliferation

The argument that a reductions agreement at SALT would strengthen constraints against the further spread of nuclear weapons may also rest on some dubious assumptions. The very size of the super-powers' forces serves to weaken incentives for potential adversaries to acquire nuclear weapons. The idea that China, France, Britain or some new nuclear state might seriously compete with either of the super-powers is hardly credible at present. Given the size of medium-level nuclear arsenals, a 25 per cent reduction in super-power launcher numbers would not affect this situation materially, but it is conceivable that cuts on this scale might bolster arguments in these countries for maintaining, if not expanding, their present capabilities. Moreover, reduction agreements that limited American European-based systems (aircraft or cruise missiles) might also generate renewed Western European interest in independent deterrent capabilities.

While Soviet–American reductions might spur *vertical* proliferation on the part of medium nuclear powers, they would still be attractive if they contributed to the halting of further *horizontal* proliferation. This seems highly unlikely, however. To begin with, a 25 per cent reduction in super-power strategic forces would not necessarily dampen the criticism made by the non-nuclear states of Soviet–American arms competition. If, as is probably the case, reductions stimulated super-power force modernization, non-nuclear critics could legitimately claim that the arms race had not been slowed down, but only channelled into new directions. More important, the premise that would-be nuclear states are likely to base their behaviour on the model provided by the super-powers is highly questionable. Whether South Korea, Iran, Brazil or Pakistan decide to acquire nuclear weapons over the coming decade will depend primarily on regional security considerations, not on what the super-powers do or do not do at SALT.

### Conclusion

Despite the fact that fashions in arms control are ephemeral, questioning popular concepts is never easy. The growing interest in mutual reductions at SALT is understandable. To date, the SALT process, while placing ceilings on strategic forces, does not seem to have affected seriously the weapons programmes of either super-power and, in some cases, it has even served to increase spending and accelerate the acquisition of new weapons. Yet, as this essay has attempted to demonstrate, reductions in themselves offer few important gains. As we have seen, the most attractive reduction schemes are those, like the Carter Administration's proposals of March 1977, that linked cuts in aggregate forces with sub-ceilings and modernization constraints in an effort to rectify specific imbalances within the overall Soviet–American balance. However, these imbalances reflect deeper asymmetries in the Soviet–American strategic relationship – in technology, geography and doctrine. Efforts to redress these asymmetries at SALT are thus likely to be non-negotiable.

Aggregate reductions schemes, on the other hand, while more negotiable, are hardly desirable. At best, reductions in aggregate forces would be irrelevant to the new array of problems that now confront the super-powers at SALT; at worst, they could exacerbate them. As we have seen, reductions could speed up American land-based missile vulnerability, heighten the problem of dealing with peripheral systems at SALT, unsettle American relations with allies, and have little impact on spending or the spread of nuclear weapons.

It is important, therefore, to see the issue of reductions in the light of what SALT can reasonably be expected to accomplish. While the existing inventories of the two sides are not the product of any strictly rational process of setting requirements, the ability of the two sides to negotiate at SALT is largely based on their possession of large and redundant weapons inventories. Large reductions, by creating concern about the survivability of forces or by generating tensions within the Alliance, could, in turn, cause governments to question the stability of the strategic balance and the efficacy of deterrence. Thus the argument that SALT is a charade used by the two super-powers to codify the arms race betrays a fundamental misunderstanding of what the talks are meant to accomplish. The objectives of arms control, of course, are not synonymous with those of disarmament: with regard to arms control, reductions cannot be viewed as an end in themselves, but must be judged in terms of their impact on the character of the strategic relationship. As was noted above (p. 4), during the 1960s the goal of strategic stability was thought to require more forces, not less.[10] It is difficult, at present, to envisage either side needing to increase its forces above existing levels; but because of the problems that would be likely to occur under reductions it is equally hard to see how arms-control objectives would be served by attempting to reconstitute the balance at lower numbers.

Yet the tension between arms control and disarmament must also be placed in a wider political context. While reductions might generate greater asymmetries in the military balance or disturb Alliance understandings, they could also impart a new momentum to Soviet–American relations which might, in the short term at least, diminish the political importance attached to these problems. Ultimately, however, the future of SALT, as well as the wider phenomenon of Soviet–American detente, will require both sides to come to grips with such issues as missile vulnerability or cruise-missile deployment. This is because SALT depends for its success on the very political trust that it is supposed to generate.

Thus, whatever momentary political boost a reductions agreement might give to relations between the super-powers, the strategic problems that might arise under a reductions regime should be taken seriously. At the same time, it is vital to recognize that mutual reductions would not be the *cause* of the problems discussed here, they would only aggravate difficulties that already exist. Undoubtedly, reductions agreements could create new headaches for the super-powers. But, with or without reductions, new problems presented by force modernization and the deployment of new technologies will certainly test governments. In some cases this may necessitate some fairly radical changes in approaches to arms control. The problem posed by peripheral weapons such as the cruise missile or the SS-20, for example, may require alterations to be made to the existing framework of East–West arms control; if SALT is to encompass a wider range of weapons to be effective, it may have to evolve towards a multilateral forum with direct ties to the negotiations on force reductions in Vienna. The possibilities clearly need to be examined. The weakness of the reductions approach to SALT is that it is not daring enough. In engaging the energies of analysts and policy-makers, the reductions concept could prove to be a distraction from some more pressing items on the arms-control agenda.

A note of caution seems appropriate. Even if a reorganized SALT process were able to surmount some problems, others would still remain. These are problems that cannot be solved through mutual agreement and which therefore must be resolved unilaterally. Land-based missile vulnerability seems to be such a problem. Policy-makers worry about ICBM vulnerability because it runs counter to the deeply-ingrained Western conception of what constitutes strategic stability. But stability is in the eye of the beholder, and Soviet doctrinal preferences differ markedly. There are dangers, therefore, in asking more from formal negotiations than they can be expected to accomplish. First, this fosters the belief that strategic problems can only be solved through mutual agreement. In fact, because the super-powers are often unable to agree on what is a problem, attempts to use reduction agreements at SALT to solve such differently perceived problems as ICBM vulnerability may, in the long run, do more harm than good. SALT is probably most useful as an instrument for formalizing the existence of rough parity between the super-powers, a task that is most easily performed when both sides possess large strategic inventories. Arms-control proposals that depend on the mutual acceptance of idiosyncratic concepts of strategic stability stand little chance of success.

A second danger is that the tendency to expect too much from SALT creates expectations that cannot easily or safely be satisfied. The wide-spread public cynicism that greeted President Ford's claim in 1974 that the Vladivostok understanding had 'capped' the arms race has led the new Administration to outline a far more ambitious set of objectives for arms control. In the short term, emphasizing the importance of reductions at SALT may be a necessary means of creating a strong domestic arms-control constituency. In the longer term, however, this tactic could rebound. Objectives that are unrealistic or irrelevant will only reinforce the frustration of many at having to live in a nuclear world.

---

[10] This view has not entirely withered away. Paul Nitze, for example, has suggested that one theoretical solution to the problem of land-based missile vulnerability would be for both sides to scrap missiles with MIRV and deploy some 5,000 single-warhead ICBM.

# Verifying SALT in the 1980s

ROBERT PERRY

Only two kinds of arms-control agreement do not include verification provisions. In the one, the signatories trust one another sufficiently. In the other, violations will either be so obvious or their consequences so unimportant that verification becomes needless.

Neither of these observations applies to the several Soviet–American arms-limitations agreements generally treated as SALT I – the 1972 ABM Treaty and Interim agreement on Strategic Arms, and the Vladivostok protocols of 1974. The two sides do not trust one another, and at least one, the United States, hold that violations, whether obvious or not, can be of vital importance. Thus, from the American point of view, verification is 'the critical element of arms control'.[1]

Verification clearly was an important consideration in the early negotiations for a SALT agreement. In the future, the chief difficulties could lie in the prospect that weapons limitations imposed by SALT agreements may not be as readily verifiable as those of the early 1970s. If that is indeed the case, and verification nevertheless remains as critical to the American view of arms control as in the past, this will be more than a technical problem: it will be a major political problem for the future of strategic arms control.

## The Background

The arms-control agreements of 1972 were the products of negotiating initiatives of the early 1960s which acquired form and substance in the late 1960s and were formalized nearly a decade after the weapons they had originally addressed had been developed and (to some extent)

deployed. The means of verification were of similar vintage. Thus the verification measures agreed upon in 1972 were those deemed adequate, largely on the basis of experience in the late 1960s, to confirm mutual compliance with agreements limiting the numbers and quality of strategic weapons from the mid-1960s period.

Well before SALT, verification issues had been tentatively addressed. In the course of the 1958 Geneva conference of Western and Soviet bloc representatives, concerning the reduction of force levels in Europe, the Soviet Union proposed a warning system involving aerial reconnaissance plus observation posts along the East–West border. It was then that 'the technical possibilities of photographic and radar reconnaissance by orbiting space satellites were first explored'.[2] The phrase 'existing means of detection' entered discussions of a ban on atmospheric nuclear tests in 1961 and became 'national technical means' (NTM) in the Limited Test Ban Treaty of 1963. The qualification 'technical', which could mean so little or so much, was of Soviet origin.

In all Soviet–American discussions about arms limitations from 1946 to 1970, the United States had insisted that verification provisions must include some form of on-site inspection, while the Soviet Union usually, but not invariably, responded that any inspection in advance of general and complete disarmament was neither more nor less than an excuse for espionage and thus unacceptable. That impasse extended right through discussions of nuclear test bans, troop

---

[1] *Verification: The Critical Element of Arms Control*, (Washington DC: ACDA) No. 85, March 1976.

[2] *op cit.*, p. 12. But note also that as late as 1960 Soviet spokesmen were proclaiming that 'efforts . . . to employ artificial satellites for the collection of intelligence data are unlawful'. See G. Zhukov, 'Space Espionage Plans and International Law', *International Affairs* (Moscow), 1960, No. 10. pp. 53–58.

124

reductions in Europe, and the prohibition of weapons in space (although, it later became apparent, the Soviet Union had no philosophical objection to on-site inspections of *other* states' national territories).

As early as 1965, some members of the American arms-control community concluded (and argued) that treaty limitations on the numbers and kinds of Soviet and American missile launchers could be adequately verified without on-site inspection. In October 1967, Assistant Secretary of Defense Paul Warnke publicly suggested that the United States could avoid the issue of on-site inspection by agreeing to rely on 'our own unilateral capability' for verifying Soviet compliance, and after July 1968 the United States was unofficially prepared to accept arms-control agreements on that basis.[3] Nevertheless, until 1970 it remained official American policy to press for on-site inspection privileges. In the same year, the Soviet Union rejected any further consideration of the option,[4] came out in favour of verification by national technical means but made it plain that she intended to differentiate between permissible 'national means' and 'espionage'.[5] The American delegation did not inquire too closely into the fine implications of the Soviet position. The ABM Treaty and the 1972 Interim Agreement on offensive strategic weapons specified that 'assurance of compliance with the provisions of this Treaty' would be provided by each party's use of 'national technical means

of verification . . . in a manner consistent with generally recognized principles of international law'. A second clause prohibited interference with NTM '. . . operating in accordance with Paragraph 1 of this Article', and a third outlawed 'deliberate concealment measures which impede verification'—except for 'current construction, assembly, conversion, or overhaul practices' which have concealment effects.[6]

Those terms implicitly expressed both American assumptions about the adequacy of NTM for the purposes specified in the agreements and Soviet understanding of what constituted 'acceptable' compliance. Both have presumably changed since 1972, as suggested by American charges that the Soviet Union has taken unfair advantage of the execution clause on construction practices, and by other American allegations of Soviet evasions.[7] Over the past five years, American negotiators have come to appreciate the literal way in which the Soviet Union interprets the terms of the agreements and the associated protocols and interpretations. As Secretary of Defense James R. Schlesinger said in 1975, in response to Senator Henry Jackson's question on whether Soviet ICBM changes represented a 'clear violation' of the Vladivostok understanding: 'the point is, we can say there is violation of our interpretation of our unilateral statement, but I am not sure what binding force that has on the Soviets'.[8]

Of course, such differences of interpretation affect differences of view on the need for adequate verification. John Newhouse has expressed it well:[9]

The Americans can neither propose nor accept anything that cannot be verified with reasonably high confidence. The problem is less severe for the Russians. Their detection

---

[3] John Newhouse, *Cold Dawn: The Story of SALT* (New York: Holt, Reinhart, and Winston, 1973), p. 99.
[4] A carefully limited on-site inspection privilege was admitted into the Peaceful Nuclear Explosions agreement of May 1976.
[5] Robert Perry, 'Breakout Warning: A Problem of Verification', unpublished (Santa Monica, Ca.: Rand, February 1977). [No formal treaty language defining the distinction ever emerged. What did appear was an informal Soviet representation that the U-2 overflight programme was an example of espionage, although it was never established whether the Soviet Union objected to the means (overflight in the atmosphere) or the specific details of the U-2 operations. The deliberately ambiguous wording of the verification clauses in the 1977 SALT I documents resolved none of these uncertainties. It seemed possible that the Soviet Union considered the 'national technical means' available to the United States in 1970–72 inferior in one respect or another to 1960-vintage U-2 capabilities and therefore permissible; on unilateral redefinition of 'permissible' NTM the Soviet Union might at some future time allege that certain of them were espionage devices not protected by the agreement.]

[6] *Arms Control and Disarmament Agreements: Texts and Histories of Negotiations* (Washington DC: ACDA, 1975) pp. 135, 140. Except in substituting 'interim agreement' for 'Treaty', Article V of the Agreement was identical to Article XII of the Treaty.
[7] The literature on the 'evasion' furore of early 1975 is voluminous, but the heart of the controversy is summarized in 'Soviet Compliance with Certain Provisions of the 1972 SALT Agreements', *Hearing before the Sub-Committee on Arms Control of the Committee on Armed Services*, US Senate, 94th Congress, First Session, March 6, 1975.
[8] *Ibid.*
[9] Newhouse, *op. cit.* in note 3, p. 14.

systems, like America's, are constantly improving and may have achieved comparable performance. Their advantage is that of a closed society competing against an open society. It is a major advantage. Their aversion to on-site inspection is doubtless genuine, but apart from a passion for secrecy, their position owes something to the small benefits they would obtain from having direct access to what the United States does, not much of which is concealed.

To what extent, therefore, did the United States in 1972 assume that the 'national technical means' authorized in the SALT agreements would provide credible verification of Soviet compliance? The answer can be given in three assumptions.

(1) American NTM can provide conclusive evidence of non-compliance with the terms of the agreements.
(2) No expansion of Soviet strategic capabilities could be concealed long enough, or well enough, to support the development of a serious Soviet threat to the established strategic balance.
(3) So long as the Soviet Union supports those assumptions, no serious effort to evade the terms of the arms-limitations agreements will occur.

The third of those assumptions is self-fulfilling so long as the first two remain valid. However, the first two reflect premises – first about American NTM capabilities, second regarding Soviet deception talents, and third about the stability of weapons technology – which, if even modestly discredited, could bring down the entire structure of the arms-control agreements.[10] Finally, only weapons and activities explicitly defined by the agreements and the jointly accepted protocols are controlled, and (as Secretary Schlesinger's observations make plain) in the future both parties are likely to pay greater attention to the fine details of phrasing.[11]

Neither the Soviet Union nor the United States has officially revealed what qualities lie behind that interesting term 'national technical means'.[12] Nor have unofficial appraisals been much more helpful. That is of little importance if one proceeds from the assumption that whatever the capabilities, they are, or were, sufficient to satisfy the perceived needs of the United States yet not so marvellous that the Soviet Union felt the fine line between verification and espionage had been critically broken. However, continuing discussions and the recent American furore over alleged Soviet violations also suggest that existing capabilities may not be able sufficiently to assure the United States authorities of Soviet compliance with future arms-limitation agreements extending to newer, more readily concealable weapons.

The capabilities of NTM are inseparable from their vulnerabilities, and perception of capability – or vulnerability – may be as important as the reality. It is the Soviet perception of American NTM capabilities weighed against assumed Soviet capabilities to deceive or degrade NTM performance that will be taken into account if an evasion effort is contemplated. If the rewards of successful tampering seem great, the probability of being caught slight, and the prospective penalty small, evasion becomes increasingly attractive.

From an American viewpoint, it is essential to obtain early and unambiguous warning that an evasion effort is underway. Ambiguity is the problem. Protracted, small-scale, low-profile

---

[10] Another little-considered problem is that the United States must be prepared to *disclose* knowledge of Soviet violations if the desired effect is to bring them to a halt. Source sensitivity is a non-negligible problem. ACDA has openly posed the question of whether the value of revealing evidence of a violation, or even the fact that the evidence exists, is worth the cost of compromising the intelligence techniques that must be disclosed if knowledge of the violation is publicized. (*Op. cit.* in note 1, pp. 29–30.)

[11] Fred C. Ikle, Director of the ACDA, in 'Arms Control in an Election Year', Speech, 26 April 1976 (reprinted in *Survival*, July/August 1976), effectively specifies that the United States will not accept ambiguities and unilateral statements in future agreements.
[12] There have, of course, been numerous public or semi-private but informal comments made by various spokesmen on both sides. The first, apparently, was Khrushchev's suggestion to the Belgian Foreign Minister, Paul-Henri Spaak, in July 1963 that satellite observation should be used instead of on-site inspection to verify a nuclear test ban. See W.H. Schauer, *The Politics of Space* (New York: Holmes and Mier, 1976), pp. 42–43, 254, citing C.H. Sheldon II, 'The Challenge of International Competition', 6 November 1964 address to AIAA/NASA, printed in *International Co-operation and Organization for Outer Space*, Staff Report for Committee on Aeronautics and Space Science, US Senate, 89th Congress, 1st Session, Document No. 56.

indicators will be difficult to detect, identify and interpret; responses may not be sufficiently prompt, positive or effective. The political and economic constraints on a rapid arms build-up are substantial. Actual military operations, even on a small scale, will be very difficult to justify if a provocation is not clearly apparent.[13]. For such reasons, 'Assured Detection' is likely to be as fundamental to American concepts of strategic deterrence in the 1980s as was Assured Destruction in the 1960s.

Assured detection will actually become a precondition of future arms agreements once rapid, major shifts in the strategic balance become conceivable, either through the quick deployment of weapons that have not been adequately identified during their development, or through the rapid exploitation of some major breakthrough in the technology of strategic weapons. It is not the immediate detection of each new missile or silo that becomes important, nor even the accumulation of such hardware and equipment, but the uncertainty that may accompany the indicated development or deployment of some weapon with ill-defined strategic potential. Arms-limitations agreements remain effective so long as each side believes that there will be enough time for an effective response if the other attempts to violate the agreed limits. For the United States, assurance that such attempts can be detected early and unambiguously identified thus becomes essential, since any agreement which the Senate of the United States might conclude was only marginally verifiable is unlikely to be ratified, and American negotiators are unlikely to risk such rejection by agreeing to arms limitations that do not meet this requirement.[14]

'National technical means' are – by definition – vulnerable to measures that may *degrade* their assumed effectiveness, *interrupt* their functioning, or *prevent* their operation. Such limitations of capability can be extended by *active* or *passive* interference or any effective combination of the

two. Passive interference could take many forms. The concealment of weapons which do not require extensive site preparations is an obviously feasible and passive measure, as are concealment measures justified under the construction clause of SALT or which can masquerade as innocuous building activites. Some events may pass by without comment merely because they seem unremarkable: they have prosaic 'signatures'. A unilateral Soviet redefinition of what is a 'permissible' type of NTM, passive and legalistic in nature, could exclude some 'means' from whatever nominal protection is afforded by the curiously worded non-interference clauses of SALT. In the aftermath of the 1972 agreement, it became apparent that the phrasing of the agreements permitted some missile development and deployment activities which the United States apparently believed had been precluded effectively. This might suggest that in 1972 and 1974 the Soviet Union had a profound appreciation of the capabilities and limitations of NTM. Post-1974 changes in the dimensions of some Soviet ICBM sites, for example, seem to have been relatively slight, since the Soviet Union seems to have assumed that they would be noticed and reported. Many interesting clues to Soviet perceptions of the vulnerabilities and capabilities of American NTM may be buried in the fine wording of the agreements themselves.

With the exception of the final stages of most weapons-acquisition programmes (operational testing and training), few of the essentials of developing, producing and deploying a new strategic weapon are difficult to conceal. The fact that detection can only be postponed, and is assured later, is not necessarily always a substantial objection to attempting concealment. Given the considerable lead times and enormous costs of introducing new weapons, being found out after having largely developed and partly deployed some device might be as advantageous as a completely undetected deployment.

Together, the 'national technical means' permitted by the ABM Treaty and the Interim Agreement, and incorporated by assumption in the Vladivostok understanding, are generally capable of confirming national compliance with the terms of quantitative limits on specified weaponry and have at least some ability to detect qualitative changes. The continuing controversy about the capability of the *Backfire* bomber and

---

[13] The Cuban missile crisis of 1962 provides an instructive example of the effects of ambiguous indications on responses to a perceived but (at least temporarily) uncomfirmable challenge. Such ambiguity disrupts the decision-making processes in a democracy.

[14] It may be safely assumed that the President and key members of the Senate would be consulted in advance, but the prospect of rejection does not lessen merely because it can occur at an early 'informed' stage.

expressions of American disquiet about the ability of the Soviet Union to convert IRBM-class SS-20 mobile missiles quickly to an ICBM configuration indicate what may be seen as 'significant' in qualitative assessments. The ability of 'national technical means' to distinguish missiles with MIRV from similar single-warhead missiles, or to detect the replacement of single warheads with multiple-warheads, is probably non-existent.[15] Therefore, the effective capability of 'national technical means' must lie somewhere within those imprecisely limiting parameters.[16]

### Verification for SALT II and Beyond
*The March 1972 Proposals*
After 1972, the United States had to change her notions about the value of unilateral interpretations of negotiated arrangements. The American proposals for a new SALT treaty made by the Carter Administration in March 1977, and the reception accorded them by the Soviet Union, suggest that earlier assumptions about the acceptable scope and compass of a new strategic arms limitation treaty have changed. The American proposals are reported to have extended to: (1) reducing the number of strategic delivery vehicles from the 2,400 accepted at

---

[15] Thomas W. Wolfe, *The SALT Experience: Its Impact on US and Soviet Strategic Policy and Decisionmaking* (Santa Monica, Cal.: Rand, R-1686-PR, September 1975), p. 217, reports that the American agreement to accept the placement of MIRV warheads on 'some' SS-18s was based on a Soviet commitment to 'display certain specialized MIRV-handling equipment alongside those missile sites where MIRVed launchers were being installed – as an aid to verification by US reconnaissance satellites'. He cites various articles in the *New York Times*, *Washington Star* and *Aviation Week & Space Technology* in May and June 1975 as his sources.
[16] On the MIRV issue, see Herbert Scoville, Jr., testimony before the Senate Foreign Relations Committee, April 1970, quoted in Newhouse, *op. cit.* in note 3, p. 16; Colin S. Gray's article 'A Problem Guide to SALT II', *Survival*, September/October 1975, pp. 230–4, treats MIRV and similar uncertainties of verification in some detail; J.I. Coffey, *New Approaches to Arms Reduction in Europe*, Adelphi Paper No. 105 (London: IISS, 1974), addresses the broader issue of what kinds of weapons can be verified without recurrent on-site inspection; capabilities assumed by various unofficial estimates are represented by Newhouse, the SIPRI articles previously cited and others. Notably, few of those evaluations give much weight to the normal and natural obstacles of verification – bad weather, night, equipment failure, periodicity of coverage, and the transient nature of many potentially significant indicators. The potential and implications of deception have been little considered.

Vladivostok to perhaps 1,800; (2) reducing the number of permitted 'heavy' Soviet ICBM from 300 to about half that total; (3) reducing the ceiling on MIRV-equipped launchers from 1,320 to a reported 1,000; (4) imposing limitations on the development and deployment of improved strategic weapons, continuing the freeze on new silo construction, limiting flight tests (and presumably also operational training launches) to a small annual number for each type of ICBM, and banning the test and deployment of new ICBM; (5) banning land-mobile ICBM, limiting cruise missiles to a range of 2,500 kilometers, and obtaining from the Soviet Union 'a list of measures to assure that the *Backfire* would not be used as a strategic bomber'.[17]

In that set of limitations, what is verifiable? The aggregate numbers of strategic launchers, the numbers of 'heavy' Soviet ICBM, new silo construction, ICBM tests, and new ICBM developments can be confirmed through the 'national technical means' permitted by earlier protocols and treaties. The MIRV genie has been out of his bottle for five years, so whatever consequences are implied by the possibility of adding warheads without increasing throw-weight have presumably been taken into account earlier. The *Backfire* guarantees would seem to be nearly valueless in terms of verification; they are not obviously verifiable by NTM, in any event. A total ban on land-mobile ICBM, which the United States has consistently sought, may be credibly verifiable, although a numerical limitation is unlikely to be so. As for ICBM 'improvements', masked changes may be difficult to detect and interpret unless they extend to new construction (which would be separately banned). The range of a cruise missile

---

[17] *The Times* (Los Angeles), 24 March 1977, quoting Secretary of State Cyrus Vance. The American approach, which envisaged substantial reductions in numbers of weapons as well as restraints on quantitative improvements in delivery systems, was rejected by the Soviet Union. The Soviet position has publicly been that both sides were committed to an agreement along the lines of the Vladivostok accords of 1974. A compromise appeared to be emerging in the late summer of 1977, but some issues obviously had not been resolved (although public statements of disagreement became less numerous and less assertive). An extension of the existing agreement seemed to be the best that could be achieved in the near term (by October 1977, the expiration date of the 1972 agreement), with negotiations for a new agreement continuing into 1978. See *The Defense Monitor*, Washington DC, July 1977.

cannot be credibly determined by any feasible inspection, although a ban could conceivably be policed if the absence of obvious test and training activities were accepted as positive evidence of compliance.

There are, therefore, three kinds of limitations in that set: (1) controls which merely continue existing practices and extend earlier assumptions (mobile and fixed-site ICBM constraints and launcher counting); (2) nominal limitations with more political than military significance (MIRV and *Backfire* clauses); (3) unverifiables with potentially major implications for the strategic balance (cruise missile range limitations and ICBM 'improvements').

On the surface, at least, the *Backfire* assurances and limitation on cruise missile range would appear to have much in common: both put greater weight on trust than verifiability.[18] Although the role of the *Backfire* can be even less credibly verified than a cruise missile range limitation, it seems improbable that *Backfire* could become a major strategic threat to the United States in the short term. In theory, the United States could develop clandestinely a true inter-continental cruise missile from one with a 2,500-kilometre range limitation, but in fact that is a most remote possibility. The United States seems incapable of devising and carrying out large-scale development or deployment programmes without great public clamour.

From time to time several alternatives to 'national technical means' have been proposed for verifying compliance with arms agreements.[19] A prohibition on certain kinds of research and development has been suggested, but without recurrent close inspection it is fundamentally unverifiable. Size constraints, chiefly for ICBM, were discussed at Vladivostok (and earlier); for a time the United States apparently believed that, although the Soviet Union had not acceded, a unilateral American statement of what constituted 'acceptable' size growth in ICBM would be honoured. The Soviet Union ignored the American interpretation, however, and proceeded to carry out a missile-replacement programme that had presumably been ready for implementation at the time of the talks. Size is, to some extent, verifiable by 'national technical means'. This is apparent from public statements by American spokesmen about the dimensions of the new Soviet SS-18. Overall size, however, reveals little about vital measures of performance (MIRV capability, guidance accuracy, silo and missile hardness, command and control arrangements, reload potential, and so on). Indeed, without making critical assumptions about throw-weight trade-offs, it is not possible to extrapolate confidently from external dimensions to missile range or warhead size.

Calculations of maximum aircraft range have been worthless since the first demonstration of aerial refuelling in the 1940s. The credibility of estimates based on tanker numbers and performance has been doubtful for nearly two decades; readily obtainable conversion kits can quickly transform almost any large civil or military aircraft into a tanker. Counting tankers is not a promising approach to controlling strategic bomber capabilities.

Monitoring military budgets to verify arms-control agreements has been suggested since the Hague Peace Conference of 1899. The Soviet Union advanced more than 20 such proposals between 1948 and 1977, but in all instances means of verification were either unspecified or were so vague as to be unacceptable to the West. The objection to budget-monitoring has been most aptly expressed by Sir Donald Maitland; in November 1973 he asked the United Nations, 'Who will take us seriously if our suggested starting point is arbitrary and unverifiable deductions from an unknown quantity?'[20]

Scepticism about the motives of the Soviet Union in repeatedly urging budget cutting as a disarmament device arises mainly because Soviet military expenditures have never been publicly detailed and from widespread conviction that the announced totals exclude substantial concealed outlays elsewhere in the Soviet budget.

---

[18] To made *Backfire* a strategic bomber, tanker support and adequate training would be essential. It would still be a comparatively minor threat to the US. Extending the range of a cruise missile requires only a small addition to fuselage length for fuel tankage; see *Aviation Week & Space Technology*, 21 March 1977 for a brief description of how to go about converting a 650-mile missile into one with a 1,300 nautical-mile range.

[19] In what follows, there is no consideration of 'verification' based on conventional espionage or defector-provided information. Credibility – the problem of ambiguity – is the source of difficulty.

[20] Quoted in A. S. Becker, *Soviet Proposals for International Reduction of Military Budgets* (Santa Monica, Cal.: Rand, March 1977), P-5837.

Indeed, although one Soviet proposal of 1955 on budget limitations provided for a control commission with 'unimpeded access' to budgetary records, that access depended on the prior acceptance of general and complete disarmament by all major nations.

The likelihood that limitations on or reductions in the size of a national military budget may become an important element of arms control is proportional to the willingness of the Soviet Union to make detailed budgeting information accessible to international inspectors. Although such an arrangement would, in effect, disclose less about the nature of military hardware than most other verifiable arms-control measures, it would also violate fundamental problems of traditional Soviet behaviour. Without a major change in the traditional Soviet refusal to release any military information, no proposal to limit military expenditures can receive serious consideration in the West.[21]

A prohibition on missile R&D testing or operational testing, or stringent limitations on their frequency and scope, have interesting implications for arms control. ICBM test controls were part of the package presented by the US Secretary of State and rejected by the Soviet Union in March 1977. They are obviously verifiable, at least for the existing type of ballistic missile, although accuracy, range, throw-weight, and MIRV capability will not necessarily be disclosed in the course of an artfully conducted test programme. If adopted, such controls would complicate if not preclude the development and introduction of new ballistic missiles. However, the unqualified assertion that 'no nation would replace existing reliable missiles and consider initiating a nuclear war with a missile which had only partly been tested'[22] is at least a slight exaggeration and is contradicted by experience.[23] Testing a ballistic missile at full range may be desirable, particularly from the point of view of prospective operators,

but it is not essential to individual tests of key sub-systems nor to their successful integration; a two-stage MRBM can rather easily become a three-stage ICBM. It is conceivable that various atmospheric missiles, aircraft, submersibles, and 'exotic' devices with application to strategic warfare could be extensively tested without attracting attention. The Soviet Union has for centuries honoured the art of *maskirovka* – cover and deception. Although arranging a covert development that did not provide for full-scale testing would be difficult enough on technical grounds, the chief difficulty is likely to lie with the institutional predilections of the Soviet R&D bureaucracy. The *willingness* of the Soviet military to risk the operational use of a partly proven system may be insufficient, even if the risk seems slight.[24]

A prohibition on mobile ballistic missiles would be verifiable to the extent that any concealable missiles can be found, counted and evaluated. A mobile missile, however, is by nature composed of elements small enough to be transportable over ordinary road and rail networks; it is, therefore, far from certain that a carefully masked deployment would be noticed or, if indications were at all ambiguous, that effective counteraction could follow.

On-site inspection, much discussed in the days when there appeared to be no substantive alternative, last received serious consideration in 1968 during early Soviet–American discussions of a ban on MIRV. It may be doubted whether the United States would have accepted such controls in the end, since Soviet inspectors could then have moved from silo to silo, tipping up the nose cones on missile warheads and viewing the details of the interior fittings at close range. Random, unannounced and total access to all national installations will not be conceded lightly to one state by another, and inspection that requires notice to be given as a matter of routine may not uncover much that the inspected party is anxious to conceal.[25]

[21] A. S. Becker, *Soviet National Income 1958–1964* (Berkeley: University of California Press, 1969).
[22] Testimony of Herbert Scoville, former assistant ACDA director, quoted in Newhouse, *op. cit.* in note 3, p. 16.
[23] Both the United States and the Soviet Union have in the past deployed 'operational' missiles which had not been fully tested – and other, if less complex, systems. No doubt they would have been used had any of the Soviet–American crises of the early 1960s escalated to war.

[24] However, it may also be true that Soviet military officials are so accustomed to receiving imperfect operational test articles that their experience would totally condition them not to accept any such risk.
[25] Coffey, *loc. cit.*, does not entirely accept this argument, but most commentators have acknowledged the inherent shortcomings of a constrained on-site inspection process. An inspection of production facilities would provide considerable, though perhaps insufficient, assurance that

*Verification through Aircraft Reconnaissance*

A more promising approach, that of permitting reconnaissance aircraft to fly freely over the territory of an inspected nation, has been mostly ignored since the early 1960s. Doubts over its political acceptability weakens its prospects. Yet the Soviet Union was willing to entertain such a scheme in early discussions of tactical arms-control measures, and the 'Open Skies' approach first suggested to President Eisenhower in 1953 has some singular attractions for a world of MIRV, land-mobile ICBM, cruise missiles, and other strategic gadgetry of a nuclear age. It lacks some of the more intrusive aspects of on-site inspection, promises a prompt and direct view of a suspect activity, and can still be conducted without exposing the military hardware of the host country to the close scrutiny of an inspector.

Concealment of any major weapons activity would be difficult because reconnaissance aircraft need follow no set path, conform to no schedule, pass no check points, and are not necessarily inhibited from performing their assignments by night or bad weather. To secure acceptance of the notion and work out operating details would not be easy. However, as a verification method inherently less intrusive than most others involving inspection, and one which can be denied success only by elaborate measures of cover and camouflage, it would provide great assurance that almost any sort of limitation – on mobility, on new developments, on numbers of missiles or bombers or tankers, on ICBM size – would be verified with high credibility. Moreover, it would be comparatively cheap, which creates the possibility that many nations could participate actively in arms-control agreements without having to rely on the good will of one of the super-powers for verification assurance.

no major evasion of a weapons-limiting treaty was in progress if access to all suspect production sites were permitted, if the suspect article were so conspicuous that it could not be built in bits for later assembly in out-of-the-way installations, and if the inspectors were permitted to make surprise visits. Whether the United States, much less the Soviet Union, would consent to such inspection by unfriendly foreign nationals is very doubtful. A most comprehensive analysis of on-site inspection was available as early as 1961; see B. T. Feld, 'Inspection Techniques of Arms Control', in D. G. Brennan (ed.), *Arms Control, Disarmament, and National Security* (New York: Braziller, 1961), pp. 317–333. Little of substance has been added since then.

As envisaged here, reconnaisance aircraft would have to be incapable of performing offensive missions, of carrying strategic weapons, or of detracting from the defensive potential of the nation being reconnoitred. That could be accomplished rather easily either by specifying that only 'pure' reconnaisance aircraft could be used, or by permitting on-the-ground inspection of each aircraft at any time, for example. In fact, however, the possibility that one or a few reconnaissance-configured aircraft could deliver weapons payloads that would appreciably alter the strategic balance is so remote as to be of no real consequence. The main objection would surely be political – that such reconnaissance verges on espionage. It is probable that political spokesmen in both the United States and the Soviet Union would object on those grounds. Nevertheless, in the absence of less objectionable alternatives aerial reconnaissance remains an attractive option, and all other options have been deemed more objectionable.[26]

Such aerial reconnaissance would indeed produce information that could be exploited for tactical and strategic intelligence purposes, but so, presumably, can information derived from 'national technical means'. The difference is largely one of perception and acceptance: the perception that, without means of providing credible verification capabilities, there may be no agreements to limit some of the new weapons, and acceptance of the idea that if the price of adequate and acceptable verification capabilities proves to be mutual abandonment of some treasured elements of secrecy (not necessarily security), it may have to be paid. In view of increased American sensitivity to possible Soviet violations of a new and enlarged SALT agreement and the suspicion engendered by Soviet actions (which, if compliant to the letter of the agreements, plainly were contrary to their spirit as represented to Congress by the American arms negotiators),[27] it seems unlikely that uncertainties of verification acceptable to technical

[26] The literature on aerial reconnaissance, 'Open Skies', and related issues is vast. Probably the best brief overviews are A. H. Katz, *Some Notes on the History of Aerial Reconnaissance* (Santa Monica: RAND, April 1966) P-3310, and *Selected Readings in Aerial Reconnaissance* (Santa Monica: Rand, August 1963) P-2762. In the latter the short articles by Colonels R. S. Leghorn and R. W. Philbrick are of particular interest.

[27] See Gray, *op. cit.* in note 15 above.

experts and arms-control specialists will survive objections likely to be made by members of Congress.

## Conclusion

Soviet military doctrine incorporates a concept which the Soviet Union has sought: strategic superiority, or the possession of vastly superior forces coupled with an ability to strike first, thus limiting damage to the Soviet Union. Soviet leaders appear to be designing their forces not merely to survive and retaliate against any attack, but to exploit – for coercion, for deterrence or, if necessary, in war – any opportunity with which the acquisition of strategic superiority might present them.

Verification of Soviet compliance with the terms of a strategic arms-limitation agreement is, therefore, an obvious and necessary but not sufficient condition for American confidence that major asymmetries in the strategic balance will not occur.[28] The aim of the United States is to obtain credible assurance that the Soviet Union cannot clandestinely acquire destabilizing strategic capabilities. While there remains any substantial doubt about American capabilities to detect Soviet deceptions, the United States will balk at accepting unverifiable Soviet assurances. So long as the Soviet Union views all non-client states as potentially malevolent, she will resist verification processes that enlarge American knowledge of her strategic capabilities. That is the dilemma of arms control.

Three principal outcomes seem possible. One is to continue the present uneasy mutual accommodation, applying arms controls only to those older weapons which can be found and counted by 'national technical means'. Newer weapons, not accountable by those means, would probably proliferate. The worst outcome could be the breakdown of arms-control negotiations. That not only invokes the prospect of a large-scale arms build-up on both sides but could encourage the Soviet Union to seek immediate advantage by coercion and intimidation, risking nuclear war in order to prevent the development of an increasingly unfavourable situation. The best conceivable outcome might be an agreement that further reduced present levels of nuclear weapons

and effectively restrained the introduction of new systems – but that cannot occur unless there is concurrent agreement on verification measures that provide high assurance of compliance. Some form of close inspection may be the *sine qua non* for the United States, perhaps as a reinforcement of 'national technical means', perhaps as a replacement.

Whether the US Congress could be brought to accept a complete ban on the introduction of new delivery systems without insisting on greater credibility of verification is uncertain. The argument that as detente progresses greater uncertainties of verification can be tolerated[29] is attractive in the abstract, but it may be inconsistent with the realities of American politics and the inventiveness of military designers. 'National technical means' have been defined by the US government as invoking 'sophisticated methods of data collection which do not operate from installations in the territory of the parties being monitored . . .'[30] If what is wanted is a means of verification that provides greater assurance than do 'national technical means' and is less intrusive than traditional on-site inspection, earlier verification concepts must be fundamentally altered. 'National technical means' do not seem to provide the assured detection capabilities that the US Congress wants and that the Soviet Union so steadfastly opposes.

At least some senior Soviet officials are sure to be aware of the technological and institutional paradoxes that inhibit the Soviet Union in her competition with the United States for strategic advantage. Without a major overhaul of Soviet political and industrial institutions, which would discomfort Soviet leadership, no effective remedy can be applied. A reasonable, if less easily accepted, alternative for the Soviet Union would be to forgo an unpromising new arms race by making verification concessions to the United States in return for a mutual ban on the development of new weapons – particularly the cruise missile, but also the land-mobile ICBM. The *quid pro quo* from the United States is not inconsiderable: abandonment of the cruise missile, a weapon that promises, relatively inexpensively, to negate an increasingly threatening Soviet

[28] A. S. Becker, 'Strategic Breakout as a Soviet Policy Option', unpublished manuscript, 1977.

[29] Jan M. Lodal, 'Verifying SALT', *Foreign Policy*, No. 24, Fall 1976, pp. 40–64, summarizes that point of view.

[30] *Op. cit.* in note 1, p. 15.

counterforce potential.[31] That concession is certain to be tenaciously resisted by those who prefer to put their trust in assured weapons superiority rather than in verification methods that promise *but cannot absolutely guarantee* assured detection of Soviet treaty violations. Lesser concessions, on either side, must lead to partial and ineffective arms limitations policed by less-than-credible verification assurances.

[31] It is not obvious that the United States can restrain her allies from developing cruise missiles, which may further complicate the arms-control negotiations and even make multi-national rather than bi-national agreements – and verification – essential. But that is a topic for another paper and another time.

# The 'Grey Area' Problem

LOTHAR RUEHL

Negotiations and agreements on the limitation of specific kinds of arms such as 'strategic offensive systems' have deliberately been limited in scope in order not to run into too many obstacles. As a result, wide areas of armaments and forces have been left outside the framework of the two existing fora for East–West arms control: SALT and MBFR. 'Grey areas' stretch over the military map between the arms or forces dealt with in these negotiations; new weapons technologies and systems proliferate outside the hedged-in terms of reference for negotiations.

The 'grey area problem' is thus the result of incongruencies between technology and the formal categories of existing arms-control negotiations. The operational qualities of certain weapons systems cannot be brought under the agreed criteria chosen for the purposes of a particular negotiation, either functional or geographic. New technologies seem to move increasingly towards multi-purpose and multi-mission systems, hybrid arms which straddle the demarcation line between different categories of weapons either for strategic or arms-control purposes. Systems cover a wide spectrum of operational characteristics – range, warhead, launcher and platform. They may be armed with nuclear, conventional, chemical or 'radiological' warheads and offer a variety of 'strategic' and 'tactical' options. They may be deployed and used in various combinations, changed at will according to need.

Some recent arms developments can be cited as examples; by virtue of their versatility and flexibility in deployment and the ambiguity in their technical nature and operational mission, they cut across all formal categories. The pair of Soviet ballistic missiles, the SS-16/SS-20, present an inter-changeable combination of an ICBM and an IRBM, each with a mobile launcher-platform and a MIRV version; the non-ballistic aerodynamic cruise missiles; various kinds of RPV; attack aircraft with variable ranges and mission profiles, armed with cruise missiles with nuclear and/or conventional warheads; all of these are typical of the systems that produce the 'grey area problem'.

The term 'grey area' has been used only recently, but ambiguous weapon systems have existed for some time. Dual-purpose delivery vehicles for nuclear or conventional warheads have been deployed in Europe by NATO for twenty years. In the Soviet inventory, SRBM for 'tactical' use, such as *SCUD*, have been deployed in Eastern Europe with nuclear or chemical warheads, but these weapons are not so significant as the combination of new technologies, strategic deployments and arms-control negotiations such as SALT and MBFR.

## The Grey Area around SALT

In past and current negotiations between the United States and the Soviet Union on the limitation of strategic arms, the primarily *quantitative* method used so far has reduced the objective of agreements to largely *numerical* balances. Even when technical, and hence operational, *quality* has been considered (as with the MIRV PBV on ballistic missiles in SALT II), the qualitative factor has been broken down into its quantitative components without including in the numerical balance any of the complex operational factors such as accuracy, penetrability, targeting flexibility (re-targeting systems and re-loading techniques) – factors which have since acquired increasing weight.

134

Thus it was agreed in 1974 at Vladivostok to limit the numbers of missiles with MIRV without limiting the quality and therefore the operational capabilities of the MIRV systems themselves. The number of warheads and penetration aids within a MIRV-PBV remains unrestricted; improvements in on-board computers for trajectory correction, MARV and advanced terminal guidance technology were not constrained. Missile throw-weight, after much public discussion in America, was also excluded; the yields of warheads remain outside the SALT limits on strategic missiles and bombers. This follows the SALT tradition: in general, improvements in weapons performance have been left free from any constraints, apart from the 15 per cent limit on the enlargement of silos for fixed ICBM launchers and the limits placed on the modification and improvement of essential components of ABM systems, by the ABM Treaty of 1972.

Strategic attack aircraft and the stand-off air-to-ground missiles and bombs they may use were taken into account in the Vladivostok accord, but without precise definition. The definition of 'strategic' bombers and that of the missiles they may carry, has been left in doubt and disagreement since 1974. The Soviet–American dispute on air-launched aerodynamic cruise missiles stems from the ambiguity of the language used at Vladivostok ('air-launched missiles' on 'heavy bombers' without specification as to the character of the 'missiles' other than 'air-to-ground', and without saying whether 'ballistic' or 'aerodynamic' or any other conceivable kind of missile was meant). As a result, the appearance of the new American air-launched and sea-launched long-range cruise missile of high accuracy (and capable of carrying both nuclear and conventional warheads) during the course of 1975 became the major impediment to a new agreement.

These long-range non-ballistic missiles compound the problem of defining and limiting 'strategic' weapon systems by agreement. They re-open the old SALT dispute between Washington and Moscow over 'forward based' or 'non-central' systems, capable of reaching Soviet territory from certain geographical bases (FBS). In the 1972 Interim Agreement on strategic offensive missiles (ICBM and SLBM, including the nuclear submarines carrying SLBM), the definition of 'strategic' arms, as in the ABM Treaty of 1972,

is rudimentary: the one objective criterion is the shortest geographical distance between the north-eastern border of the United States and the north-western border of the Soviet Union, giving an aerial route of 5,500km. For the rest, 'strategic' remains to be defined. The Interim Agreement included shorter-range SLBM on submarines, since their mobile launcher platform allows operational deployment sufficiently close to the territory of the other side as to be able to attack all or most continental targets. The SLBM is considered a 'strategic system' *per se* without regard to its operational range. While this is a reasonable assumption for all practical purposes in SALT I, it leaves an open flank: a ballistic missile of considerable range, above 3,000km for example, which can be launched from a submarine, is covered by SALT as a strategic weapon, but what if it were carried by a surface vessel, as was planned in the late 1950s and early 1960s for the *Polaris* missile in the context of the MLF project? This particular grey area is not without importance: the Soviet Navy has over the years released from the strategic role at least some of the 60 older short-range SLBM (SS-N-4 and SS-N-5 with ranges of 350 and 750nm respectively) in diesel-powered submarines which are not covered by the Interim Agreement, and has assigned them to duty with the Baltic Fleet. Others may follow or be sent to the Pacific and Black Sea Fleets. In all these cases what were formerly 'strategic' Soviet SLBM systems and their submarines, having been excluded from SALT I, could serve 'non-central' but nevertheless strategic Soviet purposes in regional theatres, for example in Central and Northern Europe, or around Japan. They would be a factor in a regional balance.

IRBM and MRBM (apart from those in nuclear-powered submarines) and bombers were left out of SALT I in 1972 and will in all probability be kept out of SALT II, despite the appearance since 1972 of new ballistic and non-ballistic systems to replace them. In 1969–70 the European allies of NATO had considered demanding that the Soviet IRBM/MRBM ballistic missile systems and medium-range nuclear-capable bombers (of which two-thirds have traditionally been targeted against Western Europe and the Middle East) be limited by SALT. However, they decided against this on the grounds that the Soviet Union would then have a valid case for demanding limitations on

135

NATO's own theatre nuclear strike forces in Europe and the Eastern Mediterranean. Moreover, it was argued that the Soviet IRBM/MRBM capabilities (some 650 SS-4 with a range of about 1,200sm and 1MT warheads, deployed in the period since 1959; about 100 more modern SS-5 with a range of up to 2,300sm and a 1MT warhead, operational since 1961; and 750 Tu-16 medium-range bombers first deployed in 1955) were mostly obsolescent and would probably be phased out in due course. As a result, the United States succeeded in keeping her FBS (*Pershing* SSM in some deployment postures, and nuclear-capable attack aircraft on carriers plus the 'non-central' long-range F-111 bombers) outside any limitations, although the Soviet Union continued to demand that they be included at a later stage in the negotiations. However, the entire Soviet IRBM/MRBM and medium bomber force also remained free from limitations. Since then, the United States has not deployed comparable weapon systems apart from more F-111s but the Soviet Union has procured and deployed a new long-range bomber with a nuclear capability, *Backfire*, and a new IRBM, the SS-20. In the near future, American LRCM could also change both the central strategic relationship and the regional balances, so long as there is no Soviet counterpart. Land-mobile, short-range tactical ballistic missiles and cruise missiles with operational ranges between, say, 700 and 1,000km, and RPV systems equipped with PGM warheads may further complicate the situation in the years ahead. They will all help to make the grey areas even larger and to overlap.

**Towards New Strategic Definitions?**
It was clear from the beginning of SALT that the distinction between 'strategic' and 'non-strategic' arms is only an arbitrary one. Militarily, arms can be considered 'strategic' or 'non-strategic' only in relation to the capabilities and vulnerabilities of the enemy. It is the combination of the value of the target in a given situation and the means with which to destroy it that confers a strategic or tactical character on a given attack capability: 'It is the objective that makes the attack and the weapon used strategic or tactical' was the formula used in 1967 by French Chief of the General Staff General Ailleret. NATO's attempt at about the same time, to refine its official terminology from 'tactical nuclear weap-

ons' to 'nuclear arms for tactical use' reflected this. A case in which the distinction is particularly clear is that of the dual-mission deployment of American SLBM in the European Mediterranean theatre: some of the warheads of these SLBM have been assigned to the tactical 'SACEUR's strike plan' while others are incorporated in the American national SIOP. The same submarine may thus be part of the central and of the regional balance, the same SLBM force available for both purposes, the same missile held ready for either mission. Similarly, heavy or intercontinental bombers oscillate between the strategic and tactical categories. B-52 and F-111 bombers were used in Indo-China in a conventional role: their ordnance and their targets determined that role, not the weapon system itself. The use of the first PGM air-to-ground weapons by American aircraft against North Vietnam made it possible to destroy targets that previously withstood conventional bombing and hence had been thought of as vulnerable only to nuclear attack. A B-52 or F-111 with an ALCM can be given various mission profiles for strategic, theatre, tactical nuclear, conventional and even strategic conventional targets.

**A Euro-Strategic Balance?**
This is more than a problem of definition; it is essentially a political problem. So long as the existing FBS were safely excluded from strategic arms limitations and the new systems not considered 'strategic', nor relevant to the central balance between the United States and the Soviet Union, SALT could be conducted in relative isolation from the European situation as from other regional balances. Theatre balances remained important but formed strategic relationships by themselves, even if they were linked to the global balance and dominated by the commitment of external forces in the event of conflict.

With the confirmation of Soviet–American nuclear strategic parity, the rather loose term of the 'Euro-Strategic Balance' has appeared. It suggests a *distinct* regional strategic balance, relevant to conflict that may arise in Europe, made up of the nuclear forces which might decide the outcome of a war in that theatre. In reality there is no equilibrium between the Soviet and the Western Euro-Strategic capabilities. A considerable disparity exists to the advantage of the East. Approximately 400 IRBM/MRBM systems and up to 500 medium-range bombers are deployed in the western Soviet Union, capable of attacking most parts of Western Europe. Thus at least 900 intermediate- and medium-range nuclear attack systems with some 1,000 nuclear warheads are available, together with about 320 nuclear-capable tactical aircraft of the Soviet air force in central Europe and another 300–400 in the western Soviet Union (this last force is difficult to pin down on the map as a permanent factor and is, of course, apt to change its deployment patterns and missions). Some 1,600 or more Soviet nuclear-capable attack systems can therefore be counted on their side of the Euro-Strategic balance. There is an assortment of systems on the Western side: 130 British and French SLBM and IRBM, plus about 30 operational French *Mirage*-IV bombers; those American SLBM which are targeted in SACEUR's strike plan; a maximum of 500 nuclear-capable American attack aircraft in Europe or aboard carriers in the Mediterranean and East Atlantic, which could be committed to operations in the European theatre; also at the most some 200 nuclear-capable NATO tactical aircraft, of which, however, only a small number are actually deployed in a strike role. Under the most favourable assumptions, NATO could therefore put up to 1,200 nuclear-strike systems in the Western scale of the balance; a more realistic count would suggest a figure below 1,000.

It is imbalance, therefore, rather than balance that characterizes the 'Euro-strategic' situation. The major components – the IRBM/MRBM and medium-range bomber forces of the Soviet Union – remain dominant. Recently, the Soviet Union has begun to change the composition of her IRBM/MRBM and medium-range bomber forces by procuring the new *Backfire* bomber and the SS-20, and in doing so has further increased her advantage. It seems reasonable to assume that within the next few years about 275 MIRV-equipped SS-20, and about 4,000 warheads overall, will be deployed in the Soviet Union, mostly in the western part. NATO estimates that by 1985 there will be 230 *Backfire* bombers. The SS-20 is expected to have a much increased range (over 4,000km, possibly up to 7,000km) and improved accuracy. The two systems will offer a wider variety of operational options and multiply the number of targets that can be covered.

The Soviet Union has thus increased her nuclear Euro-strategic potential, while at the same time strengthening her nuclear arsenal *vis-à-vis* the United States. While for the time being the United States enjoys a marked superiority in the number of deliverable warheads and might, therefore, still be able to cover the modernized Soviet potential for strategic strikes against Western Europe, this situation is changing. In the past, the function of Soviet medium- and intermediate-range delivery systems was to hold West Europe hostage, so as to offset American strategic superiority. Now that strategic nuclear parity is being achieved, this now modernized arsenal is no longer required to balance an American advantage in the overall relationship; it offers instead a separate, and new, Euro-strategic option.

Yet the degree to which this option can be exercised will not only depend on the Soviet Union, but essentially on whether or not the Western Alliance accepts the Euro-strategic balance as a separate option. Traditional Western – and particularly West European – concerns have been to avoid any 'de-coupling' of deterrence. This must continue to be the over-riding consideration, for if the new Soviet systems can be employed without the risk of escalation to strategic nuclear exchange, the European theatre forces could be 'de-coupled' from the global situation and hence the Euro-strategic balance would become a reality. On the other hand, to insist that Soviet 'Euro-strategic' systems should be subjected to limitations may imply West European readiness to bring French and British strategic systems under similar constraints.

### Options for limiting 'Grey Area' Weapons
Apart from unilateral restraint, there are essentially three ways in which the grey area problem might be dealt with in arms control: to devise a new arms-control forum covering the whole spectrum of weapons from theatre to central strategic; to set up special negotiating machinery somewhere between MBFR and SALT; or to try to include, within the framework of the two existing negotiations, those weapon systems on their periphery which, if not included, would devalue any agreements that might emerge.

While these three ways are listed here, the first two are too unrealistic to be considered seriously. To include all weapon systems – and all those that possess them or can produce them – from the theatre to the central strategic level would be a negotiating nightmare and assure failure. The second suggestion, that of setting up a special negotiating framework for grey area weapons, is no more promising. The very nature of these weapons is such that they cannot be contained in a specific forum because they cover the whole range of weaponry; they elude definition, and any attempt to define them through setting up separate negotiating arrangements is foredoomed to failure.

This leaves the third and pragmatic option: to include in MBFR and SALT such systems on the periphery as are deemed essential to the success of negotiations.

## The Periphery of SALT

The Soviet Union has always held the view that 'peripheral' nuclear delivery systems which can reach Soviet territory must eventually be constrained by SALT. At American insistence, however, existing FBS have so far been kept out of SALT I and II, though they may be made the subject of SALT III if the process continues. The main problem would be to agree on a definition of FBS on land and sea. The Soviet definition, put forward in SALT I, is strictly related to the structural asymmetry in force deployments. The Soviet Union cannot, at present, deploy peripheral or intermediate-range nuclear-capable weapon systems that can reach American territory, but the United States can deploy systems that can reach the Soviet Union by using bases abroad. The Soviet Union therefore demanded, as part of the 1972 Interim Agreement, that the American ballistic-missile submarine bases on foreign territory be taken into account when setting SLBM and strategic submarine numerical limits, so that the numbers allowed favoured the Soviet Union. Geostrategic asymmetry (access to oceans) and alliance structure (availability of foreign bases) was the criterion. The United States agreed to meet this concern up to a point but refused to accept an associated Soviet demand, that any future increase in the number of French and British SLBM beyond that envisaged in 1972 be counted against the American SLBM ceiling. Similarly Soviet negotiators raised the question of non-transfer of nuclear arms and system components from the United States to

other nuclear-armed countries, allowed under the NPT to receive such weapons, techniques and aid (at that time – 1971–72 – Britain, France and China). The United States refused to accept any limitation of this kind.

American FBS capabilities, however defined, are certainly limited in numbers of systems and deployment in relation to negotiations in SALT. In Europe and Japan, F-111 bombers and, for some deployment patterns, land-based strike aircraft such as F-4 and carrier attack aircraft are the mainstay of FBS options. Since these numbers are small, the problem is strategically of marginal importance for the Soviet Union, so long as the United States does not deploy land-based IRBM or MRBM systems in Turkey, Greece, Northern Italy, Britain, continental Western Europe, or in East Asia, in Japan and South Korea (as had been the case until 1963 in Turkey and earlier in Britain and Italy). It is also marginal for the United States; Soviet FBS are relevant only as a threat against Alaska, unless redeployed to Cuba. SALT can, therefore, exist without covering FBS.

The same cannot be said for the more recent types of peripheral systems that have made their appearance since 1974: the Soviet *Backfire* bomber and SS-20 IRBM, and the new American cruise missiles.

For the United States, *Backfire*, if deployed in a marginal inter-continental configuration and mission profile (that is, with in-flight refuelling), could change the conditions for continental air defence, though it would not constitute a decisive strategic threat. If successive American Administrations have nevertheless insisted on the inclusion of *Backfire* in SALT in some way, this is primarily for tactical reasons; if the Soviet Union insists on counting in SALT all systems which might be able to reach a part of Soviet territory, it is only logical that the United States should insist on *Backfire* also being counted. For the Soviet Union this would mean, under the combined ceilings of the (temporarily extended) 1972 Interim Agreement and Vladivostok 1974, that only 42 of the 135–150 inter-continental bombers now deployed, not counting *Backfire*, might be kept operational if 2,400 was the limit for all systems and the maximum of 2,358 SLBM and ICBM allowed in the 1972 Agreement was deployed. An increase of heavy bombers above 42 would have to be bought with a decrease in the number of missiles allowed by Vladivostok. If *Backfire* had to be placed under this overall ceiling, then the Soviet Union would have to withdraw all the older, heavy intercontinental bombers, to make room for at least 42 *Backfire*, or reduce the numbers of missiles.

The Soviet interest in not having to count *Backfire* against the Vladivostok ceiling is thus clear and compelling. The Soviet Union, under the agreed rules, is already in difficulties with her strategic force structure. She has no viable and efficient strategic 'triad' and maintains a continent-wide relatively dense and expensive air defence. She has structured her strategic forces with a heavy concentration on land-based ICBM and invested heavily in ICBM development, which is continuing. To make the best use of the options allowed for SLBM she has to dismantle part of her ICBM force and limit further investment in this technology, which has in the past seemed the most promising to the Soviet strategists and engineers. (This is the reason for the 'shock' suffered by the Soviet leaders in 1977 when US Secretary of State, Cyrus Vance, presented the first SALT proposals of the Carter Administration which offered two options: to keep the cruise missile and *Backfire* out or to include them at a level lower than that agreed at Vladivostok and, in particular, to cut the allowance for 'heavy' ICBM to less than half, from 330 to 150.)

One may conclude that, for the *bilateral* Soviet–American strategic balance, the Soviet interest in keeping *Backfire* free from SALT constraints is much stronger than the American interest in bringing it in. For alliance reasons and for regional security in Europe the American interest in constraining *Backfire* is, however, very real indeed. In this regional context it is not the marginal capability of this aircraft for strategic use against the United States that is important but its strategic significance for the neighbours of the Soviet Union – Japan, China, the Indian sub-continent, the Middle East, North Africa and Western Europe. Forty-two 'strategic-capable' Soviet *Backfire* would not make much difference to the United States, in view of the ICBM and SLBM threat. But 230 or more *Backfire* with an operational range of 2,400km, with or without nuclear-armed air-to-ground missiles and nuclear bombs, would considerably improve Soviet 'Euro-strategic' and other regional strategic

capabilities. The latter, however, cannot be constrained in SALT regional balances.

'Strategic' constraints on *Backfire* range, mission profile and deployment patterns in the Soviet Union would, therefore, be of little significance for the global balance and irrelevant to the regional balances. *Backfire* is a grey area system which need not be covered by SALT. While this weapon system is of obvious concern to the neighbours of the Soviet Union, strategic arms limitation agreements can be effective without its inclusion.

The SS-20 represents a completely different problem. If it remained outside SALT, without specific conditions for easy identification by NTM, the grey area would reach into the field of SALT and could undermine an agreement. This is due to the hybrid nature of the weapon system, the SS-20 being a two-stage version of the three-stage SS-16 ICBM; with the first stage of propulsion added it can be converted into an SS-16. Thus, the SS-16 and the SS-20 are a pair. Since the SS-20 (as a land-mobile system) could be moved around and serviced in shelters, reconversion to the SS-16 ICBM could easily be hidden from distant satellite observation and accomplished rapidly. Consequently, the United States would experience considerable difficulty in verifying Soviet compliance with SALT rules on the permitted number of both ICBM and MIRV systems. This problem would be somewhat reduced if the Soviet Union agreed to a ban on land-mobile ICBM launchers and, as American negotiators in SALT II have asked, also agreed to give the SS-20 launchers a different and clearly visible configuration to distinguish them for purposes of satellite observation from the SS-16 launchers. SS-20 in silos could not be reconverted into the larger SS-16 without technical modification which could be observed by satellites. An agreement not to deploy land-mobile IRBM SS-20 would therefore bring the problem under control.

The basic problem would, however, remain unsolved. In SALT only *launchers* for ICBM and SLBM are the objects of constraints, the missiles themselves remaining free from limitation (apart from the number of MIRV allowed on such missiles by the Vladivostok MIRV sub-ceiling of 1,320). Since SS-16 and SS-20 have the same type of warhead (with single RV or MIRV), the same missile would be covered by SALT when launched by three propulsion stages but not when launched by only two. It would be at once 'strategic' and 'non-strategic' according to SALT criteria, depending on the number of propulsion stages in the launcher. On account of this ambiguity, the system in both its SS-16 and its SS-20 modes will have to be included in the SALT ceilings, unless a reliable and verifiable barrier to rapid conversion can be established. If not, to leave the SS-20 outside SALT would threaten the stability of the agreement.

The SS-20 is, therefore, a grey area weapon that SALT must cover and cannot afford to leave unconstrained – for the sake of SALT itself. It is also an example that demonstrates very well why the attempt to set up separate negotiations to deal with grey area weapons, in this case IRBM/MRBM, would be meaningless. True, if introduced in the numbers envisaged, the SS-20 would dominate the European strategic situation, and, since the other regional strategic forces of the Soviet Union (and also those of the West) clearly fall outside SALT, a separate arms-control forum for dealing with them would seem, at first sight, to make sense. It would, however, encounter the same problem as in SALT: because the SS-20 can be converted from a 'strategic' to an 'inter-mediate-range' weapon and vice versa, it could not be incorporated within the terms of a regional limitation agreement.

Finally, the cruise missile. If cruise missiles remained completely free from constraints they would eventually restrict the usefulness of limitation agreements on inter-continental delivery systems, including ballistic missiles, despite the latter's higher performance and greater strategic capabilities. A cruise-missile competition, with massive deployment of dual-capable cruise missiles on aircraft, submarines, surface ships and land-based platforms, would cause an erosion of SALT. The cruise missile is the grey area weapon *par excellence* because of its high degree of versatility in tactical and strategic, and regional and semi-intercontinental roles.

On the other hand, SALT or any other bilateral Soviet–American arms-control negotiation is not the appropriate forum for discussion of the cruise-missile problem, as has been shown since 1976 in the SALT process and by the consultations within NATO. The European NATO allies would have to be associated directly with such a negotiation, since they are able to develop and deploy cruise missiles by themselves, with or without American assistance. Moreover, cruise-missile technology is not only for nuclear purposes. There is no reason why the European NATO allies, who are constantly asked by the United States to spend more on defence, should maintain costly conventional forces and not exploit the conventional options offered by cruise missiles, even though they may rely on the assurance of the protective power to commit itself fully to their defence with all means, including strategic nuclear arms. If optimizing the options for defence is a NATO task in the service of security, the cruise missile should not be excluded from this service merely for the convenience of a bilateral arms-control agreement between the two SALT partners. What is more, even bilateral Soviet–American agreement would not succeed in effectively excluding the introduction of the new technology into the major West European forces for long.

There are two problems in particular. First, a distinction between SALT and non-SALT cruise missiles based on range will be almost impossible to make in any agreement because the range potential of a normal cruise missile has such a wide margin of tolerance that verification becomes virtually impossible: the range limits cannot be detected by looking at the launcher even if it can be found. 'If the engines will operate over a 600km range, they will probably operate for another 600km'.[1] Therefore, even setting permitted range limits very low would not exclude ranges of more than double the distance, and permitting cruise missiles of only very long range does not exclude their use for non-strategic theatre roles.

Second, even if a solid adequate verification formula were found (which would also have to satisfy the US Congress), the United States will face opposition from her European allies. In the SALT II negotiations of 1977, the United States has reportedly proposed a three-year protocol which would limit deployment to air-launched cruise missiles (ALCM) with a maximum range of 2,100km, on heavy bombers, while SLCM and GLCM with ranges exceeding 600km would be banned.

The European allies (and Japan and others associated with the United States) need not be

[1] Jan. M. Lodal, 'Verifying SALT', *Foreign Policy*, No. 24, Autumn 1976, pp. 57–58.

concerned with an ALCM limitation of 2,500km on strategic bombers, unless they want to deploy such ALCM on their non-strategic strike aircraft, which would suppose a NATO requirement. France may have an independent national requirement to keep the residual *Mirage* IV bomber force in the semi-strategic business. However, the range of a cruise missile, like that of an aircraft, can be translated into flying time regardless of direction. A cruise missile, like a manned aircraft, can cruise without having to take the shortest route to the target and can therefore fly around areas where there are thick air defences.

For European NATO an ALCM limitation to a range of 600km would already be prohibitive, since NATO attack aircraft would come under air defence fire at the moment of crossing into East European air space; NATO aircraft could launch ALCM over friendly territory and thus improve their attack capability against Eastern Europe, but a 600km range limit would not reach deep into Eastern Europe nor threaten targets in the Soviet Union (which are not at present assigned to these aircraft). The European allies could not therefore countenance a 600km limit to ALCM on aircraft other than 'heavy bombers'.

Even less acceptable to West European interests would be 600km limits to the range of ground-launched cruise missiles, since this would restrict these systems to an operational range well below that of the short-range (750km) ballistic missile *Pershing*. Here a 2,500km limit would be acceptable and allow for a marginal and partial IRBM/MRBM counter-force capability, given satisfactory penetrability and accuracy. However, NATO ground-launched cruise missiles would need, at present cruise speed, at least three hours' flight-time to targets 2,500km away and their range would be insufficient to fly this distance at low level.

Five years or so from now cruise missiles are expected to reach and hit with accuracy targets up to 3,000km away. This would still be marginal against the SS-20 deployed in the Soviet Union, assuming it has a 4,000–5,000km range.

For NATO a 600km limit to the operational range of SLCM systems, as envisaged by the United States in SALT II, would be barely acceptable on technical grounds, but could be tolerable for most missions in the North Sea and Baltic against hostile naval forces and coasts. Such a low limit would not, however, serve the purpose of replacing obsolete SLBM with modern SLCM on nuclear strategic submarine systems, as may be considered for the British SLBM force. It would not permit reinforcement of the seaborne strategic component by long-range SLCM on other submarines or on surface combatants. (In the British and French navies the SLCM might have nuclear warheads and in other NATO navies conventional ones.)

The evolution of SALT II since Vladivostok points to a possible conflict of interest between the United States and her major NATO allies concerning the Soviet IRBM/MRBM and medium-range bomber capabilities and cruise-missile technology. The United States may find herself confronted with the choice of putting SALT at risk, or else neglecting the security interests of European NATO partners faced with the growing Soviet 'peripheral' threat.

The problem which the cruise missile raises for SALT – bilateral or multilateral – is compounded by the asymmetry of strategic interests between the Soviet Union, the United States and Western Europe (as well as, for example, Japan). The United States really does not need cruise missiles of longer ranges, apart from the ALCM for heavy bombers, tactical aircraft and theatre nuclear strike aircraft. The Soviet Union employs SLCM on surface combatants and submarines, at present up to 600km range, and will probably develop new ones to improve capabilities. Soviet forces could therefore make use of ALCM systems, but do not have the same operational requirements for them as has the United States, as penetration weapons against a dense air defence. There are no heavy air defences over North America, Western Europe or Turkey. Furthermore, for deep nuclear strike missions Soviet forces have IRBM/MRBM and medium-range bombers; the SS-20 could do anything that cruise missiles and bombers could do, and at least as well. Soviet short-range ballistic missile technology can be called upon to develop systems of a 600–1,500km operational range with nuclear warheads. The Soviet interest therefore is less in cruise missiles than in shutting-off Western options to use cruise missiles as a means of off-setting Soviet strategic and tactical options offered by other systems such as IRBM/MRBM. This became quite clear when Soviet public comments on the American decision on the B-1 bomber downgraded the threat of a new strategic bomber and focused on cruise missiles as the main source of 'danger to strategic stability and security'.

For Western Europe, cruise-missile technology offers a multi-purpose system, with nuclear and conventional capability, for deep penetration and neutralization of force concentrations and military targets in distant rear areas, as well as for theatre-wide offensives. It would also be a relatively cheap investment. The 'conventional-strategic' potential of advanced cruise missiles in the next five to ten years would seem to present Western Europe with a fair chance of reducing the superiority of Soviet theatre capabilities and enhancing Western deterrence, as well as optimizing defence options for ground and air forces.

For this reason Western European countries cannot be interested in cruise missile limitations at all – in range or numbers – unless the Soviet IRBM/MRBM and medium-bomber nuclear attack potential were included in a wider negotiation as well.

The answer to the cruise-missile problem in SALT must, because of these difficulties, be imperfect; there is no way in which arms control can cope with the grey area problem completely. Long-range cruise missiles are weapons with a strategic potential that implies their inclusion in SALT, since without this an agreement would be in danger of being circumvented to the point of becoming irrelevant as a means of regulating the Soviet–American strategic relationship. But this applies only to Soviet and American cruise-missile capabilities, not those of the allies of the United States. While the Soviet Union will no doubt press strongly for a ban on the transfer of the relevant technologies to allies, which means at the 'non-strategic' level, this demand should only be considered if, in return, the Soviet Union were to accept limitations on the same level, that is, on her own Euro-strategic forces. Cruise-missile production by West European countries does not require but would certainly be facilitated by access to American technology; it is understandable, therefore, that the Soviet Union wishes to restrict such a transfer. But West European capabilities would be designed to counter not Soviet strategic capabilities vis-à-vis the United States but vis-à-vis Europe.

This is where the *quid pro quo* of mutual concessions would have to apply, not in the SALT context. Dealing with the grey area problem is only possible if the distinctions that can be made are upheld.

### The Periphery of MBFR

At present, MBFR is more resistant to the introduction of grey area weapons than is SALT. None of the systems mentioned in the preceding section would, if left unconstrained, seriously undermine the terms of the negotiations or of any agreement that might emerge from them. This is due to one fundamental difference between the MBFR approach and that of SALT: the Vienna negotiations define their substance not by categories of weapon systems (strategic – non-strategic) but by the number of forces (and to some extent weapons) within a certain geographical area. They are, therefore, less vulnerable *within their own brief* to the introduction of new weapons technologies. Such technologies may deprive any MBFR agreement of substantive results in arms control, and it can be argued that the primary MBFR focus on manpower levels within a relatively narrow area should be redirected to address those elements of military power which, like short-warning attack capabilities, will be more relevant to East–West security stability and more influenced by qualitative improvement in weapons. But this is not the same as the grey area problem. For MBFR, this problem is relatively simple; there is no real grey area since the area is geographically defined.

MBFR comes into the discussion in relation to those weapon systems which SALT cannot encompass, not so much in its specific Vienna configuration but as a multilateral forum for regional arms control: should those Euro-strategic weapon systems which can affect SALT but do not fall under its definitions be constrained within such a framework? As a result of the geographical limits of the proposed MBFR reduction area, force reductions will be relatively irrelevant to the full offensive and defensive capabilities of both sides, to the general European strategic situation and the balance of forces between East and West. Most of the nuclear-capable systems would remain outside the reduction area, particularly in the East, where the Soviet territory presents a favourable deployment area for missiles and air forces directed towards Western Europe but out of reach of most of the theatre-based weapons of NATO.

The NATO 'nuclear' offer of December 1975 in Vienna opened up discussion on nuclear arms in MBFR. The Soviet Union showed marked interest in a substantial reduction of *Pershing* SSM, nuclear-capable SAM and strike aircraft, not only of the American forces but also of other NATO forces in the area. She also made clear her wish that the nuclear-capable force components that would be left after such reductions should not be modernized by the introduction of systems of higher capabilities (such as *Pershing* II and newer aircraft like the F-15). Although such unofficial indications must not be taken as final positions, they do show the direction in which the bargaining could go. The NATO offer of December 1975 touches, however, the limit of what NATO can offer without jeopardizing its nuclear-tactical force posture for the execution of 'flexible response' in a forward defence situation in central Europe.

To achieve significant results, MBFR would have to include all theatre nuclear forces on both sides and strike a deal on a balanced common ceiling for them, stretching into Soviet territory. This would probably overburden the negotiation and the Soviet Union would probably not accept such a geographical extension. The Soviet concern with American FBS in general could not be met in the context of MBFR in Europe since not all these systems are deployed in Europe and practically none are deployed in central Europe. MBFR in its present form is, therefore, definitely not the appropriate negotiating forum in which to discuss Euro-strategic and other peripheral nuclear-offensive systems.

It would, of course, be another and very different matter if, after finishing their current and already difficult business, the MBFR negotiations were to be replaced by a genuine forum for regional arms control in Europe, covering all of the European geographical area and including all those weapons and forces of the two military alliances relevant to conflict in that theatre: i.e., Soviet and American Euro-strategic systems as well as British and French nuclear forces, theatre nuclear weapons as well as major components of conventional military strength, air, naval and ground forces. It is, however, difficult to see much political attraction for any of the major countries in such a proposal, with the possible exception of the non-nuclear member countries of both NATO and the Warsaw Pact.

For the Soviet Union, there would be a double disadvantage of having the European part of her territory included in force restrictions, and of seeing the bilateral strategic relationship with the United States diluted by the participation of other powers. For France, without whose involvement such a departure would make little sense, the major disadvantage would be to see the independence of her nuclear deterrent forces curtailed; so long as French strategic doctrine regards the absolute freedom of national action as essential for effective deterrence, there is little prospect of French participation in a genuine, all-European arms-control effort. The other European allies, while less concerned about independence, would be worried that a separate regional arms-control arrangement for Europe might be the first step to strategic de-coupling from the United States. Lastly, for the United States, the chief concern would be less the constraints that such an agreement would impose on her forces in central Europe than the restrictions on her military flexibility on the European periphery, particularly in the Middle East.

These political considerations are, of course, subject to change. But this change does not seem imminent. Political preferences tend to display greater inertia than do technological options. In the meantime, therefore, the grey area problem will remain with us. It cannot be solved, but perhaps it can be domesticated.

# The Consequences of Failure in SALT

LAWRENCE FREEDMAN

SALT has been with us now, in one form or another, for a full decade. During the course of the ten years since their inception the negotiations have become one of the constant features of Soviet–American relations. Pundits have come to chart the health of detente by referring to progress at SALT. The leaders of both countries have found it necessary to educate themselves in the mysteries of strategic weaponry so that they can converse with their opposite numbers and answer questions from journalists with the proper degree of technical authority. No busy politician devotes many hours to being briefed on the properties of ballistic missiles unless he has a serious purpose in mind. The negotiations have been conducted in a sober and business-like manner by both sides, and till now there seemed little reason not to believe that they would eventually produce results. They have been in the interest of all. The arms race could be kept in check; defence expenditure could be diverted to peaceful purposes; a 'structure of peace' might be created to make the world a safer place; more relaxed and even amicable Soviet–American relations could evolve; non-nuclear powers could be assured that the injunction in the NPT to the nuclear powers to 'pursue negotiations in good faith on effective measures relating to cessation of the nuclear arms race' was being treated with appropriate respect. The alternative to SALT has appeared quite stark: a determined and energetic arms race; reversion to the attitudes and behaviour of the cold war; the discrediting of all efforts at arms control. If the SALT process fails, it has been asserted, the world will become a more dangerous place.

## What Kind of Failure?

There is no reason to believe that the virtues of the SALT exercise have been seriously diminished for the participants. It is true that Soviet–American relations have cooled, that the two are less sure of each other's motives, and that both have found that national security considerations leave little room for manoeuvre. Nevertheless there is every reason to believe that both desire an agreement. If they are to be disappointed the cause will lie in the intractability of the issues involved.

There is no guarantee that failure will ever be explicitly acknowledged by the parties concerned. Some have taken the visit of US Secretary of State Cyrus Vance to Moscow in March 1977 as an indication of the sort of events likely to surround the terminal stages of SALT. There were public recriminations and accusations of bad faith from the Soviet Union and rather condescending comments from the United States on the Soviet inability to cope with radical proposals. Each gave warning of its capacity to build up its military strength if the need arose. Qualifications were carefully made, however. Both wished the talks to continue, were anxiously looking for signs of 'good faith', were still desperately worried about the acceleration of the arms race, the future of mankind, and so on. 'Our tolerance', Gromyko commented at that time, 'is not yet exhausted'. These were mainly bargaining tactics. If such an event recurs, it is possible that both will retire to their corners to construct alibis and huff and puff at each other, and no further meetings will be arranged. It is more likely, however, that the formalities will

144

continue to be observed while the talks stagnate. There will be no serious agreements.

The talks, though in decline for the time being, might produce some trivial agreements. Could success be claimed? The difficulty is that, because SALT is inherently a limited exercise, it cannot solve all the problems of the nuclear arms race and it will always be a relative failure. The efforts of the negotiators will seem feeble compared with the problems. There must be, nevertheless, a minimum output if the process is to be taken seriously. To be of consequence it must produce evident constraints on the development and deployment of central strategic systems.

Such results will be progressively more difficult to achieve. In the early days conditions were particularly favourable. Detente was still being nurtured, rather than qualified and minimized. Moreover the weapons to be limited could be counted easily, and did not come in too many different shapes and sizes. The picture has now become much more complicated. Great accuracy is being combined with multiple warheads and mobility of launch platforms. Modern cruise missiles may indicate a move to versatile, modular weapons systems, equipped with interchangeable parts for a variety of roles. These weapons are also independent of specific launch platforms. None of this assists the arms-control efforts, which have been presumed to require readily accountable systems.

There is, however, another awkward feature of modern cruise missiles: they are currently an American advantage for which there is no obvious Soviet equivalent. Thus, the main effect of this technological advance is to exacerbate a more fundamental problem. The negotiating positions of the two sides are becoming more, not less, incompatible.

There are two explanations of the growing divergence in negotiating positions. First, the element of strain in Soviet–American relations has recently increased. It is no longer being said that detente is 'irreversible'. Particular irritants need not have too disruptive an effect. After all, the SALT I agreements were signed at a particularly tense stage of the Vietnam War. Foreign-policy crises such as the Cuban intervention in Angola or President Carter's human rights campaign may make it difficult to begin new negotiations now (just as the invasion of Czecho-

slovakia delayed SALT) but rarely provide grounds for breaking them off. However, if the atmosphere is becoming unpleasant, breakthroughs in negotiations are more difficult to achieve. If nothing else, domestic pressures unfavourable to an agreement will be reinforced. Questions will be asked as to the trustworthiness, good faith, intentions and the like of the other side. Even without following a policy of direct 'linkage', a general deterioration in relations can still undermine specific negotiations. It becomes difficult to create an atmosphere of compromise and flexibility.

Second, the tendency in SALT to postpone discussion of awkward issues in order to secure agreement on more readily negotiable matters has ensured that the talks become successively more difficult. Issues such as the possible inclusion of American FBS are continually reintroduced at the negotiating table. In the current talks all that is desired for the most troublesome issues is a breathing space, an agreement not to make things worse. Full development and deployment of controversial weapons is to be postponed for a limited period. This is a concept similar to that of the Interim Agreement on Offensive Arms of SALT I. The fact that the five-year breathing space has passed without producing a Treaty ready to be signed indicates that 'buying time' is no guarantee of subsequent success. Another device, which is being considered for even more difficult issues, is to agree on nothing more than a statement of principles, with the intention of defining the future course of negotiations. Such a device is rarely satisfactory, for it results either in the blandest generalities or, in so far as it is detailed enough to imply a specific commitment, is almost as hard to negotiate as more binding measures.[1]

As the talks become protracted, a vicious circle develops in which negotiating flexibility is lost and both sides begin to act in anticipation of failure. To some extent this has happened

[1] The negotiating framework proposed by the United States in May 1977 involved: (1) an eight-year agreement which would ratify the non-disputed elements of the 1974 Vladivostok agreement, and some further reductions in force levels; (2) a three-year protocol to provide temporary solutions for controversial problems; (3) a 'mutual commitment in writing' to pursue drastic, substantial reductions in a comprehensive SALT III agreement. *Transcript of President Carter's press conference*, 26 May 1977 (USIS).

already. The lack of momentum in SALT, combined with the growing suspicion of detente, has encouraged the development of a strong body of opinion in the United States unlikely to accept any agreement as being of value. Those of this opinion believe that SALT is a process biased in favour of the Soviet Union because the Soviet leaders are 'realistically' tough, secretive and devious. There is now a danger that a SALT II accord will not be ratified in the Senate, especially if the Administration aims for a Treaty (which requires a two-thirds vote) rather than merely an Executive Agreement. This would be the most disastrous form of breakdown, for it would suggest to the Soviet Union that there was little point in persisting in talks if the American Administration could not fulfil any accord.[2] Domestic support is not considered to be so serious a problem in the Soviet Union. Leonid Brezhnev now appears to be more powerful than ever before, and it is generally felt that he wishes to conclude a SALT Treaty as his valedictory gift to mankind. There are undoubtedly forces hostile to SALT in the Soviet Union and in the event of a future succession crisis they might prevent decisions being made.

Even in the most favourable of climates it needs a determined effort for negotiators to keep up with the pace of arms deployments. There is always a danger of SALT being overtaken by events, with formulae that might once have formed the basis for an agreement becoming obsolescent. It is possible that, if SALT goes into a steady decline, one side might instigate a major acceleration in weapons' programmes in an effort to shock the other side into making concessions. As it happens the United States is, at the moment, probably in a better position to do this than the Soviet Union, since decisions are pending on the MX mobile ICBM and cruise missiles.[3] Decisions to accelerate programmes

can always be reversed if the arms-control climate improves, but past experience does not encourage one to believe this option will be exercised.

Another danger is that the two powers will become more secretive. The Soviet military authorities have already indicated a preference for severely limiting American observation by the 'national technical means' strictly to matters covered by existing arms-control agreements. As the dividing line between normal intelligence work and arms-control verification is often blurred, this Soviet secretiveness has already been a source of tension with the United States. If she anticipates an acceleration in the arms race she might well try to prevent the United States getting too clear a view of her preparations.[4]

### After Failure

Therefore, if SALT is to fail, this is as likely as not to occur gradually as negotiating momentum is lost and the problems become more intractable. As neither side seems prepared to abandon a SALT treaty as a foreign policy objective, and as neither side will wish to assume responsibility for the drastic step of breaking off negotiations and so endangering world peace, SALT could drag on for many a year. Though the formalities will be honoured, future negotiations will be substantially different from those of the past. We might expect two things to happen. First, the negotiations will be handled at a lower level than before. Second, they will be used for propaganda purposes. Proposals will be more public and more radical. I would predict that the decline in SALT will be marked by the protestations of peaceful intent becoming ever more fervent and the negotiating positions becoming ever more unrealistic and utopian. If the Soviet Union also

---

[2] Advanced warning of this possibility came with the close Senate vote (58 to 40) to confirm Paul Warnke as the chief American negotiator at SALT. Warnke was challenged because of his 'doveish' reputation. One possible compromise, in the event of strong Senate hostility to a SALT II agreement, might be to trade an endorsement of SALT II in return for an acceleration in prized weapons programmes not covered by the agreement. This is what happened in 1972.

[3] The recent decision to put the new Mark 12A warhead on top of the *Minuteman* III ICBM in 1979 may come into this category. If this is meant to warn the Soviet Union

of the dangers of inflexibility in SALT negotiations, it is probably directed at Soviet disinclination to take seriously American views on the destabilizing consequences of chronic ICBM vulnerability. The American message with this improved hard-target warhead is that if the Soviet Union does not currently take this problem seriously she will be given reason to do so. A variety of messages to the Soviet Union could be seen in the decision made in June not to procure B-1 bombers but to proceed with air-launched cruise missiles. However, this decision was determined by budgetary factors, and not SALT. That does not mean, of course, that the decision will not have important influences on the SALT process.

[4] On this problem see *Strategic Survey 1975* (London: IISS, 1976), pp. 111–6.

expects this, she would not have been impressed by the American performance in the preparations for Secretary Vance's visit to Moscow. The combination of a public disclosure of the bold new American initiative with a tardy private disclosure to the Soviet Union, including a proposal with an impressive and appealing formula that just happens to require the major concessions from the Soviet Union, could well have been taken as a signal that the new Administration was more concerned with addressing the gallery than with serious negotiations. If the Soviet Union had acted in the same way this would certainly have been the assumption made in the West. If attempts to put the other side 'on the spot' become a regular feature of negotiations we can expect little progress.

One model for the future of SALT is the Vienna negotiations on MBFR in Europe, where there is virtual deadlock, with neither side inclined to make basic concessions or to take the blame for causing the negotiations to be abandoned. Another model is offered by the CCD in Geneva. A negotiating forum is maintained into which, when convenient, an arms-control proposal can be inserted. The CCD alternates between discussions of the most marginal proposals (where it occasionally has some success) and the most radical. Thus SALT could be maintained to discuss non-controversial matters of bilateral interest. Another model for the future of SALT is provided by the Sino-Soviet border talks. Meetings are irregular, with most interest centring on the form rather than the content (how senior is the chief negotiator, who meets him at the airport, and so on).

It should also be remembered that, even if the present round of talks breaks down and nothing is planned to take its place, the Standing Consultative Committee set up to monitor compliance with SALT I and to discuss problems of implementation will remain in being (for the ABM Treaty if not for the Interim Agreement). Problems could well arise on this body too, even if it concentrates only on issues arising out of the implementation of SALT I. There are no third parties available for arbitrating on disputes. The alleged ambiguities in Soviet compliance raised hitherto at the SCC appear to have been dealt with in a constructive and satisfactory manner, but if the two sides begin to fall out over strategic arms, relations in the SCC could become strained.

Allegations of cheating might be made without a serious effort to refute them, or to acknowledge and correct unintended violations, being made in reply. Instead counter-allegations might be preferred, and relations could deteriorate further.

### The Effect on the Strategic Balance

The alternative to arms control has always been thought to be an unrestrained arms race. Cynics may point out that involvement in arms control and an arms race do not appear to have been mutually exclusive activities over the past decade. The SALT I agreements and the Vladivostok proposals have been quite permissive. Little has been done that might upset current or planned force structures. It might therefore be felt that the subtraction of SALT from force planning calculations would not necessarily have a major impact on future deployments of strategic weapons. To examine this proposition further we can look at two types of SALT objectives: those concerned with public appearances and those concerned with specialist strategic problems.

The main effort in SALT II has been to find a formula to demonstrate that, in aggregate and in key components, the two super-powers have rough equivalence. Both must be able to say they are 'second to none'. Though visible disparities in the strategic balance might be utterly irrelevant if it ever came to a nuclear exchange, it is felt important that the peoples of the world, and in particular key allies and potential enemies, should have no grounds for thinking that one side has a significant superiority over the other. This sort of concern, which has sometimes been taken to absurd lengths, has been stimulated by SALT. The insistence of Senator Jackson after SALT I (which did allow for some visible disparities in numbers) that there must be 'essential equivalence' in any future agreement has concentrated the minds of policy-makers on comparing and contrasting the American force structure with that of the Soviet Union. If SALT is unable to provide a means of dealing with this there will perhaps be a determined effort to redress imbalances large and small.

The more technical side of SALT has been concerned with the problems that may arise out of the destabilizing properties of new weapons. The main achievement of SALT thus far – the ABM Treaty – removed a weapons system that was theoretically the most destabilizing of all, because it held out the prospect of victory in a nuclear exchange, even if in practice it was both technologically and economically unattractive. Unlike ABM, which were relatively easy to control because of their evident shortcomings, the technology of the strategic offence has been making rapid strides – primarily in the area of guidance systems. Exploitation of this technology can create a number of options for limited nuclear exchanges, though none for successful all-out exchanges. Most of the limited nuclear options would be unaffected by any SALT Treaty. The option that has caused the most concern – a pre-emptive attack on fixed-base ICBM – would not be limited by the Vladivostok accord but would be limited by the comprehensive Carter proposals of March 1977. It is to be doubted whether the Soviet Union will sign anything in the near future which requires her to undo all that she has recently achieved with her massive investment in ICBM, so the problem of ICBM vulnerability may well be with us in the 1980s, even if some SALT II Treaty is signed. If this is so, there are two basic options available to defence planners. One is ABM site defence; the other is extra mobility to complicate the attacker's calculations. Active defence of ICBM silos is ruled out by SALT I. The use of mobility as an answer to the vulnerability problem has also been considered unwelcome in the United States, because mobile systems are hard to verify. This is the objection to the mobile variant of the SS-16 and MX ICBM and cruise missile. This objection is valid only in an arms-control regime. Doctrinally there can be few objections to mobile systems. If anything they are stabilizing. They render first strikes difficult because they are hard to find and up till now have lacked the accuracy for a first strike of their own. That mobile systems have a second-strike character is after all why nuclear submarines have been considered stabilizing. The point is that the objections to mobile systems are connected with an arms-control regime and the consequent desire for accountable weapons. Without SALT these objections would diminish. Any attempt to revive SALT would then be inhibited by the problems of verification and the lack of a reliable data base.

The Soviet Union, who has always suffered from a feeling of technological inferiority vis-à-vis the United States, will attempt to build her own modern cruise missiles, though it is hard to identify a significant Soviet requirement for them. As the United States lacks an air defence system and the Soviet Union a substantial fleet of heavy bombers, the value of air-launched cruise missiles as a means of penetrating heavily-defended air space does not seem relevant. Nor is the Soviet Union short of medium-range missiles for use in the European theatre. Nevertheless, the Soviet Union will have to show that she can master this technology just as she once mastered the MIRV.[5] In this way strategic arms *limitation* might give way to strategic arms *imitation*. Strategic arms competition along these lines will be very expensive since the real strategic and political advantages that either side can hope to gain in this way are minimal. Without agreed ceilings it is also likely that the Soviet Union will not remove old weapons when deploying new. The American habit of scrapping a perfectly adequate weapon just because it is old has never come naturally to the Soviet Union. Overall numbers of her missiles will probably grow.

There may, however, be renewed interest in the United States in building up quantitative indicators of strategic strength. As the *Trident* submarines become operational some of the *Polaris* submarines may be maintained and there might be renewed interest in maintaining the *Minuteman* III production line. Deployment of the large MX ICBM would allow the United States to build up warhead numbers and throw-weight. The main effort, however, will be directed to the replacement of older weapons with a new and more sophisticated generation. It has been said that new advances in ABM technology are making active defence an attractive option once more. In June 1972, the United States government did announce that the failure to replace the Interim Agreement with a more permanent arrangement might lead to a reconsideration of ballistic missile defence options. It is quite likely that if there is a patent failure in SALT all sorts of weapons lobbyists will insist that, if the arms race is to be fought in earnest, such a weapon is absolutely vital, and will provide a war-winning capability and so on.

---

[5] Soviet commentators have insisted that they are capable of building modern cruise missiles and will do so if necessary. American estimates on how long this would take the Soviet Union vary from five to ten years.

Some of these lobbyists may well be successful but I think Soviet–American relations will have to deteriorate dramatically before the United States would consider abrogating the ABM Treaty. It is generally worth remembering that weapons decisions are the product of a variety of factors, including strategic doctrines, the state of the technological art, internal politics and resource constraints. The absence of arms control does not mean that governments can afford to let their defence budgets go out of control.

One of the problems with SALT has been that the weapons programmes of the two sides have been out of time. When SALT was first mooted in 1967 the Soviet Union was some five years behind the United States in the deployment of her second-generation ICBM (SS-9/11/13 as compared with *Minuteman* I and II). By the time SALT I was underway in 1970 the United States was moving to her next generation of ICBM, characterized by MIRV (*Minuteman* III). It took the Soviet Union another five years to catch up with MIRV (SS-17/18/19). Now the United States is considering starting the 1980s with an even more sophisticated ICBM (MX) which will embody all the most advanced technology. It is likely to be well into the next decade before the Soviet Union starts deploying a comparable generation of ICBM. The gaps are even more marked when SLBM are considered. There is nothing automatic in this process, but it may be that the most opportune moment for a SALT Treaty comes after the Soviet Union has caught up with the United States (technologically) in the current stage of the arms race and before the United States has fully defined the next stage. If the United States moves ahead with the MX, especially in its mobile variant, the Soviet Union will feel she must plan to modernize her ICBM force in the second half of the 1980s. A decision to deploy MX and cruise missiles will probably mark the start of the next stage of the arms race. In anticipation of the American surge in new weapon deployment the Soviet Union may currently be extremely interested in a SALT agreement. Once this surge is underway she may feel that she has little choice but to attempt to catch up. I suspect the effort would put more of a strain on her technical and economic resources than comparable efforts in the past.

If the next generation of mobile and highly accurate strategic weapons comes into being, it will be very difficult to recover the ground lost in strategic arms control. New agreements will have to be much more imaginative and take much more on trust. The immediate impact of a decline in SALT on other arms-control negotiations is hard to tell. One of three things may happen. These arms-control agreements may carry on in the same desultory fashion as now; they may become even more half-hearted or be abandoned; they may be given fresh life as the super-powers decide to demonstrate that they are not completely incapable of reaching agreements in this sphere. The latter possibility is illustrated by recent attempts to extend the partial test ban treaty of 1963. In order that the whole effort should not appear fruitless, a rather trivial and undemanding agreement was reached on underground testing. The danger is that if arms controllers continually promise mountains and bring forth mole-hills the entire effort will be discredited. Nevertheless, if we are now to enter a lean period of arms control we can expect it to be occasionally punctuated by some accord on a minor or non-controversial matter (perhaps the product of one of the Soviet–American working groups which were set up at Moscow in March 1977).[6]

It has always been assumed that the snail's pace at which the MBFR negotiations have been conducted would be speeded up once a SALT Treaty had been concluded. If 'waiting for SALT' is now to produce complete stagnation, the participants at these MBFR talks may feel that, for the good name of arms control and to show that the long and tedious negotiations have not been a complete waste of time, some First Phase (Soviet–American) reductions ought to be agreed. This effort might be revitalized by top-level negotiators released from SALT duties. However, this is entirely unlikely since the issues here are even more intractable than those at SALT.

## A Return to the Cold War?

The discussion so far has implicitly assumed that the collapse of SALT will not be utterly disastrous for Soviet–American relations. It is true, of course, that progress in detente has been bound up with SALT and it may be felt that a

---

[6] In the midst of the present strain, on 18 May 1977, the United States and the Soviet Union became the first signatories to a convention banning the hostile use of environmental modification techniques.

149

failure here will set back the detente process. However, relations between the two super-powers may have become as warm as possible for the moment, and may well be cooling significantly irrespective of what happens at SALT. A failure in arms control will be symptomatic of the difficulties both sides have faced in establishing close ties. They have found that national security considerations, the anxieties of allies and the marked difference between the two socio-economic systems has allowed less room for manoeuvre than was anticipated during the balmy days of the first Nixon–Brezhnev summit. This does not mean, however, that we are doomed to another round of the cold war and a period of heightened tension. The mechanisms for consultation and communication still exist; the 'hot line' still works and the conventions of crisis management are still in force. The extent to which a breakdown in SALT does have a deleterious effect on detente will depend in the end on how it is managed. If there is little more than a mutual acknowledgement that the problems appear for the moment to be so intractable that it seems sensible to retire for a period of contemplation, no permanent harm need be done to detente. If it collapses into a slanging match, the consequences will be more far-reaching.

Europe views the prospect of a resurgence of cold-war attitudes and behaviour with some ambivalence. There are many who have misgivings concerning SALT. Important matters are discussed in negotiations to which Europe has no access; technological transfers from the United States may end because of non-circumvention clauses; exciting military options may be denied because the weapons in question (e.g. cruise missiles) become forbidden; American forces in Europe may be limited by some compromise. Those of this opinion would prefer the United States to rely for her security on a strong alliance rather than tentative deals with potential enemies. However, Europe lacks both the resources and the inclination for an arms race, and has enough problems on its hands without the added tensions of East–West confrontation. The Conservatives and Christian Democrats who are currently waiting in the wings in Britain and Germany may well be happy with a tougher line with the East. But the incumbent governments of these countries are not particularly pugnacious, and the up-and-coming parties of the Left, in France and Italy, have a positive interest in promoting detente. Francois Mitterand, First Secretary of the French Socialist Party, has expressed interest in a greater French involvement in arms-control efforts. Europe can be expected to adopt a moderating role, reminding both super-powers of the dangers of conflict. Again, however, it is important to add the qualification that European policies on East–West relations are determined by a variety of factors. SALT is of small importance, the general tenor of Soviet–American relations is of greater importance, but neither is decisive.[7]

A final note. The current situation is not unique. There have been periods of relatively friendly East–West relations, matched by a spurt of arms-control activity, that have come to a close. Arms-control activity has withered, but rarely died, in the past. The active period in 1955–58, with its thorough discussions of test ban treaties and measures for reducing the danger of surprise attack, was followed by the tense years of Khrushchev's hard-line diplomacy based on Soviet achievements in missile and space technology. The post-Cuba detente was particularly fruitful, when the Hot Line, the Test Ban Treaty, the groundwork for the Outer Space Treaty and a series of non-binding but reciprocated gestures were made. This activity went into decline in 1965 following the intensification of the Vietnam War but picked up again in 1967 to the extent that we have had a decade of arms control and some limited achievements. It may be that this effort is now grinding to a halt and we must now expect a period of reflection and recovery from the exhausting experience of a series of negotiations on difficult and sensitive matters. The interest and the need for arms control remains and the effort will probably be taken up again in a few years time though the problems will grow in complexity in the meantime. Many have remarked on the difficulties

---

[7] As has already been indicated, arms-control efforts directed towards controlling the spread of advanced conventional and nuclear technologies demand delicate negotiations between the United States and Western Europe as much as with the Soviet Union. If, following a SALT success, President Carter is filled with enthusiasm for arms control and pushes the goals he has already set to their limits, relations between the NATO allies could become tense.

caused by the over-selling of the benefits of detente in the early 1970s. We must guard equally against excessive alarm about the consequences of failure. This would obviously not be a time for undue optimism, but nor would it be a time for utter despair.

# 5 ARMS CONTROL AND TECHNOLOGICAL CHANGE: ELEMENTS OF A NEW APPROACH

CHRISTOPH BERTRAM

## INTRODUCTION

For the past two decades, the control of arms through mutual agreement has seemed one of the most promising ways to pursue stability and rational accommodation between East and West in the nuclear age. The concepts of arms control, articulated and refined in the late 1950s and early 1960s, were soon tried out in practice. In 1969 the Soviet–American talks on the limitation of strategic arms (SALT) got under way, leading to a series of treaties and agreements in 1972 and 1974. Since 1973, delegations from member states of the two East–West military alliances, the Warsaw Pact and NATO, have met regularly to seek agreement on the reduction of theatre forces in Europe, so far without result. However slow the process, advocacy of arms control remains the symbol with which politicians in East and West seek to demonstrate the sincerity of their desire for peace.

After almost four years of negotiation, the Soviet Union and the United States now seem on the threshold of a new SALT agreement, forecast for 1978 and to run until 1985. Yet one should be careful not to hail the new agreement too enthusiastically as evidence of successful arms control. It is more the result of the determination of both sides to overcome that major obstacle to agreement that has, in recent years, increasingly tended to render compromise more and more difficult: the dynamics of technological change in modern arms competition.

At first glance, this is no more than a banality. After all, there has rarely been a period in which the characteristics of weapons have remained unchanged. The dynamics of military technology have often exceeded and even defined those of civilian industrial technology; they have never stood still. Arms controllers have always been familiar with this problem, and when they have negotiated quantitative restrictions on weapon systems, they have defined them not just in terms of numbers but in qualitative terms as well: battleships, ICBM, MIRved launchers, etc. This measure is adequate at times when the dynamics of technological change are relatively restrained, but it ceases to be sufficient when military technology undergoes major qualitative changes, when the performance of weapon systems alters so drastically that the categories of agreement can no longer embrace them and when all consensus on quantities of weapons inherent in a mutual arms limitation accord is jeopardized by performance improvements on one side which are not matched by equivalent advances on the other.

I shall argue that, because of technological change, there is an urgent need for a new approach to the control of arms. The instrument chosen to effect arms control in both SALT and the Mutual and Balanced Force Reductions (MBFR) talks – that of quantitative restriction of numbers of men and weapons between East and West – is no longer adequate. The tool no longer fits the task. Unless we can develop a better tool, the task itself may fall into disrepute.

This paper will first examine more closely the dilemma created for the existing arms-control approach by the rapid change in military technology. Second, it will discuss whether it is worth the effort of retaining arms control as a viable instrument of international security policy and, if so, whether there are ways of moderating the effect of the dynamics of technological change on the control of arms. Third, the paper will suggest an outline for a new approach which may help to incorporate provision for techno- logical change in the effort to control arms competition more effectively than the quantitative method of arms restriction tried and applied so far in East–West relations.

## I. THE DILEMMA

Technological change has characterized much of the competition in arms between East and West over the past three decades. Sometimes new technologies were the result of major breakthroughs, in concept at least, if not always in implementation: reliable intercontinental delivery systems carrying nuclear weapons against far-distant targets; multiple and independently targetable warheads which increased the destructive capability of each missile launcher; antiballistic missile technology; sea-based missile launchers; satellite reconnaissance – to name a few in the strategic nuclear field. Others were the result of a cumulation of evolutionary improvements; much of the technology of precision guidance and target acquisition which will considerably affect the performance of both strategic and conventional weapons belongs in this category. Yet the problem of technological change, while always present, did not seem to worry arms controllers unduly until very recently.[1] They felt that priority had to be given to restricting the numbers of specific weapon systems and that this would also restrict the weapon technologies that went with them. Qualitative arms control was, in this sense, a by-product of quantitative arms control.

This approach was never satisfactory, though perhaps the best available. Today it is in danger of becoming inadequate for three reasons, one political, the other two technical.

### Political Strains
Politically, arms control has been seen as a symbol of East–West detente, perhaps the most tangible and unambiguous of all such symbols. If East and West are able to agree on limiting or reducing the forces they have available to pit against each other, this will indeed be one token of their sincere commitment to peace and accommodation. But arms-control agreements will only acquire this politically important symbolic significance if they are regarded both in East and West as fair and equitable: if not – if public or official opinion on one side feels 'we have been had' – an agreement will not be interpreted as a genuine gesture towards detente but as a confirmation of long-held suspicions.

The trouble is that, because of technological change and the difficulty of incorporating it in an agreement, it has become almost impossible for arms-control negotiators to produce treaties which will be unequivocally fair and equitable. A bargain struck on the basis of the technological characteristics of specific weapons existing at the time of agreement will become inequitable as one side or the other introduces qualitative improvements which have not been ruled out, or deploys alternative weapon systems which bypass the restrictions agreed upon. Theoretically, it might be possible to resolve this problem by entering into new negotiations once the base of the old agreement shows signs of erosion. However, given both the inherent speed of technological innovation and the wide-spread tendency of politicians, analysts and the media to speed it up further in their minds by assuming that a known technology is already a deployed one, the intervals between agreements would have to become very brief indeed. The complexity of negotiating new, or renegotiating old, quantitative restrictions would undermine the hope that new and more durable results could be achieved in time. As a result, arms-control treaties and agreements which consist of striking numerical balances are drawn into inevitable political controversy, generating doubts over, rather than promoting confidence in, detente and increasing the political risk for the leaders on both sides.

The fate of the Soviet–American Interim Agreement on the Limitation of Offensive Strategic Weapons of 1972 is a case in point. The numerical balance struck in the agreement soon appeared, rightly or wrongly, to many in the

United States to give a one-sided advantage to the Soviet Union, as Soviet weapons developments were catching up with American qualitative superiority. Rapid renegotiation became necessary, not least for domestic political reasons, which gave rise to the Vladivostok Accord only thirty months later. But even this compromise, which granted MIRV parity to the Soviet Union in exchange for an equal ceiling of total strategic forces, did not remove SALT from political controversy in the American debate. The dynamics of technological change eroded not only the basis of the original agreement, but also – and more importantly – eroded much of the desired political effect which both sides had sought to achieve. Rather than being a promoter of detente and political trust, inadequate arms control has become a consumer of trust.

## Limits to Verification

The second reason why technological change is rendering inadequate the current practice of negotiating quantitative restraints is the increasing difficulty of verification. That agreements on arms limitation must be adequately verifiable has been accepted wisdom for a long time, and technological inventiveness has indeed made this a realistic and unobtrusive principle in permitting the detailed observation of the military effort of another country through satellite reconnaissance. But verification depends on what is observable. Today, significant improvements in military forces and weapons are becoming less and less observable and may be concealed altogether. This poses an awkward dilemma: if a major determinant for arms control is verifiability, and verifiability is less and less assured, then fewer and fewer arms can be covered by agreement, and arms control becomes more and more irrelevant. But, without adequate verification, how can even the most promising arms-control agreement provide both sides with the trust in compliance by the other?

Neither of the two techniques for solving this dilemma suggested in recent arms-control negotiations justify much optimism. The first is to verify compliance to qualitative arms restrictions – for example, which missiles are equipped with MIRV – through the observation of weapons tests. This is based on two questionable assumptions: first, that responsible governments and cautious generals will not entertain the idea of deploying new weapons technology without thorough testing; second, that all tests will be adequately observable. While adequate testing is desirable, it would scarcely be undertaken if camouflage were seen to be of higher importance, particularly since military planners are used to living with a high degree of uncertainty anyway. In addition, much of the more important new weapons technologies in command, control and communications, guidance and target acquisition elude observation altogether.*

The other technique for rendering accountable the unobservable characteristics of weapons is the 'counting as if' method: a weapon system (say, an intercontinental missile of uncertain performance) is regarded, for assessment's sake, as if its performance were certain. The SALT II negotiations have already provided one such example: since the Soviet ICBM SS-18 had been tested both with MIRV and with a single warhead, the United States declared that within the Vladivostok limit of 1,320 MIRVed launchers, it would count each Soviet SS-18 *as if* it carried more than one independent warhead. This may be helpful in specific cases, but as a general device its efficacy is more than doubtful. Elevated to a standard measure for assessing qualitative, non-observable weapons improvements, 'counting as if' is a positive stimulus to maximum exploitation of qualitative advances and hence to qualitative arms competition: why should either side maintain a single warhead on a missile if it is counted as a multi-warhead missile anyway? Moreover, it only makes sense if the weapons characteristics are known and form the subject of agreed numerical limitations. 'Counting as if' is at best an auxiliary device, but it is not a satisfactory answer to the verification problem at a time of technological change.

## Multi-mission Weapons

It might still be possible to make do with a less than satisfactory answer if it were not for another, and probably the most important, feature of current weapons technology: the defiance of traditional categories of weapons definition. Not only does technology improve performance within existing and defined weapons categories; it also makes possible multi-category and multi-mission weapons. The distinction between

---

* For a more detailed discussion, see pp. 162-5.

nuclear and non-nuclear systems, or strategic and theatre weapons, was never absolutely clear-cut but it was sufficiently precise to allow arms-control negotiators to operate with it, incorporate it in treaty language and provide governments with a relatively unambiguous notion of their mutual obligations. It was possible, by restricting certain weapon systems, to restrict certain military missions: a limit on battleships limited also the amount of fire-power a navy could project beyond the shores; a ceiling on offensive intercontinental missiles also restricted the ability to launch a first strike against the other side; a freeze on theatre nuclear delivery vehicles also curtailed the destruction of specific theatre targets beyond the range and yield of conventional systems.

The trend towards multi-category and multi-mission systems is rapidly eroding this link between restrictions by category and curtailment of military performance. Limitation of the numbers of a particular category of weapon system no longer restricts the military mission the system used to support, since that mission can be allocated, albeit sometimes less effectively, to other, unrestricted systems. The particular feature of technology which makes this possible is the interchangeability of those factors which define weapon performance: range, yield and accuracy. In the past, a weapon of intercontinental range had to have a warhead which was both nuclear and high-yield, in order to make up for the inaccuracy caused by distance, and both features were more or less rigid requirements: there was no way of replacing the nuclear by a conventional explosive, since the weight differential would significantly reduce the range of the delivery system, and no way of substituting the high nuclear yield by a lower one, since this would drastically reduce destructive efficiency. But increasingly over the past years these absolute thresholds for performance requirements have become relative, largely as a result of the dramatic improvement in missile accuracy. Accuracy is no longer a function of range, as inter-continental delivery systems can attain CEPs as low as 300 ft over thousands of miles.[2] Low accuracy no longer has to be offset by high explosive yields, and conventional explosives, guided to the heart of a point target, can sometimes produce destructive effects of a kind previously reserved for certain nuclear missions.

The initial motivation for these performance improvements was to render delivery systems more effective, i.e. to produce better strategic or better theatre weapons. Their real and long-term significance, however, lies elsewhere: the visible size and configuration of a weapon system are no longer reliable indicators of its performance and mission, as performance elements within the same shell can be allocated differently and can even be changed rapidly to produce a wide range of mission capabilities.

The most obvious example of this development is the modern cruise missile: it can be a tactical or a theatre weapon, but with a smaller warhead load and the resulting increase in range, the same system can also be turned into a long-range weapon, capable of reaching strategic targets deep inside enemy territory. It can, at least theoretically, carry a nuclear or a conventional warhead. Cruise missile ranges can be as high as 4,000 kilometres and as low as desired, and their mode of launch – from the air, from sea-based launchers or from the ground – is equally variable.[3]

Variability is also the feature of another weapon system, the Soviet SS-20 IRBM. Its booster consists of the last two rocket stages of the three-stage ICBM SS-16. By adding the third stage, an intermediate-range ballistic missile targeted on Europe or China can be turned into an ICBM targeted on the United States. The time required for conversion is estimated by some to be no more than a few hours.

It would, of course, be an exaggeration to claim that this trend towards multi-category, multi-mission weapons is entirely new. Theatre arms, like artillery, air-defence systems or tactical aircraft, have for long been 'dual-capable', i.e. able to deliver both nuclear and conventional explosives with resulting variations in range and destructiveness. Manned bombers often span strategic and non-strategic missions if their range permits. The American B-52 force has today a primary strategic nuclear mission, but many of the aircraft were used during the Vietnam War for conventional area-bombing against targets in South-East Asia. The Soviet *Backfire* bomber, although probably not intended for use against strategic targets in the United States, has caused problems of definition and accountancy in the SALT negotiations because of its theoretical ability to reach American territory on some missions with in-flight refuelling. Equally, ship-based delivery systems have enjoyed considerable variability – witness the decision of NATO's Nuclear Planning Group in May 1976 to include *Polaris/Poseidon* SLBM in the theatre nuclear forces assigned to the Supreme Commander in Europe (SACEUR).[4] So the multi-mission phenomenon is, indeed, not entirely new. But while it had seemed relatively marginal during the development of intercontinental missile systems, it is now becoming much more central, challenging notions that have been essential to arms-control policies of the past twenty years. It is blurring the distinction between strategic and non-strategic weapon systems and making the verifiability of agreements uncertain.[5]

The answer to the problem cannot lie in singling out the latest and most obvious of these new systems, the cruise missile, and trying to find ways of making it conform to familiar arms-control definitions (for instance, by prohibiting all cruise missiles, or by so restricting cruise missile sizes that trade-offs between range, guidance, nuclear and non-nuclear use have little or no relevance to the performance). The inapplicability of the approaches of traditional arms control to the cruise missile is a product not so much of any particular characteristic of this specific weapon system as of the technological elements that are responsible for its performance: the miniaturization of guidance and engine, the increased accuracy of delivery, the development of explosives tailored to specific targets and the relatively low cost which allows production in large numbers. If the cruise missile were banned altogether or in specific configurations, other combinations of these elements would still be conceivable and conceived and would pose the same problem again, possibly within a short time.

Nor can the answer to the erosion of existing weapons categories – strategic/theatre, nuclear/non-nuclear – lie in the setting up of a third or fourth category or of a new arms-control forum designed to cover systems below SALT and above regional negotiations such as MBFR. These systems have often been referred to as 'grey area weapons', but this is a misleading term, since it suggests that defining the 'grey area' between strategic and regional arms control would make it possible to subject them to a specific arms-control regime. The particular significance of

multi-mission weapons is precisely that they cannot be pinned down in any category; they can span the whole spectrum. Attempts to deal with them with the help of a new category or a new arms-control forum will, therefore, be irrelevant to the problem they pose.[6]

For the same reason, the answer to the challenge of the new technologies is also unlikely to lie in an attempt to squeeze them into the framework of existing arms-control negotiations. Splitting up the 'grey area' between the more SALT-related systems (such as long-range nuclear cruise missiles or versatile medium-range ballistic missiles of the SS-20 type) and systems more related to regional security concerns and regional arms-control fora (such as the short-range cruise missile or the *Backfire* bomber) can be no more than a temporary and makeshift measure. Not only would verification – which is which in what context? – soon prove frustrating but, even if verification were attainable, any arrangement in one forum would deeply affect and disturb the considerations of the other. A severe restriction on cruise missiles in SALT would not only curtail the ability of the super-powers to carry out other military tasks with these systems that they would not want to forgo, but it would also, at least indirectly, circumscribe the use of these weapons by their allies (a problem peculiar to allies of the United States) in purely regional roles and would cause strains in the Alliance. Conversely, the inclusion of theatre cruise missiles in MBFR, even if compliance were verifiable, is bound to affect the balance of strategic forces discussed in SALT and with it political relations between the super-powers as well as between America and her allies. Much of the 'grey-area weapons' technology is not exclusive to the super-powers; refusal by their allies to conform to rules framed by Soviet and American negotiators (leading perhaps to national development of cruise missiles) would limit the scope of super-power agreement while potentially undermining cohesion within the Western alliance.

These, then, are the three problems that technological change poses for the future of East–West arms control: first, the speed of technological change injects a high degree of ambiguity into restrictions directed primarily at quantitative levels of forces, and not only complicates the negotiations but, more important, endangers the political acceptability of their outcome; second, qualitative improvements are often more significant and less verifiable than quantities of weapons, so that arms controllers have to choose between agreements that are fully verifiable but increasingly irrelevant for the control of military potential and agreements that may be relevant but cannot be adequately verified; and third, the trend of technological change is towards multi-mission weapons which undermines the definitional categories which have, in the practice of East–West negotiations, been a primary 'organizing principle'.[7] If arms control continues to encompass only the existing categories, it will fail to cover much of the new weaponry, which, as a result, will acquire increasing importance in the arsenals of both sides and will reduce the relevance of existing and future control agreements; if new categories were defined, these would prove equally elusive.

Attempts to cover the whole range from strategic-nuclear to regional-conventional weapons in one framework of negotiation and agreement could scarcely be promising: not only would the process of negotiation be even more cumbersome and agreement delayed beyond relevance but, more important, the wider framework would not do away with the problem of comparing categories and numbers of weapons. The search for strategic stability would be frustrated by the specific concerns of regional security. In this situation the United States may well decide that the former is more important than the latter; that if the security of the regional alliance were to interfere with the Soviet–American strategic relationship, then the Alliance would have to take second place. It is a choice which America has so far refused to accept.

This analysis of the dilemma is, of course, based on two assumptions: first, that the dilemma matters and that arms control remains an important instrument in the search for East–West security; second, that technological change, which has largely caused the dilemma, cannot be effectively controlled. Both assumptions will be examined in the following two chapters. If arms control had outlived its usefulness, or if the disturbing features of technological change could be domesticated, the need for a new approach would not arise.

## II. WHY ARMS CONTROL?

The traditional objectives of East–West arms control have been three: to reduce the likelihood of war by increasing stability; to reduce the damage of war if war does break out; and to reduce the economic cost of preparing for war. If arms control today has lost much of its initial popularity, this is due not only to a greater recognition of the complexities involved, but also to doubts about whether arms control can realistically achieve these objectives.

### Stability?
Current East–West arms-control negotiations – SALT and MBFR – are concerned with aspects of the strategic and theatre balance, both of which have, after all, been marked by a relatively high degree of stability in the past. The major change in the strategic relationship between the United States and the Soviet Union has been Soviet accession to parity. But that, it can be argued, is a condition for stability. In spite of the introduction of new weapons on both sides, in spite of a multiplication of deliverable warheads, a dramatic increase in the precision of delivering destructive power and a combination of symmetries and asymmetries in the force posture of both the Soviet Union and the United States, the post-1970 balance has shown remarkable resilience.

Although a very great deal of thought and diplomatic effort, hard bargaining and political courage has been invested by both sides in the process of strategic arms control, it is difficult to prove that without any of it – with the possible exception of the Anti-Ballistic Missile (ABM) Treaty – the stability of the central balance would by now be seriously undermined. The current discussion on limited strategic options, scenarios of limited first strikes against vulnerable ICBM and the inadequacies of 'mutual assured destruction' concepts for deterrence indicates that the stability of the balance is under strain, and no more.[8] The fact that much of this discussion fails to excite fears and concerns beyond the small society of strategic analysts

157

rather confirms the resilience of the existing strategic relationship between the two superpowers, arms control or no arms control.

The European theatre balance, now the subject of East–West negotiation on force reductions, has shown an equally impressive degree of stability, in spite of the absence of any arms-control agreement. This is not to say that the balance is perfect in all respects, nor that there are not very real and sincere doubts over its future in the light of a continuous Soviet build-up which exceeds NATO efforts. But it does indicate that, in spite of changes in force ratios, political crises and the impact of technological innovation on the military arsenals of both sides, relative stability has in the past been obtained without arms control.

That is, of course, not really surprising. After all, there are other means for obtaining and maintaining stability than arms control, in particular that of offsetting through military efforts any threats to the balance as each side perceives it. The test for arms control is, therefore, not whether stability has been present without it but whether it has contributed to *more* stable military relationships. Here the record is at least ambiguous. Arms control has made the military relationship between East and West more calculable, and therefore stable, when it has been preclusive in character, i.e. when its aims have been to restrict the emplacement of weapons on the seabed, to prohibit the development and deployment of biological weapons, to reduce anti-ballistic missile defences to the point of insignificance, as in the 1972 Soviet–American treaty. However, where negotiators have sought not preclusive arrangements but quantitative limitations and reductions of existing arsenals, the contribution to stability has been less evident. Details of military force relationships have often received emphasis beyond their real strategic significance; reductions seem to have been contemplated primarily in connection with older and more obsolete weapon systems, and new programmes have been entertained both to provide a card in the bargaining with the opponent and to mollify domestic political and military opposition.[9] In this respect the relevance of arms control to strategic stability has been doubtful. While it is impossible to judge with any certainty what would have been the state of the strategic balance without SALT, it is clear that the negotiations and the political ambiance they have created have generated at least some dynamics which have favoured arms competition rather than control.

In the European context, the effect of quantitative, systems-orientated arms limitation on stability is equally ambiguous. While reductions of arms and forces in the potential conflict area of Central Europe might make war preparations more visible and therefore perhaps less likely, they could weaken political stability in a continent where military and political relationships are so closely intertwined: in Eastern Europe, where Soviet political control is underpinned by military presence, and Western Europe, where the strain of negotiations could emphasize differences between allies at the cost of alliance cohesion, and where the establishment of certain arms-control zones could lead to political divisions.[10] This need not be so – but the contribution of arms control to stability is not so clear-cut and obvious as to warrant, for this reason alone, a major political effort.

**Damage Limitation?**

Nor is the need for arms control all that obvious when it comes to the second objective: reducing the damage if war should break out. Paradoxically, the introduction of new weapons technology has sometimes been more successful in this respect than have efforts at controlling arms. The increased accuracy of delivery systems, both for strategic and theatre use, means that collateral damage (that is, unintended damage) can be considerably reduced. New precision-guided weapons with conventional warheads may, in the European theatre, be able to perform tasks that before had been allocated to nuclear weapons, thus raising the 'nuclear threshold'. As strategic systems can be used more selectively, because of refinements in command and control as well as accuracy, the threshold of all-out nuclear war is further removed from regional conflict, and military installations replace urban centres as the primary targets in the echelon of escalation below that upper threshold. These technologies may well be 'destabilizing', in that they remove one barrier against their employment, that of uncertainty of effect; as the effect of weapons becomes more calculable, the decision to go to war may also. But if war does break out, the new technologies allow for a more discriminating and controlled use – an important objective of arms control. This, again, is not an argument *against* arms control; efforts at damage limitation, like the current Red Cross talks on incendiary and other weapons,[11] or the negotiations of the United Nations Disarmament Conference in Geneva on chemical weapons, weather modification and weapons of mass destruction, may also contribute to making war less indiscriminately destructive. The point is merely that arms control, contrary to the beliefs and hopes of some, is not the only, and often not the most effective, way of achieving this goal.

### Reducing Military Costs?

The third objective, that of reducing the economic burden of the military effort, has been both the most pragmatic and the least successfully attained to date in East–West arms-control negotiations and agreements. The promise of savings in defence expenditure has been offered by political leaders in East and West every time they have embarked on negotiations over the limitation of arms. Yet the results have rarely matched the promises. In connection with the SALT I experience, Allison and Morris have noted: 'After a decade of steady decline in [American] strategic expenditures – in the absence of a SALT Treaty and attendant principles and agreements – defence budgets submitted to the Congress [after the 1972 SALT Agreements] .... called for a levelling off of that decline and, indeed, for increasing strategic expenditures.'[12] On the Soviet side, judging by the range of new deployments and newly started strategic programmes, the discrepancy between expressed economic hopes and actual expenditure, although less verifiable, has been no less and probably much greater than in the United States. Even if future SALT negotiations should produce sizeable reductions, as opposed to ceilings without cuts, in the strategic arsenals of both sides, these are not likely to produce major economies but would probably involve the phasing out of old systems in favour of new and more expensive ones. The major exception to the rule has been the ABM Treaty, in which both sides agreed not only to limit, but in reality to forgo the investment for, a functioning ballistic missile defence, an example to which we shall return later.

No practical experience with mutual arms limitation has so far been gained in the European theatre. The MBFR negotiations have been accompanied by publicly expressed hopes that they would result in the maintenance of security at lower costs. This might be the case if negotiations were to lead to a sizeable cut in military manpower; but the Western reductions envisaged by NATO's proposals – 20,000 US forces in the first phase and a further 53,000 US and Allied in the second – would not go far in producing savings for the six NATO forces involved in the prospective reduction area[13] (even assuming reductions would lead to the units' being disbanded rather than redeployed elsewhere). Savings would certainly be much less than the £10 billion per annum which, it has been argued, could result from NATO weapons standardization.[14] Where not manpower but weapons cuts are considered, as in the December 1975 NATO proposal to withdraw from West European territory 1,000 nuclear warheads with launchers in exchange for a withdrawal of 1,700 Soviet tanks from Eastern Europe, any savings are likely to be largely offset by the cost of modernizing those that remain.

This assessment is, of course, open to the criticism that it concentrates on savings against actual but not against potential expenditure. In the absence of negotiated restrictions, it has been argued, the arms race would have continued unabated and major new weapon investments would have been necessary to keep ahead in the race. This might well be true but it is not self-evident. For one thing, the contention rests on a hypothetical comparison – between that which is and that which might have been. As the point raised by Allison and Morris makes clear, it is by no manner of means certain that the absence of arms control would have promoted arms competition more than has the negotiation of formal agreements. For another, it assumes that the primary driving force of the arms race is the action–reaction process by which the weapons procurement of each side is a response to that of the other. However, this is an assumption which has been increasingly and persuasively challenged by recent academic studies;[15] at worst it is erroneous, at best too simple.

If the economic rewards of arms control have generally been disappointing, some kinds of arms control seem to have yielded more tangible results. The ABM example is, after all, impressive as a preclusive arms-control agreement which rules out of the legitimate arsenals of both sides the specific military mission of ballistic missile defence and prohibits investment on production and deployment (not research or development) of weapons designed to provide it. Quantitative limitations, however, if they imply reductions at all are likely to produce only marginal savings, because in the bargaining of mutual concessions both sides will tend to seek the smallest common denominator, which often means retention of the largest force. It is also easier to agree on phasing out obsolete weapons which are obsolete precisely because new and more expensive systems have superseded them, thus offering economies in maintenance but not in investment as the most likely saving. Moreover, quantitative restrictions of specific systems encourage the search for alternative, non-restricted systems in a world of technological change. It is therefore not surprising if the economic advantages of quantitative arms control have been less than impressive and represent, by themselves, an insignificant dividend for the effort invested.

Has East–West arms control then outlived its usefulness? The balance in the strategic Soviet–American relationship and in the European theatre is not ideal but it is still relatively stable. Potential damage in war could be reduced with the help of some of the new military technologies that are being introduced over the next few years. The tangible economic dividends of arms control have generally been meagre.

And yet the reasons why, in spite of doubts, disappointments and disillusionment, attempts at arms control between East and West must be continued remain powerful, perhaps more powerful than in the past.

**Arms Control as Conflict Management**
Much of the original American enthusiasm for arms control was shaped in a period of clear American superiority, and more recent disappointments may have much to do with the difficulties of living in a state of nuclear strategic parity. Both the Soviet Union and the United States face a tough learning process. The Soviet Union must learn that catching up with the leader is one thing, gaining superiority over him quite another. The Americans must learn that parity is a combination of asymmetries and that marginal advantages on one side or the other do

not undermine stability. This learning process will be made even more difficult by the fact that some of the basic elements of nuclear deterrence will be called into question by technological change and will require careful deterrence management. The most important and potentially the most disturbing of these changes is the vulnerability of second-strike forces to strategic counter-force action. With growing missile accuracy, land-based ICBM (even those in hardened silos) will become, sooner for the United States or later for the Soviet Union, targets that can be destroyed by the other side with a relatively high degree of reliability.[16] As to sea-based nuclear missile forces, the anti-submarine warfare (ASW) effort continues and may, over time, decrease the margin of invulnerability which they enjoy today. These developments will not only raise the general level of strategic nervousness; they may also reopen the question of ballistic missile defence which has been presumed closed since the ABM Treaty of 1972. The degree of strategic turbulence will therefore be considerable over the next decade; probably much greater than that provoked by the relatively simple process of adjustment to the Soviet–American parity of secure second-strike forces which has marked the previous one. During this period of pronounced sensitivity, with its concomitant risks of miscalculation and misinterpretation, arms control will provide an essential framework of management.

**Nuclear Proliferation**
The other development which will confront the two strategic superpowers in the decade ahead is nuclear proliferation. As other countries demonstrate their real or potential status as nuclear-weapons powers, the need is becoming manifest for the Soviet Union and the United States to keep their strategic relationship clear of the impact of third-party proliferation. Not that, in the foreseeable future, there will be serious rivals to the status of the super-powers, nor that the next decade is likely to see the emergence of many fully-fledged nuclear-weapons states; the situation will be much less clear-cut. Some states will visibly invest in a nuclear-weapons option without proceeding to its implementation; others will set up a minimum force, primitive by super-power standards but nevertheless frightening to neighbours; other states again will keep the

160

world guessing as to whether or not they have acquired the capability to deliver nuclear weapons against an enemy; and a further group will make their continued non-nuclear status dependent on the co-operative behaviour of others, including the adequate supply of conventional weapons. As a result, nuclear power will be brought into international politics much more actively than before, in spite of the continued military pre-eminence of the United States and the Soviet Union. It is against this background that the super-powers must seek to protect their relationship of mutual deterrence through the continued process of dialogue which is arms control.

Finally, the arms-control process between East and West should be sustained in order to constrain the use of force in the period of international change, potential conflict and gradual adjustment which the world will be facing over the next decade or two. There is a risk that wars in the Third World could embroil the Second and First worlds as well, that domestic change in East and West European countries could blur the European dividing line and introduce, into a continent which has owed much of its stability of the last thirty years to the predictability of alliances, a degree of unpredictability which could jeopardize security in the short run. And there is a risk that the Soviet Union, faced at home with the dilemma of the continued postponement of needed modernization of her political system for fear of its survival, and abroad with her inability to influence events other than by military force, might seek via the active employment of military resources an expansion of her influence and release from internal deadlock. Arms-control negotiations and agreements will not be capable of repressing the use of force on their own, but they may contribute to restraint, however modestly, in a period when the world will need all the barriers against conflict it can construct.

The requirement for arms control follows, therefore, from the need to manage and control military competition between East and West in the years ahead. Can this not be done adequately by dialogue, by discussion and by the explanation of respective doctrines – in other words, without specific agreements on subjects which, like force reductions and weapons deployment, are affected by technological change? Dialogue and discussion are, no doubt, an important ingredient of the management of arms competition, but they must be expressed in agreements in order that their success can be assessed and so that they may receive and maintain political support. Results mean visible restrictions, reductions and constraints. As these will be affected by changes in military technology, arms control will either have to develop the means to slow down and control technological change, or it will have to devise other methods of restraint which are less subject to the dynamics of technological innovation and change than the existing method of primarily quantitative limitation.

## III. CAN TECHNOLOGICAL CHANGE BE SLOWED DOWN?

Clearly, not all technological changes are undesirable and some, indeed, are essential to the maintenance of national security. But even assuming that they were undesirable, could they be prevented? On the face of it, the most obvious way of slowing down the rate of technological innovation and development would be an East–West agreement to cut military research and development (R&D) expenditure: less funds, less change. But even on the assumptions that East and West could agree on the size of their respective expenditure on military R&D and

that verification were considered adequate – and these are big assumptions – there are two important reasons why the supposedly simple device of reductions in funds will not work. The first is inherent in the term R&D. The results of R&D efforts are, to a large degree, unplannable. Major improvements in weapons characteristics need not be, and often are not, the result of the sustained expenditure of large sums of money. Indeed, major improvements need not be the result of major innovations at all but simply of introducing already known ingredients into a

161

new system, ingredients that may, moreover, have stemmed from civilian rather than military R&D programmes.

It is not only that some of the small changes involved may be relatively inexpensive and others not. It is that the costs and the development are unrelated to the recognized administrative and budgetary categories of R&D, may not become apparent until after they have happened, and even then, though apparent in the aggregate, seem difficult to identify in detail.[17]

This means that *specific* cuts in *specific* R&D programmes are likely to produce results that are different from the ones intended. The attempt to slow down the rate of technological change for specific weapon systems in a quantitative arms-restriction agreement is, therefore, bound to fail, if only because of the high degree of uncertainty that must accompany it for both sides.

This leaves the alternative of major cuts in overall military R&D spending, on the assumption that a general reduction in all R&D activity would reduce the general rate of technological innovation. But – and this is the second reason why cuts in R&D expenditure are not a realistic method of restraining the technological momentum – no responsible government can be expected to agree to such a proposal, since it would risk the suppression not only of innovations that complicate arms control but also of those that promote national security. Moreover, the knowledge that R&D will not be constrained is essential if governments are to accept the risks of agreeing to restrictions in their existing military arsenals.[18] They may be ready to accept a cut in actual military power but not at the price of forgoing future developments.

Other, more pragmatic suggestions have been made for keeping technological change from upsetting quantitative East–West arms-control agreements. Two suggestions in particular merit closer examination. They have one basic idea in common: if it is impossible to restrict military R&D as such, at least it should be possible to restrict the procurement and deployment of new weapons. The first suggestion is to limit the number of tests for new systems; the second to restrict the frequency with which new weapons are introduced into the military arsenals. Both have been referred to by President Carter and

are under consideration in the current round of Soviet–American SALT negotiations.[19]

## Limits on Testing
This is a popular suggestion among those who are concerned, in particular, with the impact of new missile technology on the Soviet–American SALT agreements and negotiations. Harvey Brooks puts the argument succinctly:

Experimental launchings are an essential part of missile development and are at the same time readily detectable by unilateral methods. Therefore, limitation of the number of test firings is a potential means for retarding innovations in missiles that can be verified unilaterally.[20]

But it is important to realize that the term 'essential' is relative, not absolute. Testing is essential to promote a degree of confidence that a weapon system will function reliably – but only in circumstances where testing is possible and not restricted. All that restriction of the number of permitted weapon tests would assure is that, provided verification were adequate, no further *tests* were being undertaken. What it would not assure is that no further *weapons* were developed and deployed or that no further qualitative improvements in existing weapons were implemented.

Those who argue that a limitation on weapon *tests* will produce a limitation on weapon *acquisition* do so on the assumption that governments, technologists and military men will refrain from procuring a weapon system they do not regard as sufficiently reliable. This may be the case. But it is an unproven contention, and a number of arguments raise considerable doubts about whether it can ever be proven to the degree required to make a limitation on weapon tests an effective measure for qualitative arms control.

The main reasons for doubt are that the reliability of weapons is a relative notion, that uncertainty has not prevented governments from acquiring modern weapon systems in the past, and that test restrictions are unlikely to increase the relative uncertainty about actual weapons performance to the point of creating an absolute barrier against further procurement.

None of the strategic weapon systems in existence today has been fired in anger over the past thirty years. It is true that modern weapons have been used in other, non-central conflicts like Korea, Vietnam or the Middle East, but these have at best provided limited experience which cannot be applied automatically to the specific conditions of other theatres, and they do not substantially alter the fact that assumptions about the actual performance in an East–West conflict of most of the weapons designed, procured and deployed over the past three decades are based on estimates, not certainty.

In fact, the reliability of specific strategic weapons, such as the *Minuteman* or *Poseidon* missiles, has been questioned, in spite of repeated test firings. If one system of a specific type functions properly in a test, this does not guarantee that it or other identical systems will function when the military need arises. All that can be statistically derived from tests is a probability that a certain percentage of systems will function as designed.

This uncertainty has not prevented governments, technologists and military men from acquiring the military arsenals that East and West possess today. Absolute certainty over performance does not, therefore, seem to be the decisive factor in a procurement decision. Why then should a restriction of weapons tests provide the decisive barrier against procurement?

There are other, more specific factors which make the link between the number of tests and new weaponry still more tenuous. For one, 'the cumulative effects of many small evolutionary improvements in the parameters of component technologies can often be as revolutionary as such dramatic, basic developments as the transistor or the hydrogen bomb.'[21] Much of the 'new' weapons technology consists of a combination of trusted 'old' technologies, for which testing to ensure reliability is of lesser importance. The uncertainty pertains not to the components themselves but to the systems of which they are a part, and consequently may seem more tolerable and less inhibiting.

It is true that incrementalism of this kind is often more characteristic of the Soviet procurement process than of the Western. Soviet weapon systems are marked by the care with which their designers seek to maintain as many as possible of the trusted features of previous generations of weapons, adding only those new elements required to give the systems particular performance. The American approach, however, is generally more innovative and directed towards entirely new systems with a wide range of new components, which probably require more intensive testing before procurement than is the case with Soviet military products.[22] We know that the Soviet Union is conducting many more tests now than the United States, but this is under present conditions, i.e. when there is no test limit. If one were agreed, this pattern could change and Soviet testing habits may turn out to be a luxury which is expendable. At any rate, an agreement to limit testing is likely to have a different effect on Soviet than on Western military modernization.

A serious restriction on the number of missile tests on both sides will, moreover, encourage the search for test methods which are not excluded but can still promote a degree of confidence in performance. Features of a long-range cruise missile, for instance, like guidance and other key systems, can be fully tested on a short-range missile since they do not change their method of operation with greater range, and 'system endurance can be tested by running the engines and components for long periods of time in a fixed stand without flying the missile at all'.[23] Simulation conducted below the specific level prescribed by agreement would thus acquire an even greater importance than today. Even a severe test limitation might prove no serious obstacle to modernization. Similarly, since a complete ban on tests for strategic delivery vehicles would conflict with the needs of East and West alike to demonstrate the minimum functioning of their deterrent forces, a limited number of 'confidence tests' would have to be permitted in any case.[24]

No less important than the question of the effectiveness of test limitations is, finally, that of their impact on strategic stability. Weapon tests, however imperfect the assurance they provide, constitute one objective yardstick for weapons performance and programme intent. If they were to be seriously curtailed, criteria which are much less verifiable – not only by the opponent but by the procuring government as well – may well take their place: producers' claims, laboratory tests or even unsubstantiated accounts in the specialized press. Strategic analysts are prone, as it is, to assume the full-blown existence of a new weapon system long before it is deployed; the current debate about new conventional weapons

163

technologies is one of the many examples of this failing. In the absence of a sufficient number of actual tests, these subjective criteria will acquire even greater weight in judging the performance of new weapons. As a result, the dynamics of technological change, far from being slowed down, could, on the contrary, be speeded up. There will be fewer reliable criteria on which to base the decision to stop weapon development and deployment. In the absence of verifiable tests indicating the state of the weapons programme of the other side, military planners and technologists will tend to prepare for the worst case, namely that the opponent's procurement programme goes far beyond its tested elements. An agreement to limit tests for new weapon systems can, therefore, be highly unstable. It can lead on to technological over-insurance, however untested, as well as to a high degree of mutual suspicion that tested systems, far from representing the total of new weaponry, will represent but the tip of the iceberg of the opponent's programmes.

This is also why, in the one respect in which test restrictions would appear to enhance stability, the effect is likely to be much less certain. This is the issue of the reliability of a disarming counter-force strike against, say, American ICBM forces. The argument runs that confidence in the success of a pre-emptive first strike would be impossible without testing, since the weapons needed to support such a strike must rely on the proven reliability and precision of a complex system.[25] There are, however, three flaws in this argument. The first is that it is difficult to imagine that either the United States or the Soviet Union would at any point be reckless enough to risk all-out nuclear war by destroying part of the other side's deterrent forces in a limited strike, even if they were technologically in a position to do so. Second, the confidence that such a strike will be successful can never be absolute, however successful the tests. No Chief of the Soviet General Staff, and no Chairman of the American Joint Chiefs of Staff, can guarantee to his political masters that the operation, if it were indeed contemplated, would work as planned. Third, confidence is subjective; in the absence of tests, worst-case speculation may take over where hard-fact analysis has to stop. American analysts could easily attribute to Soviet leaders a confidence in

the performance of their own weaponry which in reality does not exist.

It would seem unjustified, therefore, to hope that test restrictions can seriously and significantly inhibit the introduction of new weapons technologies. They may do so marginally, but unless we can be sure that their effect would be unambiguously beneficial, we should not see in them a solution to the problem of controlling technological change.

## Limits on Procurement

Could the *decision to procure* be subjected to agreed restrictions, thereby slowing down not the rate of technological change but the rate at which military arsenals are modernized? This might be done in a variety of ways: by regulating the replacement of individual weapons; by stipulating a minimum period in which specific types of weapons should not be replaced or modernized; or by limiting the numbers of new weapon systems each side can deploy within an agreed period.[26]

The first of these approaches (regulation of the replacement of individual weapons) has been tried repeatedly in the history of arms control. For the inter-war years, the restrictions imposed on the German *Reichswehr* by the Treaty of Versailles are perhaps the most obvious example, as well as the most obvious failure. More recently, the 1953 Korean Armistice Agreement sought to regulate weapons replacement by insisting, for instance, that combat aircraft of 'the same effectiveness and the same type' (Art. II 13(d)) would be introduced only on a one-for-one replacement basis. The failure of the Agreement has been marked in this respect (as in others).

These examples may be a little unfair. They failed because of the lack of will to abide by them. No arms-control agreement, however ingenious, would succeed in those circumstances. But even assuming political will among the contracting parties to honour an agreement which restricts their ability to replace existing or introduce new weaponry, there are still formidable obstacles to the effectiveness of this type of limitation.

The first and most obvious one is that of definition: which weapons are 'identical' and hence allowed, which are 'new' and hence forbidden? In order to satisfy the concerns of both sides, a restriction on modernization would have to go into considerable detail about all the relevant technologies of existing weapons; in the case of tanks, for instance, it would have to cover at least range, speed, weapon performance, armour and electronic equipment. The tendency towards modular building-blocks in modern weapons components would further exacerbate the problem. The very complexity of modern weaponry, both conventional and nuclear, defeats the simple device of defining as 'new' everything that does not yet exist. To provide this catalogue of permitted and non-permitted elements of weapon modernization, negotiations would at best be protracted, at worst impossible. As an example, Soviet and American negotiators at the climax of East–West arms control in the 1972 SALT accords were unable to agree on the definition of what should, and what should not, constitute a 'heavy' ICBM; the prospects for a more detailed definition of weapon characteristics which would be required by an agreement to slow down modernization are therefore not promising.

Second, even if such an agreement were negotiable, its relevance as a means of stopping technological momentum is doubtful. By definition, it could only cover those technologies that were known at the time of agreement and could, however imperfectly, be defined as 'new' by contrast with existing weapon systems; such an agreement might then succeed in delaying the introduction of a 'new' tank, a 'new' aircraft, a 'new' missile or components of these systems. But an agreement that concentrated on existing weapons could not cover alternatives yet unknown which could perform similar military missions, e.g. the cruise missile as an alternative to interdiction aircraft, the missile as an alternative to the gun, the helicopter as an alternative to the tank, etc. The restriction on modernizing existing types of weaponry would positively encourage the search for alternatives that are not covered by agreement. One set of technological dynamics would merely be replaced by another; the dynamics themselves would continue unchecked.

Finally, by regulating the cycles of weapon modernization, such an agreement would push both sides towards great efforts to secure modernization at the end of the cycle. The Protocol on cruise missiles, for instance, that is currently proposed in SALT II is likely to ensure that both the United States and the Soviet Union will undertake major efforts to seek a better bargaining position once the three-year period stipulated by the Protocol comes to an end. Regulating the frequency of procurement would maintain the level of weapons performance at best for the duration of the agreement, but only at the price of ensuring major qualitative changes at the end of that period. In the final analysis, regulation of modernization would therefore only make more fitful the qualitative arms competition between East and West; it would hardly slow it down.

For these reasons it seems doubtful whether a direct effort to reduce the rate of change in military technology will have the desired effect. One or the other of the proposals discussed above may have some temporary impact; for instance, it will take some time before design bureaux, laboratories, military organizations and political leaders will have learned to operate military programmes under the restrictions of a limitation on weapon tests. But once this impact has faded, as it is likely to do, the dilemma posed for arms control by technological change will reappear. The discovery that remedies which were regarded as promising have failed could result in a general disenchantment with arms control.

For the reasons set out in Chapter II, the instrument will continue to be needed, in the future perhaps much more than in the past. The failure of existing arms-control methods to come to grips with the challenge of technological changes is the fault not of East–West arms control as such but of the specific methods employed: the placing of emphasis on mutual agreement rather than on unilateral restraint, and the concentration on quantitative restriction of specific types of weapons or forces. Technological change might be easier to check through national decision than through international agreement, and arms-limitation agreements based less on specific types of weapons which are particularly vulnerable to changes in the technology than on the military missions they can perform might avoid the pitfalls of the existing approach. Both of these propositions will be examined in Chapter IV.

# IV. ELEMENTS OF A NEW APPROACH

## A. UNILATERAL RESTRAINT?

One of the major causes of the difficulties encountered in the attempt to devise an effective method for regulating technological change lies in the nature of agreed, reciprocal East–West arms control. It is one thing for a government to decide on its own, and without any treaty obligation, to forgo the procurement of a particular type of weapon, to cut its defence expenditure or to allocate fewer funds to a specific technology area. It is quite another thing to negotiate, and agree on, a treaty concerning reciprocal obligations and rights. The consequences for the control of arms are profound.

The first is the *quid pro quo* character of all mutually agreed arms limitations. The extent of each side's readiness to reduce its military strength depends on the readiness of the other side to do the same; cuts are made because they can be negotiated, not because they are optimal from the perspective of national security. Decisions which, in the absence of negotiations, would be determined by their relevance to the security of the state are now regarded as potential concessions in the bargain and are determined by their effect on that bargain. Even if one side were convinced that it could afford much larger cuts than those agreed, it will not implement them since this might weaken its negotiating position in a next round. Mutually agreed quantitative arms control generally makes for timid and cautious deals.

Second, by establishing a visible and formal framework of what is permitted, mutually agreed arms limitations tend to encourage each side to push the military effort to the maximum of what is permitted, rather than accept less. Shortly before the conclusion of SALT I in 1972, Abram Chayes sought to demonstrate that the large bureaucracies involved in implementing the agreement would be careful not to push it to its limits and would not risk jeopardizing it by expansive interpretations. They would generally shield the agreement from disruptive influences.[27] Five years later, however, this must be recognized as an expression of hope rather than an analysis of reality. Not only bureaucracies and military men, but political leaders, government critics and industrialists have in most cases combined to turn the *permission* granted by an arms-control agreement to build up to a certain level of military strength into an *obligation* to do so. The existence of a formal accord in a specified area of arms competition has tended to encourage increased attention to and investment in weapons technologies outside the agreed limitations.[28]

This effect of negotiated mutual agreement may be more marked in the strategic-nuclear field of East–West arms control than in the context of, say, conventional force reductions in Europe. In Europe, some fear that an agreement between East and West to reduce military forces would lead to further, unilateral reductions in some NATO countries rather than being regarded as an implied obligation not to cut beyond the agreed level. But even here, the mere fact of the Vienna MBFR negotiations has quashed the temptation in some West European countries to seek unilateral cuts in the forces covered by the negotiations.

Observation of these effects has led, in the academic debate on arms control, to renewed interest in unilateral rather than mutually agreed measures to reduce the size of military forces, increase savings and avoid the repercussions of negotiated arms-control treaties. This is an attractive thought for a number of reasons.

First, armed forces are not constituted by agreement with the opponent but by unilateral (or alliance) decision. The control of arms should, therefore, also be facilitated by unilateral (or alliance) decision and by unilateral acts rather than by a search for reciprocity.[29]

It has become clear that military procurement decisions are much less a reaction to the military efforts of the potential foe than the result of domestic processes and pressures. 'While actions of foreign governments and uncertainties about the intentions of other countries are obviously important . . . . the weapons in the American and Soviet force postures are *predominantly* the result of factors *internal* to each nation.'[30] More promising than the control, through negotiated agreement, of the secondary causes of arms competition should be the attempt to address the predominant cause, and this depends not on the wording of international treaties but on the efficiency of domestic political control.

Second, as Thomas Schelling has pointed out, even in reciprocal, formal arms-control agreements, the only real sanction against non-compliance by one side is non-compliance by the other.[31] Since the sanction is unilateral, why should arms control be complicated by the problems inherent in a formal, bilateral agreement?

These arguments have a good deal of logical merit. In a recent paper, Herbert Scoville Jr, for many years closely involved in the American arms-control debate, has developed them into a concrete proposal linked to the principle of reciprocity:

One nation could announce that it was not going to proceed with a new weapons development or deployment provided that future events did not indicate that such restraint would prejudice its security. It could then watch the reaction of the other side which, in turn, might exercise reciprocal restraint either in the same or a related area.[32]

President Carter seemed to have such an approach in mind when he suggested that the US might delay implementing the MX ICBM programme if the USSR would forgo deploying the SS-20 IRBM[33] and when he decided to delay production of the 'neutron weapon', provided the USSR responds by co-operating in arms control.

This expedient might be of limited use in *supplementing* negotiated agreement (as indeed suggested by Scoville). But to go further and *replace* negotiated agreements by unilateral acts, reciprocal or not, seems unrealistic. The penalties for misunderstanding could be severe. It might do away with some of the inadequacies of negotiated arms control, but only at the price of creating new inadequacies. Formal negotiation and mutual agreement will have to remain the basis of East–West arms control.

This is, above all, because the decision by a government to forgo certain types of armaments or to restrict its military arsenal is, in the East–West context, a political act of such significance that it must be expressed through the ritual of negotiation and agreement. Military force relations between East and West have consistently commanded, and will continue to command, a high degree of political attention. Governments must be able to show what they have received in return for the concessions they have made, and no vague expectation of reciprocal unilateral restraint by the other side will provide this – only a formal agreement would do so. This may be a pity in the context of effective arms control, but it is a fact of political life.

Moreover, unilateral decisions can be changed by subsequent unilateral decisions. There is no certainty, not even the limited certainty of an agreement which cannot be enforced, that a measure taken today will not be reversed tomorrow. This would not only perpetuate domestic political controversy (had there been no ABM Treaty in 1972, but instead a unilateral American decision to forgo the ABM programme, the protracted, inconclusive and often bitter internal American debate on the faults and merits of ballistic missile defence might well be still with us today); it would also encourage the services, industry, government and legislators alike to hedge their bets, to retain options and to avoid decisions which cannot be reversed – hardly an atmosphere conducive to serious arms control. A formal agreement does not obviate all these pitfalls, nor a good many others, but it does achieve one politically important effect: it settles the issue for the time being. To quote Schelling:

There is something about the formality of a treaty, including making people stand up and vote . . . . twisting their arms if necessary, something even about making it costly to have a treaty, costly in legislative time, that makes a lot of people who otherwise would work to undermine the treaty give up the attempt. This works on one's own populace, it works on agencies of one's own government, and it probably works on allies.[34]

This is true not only in the American but also in the Soviet political context (perhaps even more so). A treaty may be the one unambiguous way for the Soviet leadership, which tends to leave military matters for the military to decide, to exert political control over specific military programmes.

Finally, a formal agreement specifies the *quid pro quo*. The greater flexibility of response that unilateral action provides has its attractions, no doubt. The choice of what to do if the other side does not react positively is then a matter to be decided by each government as it sees fit, unhampered by the strings of a formal agreement.

167

The problem, however, is how to reconcile flexibility with credibility of response. Supposing the United States were to announce that she would not go ahead with the MX programme if the Soviet Union, in turn, were to forgo further deployment of the new medium-range ballistic missile SS-X-20. The Soviet Union might have perfectly good reasons for thinking that such a deal would not be in her interest and might either refuse or suggest a different trade-off in unilateral restrictions. Would the United States then automatically go ahead with the MX development, and would those who argued against it on purely military grounds be overruled just to save the credibility of the threatened sanction? And if the United States did not proceed with the development, would future unilateral restraint by the United States be honoured by Soviet reciprocity?

Credibility is at stake, of course, not only when a response to unilateral initiatives fails to materialize. Non-compliance with a treaty obligation raises the issue as well. But by spelling out in a formal agreement the specific obligations of the parties towards each other, by creating a specific relationship of mutual restraint in defined areas, countries not only commit themselves to compliance, they also commit themselves implicitly to counter-measures in the case of non-compliance. These can range from putting specific treaty obligations in abeyance to the abrogation of the agreement as a whole – sanc-

tions which could not be made in the absence of a formal agreement, since there would be nothing to abrogate. A formal agreement provides, therefore, firmer assurance that violations by the other side will be met with sanctions than does a web of unilateral undertakings.

The fate of the SALT accords bears this out. Where both sides have agreed formally, the obligations have been respected. But the unilateral declarations by the United States – attached to the text but not written into the agreement – have failed to make an impact: the American delegation declared that the development of mobile ICBM by the Soviet Union would prompt reconsideration of the ABM Treaty, and yet the new Soviet SS-X-16 is a mobile system of intercontinental range.[35] Similarly, the unilateral American definition of a 'heavy' missile was rejected by the Soviet Union, and the throw-weight in a number of the latest Soviet ICBM is substantially higher than that definition would seem to allow. To replace arms-control accords by a web of unilateral undertakings is, therefore, no realistic way out of the arms-control dilemma posed by technological change. Arms control between East and West will remain primarily a negotiated contract. Unless we can think of ways in which to make it more promising within that context, all suggestions for a new approach to arms control will fail the test of political practicability.

## B. New Units of Account: Missions Instead of Weapons

It has been the very precision of quantitative arms-control agreements which has exposed them most to the impact of technological change. SALT I deals with precise quantities of ICBM, nuclear ballistic submarines and sea-launched missiles, and MBFR proposes specific reductions in forces and in weapons. As a result, changes in military technology will affect them directly; the introduction of Soviet MIRV has altered the balance of the bargain struck in SALT 1972, and the introduction of more effective anti-tank technology may affect that proposed for MBFR. Verification has been directed towards counting the numbers of weapons, while many of the more important increases in military potential have been qualitative rather than quantitative, and

hence verifiability has become increasingly doubtful. Multi-mission weapons like the cruise missile cannot adequately be counted in an agreement which aims at including all weapon systems in a specific category, because they do not belong to one category alone but can be allocated to others as well. The emphasis in SALT and in MBFR on the sizes of the existing military arsenals has largely precluded control of forthcoming new military systems.

### Lessons from the ABM Treaty[36]
In recent East–West arms control there is one exception to this analysis: the 1972 Soviet–American treaty on Anti-Ballistic Missile (ABM)

systems. Some of its features adumbrate a more promising arms control approach.

(1) The Treaty is primarily directed at prohibiting a military mission – effective defence against ballistic missiles – not at simply limiting or reducing the number of permitted ABM systems. The quantitative restrictions in the text have the function of implementing this primary objective; they are not an objective in their own right.

(2) The Treaty covers not only existing ballistic missile defence (BMD) technology (Art. II(1): '. . . an ABM system is a system . . . *currently* consisting of . . .) but also future technological alternatives (Agreed Interpretations, paragraph (e): '. . . ABM systems based on other physical principles and including components capable of substituting for ABM interceptor missiles, ABM launchers, or ABM radars').

(3) The Treaty is of 'unlimited duration' (Art. XV) but includes a withdrawal clause as well as provisions for adjustment of implementation to changing circumstances.

These particular features help to explain why the ABM Treaty has provided more effective arms control than other agreements. Linking the treaty's purpose not to specific weapons systems but to a defined military mission and existing and potential technologies that might serve it, has made it relatively immune to technological change. This is the reason why it was possible for both sides to commit themselves to a treaty of unlimited duration. While there is the explicit provision that modernization of the existing ABM systems is permitted as well as R&D on BMD, technological innovation does not seem to have occurred in this area to the extent it has in others, despite the mounting concern over the vulnerability of ICBM forces.

Moreover, the agreement has led to genuine and major reductions. Instead of maintaining the 200 launchers in two sites permitted under the 1972 Treaty, both sides agreed to reduce this to 100 launchers in one site only in July 1974, and the United States did not even take up that option. This striking contrast to the difficulties of negotiating arms reduction in other areas can again be explained by the fact that the ABM Treaty is not primarily concerned with numbers of weapons but with proscribing their military mission: the permitted level of numbers is set so low that the mission cannot be performed. It

does not make sense, therefore, to maintain the highest permitted number of launchers. Reductions are related to their impact on the military mission, not – as is normal in East–West arms control – to the number of systems the other side is willing to relinquish. In sum, because quantities are not the primary focus or an end in themselves, it becomes possible to reduce numbers significantly.

This fact also explains two further important consequences of the agreement which differ from many other types of arms control. The first is that the ABM Treaty has permitted major economic savings which small percentage reductions in the military arsenals of the two sides would never be able to achieve. Second, neither side has pushed its military efforts to the maximum limit permitted under the Treaty; on the contrary, both have done less than allowed for in the agreement.

Finally, the ABM Treaty has significantly facilitated the task of verification. By focusing its concern on the prevention of the mission of BMD, verification of the treaty arrangements need be directed less at isolated incidents of non-compliance or at the difficulty of ascertaining qualitative improvements through aerial reconnaissance. While there have been allegations that the Soviet Union has occasionally gone beyond the range of permitted activities,[37] nobody has seriously claimed that, even if these claims were true, such infringements would bring the Soviet Union significantly closer to an effective system of ballistic missile defence. An agreement concerned primarily with limiting the numbers of certain types of weapons hinges on verifiability of numbers; the ABM Treaty, which is primarily concerned with prohibiting the military mission of missile defence, requires verifiability only of significant thresholds of capabilities, not of incremental increases in the number of ABM installations. A hundred more ABM launchers would not provide the Soviet Union with an effective missile defence – they would represent a violation of the text but not of the intention of the treaty; one more ICBM under the Soviet–American Interim Agreement on Offensive Missiles would violate both the text and the intention. Verification of capability thresholds instead of individual weapon systems also increases the verifiability of qualitative weapon improvements: while difficult, if not impossible, to detect in isolation, qualitative changes of the magnitude required to constitute a new mission capability are much less likely to escape detection.

These are very significant achievements by any yardstick. Can they be repeated elsewhere? It may, of course, be argued that the ABM Treaty is a special case and therefore of only limited relevance for other areas of arms control. Perhaps the reason why the Treaty has worked lies in the recognition of both sides that an effective BMD technology is simply not within reach, and it is for this reason that technological pressure has been low, compliance high and economic dividends tangible, but this is by no means certain. In the absence of an ABM Treaty public awareness and governmental concern would have tended to push for special efforts in the field; if there is less technological, military and political pressure, this must be attributable to the Treaty. Moreover, the ABM Treaty is not the only arms-control regime in which the features mentioned above can be observed: they are general to all agreements of a preclusive nature (the agreements prohibiting biological weapons is another example) in which the unit of account for arms control is not a quantity of weapons or of weapons with specific performance but the mission these weapons can perform. It is in this direction that the search for a new approach to arms control, more capable than the existing one of accommodating the dynamics of technological change, might profitably start. The following sections describe the steps which such an approach might take, before they are exposed to a specific critique in Chapter V.

**The First Stage: Agreement on Military Missions***
Instead of dealing immediately with the numbers of weapons to be curtailed, this approach would explicitly emphasize agreement on the military missions that neither side should seek.

In present arms-control procedures, desire to curtail certain military missions is implicit. If the Soviet Union and the United States agreed in 1974 in Vladivostok to limit the total number of MIRVed launchers, the mission they sought to curtail was that of a pre-emptive strategic strike: the more MIRV, the greater the vulnerability of land-based strategic forces to an attack.

---

* The term 'mission' is used here to describe specific tasks to which military capabilities can be put.

President Carter, in his SALT proposal of early 1977 for a 'deep reduction' of the land-based launchers of both sides, had the same objective, as has the reported provision of SALT II for the limitation of MIRVed ICBM. The Warsaw Pact, in trying to include NATO's theatre nuclear weapons in an MBFR agreement seeks (along with political objectives) to prohibit or at least to restrict a military mission of nuclear war-fighting, just as NATO, in urging a cut in Soviet tank forces in the front line area, seeks to curtail the military mission of surprise attack by making it less promising. In other words, governments and negotiators have tended to proceed from an *implied* understanding of the military missions of the other side which they wanted to cover by arms control. To suggest that future arms-control agreements should make the military missions to be restricted *explicit* is, therefore, less radical than might appear at first glance.

It would, however, be wrong to pretend that no more is suggested here than merely a slight shift of the vantage point from which arms control should be approached. Because it concentrates explicitly on what the other side can do rather than on what military quantities it has at its disposal, this approach represents a fundamental change, a change from a focus on the military input – men, tanks, missiles – to a focus on the military output – surprise attack, pre-emptive nuclear strike, etc. *Its significance lies in the fact that at a time when – due to technological innovation and qualitative improvements – quantitative definitions can no longer fully encapsulate the military mission that is to be curtailed, that mission itself must be made the primary and explicit focus of agreement.* Its promise lies in the fact that agreements on mission restrictions are more resistant to technological change than those that seek to limit the numbers of specific weapon systems.

What are the military missions that should be addressed in future arms-control negotiations and agreements? In the strategic nuclear field, three potential military capabilities give most cause for concern: the ability to destroy, through a pre-emptive strike, vulnerable land-based missiles in silos; the possibility of effective strategic anti-submarine warfare against SSBN, the major second-strike launcher platforms; and anti-satellite capabilities. Future SALT negotiations might, therefore, seek an explicit understanding that these missions will not be pursued by either side. In regional arms control, in the context of Europe, it seems much more important to curtail the ability of the Warsaw Pact forces to launch a successful massive surprise attack than to get an agreement, however politically symbolic, of equal-force ceilings in the two parts of Europe included in the MBFR guidelines. Elsewhere, the mission of cutting vital supply lines at sea might be subject to restriction, or, in specific regions such as Africa, that of projecting power ashore.

Seeking agreement on the military missions that should be prohibited or discouraged might, therefore, be the first stage in future East–West arms-control negotiations.

### The Second Stage: Agreed Implementation

Once there is an agreement on the missions neither side should be allowed to seek, this must be translated into restrictions on arsenals and military programmes.

In the primarily quantitative approach of current arms control, numbers are the basis of all agreement; they must therefore be defined precisely. Changes in technology can rarely be covered, so verification is again addressed to numbers.

If, on the contrary, military missions were the basis of agreement, the function of quantitative measures would be different. The reduction or limitation of numbers of forces each side accepted would no longer be defined by the readiness of the other to do likewise but by their relationship to the mission both sides had agreed not to pursue. This expedient would be distinguished from present practice in two important respects: (1) limits and reductions of forces would not always need to be identical for both sides; (2) specific quantitative implementations could be changed to respond to the basic agreement, should technological circumstances change.

A few examples may illustrate this. Supposing the United States and the Soviet Union had agreed that neither should have the capability to launch a successful first strike against the land-based strategic missile forces of the other. This could be implemented in a variety of ways. It could be effected by reducing the number of MIRVed launchers so that fewer delivery systems possessed the accuracy to destroy a missile silo, or by cutting down on the throw-weight of delivery systems so that they could not carry the kind of nuclear yield required for destroying a hardened silo. Another possibility would be to reduce the number of land-based ICBM significantly, both because these are the systems most capable of exact guidance and because they do not pose the command and control problems of the sea-based deterrent forces. In order to implement the basic agreement, both sides could choose the same method of implementation, or they could make different choices if they preferred, within a range of agreed alternatives. Moreover, having made a choice, they could alter it later within an agreed range of options.

Or consider an agreement between NATO and the Warsaw Pact countries that neither side should maintain or develop the ability to launch a major surprise attack. This could be implemented by increasing the dependence of front-line units on reinforcements of men or equipment, by reducing the mobility of front-line forces, by curtailing attack capabilities such as tanks or APCs, or by each side accepting aerial and other reconnaissance by the other side in a defined zone of its territory. Again, both sides might choose identical measures of implementation, but they might also choose different ones. And they could alter their choice within a range of agreed alternatives if they should find the original one less attractive.

The particular advantages for arms control of this flexibility of choice are three-fold. First, Soviet and Western strategic and military doctrines are clearly different, and the hope held out by some in the early days of SALT that both sides could share the same doctrinal notions has long been dispelled. Flexibility of choice would allow each side to adopt the implementation that fitted best its military or strategic doctrine. Doctrinal differences would no longer be the major obstacle to arms control that they have so often been in the past. Second, since choices could be altered, the risk that new technologies might offer an advantage to one side or the other in a particular implementation agreement would become less important. While military choices clearly could not be revised that frequently, the knowledge that neither side was pinned to a particular posture for the whole duration of an agreement would be likely to facilitate the search for compromise. Third, by removing the need for identical reductions, limitations or restraints, the actual reduction of forces would become easier; forces would not be maintained or reduced according to whether the other side maintained or reduced them but because they did or did not perform a permitted military mission.

### The Third Stage: Justification by Challenge
By making military missions the primary unit of account, and by allowing flexibility in implementation, the approach suggested here provides for arms-control agreements that depend less on a specific state of military technology. They could incorporate changes in technology without undermining the balance of concessions expressed in the terms of the accord. Any new development in military technology that threatened to upset the basic agreement on military missions would, once deployed, violate the agreement and would, therefore, also be prohibited. If new military technologies indicated a better way of implementing the agreement than the one originally chosen, each side could decide to change its hardware accordingly, within the range of agreed parameters.

However, this implies that both sides would interpret both the basic agreement and the nature of new military technologies in the same way, and this is unlikely. What is more likely is that each side would choose an interpretation which offered it the greatest advantage. And agreement would be further complicated by the fact that most modern weapon systems, particularly multi-mission weapons, are ambiguous in their impact. Many of the recent difficulties in SALT are largely a product of such different interpretations: for instance, whether the *Backfire* bomber is a 'strategic' or merely a 'theatre' system. The 'mission approach' would reduce some of the ambiguities simply by providing less vague definitions. It would not be concerned with whether or not a system is 'strategic' but with whether or not it served a prohibited military mission. If there were an agreement on, say, banning a serious first-strike capability, the current SALT difficulties would not arise. *Backfire* or the SS-20 would not significantly improve the Soviet capability to deliver a successful pre-emptive strike against American *Minuteman* silos, nor would deploying American long-range cruise missiles provide the United States with a pre-emptive capability.

Nevertheless, considerable differences of view would emerge even in the type of agreement suggested here, and ambiguities of weapon developments could not be totally avoided, however careful the definition of the military missions to be prohibited. The method of coping with disagreement – and it would by no means be foolproof – would be 'justification by challenge'.

This would consist of two obligations: first, to notify the other parties to the agreement about intended procurement programmes and, second, to explain, when challenged, why the proposed introduction of new weaponry, or a change in force deployment, does not contradict the obligation to eschew certain mission capabilities. In order to be satisfactory, justification would have to go beyond information provided by national means of verification and beyond the provision of military statistics. Both of these would be inadequate, since they would only provide information about existing systems or current tests, not about intended programmes. Moreover, in order to justify the claim that a new weapon system does not infringe the obligations of the basic agreement, the information provided would have to cover the intended mission of the new system, its performance, the total number envisaged for procurement and which equipment it is intended to replace.

This would imply a very significant departure from the kind of verification formalized by the first SALT agreements. The importance of satellite reconnaissance – the major element of what is euphemistically called 'verification by national means' – lies in the fact that it has allowed the by-passing of much of the fruitless dispute of earlier years, when on-site inspection was regarded as the only reliable means for verifying compliance but one which, because of its interference with national sovereignty, was at the same time unacceptable to the Soviet Union as well as to many other states. But satellite reconnaissance will no longer suffice, because if agreements seek to curtail military missions, rather than restrict the number of delivery systems, the motivation behind a new weapons programme or behind a change in deployment become central factors for the assessment of compliance. Therefore, justification by challenge must include explanation of the military purpose new weapons programmes are intended to serve.

172

This will inevitably be more intrusive than verification by national means, since it will require the co-operation of the other side. It will, for this reason, be more difficult for governments to accept, particularly the Soviet government with its insistence on secrecy and its tradition of keeping military and policy matters separate.

However, it is worth remembering that both the Soviet Union and the United States have already agreed to a procedure of justification by challenge in the 1972 ABM Treaty. Article XIII of that Treaty stipulates (italics added):

To promote the *objectives* and *implementation* of the provisions of this treaty, the parties shall establish promptly a standing consultative commission within the framework of which they will:
(A) Consider questions concerning compliance with the obligations assumed and *related situations which may be considered ambiguous;*
(B) Provide on a voluntary basis such information as *either party considers necessary to assure confidence in compliance* with the obligations assumed;
(C) Consider questions involving unintended interference with national means of verification;
(D) Consider *possible changes in the strategic situation* which have *a bearing* on the provisions of the treaty . . . ;
(F) Consider, as appropriate, possible proposals for further increasing the viability of this treaty, *including proposals for amendments* in accordance with the provisions of this treaty;
(G) Consider, as appropriate, proposals for further measures aimed at limiting strategic arms . . .[38]

The usefulness of the Standing Consultative Commission (SCC) has so far not been fully tested in SALT, because the main issues of mutual concern have been handled in the ongoing negotiation or through direct contacts between the two governments outside the SCC. It has been used on occasions when there have been doubts over detailed compliance with agreements, for instance in the blinding of a US reconnaissance satellite, or in the delay in the dismantling of Soviet land-based missiles as new SLBM came into the inventory. But if arms control is to have an effect on new military programmes and not just on existing arsenals, there must be a place where new programmes are reported and, when these are challenged, assurance is provided of the conformity of the new measures with earlier undertakings. Indeed, if missions and not individual weapon systems are the chief units of account in an agreement, the intention behind a weapons programme becomes one of the major elements of compliance. 'Justification by challenge' reflects this fact.

### The Fourth Stage: Verification and Sanctions

However, compliance with the agreement will also have to be verified by national means, infringements will have to be acted upon, and a mechanism for settling disputes will be required in case both sides disagree on whether a particular type of weapons programme can be justified under the agreement.

Verification itself will become easier when mission capabilities, not the numbers of individual weapons (that is, military outputs as opposed to military inputs) form the major unit of account and verifiability. The reason is simple: theoretically, to assure compliance with an agreement which is purely quantitative, verification has to confirm that the numbers agreed are not exceeded even by one; to assure compliance with an agreement controlling military missions, verification has only to assure that those thresholds are not exceeded above which an accumulation of military hardware can provide the nucleus of an effective military option. In the case of ABM, both the United States and the Soviet Union could double the number of their available launchers and still remain below the threshold of an effective defence against ballistic missiles, and such an increase would not escape notice. The margin of acceptable uncertainty may be narrower in the case of other missions, but still significantly wider than in agreements which define specific numerical ceilings. In fact, 'threshold verification' is already practised in the SALT context on systems whose utility as strategic delivery systems is ambiguous, such as the Soviet 'bomber variants' or the *Backfire*.[39] A mutual reduction of forces on both sides in Europe would be fully verifiable only if they exceeded the 'noise level' of continuous movement of military personnel between units caused by

173

training, new intake of recruits, manoeuvres, etc. But while it is very much a second best when applied to quantitative arms control, threshold verification would be adequate for agreements on military missions.

## Sanctions

In the approach suggested here, the issue of sanctions comes up in different contexts. First there is the familiar one which needs no elaboration: what should one side do if the other side does not honour the agreement? Verification alone is not enough to ensure compliance if the other side does not want to comply. The most obvious sanction in that case would be to abrogate the agreement.

But with an agreement curtailing or prohibiting certain military missions, assessment of compliance on the part of the other party or parties is complicated by the fact that certain weapon developments introduce considerable ambiguities. Clarity is not easy even in quantitative agreements of the SALT type when the character of a particular weapon system – like the *Backfire* bomber, the SS-20 or the cruise missile – as a *strategic* system is in dispute. It will be much more difficult when the relevance of a specific weapon development, or a specific type of military deployment, to a defined military mission has to be determined. A considerable degree of ambiguity will be inevitable, given, on the one hand, the trend to multi-mission weapons and, on the other, the fact that below a certain numerical threshold the introduction of weapons which in greater numbers might serve to perform a certain military mission may still not contravene the basic agreement. This is the other side of the coin: while mission-oriented arms control would facilitate verification, it would also lack the precision with regard to contravention inherent in quantity-oriented arms control.

With ambiguity come differing interpretations and disputes over which interpretation is the correct one. Suppose that both sides have agreed not to develop the capability for a pre-emptive first strike, and that to implement this agreement the United States has chosen not to deploy a new strategic delivery system of greater accuracy and throw-weight, while the Soviet Union has chosen to limit the number of her MIRVed land-based strategic launchers at, say, 600. Then the

Soviet Union tests a new system, the SS-25, of variable – including strategic – range, mobile and with highly accurate MIRV. When challenged by the United States in the SCC, the Soviet delegation explains that this system is intended to deter China, that it will be deployed in the eastern USSR only, and that, while theoretically capable of reaching targets in the United States, this would not be its mission. They declare, moreover, that only 100 will be deployed, so that, even though the new weapon can reach American targets, this will not – in terms of the basic agreement – constitute a Soviet capability to launch an effective first strike against American *Minuteman* silos.

For the United States there would be three possible reactions. The first, uncontroversial one would be to accept the Soviet explanation. The second would be to regard it as insufficient but tolerable, since the numbers of the new system to be deployed would not amount to a significant Soviet first-strike capability. The third possibility is that the United States government would see the new Soviet weapon development as a major threat, as incompatible with the basic agreement and the agreed parameters of implementation, and – if it goes ahead – as requiring American counter-measures. The American government would then express its concern in the SCC and, should the Soviet Union persist in her plans, announce specific measures to offset the effect of the new Soviet development if the Soviet Union were to go ahead.

This kind of sanction is not unfamiliar to the history of post-war arms control and defence policy: because the other side does this, we must do that. The effect has not, in general, been one conducive to arms control – rather the opposite. Why should this be otherwise in the approach suggested here?

First, the threat to take counter-measures would be made before the full implementation of a new weapons programme, to deal with an impending infringement of the agreement, not with a *fait accompli*. It would spell out the consequences for the Soviet Union or the United States, the East or the West, if either should go ahead with a plan challenged by the other, and would thereby define the price which would be exacted for full implementation. Today this price is not precisely defined; all Washington or Moscow know is that if they undertake a major new effort in strengthening their strategic potential, the other side will respond to it somehow. But if the political and military leadership in each country realized the counter-measures its own action would provoke, this would have a much more direct and powerful impact on the decision about whether to go ahead or not. It would also tend to enhance political control over weapons procurement in sensitive areas of the agreement.

Second, the range of counter-measures would not, in the first instance, be unlimited. Each counter-measure would remain subject to the basic agreement and could be challenged by the other side on the grounds that it furthered mission capabilities which both sides had agreed to curtail. This is unlikely to be a very powerful constraint in the absence of a court of law. But the contrast to the situation under the present type of agreement is nevertheless real and helpful to the purpose of arms control. Counter-measures would not necessarily abrogate the basic mission agreement, as they tend to do if quantitative restrictions alone are agreed; the framework of agreement could be maintained, and governments would probably want to justify their counter-measures not only by reference to the proposed action of the other side but also by reference to the basic agreement itself: the dialogue would continue.

Third, a spelling out of the specific consequences of a decision by the other side to proceed with a seriously contested programme would also add credibility to the threat to counter-act and would thus give it greater political weight than would the vague promise of 'appropriate reaction'.

Finally, by directing sanctions against specific infringements of mission-oriented control agreements, it should be possible to reduce what has been called the 'bargaining-chip' effect under existing arms-control efforts; that is, the tendency to promote new weapons programmes or to procure additional quantities of arms, not, in the first instance, for essential reasons of national security but in order to trade these in against appropriate concessions by the other side in arms-control negotiations. The best-known instance of the use of the 'bargaining chip' has been the American cruise missile. Originally encouraged by Dr Kissinger for the purpose of enhancing the American negotiating position in SALT, its development only gradually attracted the powerful military interest it enjoys today. While the 'bargaining-chip' effect will never be totally absent from any kind of negotiation, it is likely, however, to be much less conducive to continuous arms competition in the arms-control approach suggested here. The threat to apply sanctions against a specific weapons development on one side, which is judged incompatible with the basic agreement, by a specific offsetting development on the other side will lead to a new spiral in the arms competition only if both sides persist. But if the threat is successful, it would reverse the 'bargaining-chip' effect: both sides would agree not to pursue programmes whose effect on the basic mission agreement is doubtful. Moreover, as not only existing military hardware but new technologies as well would be covered by the agreement, it would no longer be necessary, as is the case today, to nurture a bargaining-chip technology to procurement maturity in order to give it effect in the negotiations. Today it is difficult (even impossible at times) to push the genie back into the bottle; military planners now have to develop a military rationale for the cruise missile, since, even if it provides a useful negotiating counter, it exists – in prototypes, procurement programmes and vested interests. If, however, the threat of *embarking* on a particular programme, rather than deploying the developed weapon, is the 'bargaining chip', this programme will be easier to arrest if successful in discouraging undesired action by the other side.

These, then, are the four stages of what might be elements of a new approach to arms control that would be more independent of the dynamics of technological change: a basic agreement curtailing specific military missions which could endanger strategic or regional stability; flexible implementation within agreed parameters; justification by challenge, including a mutual obligation to provide full information on the nature and purpose of new weapons programmes; and, finally, verification and specific sanctions against infringements. The next and final chapter will examine some of the particularly critical points of this suggestion, especially whether it can succeed where the existing arms-control approach has failed.

This paper can provide no more than a rough outline of a new approach to East–West arms control; still, it aims to show why this approach is likely to have a better chance of producing effective arms control than the present one. Three questions in particular have to be addressed: (1) is the approach outlined here really all that different?; (2) if so, can it succeed where the other is facing failure, in the light of previous arms-control experience?; and, in particular, (3) even if the West were to adopt it, would the Soviet Union be at all likely to accept it as well?

**What is Different?**
Clearly, there are differences between the procedure outlined here and the present practice of East–West arms control, but are these significant enough to justify the expectation of better results? After all, the desire to proscribe particularly undesirable military missions for an opponent has always been an underlying motive for quantitative arms control. In order to reduce first-strike vulnerability for ICBM forces, the United States has sought to limit the number of Soviet heavy missiles, and Soviet tank reductions are demanded by NATO in the Vienna MBFR talks precisely in order to curb the threat of conventional surprise attack. Verification, it can be argued, does not have to ascertain every single form of infringement, even under conditions of quantitative arms control, but need only detect really significant violations. The 'mission' approach will not do away with quantitative definitions altogether; indeed, agreed implementation will depend on quantitative restrictions. So, are the differences proposed here really significant? Do they offer a new direction for arms control or only more of the same?

No new approach to arms control can do away with all the familiar problems of limiting and restricting military capabilities. This is true of the 'mission' approach as it is of any other. There is no perfect way to achieve arms control, only ways that are more or less imperfect. The 'mission' approach is characterized not by a radical departure from all previous arms-control efforts but by a change in emphasis. This change of emphasis, however, is significant; it avoids some of the major difficulties encountered in present East–West arms control (although it does not resolve all problems). First, by making the military missions that should be prohibited explicit rather than leaving them implicit, and by making agreement on these missions the central focus of the arms-control effort, agreements could incorporate technological change rather than be threatened by it. Suppose, for instance, that both sides in SALT agreed on the principle of avoiding a first-strike capability. Hybrid weapon systems like the cruise missile or the Soviet *Backfire* bomber, which currently constitute the greatest obstacle to SALT, would no longer do so under the new approach. Since neither of them is a first-strike weapon, neither would be subject to restrictions. The reason why these hybrid weapon systems challenge SALT today is not that they are first-strike weapons but that they do not fit exactly the definitions of the SALT negotiations.

Second, while in both the quantitative and in the 'mission' approaches numerical balances have to be struck, the difference in emphasis is nevertheless significant because the latter introduces into the negotiations a degree of flexibility which has so far been absent. At the moment, both the Soviet and the American governments have to commit themselves in advance to agreements in SALT of a duration that often exceeds their technological foresight. Once made, their choice cannot be altered. Moreover, for reasons of political acceptability, they have to insist on numerical symmetry. The result is considerable caution, which makes agreement on numerical ceilings, particularly if they are lower than existing arsenals and imply reductions, difficult to obtain. In the 'mission' approach, not *numerical symmetry* but *option symmetry* would be required: neither could have the capability to perform the proscribed military mission. This could, in most cases, be achieved not by one method only but by several: to honour, say, a commitment not to seek a first-strike capability against the ICBM forces of the other, each side might choose between limiting the number of MIRVed launchers, reducing the total number of ICBM or not exceeding a certain throw-weight limit. Neither side would be tied to its choice for the total duration of the agreement but could revise its initial preference if it should find later that one of the other options offers greater advantage. This built-in flexibility should make compromise and agreement easier to reach. To this must be added another advantage which would follow from the 'mission' approach: each side could choose whichever implementation option was most compatible with its strategic doctrine and posture. The sacrifice entailed by choice would be less of a constraint than under present procedures. So, while there would be tough negotiations over the quantitative restrictions required for adequate implementation, conditions under the 'mission' approach should make compromise and bargaining somewhat easier.

Third, verification of numerical limits would differ significantly under the 'mission' approach. It is true that in both cases numbers of weapon systems would be constrained and violations would have to be detectable to some degree. The difference, however, would lie in the definition of what constitutes adequacy. In both cases not all violations would have to be detected but only those that matter. Under the quantitative approach, what matters is related to the total number of permitted weapons: a margin of error exceeding, say, 3 per cent may be strategically tolerable but it so undermines the credibility of verification as to be unacceptably high. Under the 'mission' approach, the credibility of verification would be measured by a much wider margin, e.g. when the accumulation of particular types of weapons approaches the threshold of a new mission capability. The lower the ceiling established in the implementation agreements and the higher the performance requirements of that capability, the wider that margin can be, even – as in the ABM agreement – going beyond 100 per cent.

The approach proposed in this paper is, therefore, not just the familiar one dressed up differently. The differences do matter, and they should help in overcoming if not all, at least some of the obstacles the present approach to arms control has recently encountered – at least in theory. But how practical is it? While it might avoid some of the obstacles in the current approach, it may well encounter others that are no less difficult to overcome.

### Can the 'Mission' Approach Work?

The 'mission' approach is based on the example of the ABM Treaty, but is this an example that can be applied to other areas of weapons competition as well?

There were, indeed, special circumstances that led to the ABM Treaty. One major reason for its successful conclusion was probably that the technology for effective BMD was not in sight for either the Soviet Union or the United States. In most weapons areas, however, the technology is often not only in sight but already available. More important, the relationship between the prohibited mission and the weapon systems covered by the treaty is a very close one: by restricting the number of delivery launchers and radars, the mission of BMD is itself restricted. Moreover, it is possible to distinguish relatively easily between forbidden and permitted systems. With the possible exception of satellite protection against attacks in space, it is difficult to think of any other mission that defines the relevant weaponry with similar clarity. In fact, most other mission definitions will not. This is so for two reasons. First, other than the ABM mission, most mission definitions will not be preclusive. An agreement to ban the ability to launch a pre-emptive first strike does not ban all offensive weapons but only that combination of numbers and performance characteristics (in relation to the weapon systems of the other side) which makes a pre-emptive first strike a serious option. An agreement to forgo a surprise attack capability will not rule out all armoured forces but only those which, through a combination of numbers, performance and deployment seem to offer a serious option for effective and successful aggression. Second, most weapons are multimission systems: the tank is suited not just for surprise attack but also for defence against it; anti-submarine warfare cannot distinguish sufficiently between strategic and non-strategic targets.

To apply the 'mission' concept to these more ambiguous areas of definition could, therefore, never be a precise exercise. It would have to be based on approximation. The ambiguity of role allocation (particularly with non-strategic weapon systems) could not be wholly overcome. It would be a matter, rather, of distinguishing between combinations of weapons and deployments that tend to favour surprise attack, say, more rather than less, of banning only those combinations of force and deployment which especially serve the purpose of attack. While this would, no doubt, be imperfect, fraught with problems of definition, difficult to negotiate and unsatisfactory to implement, it would still seem better than doing nothing at all about these systems. What is more, the ambiguity of mission characteristics of particular weapon systems, especially in the conventional field, can be reduced through a combination of other factors, such as readiness of units or advance warning. A tank may be both an offensive and a defensive weapon, but it is likely to serve the former rather than the latter if deployed (a) close to the borders of a potentially hostile neighbour, (b) in units of a high state of readiness, and (c) in numbers greatly superior to those of the other side. Particularly in conventional arms control, factors other than the ambiguous nature of multi-mission weapons could help to define that military capability which is to be covered by an agreed mission-ban. For that very reason, numerical reductions or ceilings may often be less promising than restrictions on deployment areas or troop readiness.[40] In spite of the obvious difficulties, it does not seem that it would be inherently impossible to apply the mission approach realistically to areas outside the defined and clear-cut one of the ABM Treaty.

There are, however, two precedents in recent arms-control history that put the feasibility of a 'mission' approach in doubt. The first is the fruitless attempt by the United States in the early stages of SALT to engage the Soviet Union in a discussion about strategic principles.[41] Why should agreement on missions be possible where an understanding on principles proved elusive? The answer lies in the definitions. In early SALT, the United States sought to reach an understanding on notions such as 'crisis stability', 'arms-race stability', the importance of invulnerability for second-strike forces and the risks for stability caused by the mounting vulnerability of ICBM launchers. These are all concepts which are part of American but not of Soviet strategic doctrine, and it is not surprising, therefore, that no understanding was reached. Missions, however, that were prohibited in the basic agreement would have to be compatible with the doctrines of both sides, permitting restraints not on the basis of shared doctrines but in spite of doctrinal differences. The examples given in this paper would satisfy this requirement. The Soviet Union has constantly denied claims that she is

aiming at the capability to launch a successful first strike against major elements of the American deterrent forces: it does not matter whether this is for political reasons, out of concern for 'crisis stability' or because such an attempt would appear foolhardy. As to an agreement to ban the mission of conventional surprise attack, the same would apply: it would not be determined by doctrinal preferences. The Soviet Union has never claimed that she seeks the capability to wage a surprise attack against Western Europe. In a letter to President Eisenhower on 2 July 1958, Soviet Premier Krushchev wrote of 'the importance that an agreement on joint measures for the prevention of surprise attack by one state against another would have for the preservation of universal peace',[42] and nothing has since been said by Soviet leaders to suggest that they would not subscribe to a similar statement today. Doctrinal differences do not, therefore, seem to rule out agreement on prohibiting military missions of the kind suggested in this paper – just as they did not rule out the agreement banning the mission of BMD in 1972.

The other precedent which counsels caution in consideration of the feasibility of a mission-oriented approach to arms control is the fate of the 'East–West Conference of Experts for the Study of Possible Measures Which Might be Helpful in Preventing Surprise Attack', which was held and adjourned *sine die* without result in late 1958. One might argue that this is evidence that differences in the meaning of agreements on basic missions are likely to be so marked that implementation along agreed lines becomes virtually impossible.

However, a closer look at that conference reveals that the reason for its failure did not lie here. There was considerable confusion over the task of the meeting: the West wanted to talk primarily about controls on surprise attack that did not imply arms reductions, while the Soviet Union, tabling an extended version of the Rapacki Plan for a nuclear-free zone in Central Europe, was willing to accept controls only as a corollary of reductions in nuclear and conventional forces.[43] While some of these differences are inherent in any negotiation on arms control, the failure of the 1958 Surprise Attack Conference was attributable less to these than to the absence of a specific mission definition at the outset. If anything, the Surprise Attack Conference demonstrated the need for a clear and agreed brief *before* embarking on technical negotiations; in other words, for a definition of the mission which should be prohibited. In the Conference of Experts, East and West tried to address the technical issues before agreeing on such a brief. As William C. Foster, head of the American delegation, summed up the lessons of the Conference before the Senate Subcommittee on Disarmament: 'We also have now a much more precise notion of the difficulty of separating the technical from the political in analysing the problems of surprise attack and of the need, in pursuing technical discussion on the subject, to have agreement all around on what questions should be answered.'[44] The experience of the 1958 Surprise Attack Conference does not, therefore, suggest that negotiations on the implementation of agreed mission prohibition would be so fraught with difficulties as to be virtually unattainable; in fact, it shows the opposite – that without an agreed aim, implementation talks will be useless. The Surprise Attack Conference confirms rather than contradicts the potential of the 'mission' approach for East–West arms-control negotiation.

**Will the Soviet Union Accept the New Approach?**
There is nothing in the history of East–West arms control in the post-war era to suggest that the Soviet Union will find it impossible to go along with three of the four aspects of the 'mission' approach: the basic agreement, the negotiation on implementation, and verification. The basic agreement may even be easier for the Soviet Union to accept than for the West due to a traditional Soviet preference for principles (although those principles offered by Soviet negotiators in the past – such as equal security – are much more vague than the mission definitions required in the basic agreement). Perhaps there are, from the Soviet perspective, real advantages in the quantitative as opposed to the 'mission' approach. The latter does not cover all weapon systems which can be directed against Soviet territory but only those related to banned missions. Moreover, vulnerability to conventional surprise attack in Europe or to a pre-emptive first strike against ICBM forces will, for the next few years, be more of a Western than an Eastern security problem. Finally, the Soviet

Union, worried over the Western technological potential, may initially see few benefits in an arms-control procedure which seeks to accommodate technological change; Soviet insistence on the inclusion of cruise missiles in a SALT II agreement is an example of a Soviet tactic which uses quantitative agreements to impose restrictions on specific technologies. But these are not immutable positions; they depend on the balance of perceived advantage alone. By the mid-1980s, ICBM vulnerability could become a Soviet problem, too. An earlier agreement which banned effective first-strike capabilities might enable the Soviet Union to weaken support for the American MX programme.[45] An agreement to curtail the mission of pre-emptive attack, therefore, might well become attractive. Similarly, as the Soviet Union realizes the difficulties of controlling American technological innovation by quantitative restrictions alone, her leaders might see advantage in an arms-control method that discourages Western technological effort in salient areas, just as they saw advantage in the 1972 ABM Treaty. There seems to be nothing, therefore, in this aspect of the 'mission' approach which would be unacceptable to the Soviet Union.

The same can be said of two other aspects: implementation agreements and threshold verification. The first is a more or less familiar stage of East–West arms control and its particular features in the context of the 'mission' approach – freedom to mix and freedom to choose among different options – might be an added attraction. Threshold verification would pose the least serious problem from the Soviet perspective: the openness of the American security debate has always provided Soviet intelligence and analysis with more information than would be obtainable through 'national means of verification', and explains why the verifiability of arms-limitation agreements has never been a major Soviet concern.

It is the fourth aspect of the 'mission' approach – justification by challenge – which would be the major cause of Soviet reluctance. It would require the revelation of detailed information on military programmes and their rationale. The Soviet Union has so far received such information from the West as a result of the openness of the Western (in particular, the American) debate but she has been opposed to providing detailed

179

information herself, claiming that any such demands would be an unacceptable interference with her internal affairs. The demand for greater transparency would indeed interfere with Soviet internal affairs because of the nature of Soviet society, where secrecy is not just a conscious tool of government but a deep-rooted cultural tradition, especially in military and security matters. Nor could any Western negotiator guarantee to the Soviet Union that classified information exchanged in a Standing Consultative Commission or similar body would not leak into the Western debate. The decision to provide the West with information concerning her military effort would therefore amount to a major domestic political reform within the Soviet system – one that any leader, conscious of the need to maintain the support of the military, might find it too risky to take. This, therefore, is likely to be the main obstacle to Soviet acceptance of the 'mission' approach to East–West arms control.

There is no fully satisfactory answer to this problem but two considerations might put it in perspective. First, some mission restrictions will require a greater degree of transparency than others. In the strategic-nuclear field, most new military programmes, particularly if there are no test limitations, seem to be detectable through 'national means of verification' at a relatively early stage, and the need for additional information may, therefore, be more modest than in an agreement dealing with conventional military forces. Just as, in the words of Gerard Smith, 'the first SALT agreements were carefully tailored so as to be simple to verify',[46] so the 'mission' approach might start with those missions which demand only moderate increases in information beyond what can be provided by satellite reconnaissance.

Second, the Soviet record on inspection is one of rigidity combined with political pragmatism. If the political advantage of an agreement is judged to be high, concessions in providing some transparency are not excluded. The developments leading up to the 1958 Surprise Attack Conference are a case in point: it was the Soviet leader Bulganin who, in a letter to President Eisenhower of 17 November 1956, announced that the Soviet Union was prepared to consider aerial inspection in a zone in Europe 800 kilometres on each side of the East–West demarcation line,[47] and the proposal was to include the setting up of ground observation teams at crucial points within that area.[48] The motive was political and not concerned primarily with arms control: 'The Soviet Union was willing to pay a price, though not a high one, in terms of penetration of the iron curtain for some assurance that Germany would not become a nuclear power.'[49] William C. Foster, in his report on the Surprise Attack Conference, comes to a similar conclusion:

We were much impressed by the importance which Soviet representatives attached to secrecy as a military asset. In effect, they seem to believe it enables them to possess a form of 'hardening' of their bases which we do not have. Thus they regard any encroachment upon this secrecy as a unilateral disarmament step . . . on their part which must be compensated for by other measures.[50]

A penetration of secrecy is, therefore, to some extent a negotiable issue for the Soviet Union – if the dividend is high enough to justify the cost.

In future, the price of *not* allowing greater transparency of her military programmes may be very threatening indeed, and Soviet leaders should become aware of it. The political cost involved in not paying that price could well be a break-down in arms control. Given the growing significance of qualitative weapons improvements for the assessment of the military balance, there is no way in which future arms-control efforts can be reconciled with the maintenance of the obsessive screen of secrecy with which the Soviet Union shields her military programmes – whatever the specific arms-control approach. Even more costly will be the political price. For the Soviet Union, SALT has essentially been the vehicle to establish a special political relationship with the United States. If arms control were to become increasingly ineffective, it would also become increasingly controversial and ultimately counter-productive; it would no longer serve the primary purpose which the Soviet Union ascribes to it. There can be no guarantee that the Soviet Union will understand that these costs, a product of her excessive military secrecy, are not worth supporting, particularly at a time when uncertainty over the succession in the Soviet leadership may give added weight to military influences within the Soviet Union. She may prefer to leave her institutional preferences for secrecy unchallenged. But, over time, the Soviet

Union may recognize that the political disadvantages of secrecy far outweigh the risks of controlled transparency. If this is not the case, there is little hope for effective and politically beneficial East–West arms control.

## Conclusion

It would be presumptuous to claim, at the end of this examination of the future problems of East–West arms control, that the 'mission approach' suggested here – that is, the explicit focus on constraining military 'outputs' rather than limiting military 'inputs' – provides an answer to all the problems. It clearly does not. Whatever the approach, arms control deals with issues which are too complex, with audiences which are too varied and with a military, technological and political background which is too dynamic, for its progress ever to be plain sailing. Even with the best approach, the going will be rough and frustrating.

However, in spite of the temptation to continue with approaches that have become familiar, it is important to take stock and see whether things that have worked will continue to do so. This paper has argued that the present approach to East–West arms control has come to the end of its usefulness for one major reason: namely, that it is incapable of coping with the qualitative arms competition. Unless we succeed in adapting the instrument of arms control to new requirements, that instrument will itself become blunted, ineffectual and, what is worse, politically counter-productive.

The 'mission approach' suggested here is no panacea. It is, in many ways, more modest than quantitative arms control: it concentrates on those aspects of military power which are most threatening to the stability – military and political – of the military balance, rather than trying to provide limitations across the board. It is this modesty which might enable it to cope with some of the issues on the agenda of current and future East–West arms control. Cruise missiles cease to be a threat to arms control because they do not provide a destabilizing military capability, such as pre-emptive nuclear counter-force or surprise attack. The thorny issue of Forward Based Systems – those American delivery systems which have a theatre role but can also reach Soviet territory – would only require inclusion in arms-control agreements where they serve a prescribed military mission, not just because they might or might not qualify for being squeezed into definitions of strategic delivery systems. 'Grey-area weapons' cease to be an arms-control problem so long as their military potential does not provide the basis for any armed mission. To focus on curtailing specific military missions, rather than on weapons, is to recognize that across-the-board arms control is unrealistic and priorities must be established in relation to the military capabilities most disturbing for detente and national security alike.

It is, however, more than just a modest approach. One of the major problems of quantitative arms control is that it is becoming increasingly removed from the centre of Western concerns over military power. New weapons technologies have come to be regarded as dangerous not because of their impact on East–West security but because of their impact on definitions in arms control. The strategic cruise missile is a case in point: as a first-strike weapon it is, in its foreseeable potential, largely useless, because of its flight-time, and hence much less threatening to strategic stability than any intercontinental ballistic missile. The reason why this weapon system has caused so much anxiety in the arms-control community is that it has generated concern over the maintenance of the definitions of current negotiations. Its impact on military potential has been a secondary issue. Arms control has come, in much of the Western discussion, to exist quite separately from national security policies and this is the main cause of the political controversy which surrounds it. Since security concerns are essentially determined not primarily by the number of forces an adversary has but by what he can do with them, an approach which seeks to constrain the 'military output', i.e. the ability of military forces to perform specific tasks, can offer more than merely a more promising way of coping with technological change. It may reconcile arms control as an instrument with the purpose it should serve – the pursuit of national security.

The 'mission approach' is no more than one suggestion for a method of achieving this. Whether or not it stands up to more detailed assessment remains to be seen. Whatever the result, three of its key assumptions are likely to be elements in any successful future arms-control approach: first, that the definition of military potential primarily by quantities of weapons and men and the effort to curtail these are no longer sufficient at a time of rapid technological change; second, that technological change needs to be discouraged not by the restriction of specific weapon systems but by the proscription of specific military mission capabilities; and, third, that verification in future will have to be supported by much greater willingness to make military efforts more transparent.

To argue in favour of a new approach is not to suggest either a radical break with past efforts or the demolition of existing arms-control structures. The fate of President Carter's March 1977 proposal for 'real' arms control is a case in point: arms control is too sensitive to tolerate a radical change of course in mid-stream. It takes a long time to develop a working relationship between military adversaries that allows for the discussion of force restraints. However urgent the need for a new approach, the working relationship must not be jeopardized. Indeed, the prime condition for moving towards new and more promising attempts at rational arms control is the maintenance of the East–West dialogue on arms control and the framework that makes it possible.

Elements of what is suggested in this paper can already be seen in arms-control negotiations today. That governments in East and West recognize the new challenges is manifest when one compares the 1972 SALT agreements with the emerging contours of the SALT II accord: there *is* an attempt to allow flexibility according to doctrinal preferences under the proposed MIRV ceiling; there *is* likely to be a distinction between the longer-term treaty and a shorter-term protocol for dealing with new weapons technologies; and (perhaps most significant) there *is* likely to be an 'agreement on principles' which should govern negotiations for a SALT III accord. Similarly, in the context of European regional arms control, there is greater interest in 'confidence-building measures' which would leave the size of military forces intact while curbing their potential for surprise attack,[51] just as there is a growing recognition that quantitative restrictions alone might not serve to enhance security confidence and political detente in Europe.

It is not enough, however, for governments to recognize the challenges. It is important that they get the answers right. Arms control in the 1970s has largely relied on concepts developed in the 1950s and 1960s. If governments are to get the answers right in the 1980s, the new concepts have to be developed now.

# NOTES

[1] Hedley Bull, for instance, in his comprehensive discussion of arms control in the early 1960s, *The Control of the Arms Race* (London: Weidenfeld and Nicolson, 1961, for the IISS) discusses the problem, suggesting no more than that arms control cannot operate against technological change but should keep abreast of it (p. 199).

[2] Colin S. Gray, *The Future of Land-Based Missile Forces*, Adelphi Paper No. 140 (London: IISS, 1978), p. 17.

[3] For an excellent and detailed discussion, see Richard Burt, 'The Cruise Missile and Arms Control', *Survival*, Jan./Feb. 1976, pp. 10–17.

[4] Reported in *Atlantic News*, No. 839, pp. 1–3.

[5] See also Richard Burt, 'Technology and East–West Arms Control', *International Affairs*, January 1977, pp. 51–72.

[6] For a detailed discussion, see Lothar Ruehl 'The Grey Area Problem', in Christoph Bertram, ed., *The Future of Arms Control: Part I: Beyond SALT II*, Adelphi Paper No. 141 (London: IISS, 1978), pp. 25–34.

[7] The term is Richard Burt's, *op. cit.* in note 5.

[8] See Gray, *op. cit.* in note 2.

[9] For an example following the SALT I negotiations, see J. Steinbrunner and B. Carter, 'Organizational and Political Dimensions of the Strategic Posture: The Problems of Reform', in F. A. Long and G. W. Rathjens, eds, *Arms, Defense Policy and Arms Control* (New York: Norton, 1976).

[10] See Christoph Bertram, *Mutual Force Reductions in Europe: The Political Aspects*, Adelphi Paper No. 84 (London: IISS, 1972), pp. 22–3.

[11] See G.I.A.D. Draper, 'The Emerging Law of Weapons Restraint', *Survival*, Jan./Feb. 1977, pp. 9–15.

[12] G. T. Allison and F. A. Morris in Long and Rathjens, eds., *op. cit.* in note 9, pp. 99–100.

[13] For a recent description of the current state of the negotiations, see *Strategic Survey 1976* (London: IISS, 1977), pp. 107–111.

[14] *Survival*, May/June 1975, p. 129.

[15] See Albert Wohlstetter: 'Is There a Strategic Arms Race?', *Foreign Policy*, Summer 1974, pp. 3–20, and the Debate in the Winter 1974 and Spring 1975 issues.

[16] For a fuller discussion, see Gray, *op. cit.* in note 2.

[17] Harry G. Gelber, 'Technical Innovation and Arms Control', *World Politics*, July 1974, p. 521.

[18] In the 1972 Soviet–American ABM Treaty, Art. VII (reprinted in *Survival*, July/Aug. 1972, pp. 192–4) specifically maintains the right to continue with R&D.

[19] President Carter's Press Conference, 24 March 1977.

[20] Harvey Brooks, 'The Military Innovation System and the Qualitative Arms Race', in Long and Rathjens, eds, *op. cit.* in note 9, p. 84. Similar suggestions were made by the American Secretary of Defense, Mr Harold Brown, in a paper given before the Institute for Studies on the USA and Canada of the Soviet Academy of Sciences in 1975, reported in the *International Herald Tribune*, 28 December 1976, p. 2.

[21] *Ibid.*

[22] For a comparison of the approaches in Soviet and American military technology, see *Strategic Survey 1976* (*op. cit.* in note 13), pp. 13–18.

[23] Jan M. Lodal, 'Verifying SALT', *Foreign Policy*, Fall 1976, p. 58.

[24] See Brooks, *op. cit.* in note 20, p. 86.

[25] Sidney D. Drell, 'Beyond SALT II – A Missile Test Quota', *Bulletin of Atomic Scientists*, May 1977, p. 41.

[26] As suggested by the American Secretary of Defense, Mr Harold Brown, *International Herald Tribune*, 28 December 1976, p. 2.

[27] Abram Chayes, 'An Inquiry into the Workings of Arms Control Agreements', *Harvard Law Review*, March 1972, reprinted in parts as 'Bureaucracy: An Ally in Arms Control', in *Survival*, July/Aug. 1972, pp. 183–7.

[28] The important exception of the Soviet–American 1972 ABM Treaty, where neither side exploited the scope permitted to the full, will be discussed below.

[29] See Bull, *op. cit.* in note 1, p. 77.

[30] Allison and Morris in Long and Rathjens, *op. cit.* in note 12, p. 126.

[31] Thomas Schelling, 'The Importance of Agreements', in David Carlton and Carlo Schaerf, eds, *The Dynamics of the Arms Race* (London: Croom Helm, 1975), p. 72.

[32] Herbert Scoville, Jr, 'A Different Approach to Arms Control – Reciprocal Unilateral Restraint', unpublished paper presented at the ISODARCO Conference, Italy, June 1976, p. 4.

[33] President Carter's Press Conference, 30 March 1977, reprinted in *Survival*, May/June 1977, pp. 129–31.

[34] *Op. cit.* in note 31, p. 73.

[35] See Treaty on Anti-Ballistic Missile Systems, reprinted in *Survival*, July/Aug. 1972, pp. 192–4.

[36] *Ibid.*; see also p. 196.

[37] See Colin S. Gray, 'SALT I Aftermath: Have the Soviets been Cheating?', *Air Force Magazine*, Nov. 1975, pp. 28–33.

[38] *Op. cit.* in note 35.

[39] See Lodal, *op. cit.* in note 23, p. 58.

[40] As envisaged, on a purely voluntary basis, by the 1975 Helsinki Final Act, which stipulates that military manoeuvres beyond a certain size must be notified in advance, as a 'confidence-building measure'. For a recent discussion, see J. J. Holst and K. A. Melander, 'European Security and Confidence-building Measures', *Survival*, July/Aug. 1977, pp. 146–54.

[41] See J. Newhouse, *Cold Dawn – The Story of SALT* (New York: Holt, Rinehart and Winston, 1973), p. 176.

[42] Quoted in Bernhard G. Bechhoefer, *Postwar Negotiations for Arms Control* (Washington, DC: The Brookings Institution, 1961), p. 466.

[43] For a detailed discussion of the 1958 Surprise Attack Conference, *ibid.*, pp. 464–87.

[44] Quoted in *ibid.*, p. 484.

[45] A new mobile missile system, to be deployed in tunnels, with significantly greater throw-weight than *Minuteman* ICBM. See Colin S. Gray, 'The MX Debate', *Survival*, May/June 1978, pp. 105–112.

[46] Gerard C. Smith, 'Negotiating with the Soviets', *New York Times Magazine*, 27 February 1977, reprinted in *Survival*, May/June 1977, pp. 117–20.

[47] Bechhoefer, *op. cit.* in note 42, p. 378.

[48] *Ibid*, p. 479.

[49] *Ibid*, p. 481.

[50] Quoted, *ibid.*, pp. 484–5.

[51] See Helmut Schmidt, The 1977 Alastair Buchan Memorial Lecture, *Survival*, Jan./Feb. 1978, pp. 3–5.

# 6 CONFIDENCE-BUILDING MEASURES

## Introduction

JONATHAN ALFORD

The following four papers were presented at a Conference held by the Institute in May 1978. The Conference was one of a series on the future of arms control, which is a central aspect of the Institute's current research programme. The papers are the result of an effort to see how the confidence-building approach to arms control can be pursued.

Confidence-Building Measures (CBM) can be viewed both as an underpinning for more conventional types of arms-control agreement and as alternatives when traditional types of agreement prove impossible to negotiate or sustain in the face of rapid technological change. It was at the Helsinki Meeting of the Conference on Security and Co-operation in Europe (CSCE) that the acronym CBM first seeped into the general consciousness, but the idea of confidence building through bilateral or multilateral arrangements pre-dates Helsinki by many years, and the building of different kinds of confidence was incorporated either implicitly or explicitly in many earlier international arms-control agreements. One could cite the Rhineland demilitarization arrangements after the 1914–18 war, the 'Hot-line' Agreement of 1963 and the American–Soviet Agreement on the prevention of incidents on and over the high seas of May 1972 as examples of treaties which were designed to foster confidence.

Nevertheless, these papers look beyond CSCE to the possibility of extending CBM in Europe, in the Middle East and in more contentious areas such as naval arms limitation and SALT. They suggest that there might be, beyond the limited context of CSCE, the makings of a general approach to arms control. The conclusions are necessarily tentative, for although CBM might avoid some of the problems inherent in tradi-

tional approaches, they create others, and the papers do not attempt to suggest that CBM can solve all problems. However, there is cautious optimism that CBM do indicate directions that are worth pursuing in an effort to reduce the impact of military power on political relations between East and West or further afield.

That many people sense growing a disillusionment and frustration at the inability of conventional arms control to cope with present security problems should not surprise us. Technological change is creating problems of definition which tend to blur distinctions between weapon systems; doctrinal asymmetries are clearly present, and these mean that less important than the systems themselves are the uses to which they may be put; and geographical, historical, ideological and cultural factors distort any neat theoretical balances. It is, therefore, increasingly difficult to constrain capabilities, even assuming that there is a general desire among the negotiating parties to reach substantive numerically-based agreements.

From these papers emerges a clear belief that there are psychological and physical dimensions to the building of mutual confidence between potential adversaries. On the one hand, states or groups of states will require indicators to show that the intentions of potential adversaries are benign; on the other, they will look for real constraints which will make it more difficult for states to attack their neighbours. Obviously, the price they are prepared to pay involves the acceptance of constraints on their own sovereign rights to dispose of their instruments of war as they wish in exchange for balancing restrictions on the other side.

Intentions can be divined in a multitude of ways, ranging from a vague but important awareness of attitudes, which stems from willingness to negotiate over important issues to quite specific measures which, either separately or cumulatively, are designed to act as a kind of barometer indicating fair or foul weather to come. The contributions in this Paper do not address the broader questions specifically, for they are related much more closely to the field of international relations generally than to the security field, but all would acknowledge that the state of mutual confidence between nations is the sum of many different (and often conflicting) stimuli. However, there are certain issues which, it might appear, could be agreed upon between potential opponents and which would lubricate the international machinery or allow for the rapid removal of the accidental grit which suspicion and mistrust can all too often deposit on the working surfaces. The functioning of the SALT Standing Consultative Commission (SCC) is a good example of what can be done in institutional terms to remove the smaller particles of grit before they can do damage, and each paper takes very seriously the need to build a number of similar fora in which each side can both challenge the other over incidents which appear to conflict with formal treaty undertakings and assure the other beforehand that what will be seen is not intended as an aggressive move. The announcement of exercises, naval movements and major re-equipment programmes and even, ultimately, the explanation of doctrine will help to allay suspicion or shed light on those things which, if allowed to fester, can engender suspicion and prompt escalatory counteractions. It should be emphasized that the things which can be done under this head are essentially subjective, in that they operate through the perceptions of states without imposing physical restraints. It is the totality of the almost infinite variety of stimuli which will create an overall impression of hostility or co-operation, of a willingness to control conflict or encourage it.

Moving from the subjective to the objective, there is a quite different sort of confidence which springs from the belief that one has less to fear than before. The argument runs that if states have no desire for conflict (or, indeed, even share a common desire for the avoidance of conflict), they have to be helped to wind down from a pitch of confrontation, which – given deep mutual suspicion – may be a difficult undertaking for them. Initially one looks for stabilization to ensure that things become no more dangerous than they are; subsequently potential adversaries need a framework within which small (and probably slow) backward steps may be taken towards an ultimate, albeit distant, objective. Consider as an analogy two swordsmen with their weapons raised to strike. To achieve disarmament, it may be necessary to work through a formal ritual involving withdrawal beyond striking distance, the lowering of weapons, the sheathing of weapons and the unbuckling of scabbards still to hand. Each swordsman will watch warily to ensure that his own steps towards disarmament do not so far anticipate his enemy's that he cannot reassume his guard in time.

What these papers point out is that this simple analogy is imperfect. Doctrinal asymmetry (and the force-posture asymmetries which follow from fundamentally different beliefs as to what assures security) make the creation of a ritual framework an extremely difficult process, requiring much imagination and a constant search for genuine yet mutually acceptable constraints. These will range from small steps which can accumulate into something important to large and really 'biting' restrictions on force deployments – and by 'biting' is meant constraints which reduce significantly the ability of one state or group of states to use force against another at short notice.

Cosmetic measures have their place in a political context, but no military man is likely to acquiesce in an unravelling of the structure of security unless he is sure that there is a balancing move on the other side. This raises the question of verification or monitoring. Detailed discussion of these issues is beyond the scope of the papers presented here but an important element in the confidence-building process must be to establish measures for verifying the unravelling process. Sometimes, as in the Middle East, outside agencies can help to provide the necessary monitoring of compliance, but in the main arenas of East–West conflict there can be no referee. Therefore, hand-in-hand with the design of the confidence-building framework must go measures that are adequate (a word which begs many questions) to provide each side with the assurance that the other is complying with a withdrawal in the first instance and is not covertly regaining a position thereafter. Generally speaking, the need for verification is a Western rather than a Soviet concern, since public support will not be forthcoming for CBM that provide increased warning of attack unless there is a high degree of assurance, first, that violations can be detected and, second, that there will be the time and the means to cancel out their effects. Confidence in this sense follows a slightly different logic: a state gains self-confidence to the extent that it knows that it can detect violations and react to them in time. This highlights the point that many of the CBM suggested in these papers serve to build confidence in two rather different ways. They promote confidence in one's ability to defend oneself if threatened (that is, self-confidence) and confidence that the other side is not, in fact, intending to threaten (that is, mutual confidence). There must be interaction between the two, producing a downward spiral – a counterpart of the upward spiral that results from fear and perceptions of inferiority in security terms, whereby a state's adopting measures to redress imbalances is in turn viewed as alarming by its potential opponent, who therefore takes further steps to assure his security, and so on.

What is hoped is that an acceptance of the logic of the proposals suggested in these papers will lead to a conscious search for new instruments of arms control, either to replace or to underpin existing attempts to achieve stability, and, after stability is attained, to a slow unravelling of adversaries' security structures.

# Confidence-Building Measures in Europe:
# The Military Aspects

JONATHAN ALFORD

The idea and terminology of Confidence-Building Measures emerged from the Helsinki Final Act, which set in train a rather new set of thoughts about the ways in which states and alliances might be reassured that certain legitimate military activities undertaken by potential adversaries are not intended as threatening. Initially the requirements for notification of manoeuvres were not seen as particularly restrictive on the military activities of the signatories. In a sense the Final Act was an act of faith and a declaration of intentions to proceed in particular directions. Indeed these CBM are explicitly voluntary, although there was a political commitment by the signatories of the Final Act to notify manoeuvres involving over 25,000 ground troops. The other CBM are concerned with the exchange of observers at manoeuvres, notification of manoeuvres below the threshold figure of 25,000, notification of military movements and exchange of military visits. The spirit of CBM was therefore articulated in a way which moved ahead of statutory requirements under the Final Act, and it has been quite noticeable that there has been a certain unevenness in the way CBM provisions have been applied. All seem to have abided by the letter of the law, but the West have gone beyond this – in terms of notification and invitations to observers – while the Warsaw Pact states have not. This reflects a more general attitude to detente in the two Blocs, with caution governing the Eastern attitude rather than the Western; the western bloc may have tried to go too far too fast.[1]

What the military effects of CBM already operating have been is hard to ascertain. First, it needs to be said that they *have* been put into

effect: notification *has* taken place; exchanges *have* been arranged; observers *have* been invited; and there are no proven cases in which notification has *not* taken place above the lower limit. In addition, a number of exercises have been notified below the threshold. All this has tended to increase marginally the military co-operation between the Blocs, and no exercise has been used to cover any aggressive move – but then no aggressive move has been made by either side since Helsinki. All that one could say with certainty is that had an aggressive move been made, the West would not have interpreted it as merely an exercise. This is a pretty marginal gain but it still marks an improvement in confidence. On the debit side, there have been irritations over the restrictions placed on Western observers and over the ticklish issue of binoculars (Soviet binoculars issued to observers were alleged to be unusable), but here too one is bound to acknowledge that for the Soviet Union to invite Western observers at all is a step forward. There are grounds for thinking that the timing of the first invitation (coinciding, as it did, with the Belgrade CSCE Review Conference) looked less than accidental to Western eyes. It seemed designed to show the West that the Soviet Union was doing all that the Final Act demanded of her – and just a little more. Had she not invited observers at that time, she might well have been criticized for not living up to the spirit of that provision. It remains to be seen whether she will repeat the invitation on the occasion of some future exercise. It is necessary to note, however, that Western observers were obliged to remain in prepared stands, allowed to see only set-piece manoeuvres and herded into hotels every evening.

They were only permitted to observe seven hours of a four-day exercise. Clearly, this allowed them to be reasonably certain that what they were watching was really an exercise – but as it took place in the Western Military District of the Soviet Union, it could hardly have been anything else. It must also be said that the West has not been much more forthcoming in allowing Eastern observers to roam at will.

Starting, therefore, from the premise that some CBM (none very demanding) are operable at the level agreed at Helsinki, or slightly above, the aim of this paper is to look at the possibilities for extending them, either through the CSCE or as 'associated measures' at the Mutual and Balanced Force Reduction (MBFR) negotiations in Vienna.

The failure to move forward at the Belgrade conference held to review the workings of the Helsinki Final Act was disappointing. Moderate extensions were proposed in the direction of lowering thresholds, bringing in air and naval manoeuvres and adding military movements to the list of what is notifiable. None of these proposals was very radical, but they were intended to push things forward at a modest pace.[2] Whether they collapsed as part of the general failure at Belgrade or whether, as it is said, the Soviet Union had already indicated her reluctance to extend them at the time, we do not yet know. One fears the latter to be the case. Ambassador Goldberg's final speech did not let the issue die: 'In the case of CBM, for example, we have already seen in practice how states can build from the language of the Final Act to implement its spirit. . . . In general, moreover, we can all think afresh about ways of "developing and enlarging measures aimed at strengthening confidence", a possibility the Final Act explicitly sets before us.'

This paper will avoid the procedural problems as far as possible and take, it is hoped, a fairly realistic look at what might prove workable in extending the scope and direction of CBM in Europe. Holst and Melander offer a very adequate definition when they write that 'confidence building involves the communication of credible evidence of the absence of feared threats', and they go on to make clear that the aim of CBM is to reduce the 'incentives for competition which derive from uncertainty'.[3] In this paper I shall accept both their definition of CBM and the aim they ascribe to them.

## The Theory of CBM

In marked contrast to those arms-control measures which concentrate on quantities of weapons and their physical characteristics (and thus, on capabilities), Confidence-Building Measures operate on the perceptions of those in confrontation (and particularly on their perceptions of intentions). While something of the intentions of adversaries can be learned indirectly as a result of mutually agreed arms limitations – and from the extent to which legally binding agreements are entered into and are (or are not) subsequently respected – such numerically-based treaties are primarily concerned with physical balances, as expressed in the capabilities of each side to perform military acts against the other in a future conflict. In other words, self-confidence tends to follow from the knowledge that, whatever the intentions of the potential adversary, each has the capability to match the highest level of violence that the other can employ.

In contrast, CBM can by-pass assessments of capabilities (and hence many of the problems associated with verification and accuracy of assessments) and go straight to intentions. Two rather different but mutually reinforcing kinds of reassurance are sought through CBM. The first is essentially continuous and related to the willingness of potential adversaries to demonstrate publicly their non-aggressive postures and generally defensive concerns by opening their internal affairs to examination either by the other or by independent observers. 'Associated measures' in MBFR would be of this type – that is, the monitoring of agreed ceilings and deployments. The second is designed to operate primarily in times of crisis. As a result of measures agreed between the parties, both should know that they are less vulnerable to the dangers of a surprise attack because they are assured of warning.

Although the fact that an agreement to adopt CBM has been reached may appear quite dramatic (in a symbolic sense) and therefore an important indicator of levels of detente, CBM are very slow-acting and are unlikely to give rise to any substantial reductions either in tension or in forces for some time, assuming that to be their ultimate aim. The new confidence will not be acquired overnight. The dialogue between adversaries should run something like this: if you are *genuinely* concerned about security and not about launching an aggressive war against me, then I have the right to insist that I should have adequate warning of an attack as proof of your good intentions. I accept that you may be entitled to strike first if you feel your security to be threatened, but then I am also entitled to warning. For my part, if I am assured of fair warning, I can adopt a position which is less threatening to you. As I am prepared to give you an assurance that I do not mean to attack you, I will find that a satisfactory arrangement and will reduce my readiness. I do not ask that you should not be *able* to attack me but only that you cannot do it before I am ready to meet such an attack. If I do not have that confidence, I am going to have to maintain my alert position, and so are you.

CBM are subjective in the sense that they should affect what people feel about a potential adversary, but they may also comprise an objective component, and the greater the objective component, the more likely CBM are to 'bite', for they actually impose more or less severe constraints on a nation intent on aggression. Under the purely subjective head come such things as attitudes to negotiations, openness in the exchange of military personnel, informal and formal contacts through sport and invitations of observers to exercises – in short, all those things which tend to confirm an impression of relaxation and military detente. Objective CBM which 'bite' are those which give quite unambiguous warning of intended aggression or which place physical limits on what each side can do in peacetime. Some CBM straddle the subjective and objective rather uncomfortably. Notification of exercises has a subjective component, in that each is telling the other what it intends to do, thereby reassuring him that an exercise is an exercise and not a preparation for something else. But as soon as the size or location of exercises is restricted, an objective component is introduced because a potential aggressor *cannot* (without breaking the agreement) use an unlimited exercise close to a border to mask an invasion. Even prior notification does something to restrict a nation's options.

It could be argued that it is precisely because neither side feels itself to be seriously disadvantaged by subjective CBM that they can be adopted relatively easily between potential adversaries. It is unlikely that either side would,

at least at the outset, accept objective CBM which removed existing military options altogether, even in a symmetrical sense. Asymmetrical CBM are likely to prove even less tractable.

## The Problems of Asymmetry
A's ability to act aggressively against B is a function of the numbers, equipment, organization, doctrine and deployment of both. At the same time, each will be entitled to define his own defensive needs in relation to his own security. Any attempt at classification of 'offensive' and 'defensive' weapons is likely to be unproductive, for very few weapons systems can be said to be unequivocally of one type or the other. Doctrine can differ so fundamentally between military cultures that a doctrinal approach may lead up a blind alley. Agreements to change doctrine would demand an unnatural level of tolerance and understanding on each side. Certain states – among them the Soviet Union and Israel – hold as holy writ the primacy of the offensive in all warfare. It follows that such states must organize themselves for pre-emptive attack in the event that they believe themselves to be threatened. An explicit statement of this belief appeared in *Red Star* in 1970: 'Nuclear weapons have established even more firmly the role of attack as the decisive form of military action and have made it necessary *to accomplish even defensive tasks by active offensive action*' (emphasis added).[4] One should note that it is not the advent of nuclear weapons that has altered the importance of attacking rather than defending – the doctrine pre-dated nuclear weapons. Densities, frontages and rates of advance do change, but the fundamental doctrine of Soviet land forces does not. Soviet doctrine concerning the ever-present possibility that war may become nuclear by accident or by the choice of either side is entrenched. This has led to a force structure which is designed to cope with both nuclear and conventional operations. To address intentions at the doctrinal level, therefore, is likely to be a rather sterile exercise, for it may be striking at national characteristics and fundamental military beliefs which have deep roots in history. Organization follows from the doctrine adopted, and Soviet tank armies have grown quite directly from what one suspects to be a genuine concern for defence and security. Understanding of this problem is often lacking, with the result that

Western nations tend to focus almost exclusively on what they view as an unambiguously offensive force structured to strike at the West, and they are unprepared to acknowledge that an alternative explanation might exist. One does not have to dismiss the offensive possibility to acknowledge that Soviet armoured forces can also – in Soviet eyes – be seen as essential for defence. On the not unreasonable assumption that it will be difficult or impossible to alter beliefs, one must look for ways of minimizing the consequences of this asymmetry of doctrine. It is also necessary to acknowledge that there is a secondary reason for the size and shape of Soviet forces – namely, the need to sit on top of Eastern Europe in order to quash any fissiparous tendencies. If it were possible to convince the Soviet Union that what is needed for suasion is not necessarily identical with that which is required for defence (tanks are a particular case in point), it might be possible to procure some retreat of armoured formations from very forward positions in return for a similar concession by NATO. The latter could accept infantry close to the borders of West Germany far more readily than armoured formations. Nevertheless, it must be acknowledged that the instances of Hungary and Czechoslovakia give rise to pessimism in this connection – tank units (primarily) and not infantry were used to put down these risings. The Soviet Union is likely to feel that she needs tanks in East Germany and Poland, for example, for purposes unconnected with conventional or nuclear defence.

To point up one or two further difficulties in the same general context, even the decision by NATO to arm itself far more heavily with anti-tank guided missiles than with tanks need not necessarily be viewed as an undertaking unambiguously defensive in intention, when arguably the most successful part of the Arab operation against Israel in 1973 was conducted almost exclusively with infantry and anti-tank weapons with the purpose of seizing ground and inviting attack. There is some evidence that the introduction of BMP regiments (containing large numbers of anti-tank guided weapons) by the Soviet Union is intended to give her almost precisely this option. The Soviet Union would also be entitled to argue that the armour released from its role in NATO of supporting the infantry in defence *could* be concentrated into a substantial striking force, and she need not necessarily be over-impressed by NATO protestations that it needs tanks for active defence and counter-attack. Considerations of this kind mean that there will always be a wide gulf between adversaries in terms of what each considers alarming about the posture, equipment and doctrine of the other. It is not, therefore, likely to be a very promising approach – at least in the early stages of detente. As the Vienna MBFR negotiations have shown in full measure, initial asymmetries are extremely difficult to rectify: mutual suspicion as to motives and intentions make both sides very reluctant to bridge the gulf between them in any substantive way.

## Subjective CBM

All this points to the need to start the process at the bottom end rather than at the top: that is, to take the easy things first. Those objective CBM which are likely to 'bite' hard come later in the paper. I suggest that the first step must be educational, and that it should be effected through liaison and exchanges of military personnel. Sporting links could also be encouraged. Given the needs of military communities to retain a substantial measure of security, such exchanges are unlikely to do more than establish contact at the social level, but there is some hope that this would improve relations between blocs. The fear is that each would take the opportunity of impressing the others with its prowess, and it would not be at all natural to expect soldiers to set about convincing their opponents that they have nothing to worry about.

It is very difficult to see what is really achieved through exchanges of observer teams for exercises beyond this very general benefit of social contact and the fact that a very small chink of light is allowed to penetrate the curtain of secrecy. Already we have seen that each side is concerned to circumscribe the activities of exercise observers for fear that they will discover militarily useful facts about equipment or doctrine. The notification of exercises is demonstrably more significant, and confidence follows from the fact that what is notified does occur – if what has *not* been notified occurs, there is cause for legitimate concern. The timeliness of the notification is also important, for the greater the warning that an exercise is to take place, the

190

greater the reassurance and the certainty that the exercise is neither a cover for deployment to war positions nor designed to exert political pressure; arguably the longer the warning, the better. To date the record is not good because of a discretionary clause in the Final Act, and it is worth remarking that on one occasion Hungary notified one day before an exercise and on another she left it until the day the exercise started. Between forty-five and sixty days' warning about exercises and movements would be far more reassuring. There is a counter-argument, sometimes deployed by the Soviet Union, that advance notification of exercises *could* be used to threaten or coerce even without the exercises taking place, provided that the warning period was sufficiently long. The signal conveyed would be made more convincing because it would be made under the CSCE arrangements. This is rather hard to accept, for it has always been open to a state to announce the holding of manoeuvres as far in advance as it wished. In 1968, for example, this kind of political pressure was applied to Czechoslovakia. What seems clear is that the undertaking to give warning removes one option – that of declaring an exercise at very short notice to provide cover for an invasion. Unless the areas in which exercises are permitted to take place are far removed from borders, there is no way of preventing a state from applying diplomatic pressure through the massing of forces near frontiers. All that CBM can do is to remove any possibility that an act of coercion could be confused with a genuine exercise.

Notification does not of itself restrict the military options of either side in any way, and so it cannot do a great deal to decrease tension. Pessimists could argue that it was precisely because notification of exercises (as a principle) did nothing whatever to reduce or curtail military options that this measure was agreed of Helsinki – and that this is why the idea at notifying movements was discarded by the Soviet Union. What notification can achieve is the cultivation of somewhat greater confidence on each side that it can identify normal patterns of military behaviour – as associated with unthreatening attitudes – so that departure from the norm can be spotted rather earlier and with greater certainty than before. Whether or not this is really valuable depends upon the accuracy of the intelligence-gathering agencies of both

sides. If both have a high expectation that they can in any case detect movements and exercises, notification is reduced to a symbolic gesture. To take a quite specific example outside the NATO/Warsaw Pact area, it is difficult to see what notification by the Egyptians to the Israelis of their exercises in 1973 would have done to lessen the chances of conflict. Yet it was the succession of major and almost identical manoeuvres in the spring and summer of that year that served to disguise the real attack of 6 October. It is certain that the Israelis knew about each of the exercises, and it was important – from the Egyptian point of view – that they should do so. What was not known was whether each was only an exercise or the approach march of an army intent on war. Notification *per se* would not have helped. What was needed was the addition of some unambiguous indicator that what was happening was war and not an exercise. If, hypothetically, there had been some agreement that no logistic vehicle would carry live or simulated ammunition on exercises, that vehicle canopies would always be removed on exercises and that verification of these facts could be assured by satellite photography or other means (such as stationed observers), the Israelis would have been able to rely on a measure which meant something in a way that mere notification does not. (Obviously such restrictions would place great difficulties in the way of logistic training, but arrangements could have been made for this to take place away from the Canal.) Paradoxically, notification of what is in any case likely to be detected may be of greater symbolic importance than notification of what might not be detected. The latter may mean very little if the other side has little confidence in its own ability to detect what has not been notified. It is notification plus the assurance that what has been notified will be detected that gives confidence through the operation of the mechanism of trust.

However, there are difficulties in settling the indicators that differentiate an exercise from a warlike act. Demonstrably empty logistic vehicles may be attractive as an expedient, but all nations wish to exercise their logistic services alongside and in combination with the combat arms that they must support in war. Most nations use simulated ammunition (that is, sand-filled boxes) which look like (or could hide) the real thing. Therefore such a measure could only work with intrusive on-site inspection. If observers had the right to demand the opening of boxes at random, this would work well. Aircraft and helicopters could be required to fly exercise missions without external ordnance. This would certainly be observable and would hardly detract from the training value of the exercise. The difficulty here is that it would not take long for arming to take place and, in the case of armed helicopters, this could be done in the field. One is forced to conclude, therefore, that Functionally Representational Observable Differences (or FROD, to use the latest and least attractive acronym) are likely to be as difficult to codify for conventional weapons as they are proving to be in SALT for strategic weapons.

In a sense one is trying to square the circle, for in the conventional context it will be necessary for some time to come (even assuming the continuation of detente) for both sides to present themselves as capable of deterring aggression by the other at whatever level it may occur. This requires not only that each must demonstrate power but also that each must go for very high visibility and readiness – particularly if war can start with little warning. To deter means to convince a potential opponent that the costs of any aggression are likely to exceed any benefits that might follow. If, particularly on the Soviet side, what is viewed as necessary for deterrence is almost precisely that which is seen as threatening by the other side, the building of confidence between the adversaries is likely to get off to a bad start. The only profitable line to explore is the possibility of framing a formal undertaking by both sides to forgo pre-emption, together with at least some dismantling of the structure which makes pre-emption possible and the introduction of some measures which would make pre-emption more difficult to achieve. But only the most optimistic could believe that there would be much movement in this direction in the early stages of confidence building.

It is really very difficult for either side to reconcile a drive for greater readiness with the acceptance of measures which, in their nature, are intended to make it more difficult for states to go to war and to make more visible the preparations that they must make in order to do so. As SACEUR has most amply demonstrated, the fear of short-warning attack is the driving force behind measures to increase readiness. These measures are moving in exactly the opposite direction from CBM and are almost irreconcilable with them, for readiness to defend is almost indistinguishable from readiness to attack – at least in the eyes of an adversary. To put this another way, the number of CBM which could be adopted which would *not* detract from readiness would be very small. We may have gone as far as we can without a much greater measure of political detente than is apparent at the present time.

## Objective CBM

It is important for A to convince B that the genuinely innocent act *is* really innocent. Once that confidence is established, differentiation between the malign and the benign is possible, and A has the confidence that he can distinguish between the two. He will then know how to react to what he observes: what signals to discard as essentially unalarming and what to treat as alarming.

Between adversaries with defence doctrines which are broadly similar it would be a relatively simple matter to erect a structure which increases the assurance of both that they really do have less to fear from a surprise attack than before – that is, some objective physical constraints can be imposed. This structure is likely to be partly geographical and partly institutional in the first instance, with limitations of forces and equipment by type and number following later. In geographical terms one can consider both zones of complete disengagement and zones of limited deployment of forces, either by number or by type or both. For example, one could envisage an agreement which kept all heavy armour 50 or 100 kilometres back from sensitive borders and which limited calibres of artillery in the zone. However, it is not obvious that zones of complete disengagement would necessarily favour the defence and increase the feeling of security, because the zone of disengagement of A is a hostage to the attacking forces of B, who may well be able to traverse not only his own zone but also that of A before A can move back into his own zone and organize an effective defence in it. Taking a model in which each zone is 50 kilometres deep, B (the attacker) could move his leading armoured forces unopposed across his own zone in six hours and across A's zone in perhaps a further twelve. Given that such an

192

attack could be delivered with a warning that would be of very little use to A, and that A's forces will be dispersed in their peacetime locations, it could well take A at least twenty-four hours to deploy and arrange even a makeshift defence. There would therefore be a fair chance that B could be in possession of all or part of A's zone of disengagement before A can do anything about it – except to counter-attack, which could prove costly, or to rely on air attack, which is uncertain at best and at worst can be countered by defence. The problem is that the premium on surprise (and the choice of time and place) is just as important as it is in the absence of a zone; arguably the presence of a zone tends to make a 'grab and sit' operation even more attractive than the absence of a zone.

Zones *plus* assured warning lessen the dangers somewhat, but one then runs up against discussion of what constitutes 'assured warning' and how it can be arranged. Such a concept has worked in Sinai with a combination of UN observers *and* American monitoring *and* listening posts from each of the adversaries. Translating that requirement into Central Front terms, I suggest that what works in a virtually depopulated Sinai is unlikely to be effective in a densely populated area like the borders of East and West Germany. Not only would it be technically difficult to separate 'signals' from 'noise' in that very different environment, but it would require that 'enemy' posts be established on the other's territory, which may prove unacceptable, although it is as well to remember that missions are currently exchanged between commanders-in-chief without undue difficulty and with some freedom to move about on 'hostile' territory. Each side may have sufficient confidence in satellite warning and may be prepared to sanction regular reconnaissance flights by the other over the zone; certainly, both these measures could serve to dissuade either from clandestine movements designed to break the agreements. (Weekly U-2 flights are made over the Sinai.) Nevertheless, it seems unlikely, in a confrontation between super-powers, that either will accept that its guard can be substantially lowered as a result of zones of disengagement or of limited forces unless fool-proof early warning can be guaranteed. The much-reduced warning that enemy forces were moving back into their own zone would not necessarily constitute a sound basis for adequate defensive deployment.

There is also a political component to zones of disengagement which is likely to come to the surface in an alliance. If the defence of a threatened nation rests at least in part on the contributions made by her allies on the ground, she will tend to resist rather strongly any suggestion that the forward commitment of the ground forces of her allies should be restricted. Quite specifically, West Germany is likely to oppose any scheme which limited either her own forward deployment or the forward deployment of NATO forces, for it is the certainty that her allies will be in the war from the earliest moment that underwrites the political commitment signified by the Atlantic Alliance. It also has a great deal to do with the credibility of the American nuclear guarantee, and many Europeans would be very reluctant to see anything happen that might tend to diminish linkage.

Perhaps, therefore, it may be more profitable to look at what an attacking force must do before it goes to war, and attempt to place difficulties in the way of rapid deployment, or at least establish observers to determine whether or not a particular preparatory move is going forward. An obvious choice is ammunition. Observers posted to watch all major ammunition storage facilities could not fail to detect outloading prior to war. Any interference with them or their communications would be taken as a clear indication of warlike intention. In order to permit practice in outloading procedures, rather elaborate precautions would have to be taken to ensure that such practices did not coincide with exercises and that not all depots were outloaded at the same time. It is clearly unrealistic to prohibit such necessary rehearsal altogether, for that would strike at real security needs – in this case, the ability to mobilize rapidly when under threat of attack.

Concentration on fuel stocks is likely to be unproductive, for circumvention would be relatively easy. Controls on nuclear warheads would tend to encourage the conventional option. There may be other essentially warlike preparatory moves which could be isolated but the criteria must be rather exacting: whichever ones were chosen would have to be large enough to be seen, difficult to circumvent, unrestrictive of normal training and quite unequivocally warlike. Agreement by both sides to permit observation of major ammunition storage sites (some training ammunition would have to be excluded) would be a major step forward, not least because each would be declaring its facilities and taking some risk that it would be laying itself open to a disarming nuclear or conventional air attack. It is worth remarking that one of the major trends in NATO over the past few years has been a consistent forward movement of ammunition storage sites, in recognition of the fact that dumps in the rear are likely to prolong the outloading process to a dangerous extent in the face of surprise attack. On the Soviet side the desire to be able to mount a surprise attack has also led to a forward movement of all kinds of stocks. Reversal of this trend ought logically to lead to a reduction in tension, for each side would know that preparations for war would take longer and would certainly be more easily detected. Military vehicles and trains would have to make long and readily detectable journeys. Relocation would take many years, would be very costly and would be strongly opposed by all who see readiness as the key to success. Nevertheless, if such a step were taken by mutual agreement, a reduction in tension ought to follow.

One more idea presents itself. If tactical strike aircraft were positioned in peacetime at a distance from borders that was greater than their tactical range, they would be able to act defensively against an intruder, but not to support an aggressive move unless they were deployed forwards prior to hostilities. It might not be easy to prohibit, and enforce the prohibition of, forward basing entirely, particularly for STOL aircraft, but the move forward from their permitted peacetime bases would be eminently detectable. Just how much warning that would give is uncertain, but so long as fuel also had to be moved up and there were restrictions on ordnance and forward maintenance facilities, substantial delays would be imposed on the aggressor unless he were to attack without air support in the first instance. In other words, any forward strips declared necessary for forward deployment would have to be open to inspection from time to time to verify compliance. In terms of each side's ability to disperse its own air assets, the warning that such a measure would

ensure would make it attractive as a means of increasing confidence. Clearly, the distance must be calculated on the basis of high-level transit and a significant load of ordnance. The onus would be on the side challenged to prove that its aircraft could not go beyond the border under these conditions. Any limits on the forward basing of aircraft would also have to be taken to apply to carrier-borne aircraft where these might be deployed within tactical range of possible battlefields. Arrangements might have to be worked out to cover a degree of exercising from forward bases or carriers – say a limit of one-sixth at a time. A similar restriction could be applied to bridging equipment. This is always bulky and very distinctive in shape, and without large quantities of many different types of equipment no nation – at least in Europe – could think of conducting a deep assault. There are many water obstacles and, on the Central Front, almost all run at right angles to the natural lines of advance. Although tanks can be prepared for deep fording and many armoured fighting vehicles can swim, there is no evidence that amphibious logistic support vehicles are available in sufficient quantities to allow either side to be independent of engineer support. The evidence suggests, rather, that both sides are increasing their mechanical bridging equipment. It follows that an undertaking to restrict the deployment of bridging equipment in forward areas would have a considerable impact on the ability of either side to advance at short notice; it also constitutes one of the classes of military equipment most easily identified by visual or photographic means, so that neither side would rate very highly its ability to move it forward without detection. However, it can move quickly over good roads so that it would be necessary to seek a total ban on bridging equipment within 200–300 kilometres of the border. Such a separation could give about twenty-four hours' warning of an attack and would greatly complicate the planning and preparation of any attack.

The last general approach is to attempt to identify those indicators which *must* alter before a state goes to war. No army, for example, would go to war using only clear radio transmissions. It would either use code or, until first contact, would maintain radio silence. Each side must acknowledge the other's need to train radio operators in code; at the same time each would fear that it would give away too many of its 'secrets' (in terms of doctrine and operating procedures) if it did not make intercept difficult during exercises. If each side accepted notification as a principle *and* if there were to be a numerical limit on the size of exercises, indications of changed patterns of transmission would really be redundant, but an agreement to place limitations on the use of coded radio traffic could be worth pursuing as an idea for adoption at a later stage. Such measures could be fairly easily 'spoofed' by duplicated nets or ghost formations.

So far I have avoided the question of exercise limitation. There are three possibilities: limitation by overall size, limitation by area and limitation by duration. The first is a very promising approach but not currently popular with NATO. A limitation along these lines was proposed recently by the Soviet Union. The reasons for its rejection are valid, but only in a fairly marginal sense: NATO argues that an upper limit of (say) 75,000 would be more constraining for the Alliance than for the Warsaw Pact because NATO consists of many nations, all of whom contribute substantially to the overall strength of the Alliance, whereas the Soviet Union's part in the Warsaw Pact is very dominant. It follows (so the argument goes) that NATO needs to exercise larger numbers than the Warsaw Pact if inter-allied co-operation is not to suffer. It is not a cogent argument if NATO is genuinely seeking ways of improving CBM effectiveness; in any case, as Holst and Melander have observed, there have been no exercises anywhere in Europe since the signing of the Helsinki Final Act in mid-1975 which have exceeded 75,000, and only three above 50,000 (all NATO).[5]

Proposals involving limitation by area could be much more promising, and a number of variations on a theme could be postulated:

- no exercises close to borders;
- no exercises above a certain size anywhere;
- limited exercises within border zones and larger ones elsewhere.

Certainly the removal of major exercises from sensitive areas would do much to lessen fears of surprise attack from troops deployed under the guise of an exercise, but one must also acknowledge that asymmetry upsets the neat and tidy solution. Whereas the potential attacker suffers little disadvantage in being forced to train further back, the defender loses out very substantially in being unable to train over the ground he has to defend. At least one of the factors that gives a local margin of effectiveness to the defence (in the classic ratio of $3:1$) is that of familiarity with ground. In being denied the opportunity to gain this familiarity, he would be at a far greater disadvantage than the attacker, who cannot in any case get to know the ground over which he is to attack. Therefore exercises of limited size – say divisional – will have to be permitted, even close to borders. These would, with careful planning, allow every forward division to become acquainted with its ground each year, yet single divisions would not constitute a serious threat to either side. Without over-complicating the issue, greater limits could be imposed on exercises in a deeper zone, whilst complete freedom could be permitted elsewhere. This would allow NATO the possibility of exercising very large forces (however rarely this has happened in the past), should it ever wish to do so.

Limitation by duration has only one slight advantage. It prevents either side from maintaining a threat for a long period. In the Arab–Israeli setting, this could be a major concession on the part of the Egyptians, who have in the past been able to sustain 'exercises' for long periods of time, thus forcing the Israelis to maintain an economically damaging alert, even amounting to partial mobilization, for the same length of time. In the European theatre a period of two weeks could probably be negotiated without great difficulty but, equally, it would not appear to be very significant.

To summarize, an ideal structure of CBM for the Central Front would include:

- notification of exercises and movements above a defined (fairly low) level;
- limitation of exercises and movements to a low tactical level within border zones, a higher level further back, and an unrestricted level elsewhere;
- Limitation by duration;
- prohibition of live ammunition on exercises, together with national means of verification;
- rear basing of tactical aircraft and bridging equipment;
- exchange of personnel and liaison.

## Conclusion

It would be wrong to present a picture of CBM as the easy way of getting arms control back on the road. There are all sorts of ways in which CBM could reinforce stability between states who are suspicious of each other but who basically share a desire to avoid conflict and are prepared to forgo certain military options themselves in order to negotiate the denial of similar or even different options to the potential adversary. The more nearly similar the options foresworn, the easier the negotiations are likely to be. The evidence to date suggests that the political context is crucial. To the extent that states genuinely desire a reduction in tension, CBM of graduated and increasing severity can probably be negotiated, as long as each believes its own security to be augmented thereby. CBM, which 'bite', but 'bite' unevenly, have little chance of success; only if both sides feel themselves equally constrained can anything beyond mere window-dressing be negotiated. The conclusion is inescapable that arms-control measures will work only if both sides want them to work and believe that the measures will enhance their own security and not diminish it.

Whether one should look for a package or move step by step through 'gentle' to 'severe' is a proper subject for debate. In any case CBM must be viewed in their totality; it is the sum of the CBM constraints on land, at sea and in the air which must be assessed and balanced. What has been suggested here as an ideal structure of CBM for the Central Front must be viewed against a backdrop of the overall strategic and tactical balance of forces and capabilities and in the political context which this paper has deliberately avoided.

## NOTES

[1] There is a very useful survey of the record of CBM application in Johan Holst and Karen Melander, 'European Security and CBM', *Survival*, July/August 1977. Another useful series of documents is the US Department of State Semiannual Reports by the President to the Commission on Security and Co-operation in Europe. These contain a full statement about the implementation of the Helsinki Final Act. The most recent brings the record to 1 June 1978.

[2] For the full text, see British Government White Paper, Cmnd 7126, 'The Meeting held at Belgrade 4th October to 9th March 1978 to follow up the Conference on Security and Co-operation in Europe' (HMSO, March 1978).

[3] *Op. cit.* in note 1, p. 147.

[4] General-Lieutenant I. G. Zav'yalov, 'Novoye oruzhie i voyennoye iskusstvo', *Red Star*, 30 October 1970. Translated and reprinted as 'The New Weapon and Military Art' in *Selected Soviet Military Writings 1970–1975, A Soviet View*, Soviet Military Thought, No. 11 (Washington DC: USGPO for USAF, 1977), p. 209.

[5] *Op. cit.* in note 1, pp. 150–1.

# Confidence-Building Measures in SALT: a PAR Perspective

**ALTON FRYE**

In the hills of Tennessee they still recall the moonshiners of Salt Hollow. A federal revenue agent, looking for the still one day, came across a young boy and asked where his parents were. 'Up the holler, makin' whiskey', was the answer. The 'revenooer' offered to pay the boy a dollar to lead him there, and the youngster held out his hand. When the agent promised to pay him after they got back, the boy refused, saying, 'No, sir. Pay me now. You ain't comin' back.'

This anecdote is a metaphor for the present state of attitudes about strategic arms negotiations. Before proceeding further up 'SALT Holler', many people are asking what the price will be – and whether they will be coming back. Confidence in the SALT process is at a low ebb. It has waned substantially since the 1972 ABM Treaty and Interim Agreement limiting strategic offensive weapons. Doubts have grown in many quarters and, one must add, on both sides of the great divide between East and West. The United States and her allies have valid concerns regarding the pace and scope of the Soviet military build-up in all spheres, including the rapid modernization of strategic delivery systems. The Soviet Union has shown similar anxieties regarding such American innovations as modern cruise missiles which, in some scenarios, could enable the West to proliferate its strategic delivery capabilities well beyond the levels of the ceilings sketched in the 1974 Vladivostok Accord.

Both sides have found reason for wariness in the simple fact that they failed to reach a new agreement on offensive weapons within the five years originally covered by the Interim Agreement. Some reputable analysts have begun to question the value of the entire SALT process, asking whether formal arms-control agreements are worth the cost and effort, and whether the better approach to strategic sufficiency and stability may not lie in tacit arrangements erected without laborious diplomacy. Apart from the intrinsic difficulties encountered in the long-running SALT II discussions, the atmosphere has repeatedly become soured.

This gloomy rendition of the diplomatic and political environment for SALT is but a prelude to an obvious conclusion and an evident question. The entire SALT process is in jeopardy, even if the determined efforts of American and Soviet negotiators produce an early agreement. An endeavour intended to enhance both sides' confidence in their security is itself the object of declining confidence. What can be done to serve both sides' security interests by strengthening the SALT process and by providing a prudent basis for confidence in its results? Rather than accepting the thesis that SALT may be a blind alley, the argument here is that SALT can and should remain an essential instrument for building confidence between the parties. SALT cannot be allowed to become merely a psychological exercise, an endless encounter session in which the parties play out their anxieties for one another. To fulfil their potential these talks must produce real and significant effects on the strategic programmes of the two sides. But exclusive concentration on questions of hardware and military technology may obscure the need to blend strategic, psychological and political elements in intelligent proportions. Somehow SALT must move beyond its excessive preoccupation with numbers and institute a search for ways to clarify intentions and justify strategic

197

behaviour. If procurement decisions have to be announced and explained in the light of previously declared strategic doctrine, SALT could become a way of shoring up strategic confidence. If there is mutual understanding (as there seems to be) that nuclear war must be avoided and that neither side should invoke the spectre of nuclear war, it ought to be possible to multiply those indicators and demonstrable checkpoints which serve to reassure. This is the same thing as saying that information and explanation hold the key to the building of confidence – information on testing, deployment, space launches, etc., and explanation as to why it is necessary to do what is being done.

Like tightrope walkers suspended high above the arena, the United States and the Soviet Union find themselves in a position of grave peril. To survive they must both edge cautiously along the wire – and, if possible, spread their own safety nets below them. As a strategic safety net, SALT must weave many factors together if it is to offer a basis for mutual confidence.

National security, like personal security, has both objective and subjective components. SALT must address both. Arms diplomacy must bridge dependable constraints on force posture and development on the one hand and reliable prognoses about the adversary's behaviour on the other. Unless these multiple ingredients, technology and psychology, strategy and politics, capabilities and intentions, are kept constantly in view, strategic arms negotiations are likely to be stunted or sterile.

Part of the problem in recent months has been a loss of perspective on the contribution SALT I has already made to mutual confidence in the adequacy of strategic deterrence. Had there been no ABM Treaty and had the two sides continued in their efforts to field defences against ballistic missiles, the pressures to hedge against the possible failure of their deterrent forces by further increases in their offensive capabilities would have been enormous. Considering the alarm already simmering because of incremental changes in strategic offensive forces, one can well imagine the intensity of concern that would have followed a truly rapid surge in such deployments.

Yet SALT I provided other precedents of value and relevance to later attempts to bolster confidence through negotiations. To begin with, the limitations on certain types of ABM system tests

(for example, the confinement of tests to established ranges and the prohibition on the exercise of certain air defence radars in 'an ABM mode') represented a useful step towards the solution of a problem that weighs ever more heavily on the SALT agenda – qualitative arms controls. As is now well known, quantitative arms limitations may be undercut by qualitative innovations that increase the effectiveness of any given force. Technological breakthroughs, dimly foreseen and poorly governed, may be the greatest threat to a durable and trustworthy strategic balance. In the long term, confidence in SALT agreements will hinge in large measure on their success in specifying viable restraints on destabilizing technologies.

A related and inadequately appreciated legacy of SALT I, deserves special notice in any exploration of options for further CBM. This is the Standing Consultative Commission (SCC), which has begun to fulfil its promise as a forum for relieving ambiguities in the implementation of the agreements and for preserving trust in the parties' good-faith compliance. Despite occasional intimations that the Soviet Union has violated the terms of the 1972 accords, those involved in the work of the SCC report that, when challenged on questionable activities, the Soviet Union has responded in an orderly and business-like manner. In some cases she has suspended operations that bordered on violations, for example, certain radar exercises. In others, she has been reasonably forthcoming in describing the purpose of suspicious construction and reconciling it with the terms of the agreements. In turn the Soviet Union has expressed concern over protective shelters used by the United States during winter construction at missile silos, and the United States has reduced the size of those structures to avert any suspicion that her purpose is to camouflage illicit deployments or to frustrate 'national means of verification'. As an infant institution, the Commission has shown remarkable maturity in its proceedings. It affords a unique setting for detailed technical exchanges on a number of matters concerning weapons tests and deployments.

The SCC's work points towards a major opportunity for future development of CBM in SALT. An agency now exists to which both parties have recourse to demonstrate their respect for the standards embodied in strategic arms agreements. To exploit this agency fully, the United States and the Soviet Union would be well advised to expand the number and variety of provisions subject to its review. There may be considerable advantage in the sheer multiplication of limitations within the Commission's jurisdiction. Obviously, no one would contend that every arms-control provision is of comparable value, but the availability of numerous restraints to test each side's true commitment to the negotiated regime would be useful. Increasing the number of test points on which the SCC could base its inquiries could, over a period of time, add to the force of its findings as a factor in the mutual confidence equation. Extending the range of SALT undertakings thus could have the effect of strengthening the habit of compliance and of permitting each party to gauge the other's purposes by systematic probes in the SCC.

At some point too much law may be bad – as too legalistic an approach will always be – but in this era and in this field the primitive state of the law warrants a great deal of development. In this respect formal arms agreements are clearly superior to the kinds of tacit arrangements favoured by some analysts. Explicit, verifiable and enforceable standards will usually be a sounder basis for assessing and displaying the parties' motives than informal and indirect norms. Assuming the validity of this rationale, the Commission is one of the principal means for building confidence through SALT, and its role should be reinforced so far as possible.

Granted that a modest beginning has been made, what can now be done to extract the maximum utility from SALT as a confidence-building process? An evident need is to focus the negotiations on concrete and realistic objectives, and to conduct them with an unequivocal acknowledgment of their limits and their possibilities. If that seems a truism, it is necessary in order to counter an altruism that threatens to mislead the American government. President Carter's inaugural aspiration to seek the abolition of nuclear weapons from the planet is a false start, not because the goal is unworthy but because it is impracticable. No one knows – no one has even conceived – a way to eliminate nuclear weapons completely. The manageable and appropriate function for diplomacy at present and for many years to come is to govern the nuclear capabilities that will certainly exist – to curtail their growth, to slow down their evolution, to reduce their volume and to prevent the creation of circumstances in which they might be used. Inflated hopes can only work to intensify disappointment at the rather minor changes in strategic force levels that may result from the arms agreements reached in the next few years.

Ironically, too vaulting an ambition in the realm of arms reductions may even arouse the suspicion of the Soviet Union. One wonders whether Mr Carter's inaugural invocation of the goal of complete nuclear disarmament, for all its basic honesty, increased Moscow's tendency to see the March 1977 'comprehensive proposal' as a propaganda ploy designed to put the Soviet Union on the defensive rather than to promote a more far-reaching agreement. At any rate, such pronouncements may undermine confidence instead of nourishing it.

What is required is a very broad view of the desirable long-term movement in the strategic relationship, coupled with very fine judgments regarding marginal adjustments of the balance in the short term. A vital consideration in the formulation of both types of evaluation is the nature and the implications of uncertainty for strategic force-posture planning and for strategic arms negotiations. A lucid conception of the role of uncertainty can help in the framing of useful conclusions about both deterrence and confidence – the one an essentially negative psychological phenomenon rooted in threatening behaviour, the other a more positive phenomenon associated with expectations of non-threatening behaviour. The logic of nuclear strategy is a double negative: one cannot be sure that the other side will not be able to inflict exorbitant damage.

In strategic analysis one needs to distinguish between stabilizing uncertainty and destabilizing uncertainty. A potential aggressor's uncertainty about whether he can destroy a sufficient fraction of the other side's weapons to prevent effective retaliation is stabilizing. Either side's apprehension that its own forces may be vulnerable is a destabilizing uncertainty, tending towards premature launch in extreme crisis. The quality of uncertainty may change in the transition from peace to war. The presence of thousands of theatre nuclear weapons in Europe breeds stabilizing uncertainty about whether they might be used in the event of conflict. But if war seems likely to erupt, that uncertainty could become highly destabilizing and could intensify pressure to strike pre-emptively against nuclear storage depots and delivery vehicles on the continent. Similarly, in arms-race calculations one should note the dual character of uncertainty associated with various factors. Rampant expansion and diversification of strategic arsenals generates stabilizing uncertainty about whether it would ever be rational to attempt their destruction, but destabilizing uncertainty about whether continuing force build-ups indicate that one country or another is seeking superiority, that gloating demon of paper warriors.

The guideline that commends itself in configuring nuclear forces and in conducting strategic diplomacy is straightforward: one should seek to maximize stabilizing uncertainties and minimize destabilizing uncertainties. Confidence in the mutual security provided by the strategic balance may relate directly to stabilizing uncertainties and inversely to destabilizing uncertainties. As with all simple guidelines for complex procedures, this one is easier to state than to apply consistently. Shadowy nuances affect many applications, and interpretations vary among knowledgeable people, often, one surmises, because they load into the estimate other values and concerns which they cherish. Nevertheless, on our present understanding, faithful adherence to this principle offers reasonable hope of steering diplomats and strategic planners in the right general direction, while discouraging counter-productive manoeuvres.

Another fundamental consideration in devising confidence-building measures in SALT has already been intimated. Since nuclear weapons will furnish the planet as far ahead as one can see, the urgent need is for the participants in SALT to understand that their central mission concerns the co-ordination of strategic *intentions* even more than the regulation of strategic *capabilities*. The old maxim of military intelligence that one can only deal with capabilities because they are overt, measurable and relatively slow to change, while intentions are both inscrutable and fickle, is a self-defeating canard. In fact, as frequently stated, the 'capabilities only' doctrine is a virtual guarantee that worst-case analysis will dominate the proceedings, since exclusive concentration on this aspect of the relationship breeds the inference of maximum hostility between the parties, that is, it incorporates the most extreme interpretation of each side's intentions. Of course, SALT must pay close attention to trends in strategic forces, but it could be most fruitful if it expands its purview to embrace an explicit search for methods to forge and display, if not common strategic doctrines (for that may not be possible), at least a compatible approach to strategic management.

How might this be done? Assuming that SALT II reaches a successful conclusion, one important avenue to explore in SALT III could be the formulation of an agreed policy for the avoidance of nuclear war, against which both parties could evaluate each other's development and deployment activities. This could build upon the foundation of the American–Soviet Agreement on the Prevention of Nuclear War of 1973 – itself a CBM. There have been suggestions that efforts should be made to induce some degree of convergence between the two sides' strategic doctrines for nuclear war-fighting. That there is little convergence at the moment seems certain, even if there is some overlap. But while it is probably too much to hope that either could persuade the other that its strategy was 'wrong' (it would be difficult for either to admit something so deeply rooted in history, culture, ideology and geography), the explanation of national strategy in the SCC or at the talks themselves would go some way towards clarifying intentions and thus towards building confidence. If procurement decisions or observed testing of systems appeared to be at odds with the declared strategy, the opportunity for challenge would exist. Nevertheless, even if movement towards a common strategic doctrine remains a chimera, both sides share a common need to avoid nuclear war. There are valid reasons for wishing to have a more comprehensive statement on how both mean to attain this end. Its absence from the present negotiating context tends to feed darker interpretations of the two sides' true intentions; indeed, the lack of a doctrinal consensus has eroded somewhat the favourable impact of the ABM Treaty, as Soviet civil defence efforts and the advance of 'hard-target-kill' technologies on both sides make it clear that neither wholly subscribes to the doctrine of mutual assured destruction (MAD). Apart from halting exchanges in the early months of SALT I, little has been done to identify elements of a possible doctrinal overlap, and further efforts may soon be timely.

One should stress that MAD is not a promising formulation for such a compatible doctrine in any case, even were convergence possible. Apart from its emotionally tinged acronym and its general rejection by the Soviet Union, MAD describes a technological condition rather than a desirable strategy. The capacity to inflict massive destruction is a fact of the strategic balance, not a statement of preferred or intended strategic objectives. If deterrence is to be stable, the primary *intention* must be to prevent the actual use of these forces. Nor have Soviet analysts offered any concept or rationale to fill the need for a doctrine over which the two sides could concur.

As rubric and rationale for SALT, I have proposed Programmed Assured Restraint (PAR). The PAR doctrine would take as its starting point the shared commitment to avoid nuclear war. It should elevate and broaden the discussion of strategic principles and would convey a more accurate sense of the parties' true objectives in SALT, namely to assure restraint in the development, deployment and prospective employment of their most dangerous arsenals. PAR encompasses both capabilities and intentions, subordinating MAD means to deterrent ends. It also has the attractive property of accommodating the Soviet demand that the first principle of the strategic relationship should be 'equal security', a still vague and elastic notion that tends to exaggerate the subjective requirements of security. It acknowledges the arrival and acceptance of strategic parity. It sets an affirmative tone for diplomacy. Furthermore, the hybrid concept of PAR highlights the mutual interest of the United States and the Soviet Union in co-ordinating their strategic behaviour and in programming the character and quantity of their forces with an eye to damping provocations or possible use. In short, an elucidation of a set of principles along the lines suggested by the notion of PAR might facilitate the definition of common strategic perspectives and policies.

What specific benefits might ensue from articulation of a PAR doctrine, and how might the concept inform force planning, diplomacy and other strategic behaviour? Broadly speaking, the thrust of PAR would be to discourage refinements of strategic war-fighting capabilities on both sides and to shift emphasis increasingly towards programmes that ensure the survivability of retaliatory forces. Without recognition of such an emphasis on the part of the United States and the Soviet Union, it is difficult to see how SALT or any other instrument can contribute to mutual confidence in the stability of deterrence.

This general stance would have several implications. An important topic for negotiation in SALT III should be methods for synchronizing American and Soviet behaviour in crisis, at least outside the areas of the two states' alliances. Recognizing that strategic weapons might be used either by accident or through escalation, there is a clear interest in avoiding such risks in any third-area crisis over which the Soviet Union and the United States are not obliged to extend the nuclear umbrella. To signal their commitment to contain rather than extend local crises outside NATO, Warsaw Pact and other alliances, the parties could usefully pledge not to threaten the use of nuclear weapons in any such contingency. (We have seen some tentative gropings in this direction at the UN Special Session on Disarmament.) They could, in other words, formally decouple any involvement in third-world conflicts from possible escalation to the nuclear level and forgo verbal or other attempts to extract political leverage from hints of escalation. Formal commitments are needed to reverse the negative precedents already on the record, including former Premier Khrushchev's rocket-rattling attempt at nuclear blackmail in the 1956 Suez crisis and President Kennedy's regrettable threat of a 'full retaliatory strike' against the Soviet Union during the October 1962 confrontation in the Caribbean.

To these declaratory undertakings they could add operational limits on the types of forces either side would introduce in such theatres, for example, designating certain fleet components for non-nuclear missions. Considering the dual-capable forces available to each country, there are obvious practical difficulties to be resolved (not least with American Carrier Task Forces), but there could be real advantages in segregating some capabilities for exclusively conventional application in the interest of crisis management. The value of this effort becomes all the more apparent when one realizes that, unlike the Cuban missile controversy of 1962, a future crisis will take place in a totally different strategic environment – one in which neither side will readily be able to afford to undermine the perception of strategic parity by yielding to apparently superior leverage. In the spirit of PAR it would be prudent to seek provisions for controlling the danger that direct or indirect strategic threats might inflame local confrontations in which Moscow and Washington may become embroiled.

On several fronts in and out of the SALT II discussion the United States and the Soviet Union are already groping towards measures that would serve the PAR confidence-building design. Together with Britain, they have made progress towards a comprehensive nuclear test ban (CTB) treaty for presentation to other states. The CTB would promote assured restraint in two principal ways. It would moderate the destabilizing uncertainty over the possibility, however slender, that continued tests might produce a technological breakthrough which could have a dramatic impact on the prevailing military balance. Such a test prohibition would underscore the parties' willingness to impose qualitative arms controls in order to slow the velocity of strategic innovation. Moreover, a CTB remains the pillar of a credible anti-proliferation policy, and no states should have a larger stake in that effort than the super-powers. Joint efforts to establish potent anti-proliferation barricades would represent a proper adjunct to bilateral implementation of PAR arrangements. Without in any way constituting the mythical 'great-power condominium' damned by some commentators, collaboration in this field is intrinsically worthwhile. Unless the United States and the Soviet Union work co-operatively here, they will encounter even greater difficulties in forging bilateral restraints. However, it would be right to add a word of caution at this stage. Under some circumstances, test restraint can operate against confidence, or at least against self-confidence. Given a position of strategic stability, each side must retain reasonable assurance that its own systems will work. It follows that a total ban on some activities would be less desirable than a severe limitation of numbers and types of tests, which would maintain self-confidence without allowing anything more than marginal improvements to be undertaken. There is one other way in which confidence can be affected

by test restrictions: if the only way of being sure what the other side is capable of is through observation of his tests, absence of observable tests could give rise to exaggerated fears of the other country's capabilities. It may become easier to believe in CEPs of 0·05 of a nautical mile if there are no tests to show that this *cannot* be achieved. Worst-case analysts could not easily be proved wrong. For some purposes restraint of tests is likely to prove a sounder objective than prohibition.

The central elements of a PAR approach have already been broached in SALT and substantial precedents are in place to encourage the pursuit of this path. One of the crucial bases is the agreement in SALT I not to interfere with either country's national means of verification. Later accords will surely reiterate that obligation and strengthen it as far as possible. In particular, since so many of the requisite surveillance systems are space-based, one welcomes the belated start of negotiations to ban the incipient development of anti-satellite capabilities.

There should be additional efforts to inaugurate co-operative verification techniques, not excluding occasional on-site inspection in specified circumstances. This is no longer the age of the impermeable Iron Curtain; besides opening her advanced technology to partial observation in connection with the *Soyuz–Apollo* joint space flight of July 1975 and certain other ventures, the Soviet Union has agreed to a Threshold Nuclear Test Ban with provisions for remarkable data exchanges and even on-site visits in a few instances. The United States should encourage this tendency, as far as this is practicable, but in the meantime other opportunities exist for co-operative verification endeavours. For instance, a corollary to proposals to curb qualitative change in missile forces by restricting the number and types of flight tests should be the specification of eligible ranges and impact areas chosen to maximize the visibility of tests to outside observation. Such arrangements are no longer far-fetched. They should certainly be a target for SALT III.

Despite the consternation over SALT II's sluggish pace, the current round of negotiations has moved the parties a long distance towards a significant regime of restraint. American officials have revealed that there is already agreement to lower the ceilings set tentatively at Vladivostok and to include a variety of sub-ceilings aimed at holding down the number of MIRV-equipped ICBM – the premium targets for, and instruments of, a hypothetical counter-force exchange. The accompanying protocol advances further into qualitative limitations on mobile ICBM testing and deployment; it also seeks to pin down several constraints on development and deployment of other new ballistic missiles, as well as more modest limitations on cruise missiles. While cautious analysts will withhold judgment until the final package emerges, the negotiations seem headed towards an outcome likely to offer a clear choice between a quest for security built on formal restraints and one relying on highly dynamic competition.

It is widely expected that the next phase of negotiations (SALT III) must begin to address the intricate problems of the so-called 'grey area' systems, that is, those weapons spanning the strictly strategic realm and that of tactical nuclear forces. Precisely because weapons like the Soviet SS-20 missile and certain American forward-based systems are multi-purpose, they pose acute ambiguities regarding their proprietor's intentions. A PAR perspective on those kinds of weapons would seek to distinguish ambiguities susceptible to elimination by negotiation from those that are diplomatically intractable.

For example, as SALT III works to bridge Soviet–American strategic problems and European security concerns, a promising focus for assuring restraint may centre on nuclear weapons storage and handling arrangements. Both sides have an interest in avoiding hair-trigger postures in a setting in which time-to-target for many delivery systems may be only a few minutes, and it may be feasible to contrive measures demonstrating that warheads for the numerous nuclear delivery systems are kept physically separate from launchers instead of being held in immediate readiness. Obvious difficulties will arise in averting the temptation to strike nuclear storage depots with conventional means, but the extension of warning times by keeping such depots well away from the frontiers is a partial response to this danger.

Visible segregation of warheads from theatre delivery vehicles would provide a crucial indicator of intended restraint. It would not, however, deny either side the technical capability to initiate first use in the theatre by high-readiness, central delivery systems like SLBM, which could cover time-urgent targets on the continent. Nonetheless, such arrangements could be one useful barrier against precipitate nuclear attacks. They would also introduce a potent, albeit risky, option for signalling threats in crisis, in the event that either side undertook to move warheads to their assigned launchers.

A particularly notable case involves the dual capability of certain aircraft to carry both nuclear and conventional ordnance. There is a powerful argument for restricting these planes to conventional missions, particularly when one weighs NATO's need for a surge capability to counter Warsaw Pact armour. Both alliances might find it advisable to eliminate specialized nuclear fittings from their theatre aircraft and to avoid co-locating nuclear storage facilities with airfields. These would be imperfect but worthwhile means of confirming exclusively conventional missions of the aircraft. Similar procedures might be devised for cruise missiles if they acquire a conventional function in future European deployments.

Implicit in this commentary is a willingness to accept a trade-off in the readiness to fire of theatre nuclear forces in return for the presumed benefits of confirming mutual intentions of restraint. If an intense crisis erupted, however, pressures to increase theatre nuclear readiness would certainly build up, especially while NATO considers itself at a conventional disadvantage. Over the long haul, a PAR approach to these systems will probably depend on significant progress in the adjustment of the conventional balance to lower and more stable levels. But progress in both areas is linked, and such steps as those designed to limit dual-capable systems may facilitate agreement on reductions of armoured forces in the forward areas, for the good reason that the interaction of tanks and air power is more calculable when the contingent use of nuclear weapons by the planes is excluded. Similarly, restraint in the expansion of so-called battlefield nuclear systems like enhanced radiation weapons would be more practicable if agreement could be reached to constrain concentrations of armour near the frontier. As these illustrations suggest, assured restraint in the nuclear sphere of the theatre deployments relies heavily on comparable behaviour in the conventional. This underscores the necessity for SALT III to march forward if not in step with the MBFR negotiations then at least with a clear view of the relationship between diplomatic and military moves on both negotiating fronts.

An additional cluster of problems concerns the continuing search necessary in SALT III for durable solutions to the growing vulnerability of missiles based in fixed sites. Preferable from the standpoint of a PAR regime would be regulations aimed at curbing the threat itself but, whatever is done to degrade accuracy improvements or other elements of hard-target capability, there may be a need for some responses designed to reduce vulnerability. A key principle should be that measures to increase force survivability need not be linked with simultaneous boosts in the surviving forces' counter-force capacity against the other country's ICBM. Schemes for enhancing survivability through multiple-aim-point (MAP) deployments or other forms of mobility will contribute little to assured restraint if they impede the verification of force levels or introduce more lethal forces requiring the other side to expand its inventories in order to guarantee adequate retaliatory forces. The parties need to exercise great care to harmonize their treatment of the land-based missile survivability issue with their comprehensive quest for negotiated restraints. In this context, and compared with the original MAP and MX trench concepts, recent analyses of air-mobile designs for ensuring ICBM survivability offer some hope of more verifiable and less provocative innovations during SALT III.

What is known so far of SALT II indicates that the lengthy agreements being drafted there are compatible with the PAR concept. On their own merits, the impending treaty, protocol and statement of principles deserve a fair hearing, especially as regards their utility as a preface to more far-ranging negotiations in SALT III. Assuming that the process does not falter – and no one can be confident of that – the next round of SALT will face formidable tasks. Not only should it examine additional possibilities for reducing the strategic inventories, but it should try to increase the number of indicators of intended restraint displayed by the parties. Limits on hunter-killer submarine forces and on the tracking of ballistic missile-firing submarines, controls on large power sources in space and on

exo-atmospheric tests or the deployment of high-energy lasers or particle beam systems, further deployment guidelines for cruise missiles and other new systems – all these ideas are candidates for eventual inclusion in a PAR regime. Increasingly verification may depend on the broad scope of several provisions rather than concentration on any particular case – on the opportunity to check a complex network of numerous restraints with reasonable confidence instead of demands for the most stringent verification of a few limitations. Thus, in the framework sketched here, SALT can best promote confidence in strategic restraint by spreading its net to embrace a broad array of Soviet and American capabilities and activities. Such an array would provide the maximum opportunity to gauge the parties' true intentions.

PAR as outlined here, *is* a CBM. It would shift the emphasis of SALT from a search for numerical solutions and equivalent capabilities (with all the attendant problems of assessment that the latter particularly implies) in the direction of declared intentions, intentions as manifested in procurement decisions and the specific thrusts of strategic research and development. If programmes are consistent with declared policy towards war avoidance in general and the denial of pre-emptive options in particular, the marked erosion of confidence which seems to beset the SALT negotiations at the present time could be reversed. Herein may lie the elusive link between intentions and capabilities: one expression of current intentions can be seen in the programmes embarked upon now which will confer capabilities on completion of those programmes. So long as there is a degree of transparency about the programmes, each side can see that capabilities and intentions are unlikely to get out of step in the future. Even if intentions were to change dramatically, the lack of a programme to support and sustain that change would severely curtail the options that a more aggressive regime could adopt. PAR will require the strengthening of the SCC and a widening of its scope, and it will demand much greater exchange of information and explanation than hitherto if it is to fulfil its task as a builder of trust.

Robert E. Lee once said, 'It is well that war is so terrible – we should grow too fond of it'. That same terrible fascination persists in the nuclear era and threatens to paralyse judgment. To escape that paralysis will demand vision and will – recognition that the ultimate function of SALT is to confirm the intention of restraint by manipulating strategic developments and deployments, and a willingness to choose the risks of restraint rather than of boundless competition.

# Confidence-Building Measures and Naval Arms Control

The history of efforts to place limits on naval vessels and their armaments is a small but diverse one. For the most part two approaches have dominated: those which have attempted to limit by number, size and/or type the inventories of particular states, and those which have sought to constrain deployments of vessels in specified seas.[1] The best known of the former – the Washington and London Naval Treaties of 1922 and 1930 respectively – placed ceilings on the aggregate tonnage of certain classes of ships, in addition to limiting construction and replacement schedules. The impact of these treaties was mixed. Although honoured for the most part until the years immediately preceding the outbreak of World War II, they had the effect of directing or channelling competition in naval construction into those classes of ships not affected by the agreements. Early efforts at deployment limitations also failed to establish clear and favourable precedents. The Rush–Bagot Treaty, signed by the United States and Britain in 1817, effectively demilitarized the Great Lakes – a condition likely to have evolved in any case, owing to the nature of the political relations between the countries involved. Less successful (although of more significance) has been the 1936 Montreux Convention, which has experienced difficulties both in limiting the militarization of the Black Sea and in regulating passage through the straits.[2]

This record – small, only partly successful and of considerable antiquity – has not deterred those who seek naval arms-control measures at the present time. The rationales suggested for such measures are mostly variants of traditional arguments proposed on behalf of arms-control efforts in general. Reflected are the desires to reduce inventory and operating costs, to pre-empt the possibility of arms races at sea, to avoid accidents which could bring about crises and to make the outbreak of war less likely.[3] In addition, two themes are encountered which are unique to naval arms control and the current context. Willingness to reduce the number of roles of naval vessels reflects in some instances an assessment of the lower utility of these forces in today's world. Reasons cited include the increased vulnerability of surface vessels to missiles which are capable of being fired from a variety of platforms and are in the possession of an ever-increasing number of states; the decreased political and coercive utility of 'gun-boat diplomacy'; the ability to substitute in certain circumstances other forms of weaponry less expensive and more effective than naval forces; and the constraints brought about by the global presence of an increasingly able Soviet navy. This last factor – that of the Soviet fleet – produces the other set of justifications for naval arms control: 'doves' argue the necessity of avoiding a full-scale naval arms race between the super-powers; 'hawks' see arms-control efforts as one means of placing constraints on the emerging role and capability of the Soviet Union at sea.

The corresponding Soviet attitude (or, allowing for bureaucratic rivalry, attitudes) with regard to naval arms control is difficult to assess with any degree of certainty. Secretary Brezhnev's oft-quoted comment of June 1971 ('we have never considered it an ideal situation to have the fleets of the great powers plying the seas for long periods at great distances from their own shores. We are prepared to resolve this problem, but on an equal footing'[4]) has not had a decisive impact on either Soviet naval policy or arms-control postures. Unless the increase in the quality, areas of deployment and activity of the Soviet fleet is viewed as the prelude to serious naval arms-control efforts, it is difficult to find evidence of Soviet willingness to enter into such agreements. Pronouncements on the Mediterranean continue to emphasize denuclearization and tend to be one-sided; Indian Ocean overtures, while more flexible of late as a consequence of signs of Soviet willingness to accept the American facility of Diego Garcia within a negotiated arms-control framework, are at odds with the increase in Soviet naval presence that has accompanied involvement in the Horn of Africa.[5]

This uncertain historical record and political climate notwithstanding, a number of more specific approaches to naval arms control have been voiced. These include arrangements based on the principle of reciprocal budgetary ceilings, inventory limits (both quantitative and qualitative), deployment limitations (defined in terms of some mixture of inventory, geography, mission, exercise and activity), or restrictions on bases or facilities. Yet these approaches and related ones tend to present problems of a technical or negotiating nature. (That they may suffer as well from conceptual or political deficiencies is another matter to be discussed towards the end of this paper.)

From a technical or negotiating perspective, the fundamental problem facing naval arms control (and many other kinds of arms control) is what to count and how to count it. Does one simply count the numbers of vessels in naval inventories, or does one consider as well the availability in a given part of the world of non-naval or non-sea-based forces and systems (or non-naval but sea-based vessels such as fishing ships with a communication or intelligence function)? Is the aim of naval arms control to be the limiting of naval forces *per se*, the control of all forces acting within a given maritime theatre, or the contribution made by naval and other sea-based forces to the larger theatre? (For example, advocates of Mediterranean arms control fail to make clear whether the aim is to limit only those naval forces in the sea, the overall maritime balance, which includes shore-based

air power or the possible contribution of naval forces and naval-based air power to the European theatre.) To the extent that deployments are seen as more critical than overall inventories, questions of distribution in designated seas enter into any equation. Regardless of whether one chooses inventory or deployment orientations, problems are posed by the issue of which systems of counting, or criteria for measurement, are to be chosen. No measurement standard – numbers, ship-days, tonnage, staying power, armament – is capable of providing, either singly or in combination with others, a full and accurate reflection of capability.[6] This problem is further exacerbated by asymmetries between the American and Soviet fleets at three levels: individual units of account, fleet totals and missions. To these and other problems can be added that of the definition of the role of particular ships (is the *Kiev* an anti-submarine cruiser or small carrier?), the difficulty of verifying the presence of submarines, the problem of verifying armament, the establishment of limits for the use and scope of facilities, and the growing overlap between sea-based forces and strategic arms. This last element goes beyond the SSBN role, because it must also include submarines and other units assigned an anti-submarine role and, possibly in the future, those units carrying cruise missiles of considerable range as well.

### Naval CBM: An Alternative Approach?

An alternative approach to naval arms control is that of confidence-building measures, or CBM. The impetus for this departure comes from several sources: a continued desire for progress in this arms-control area, a frustration with the technical problems associated with other more traditional approaches to naval arms control and the hope that a concept designed largely for one theatre (Europe) and one type of forces (land) can be transferred or translated into another environment to affect the use of another kind of force.

This last factor notwithstanding, it should be pointed out that CBM pre-date Helsinki. The entire process of arms-control negotiations and summitry can be seen as a basic CBM; more specific ones either proposed or effected include the 'Open Skies' initiative, test moratoria and bans, the 'Hot Line' Agreement and the 'Agreement on Measures to Reduce the Risk of Outbreak of Nuclear War'. Indeed, one can find at least two examples of naval CBM agreements to add to this list. There is the relatively obscure 1930 Protocol signed by Greece and Turkey, in which each pledged not to order, acquire or construct naval units or armaments without having first given the other six months' notice, 'so that both Governments may thus be enabled if necessary to prevent any competition in the sphere of naval armaments by means of a friendly exchange of views and explanations on either side'.[7]

A more recent, and perhaps more relevant, example of a naval CBM can be found in the 1972 American–Soviet Agreement on the Prevention of Incidents on and over the High Seas.[8] Covering both combatants and naval auxiliaries, the agreement emphasizes those measures designed to avoid accidents and incidents. More specifically, the agreement provides for:

- steps to avoid collisions;
- non-interference in the 'formations', that is, arrangements of two or more ships, of the other party;
- the avoidance of manoeuvres in areas of heavy traffic;
- surveillance ships maintaining a safe distance from the object of investigation, and avoiding 'embarrassing or endangering the ships under surveillance';
- accepted international signals being used when ships manoeuvre near one another;
- no attacks to be simulated, nor any objects launched, in the vicinity of the other party's ships, nor searchlights used to illuminate the navigation bridges of the other party's ships;
- ships in the vicinity to be informed when submerged submarines are engaged in exercises;
- aircraft not to harass the ships of the other party, nor simulate attack, nor perform aerobatics over ships, nor drop objects in their vicinity.

The agreement establishes two other precedents useful for expanding the role of naval CBM. First, some 'advance notice procedure' is called for, as each party is to provide over radio, not less than three to five days in advance, 'notifications of actions on the high seas which represent a danger to navigation or to aircraft in flight'. Clearly, the utility of this specific mechanism is low, because of the vagueness of its terms and the absence of assured direct notice or communication. The general precedent, however, may be an important one. Secondly, a communications procedure was established to facilitate the exchange of information called for by the agreement, using the offices of the respective naval attachés assigned to the embassies in Moscow and Washington.

The CBM discussed above, as well as those in the CSCE Final Act, indicate only part of the potential role for CBM in regulating arms. In general, CBM can enhance confidence in three ways:

(1) by providing for the exchange of information on standing or static presence, such as inventory levels or facility details;
(2) by providing for the exchange of information on dynamic activities, ranging from planned changes in inventories or facility infrastructure to specific advance notice of transits, deployments, exercises or other activities;
(3) through actual constraints on activities themselves.

Examples of CBM belonging to categories (1) and (2) are as follows:

(a) *Inventory.* Parties could agree to exchange information about current and projected naval inventory levels. Where observation by national means already provides evidence of the construction or existence of units, such a stipulation would at least provide a test of willingness to provide accurate information. It would be more useful if the information included the status of ships: whether a unit was planned, under construction, being tested, fully deployed, near retirement, in reserve or fully deactivated. Since numbers have proved to be a major point of contention at the MBFR talks, the political significance of this exchange would be considerable; in addition, it could help to reduce fears of major building programmes by an adversary and assist each party in its own construction planning.

(b) *Deployment information.* Parties could agree to provide, at regular intervals,

208

information concerning the presence and function of ships in designated bodies of water. Advance notice of entrances, exits, transits and deployments could also be required. The dangers of such advance notification requirements are three-fold: first, they could help to bring about countervailing responses which either might not have occurred or would have been delayed; secondly, to the extent that advance notice must be honoured at all times, the requirement to provide notice could delay the ability of each side to respond quickly in a crisis; finally, danger may arise as a result of the removal of the element of surprise and the increased vulnerability of the vessels of each side caused by the announcement of intentions in advance.

(c) *Maritime information.* A framework could be established to promote the exchange of information about the scope of non-naval maritime activities in designated seas. Such information can range from shipping volume and trade routes to fishing, mining and other oceanographic/ hydrographic activities. The aim here would be to ensure that non-military activities could be undertaken without hindrance. Again, several problems would arise. Certain data about trade routs and contents would be better left uncommunicated, and many ostensibly non-military vessels, such as fishing boats, can and do fulfil intelligence and communications functions.

(d) *Exercises.* The details of planned exercises could be given in advance. Although the question of the length of such notice would have to be considered, as well as the issue of whether any minimum level of exercise requiring notice should be designated (parallel to the troop levels stipulated by the CSCE Final Act), details to be furnished could include the time and duration of the exercise, the number and types of participating vessels, other participating countries or forces, facilities involved, the location of the exercise and its purpose. In many ways this proposal can be seen as the naval equivalent of the 'prior notification of major military

manoeuvres' section of the CSCE Final Act. For this and other 'prior notification' proposals some form of standing 'Naval Consultative Commission' could be established.

(e) *Observers.* Observers could be exchanged to view ships and/or facilities, and arrangements made to permit near observation of exercises, with limits placed on the number of foreign vessels allowed into the selected area.

(f) *Facilities.* Advance notice would be provided detailing any change in status of anchorages, facilities or bases owned or used by the countries involved. Information relating to the capabilities and use of facilities could be exchanged at regular intervals.

Collectively, these naval CBM can be seen either as tests of sincerity and willingness to enter into more structured relations or as something more. In those cases where unilateral verification confidence is high, the measures put forward will have a mostly symbolic import. However, they will add to confidence more directly in those cases where notification requirements precede any verifiable activity, where the scope for verification is limited, where accidents might occur or in times of crisis when uncertainty over intentions can be most destabilizing. This said, the question remains as to whether it is realistic to expect any degree of Soviet co-operation. The record of the Soviet Union in supplying adequate and reliable data is poor, voluntary steps mostly remain untaken and resistance is high to all forms of inspection. From the American and Western perspective, there are problems related to the entire matter of advance notification of naval activities. Even if the Soviet Union were to co-operate, the question arises of whether advance signalling or even the delaying of deployments to fulfil notification requirements would be to Western advantage.

CBM in category (3) are concerned less with facilitating the exchange of information and more with restricting particular modes of activity. Their purpose is to bring about arms regulation without having to face the many problems involved in any direct attempt to limit the quality and/or quantity of forces. More

209

specifically, the intention is to limit the use of forces so as to reduce the impact of the element of threat inherent in the possession or deployment of force, naval or otherwise. Examples of such activity-oriented CBM are:

(a) *Exercises*. Restrictions on naval manoeuvres or exercises could provide the most interesting option. Exercises could be restricted by number, location and/or scope. In the first case, limits could be set on the number of exercises involving naval forces permissible in a designated area within a given period of time. In the second case, minimum permitted distances could be established between vessels participating in an exercise and specified countries, their Exclusive Economic Zones (EEZ) or key international waterways and choke points. Thirdly, it may be possible to limit the number and kind of vessels permitted to participate, the duration of the exercise, the participation of other countries, the involvement of non-sea-based forces and the use of live ammunition.

(b) *Deployments*. Any effort to constrain deployments immediately raises the question of distinguishing between deployments and transits. Assuming this can be done, there is the possibility of limiting deployments along lines of numbers, duration, frequency and location.

(c) *Facilities*. Any attempt to introduce facilities into an arms-control arrangement again raises taxing problems associated with definition: to distinguish among facilities, bases and anchorages on the one hand, and among ownership, control and use on the other, will be difficult, if not impossible. It may actually be more profitable to ignore such distinctions and simply attempt to affect use. Certain classes of vessel, such as submarines, could be prohibited from designated facilities. Alternatively, the role of a facility could be limited to supporting only reconnaissance vessels and aircraft.

Restraints on exercises and deployments such as those presented above would be virtually impossible to make explicit within any formal arms-control agreement. There are simply too many factors to measure, stipulate and balance. This is not to say, however, that activity-oriented naval CBM have no prospect of being adopted. States can build confidence with potential adversaries not simply by what they do but also by what they elect not to do. Any state has the option of avoiding the appearance (or reality) of being provocative. Equally, any state must be aware that shows of force through the staging of exercises or deployments at certain times and locations can and will be perceived as provocative or threatening and will thus have the effect of eroding confidence. The Soviet navy would be unwise to conduct frequent and massive demonstrations of its ability to cut sea lines of communication by the mouth of the Persian Gulf; the United States would be equally foolish to deploy in force and exercise frequently near any of the choke points which potentially impede Soviet access to the oceans. Indeed, such a regime of CBM can already be said to exist, unilaterally and tacitly.

It might be somewhat easier to establish firm limits on the use of facilities, although any Soviet willingness to reciprocate remains most doubtful. In any case, whatever gains may be realized from enhancing confidence must be carefully weighed against the implications of constraining the use of facilities. Facilities, or bases, are important both as symbols of interest and as guarantees of the capacity to act. Access to a facility can be crucial for response during crises and, in both peacetime and crisis situations, such access can alleviate some of the need for 'floating' presence. One alternative to specific restraints on use may be to enter unilaterally or tacitly into a 'reduced-use posture' without in any way compromising the ability to use a facility fully if necessary.

What emerges from the above is another distinction between those naval CBM designed to enhance confidence by promoting the exchange of information and those which seek to do so by affecting activity. The former, possibly consisting of specific restrictions regarding inventories, deployment and exercise schedules, maritime activities and facilities, as well as calling for some arrangement for the exchange of observers, would best be implemented through a specific formal agreement. Confidence is most likely to

210

be increased if information is complete and accurate; random and partial information is more likely to increase uncertainty. A formal, explicit agreement provides the best means of ensuring that obligations are understood and that the flow of information is balanced. Moreover, the technical problems of establishing and maintaining a regime of information-oriented naval CBM are not so great as to preclude the feasibility of such an undertaking; the problems are far more likely to be political. By contrast, the technical problems associated with establishing and maintaining an activity-oriented naval CBM regime are likely to be formidable, as are the political ones. If they are to be tested, this will probably have to be within some unilateral or tacit framework.

A question more basic than whether naval CBM of all sorts should be approached formally or informally is whether they should be approached and considered in isolation. Increasingly weapons based on land have the capability to affect the situation at sea, while sea-based systems have long had the ability to affect the balance, both on land and in the air over it. Where a weapons system is based or mounted is not the key to its function or potential impact. As a result, CBM make more sense if conceived along lines of theatre balances rather than specific weapons-system balances. One possible means of extending CBM to embrace naval forces might thus lie within the larger context of CBM within CSCE, where the advance notification requirement for manoeuvres could be expanded to include notification of the participation of naval and/or amphibious forces.[9]

It should be pointed out that what has been presented here is not intended to be exclusive. There is no reason why naval CBM should be limited to the super-powers. They could apply equally to other areas where tension at sea exists, such as between Greece and Turkey in the Aegean. Also, they need not be bilateral; any naval CBM regime could be expanded to include a number of participants. Indeed, in the light of alliance relationships, it is likely that such expansion would follow. More important, in view of the proliferation of naval and other military systems capable of affecting the maritime environment, such expansion may become necessary in order to avoid the circumvention of any regime by third parties.

Nor is this paper intended to be all-inclusive. Possibilities exist for other naval CBM, or more general CBM involving naval forces, to be developed. One possibility is a CBM of a different kind: arrangements between the super-powers limiting the direct involvement of their naval forces on behalf of other states for certain purposes (for example, to patrol the 200-mile EEZ) or in designated parts of the world. Even more far-reaching would be an agreement between the major naval powers directly constraining their ability to project force from the sea into local disputes. Such an approach, if successful, could lay the foundation for a broader arrangement establishing rules of the road for major-power involvement in the 'peripheral areas'.

Ultimately, however, any discussion of CBM involving naval forces raises a fundamental question: is it in American (or Western) interests to have naval forces constrained? Even if naval CBM could be negotiated, would they be desirable? Analysis prompts caution, particularly over those naval CBM which limit flexibility and activity.

Several factors need to be considered. Western dependence on the free use of the sea has increased, especially in the realm of seaborne energy sources and trade. At the same time, threats to use of the sea have risen. Coastal states have developed or imported new capabilities to place forces at sea, to project force to the sea and to defend against force projected from the sea. The Soviet navy has increased both its capability and range. Unresolved issues raised by the Law of the Sea Conference could produce new sources of conflict.

Despite these and other political and technological developments, sea-based forces are still diplomatically and militarily useful. In peace and war alike, they continue to provide a major dimension of Western security. Deployments and exercises communicate the readiness and the capability to act on behalf of interests and allies, thereby promoting confidence and deterring threats. To constrain naval forces in the name of building confidence begs a key question: confidence on whose part? Some restrictions could perhaps improve relations with the Soviet Union or please those littoral states (for example, in the Indian Ocean) which fear super-power intimidation or competition. But at the same time such limits could reduce the confidence of both sides and that of their allies. At a time when the conventional balance in Europe is not without its problems and retrenchment continues in Asia, the selection of naval forces for special controls does not appear to favour the West.

## NOTES

[1] For the texts of these and other agreements, see Trevor N. Dupuy and Gay M. Hammerman (eds), *A Documentary History of Arms Control and Disarmament* (Dunn Loring, Virginia: T. N. Dupuy Associates, 1973). See also Hedley Bull, *Strategic Arms Limitation: The Precedent of the Washington and London Naval Treaties*, an Occasional Paper of the Center for Policy Study, The University of Chicago, 1971; Barry Blechman, *The Control of Naval Armaments: Prospects and Possibilities* (Washington DC: Brookings Institution, 1975); Barry Buzan, 'The Status and Future of the Montreux Convention', *Survival*, November/December 1976.

[2] Specifically excluded here is consideration of limits on sea-based platforms carrying strategic weapons such as those present in the SALT I agreement. This is not to say in any way that considerations of naval arms control can be free of ties with the strategic balance; rather, that direct examination of these issues falls more directly within the purview of a study on strategic measures. The 1972 American–Soviet Agreement on the Prevention of Incidents on and over the High Seas, also not included here, is discussed in detail on p. 25.

[3] See, for example, UNA-USA National Policy Panel on Conventional Arms Control, *Controlling the Conventional Arms Race* (New York: United Nations Association of the United States of America, 1976).

[4] *Pravda*, 12 June 1971 (*Current Digest of the Soviet Press*, 13 July 1971).

[5] For a recent Soviet statement on the Mediterranean, see Tass, 6 February 1978; on the Indian Ocean, S. Vladimirov, 'An Urgent Problem', *Pravda*, 18 January 1978; see also Ann M. Kelly and Charles Petersen, 'Recent Changes in Soviet Naval Policy: Prospects for Arms Limitations in the Mediterranean and Indian Ocean', Professional Paper No. 150 (Arlington, Va: Center for Naval Analyses, 1976).

[6] See *Means of Measuring Naval Power with Special Reference to US and Soviet Activities in the Indian Ocean*, prepared for the Sub-Committee on the Near East and South Asia of the Committee on Foreign Affairs, United States Congress, 12 May 1974; see also Richard Haass, 'Naval Arms Limitation in the Indian Ocean', *Survival*, March/April 1978.

[7] Text in Dupuy and Hammerman, *op. cit.*, pp. 168–9.

[8] Text in *World Armaments and Disarmament, SIPRI Yearbook 1973* (Stockholm, New York, London: Almqvist & Wiksell, Humanities Press, Paul Elek; 1973), pp. 36–9. For a highly individualistic interpretation of the Agreement, see Anthony F. Wolf, 'Agreement at Sea: The United States-USSR Agreement on Incidents at Sea' (unpublished paper delivered to International Studies Association Convention, St Louis, Mo., March 1977).

[9] It is interesting to note that a proposal submitted by the delegations of Canada, the Netherlands, Norway and Britain on CBM at the Belgrade CSCE Review Conference called for the expansion of advance notification to include amphibious forces (CSCE/BM/11, 2 November 1977; reprinted in Cmnd 7126, HMSO, March 1978, p. 22).

# Arms Control in the Middle East: Some Proposals and their Confidence-Building Roles

YAIR EVRON

## Introduction

Probably since as early as 1971 (when an initial dialogue about a partial disengagement agreement began), and certainly since the 1974 Israeli–Egyptian Sinai agreement, we have been witnessing a gradual process of searching for political accommodation and stability in the Middle East. This hesitant process accelerated very rapidly as a result of President Sadat's visit to Jerusalem in November 1977. He opened up new possibilities for the resolution of the Arab–Israeli conflict and for novel political departures in the Middle East. The 1974 and 1975 Israeli–Egyptian agreements had already included many arms-control measures,[1] so, in a sense, arms control preceded the political process, and it seems likely to remain an essential component of that process. This paper contends that without arms-control measures no enduring political settlement in the Middle East can be achieved, and that any political settlement that is achieved will be shaky and vulnerable. The relationship between the sphere of politics and the realm of arms control (with an emphasis on confidence-building measures) in resolving the Arab–Israeli conflict is the subject of this paper.

One important aspect of arms control is the building of confidence through specific measures designed to that end. In addition to formal arms-control agreements, the establishment of mutual confidence is needed in the Middle East as a means of underpinning any political solutions which may be found to the problems of instability and insecurity in the region. The establishment of CBM would buttress traditional arms-control measures, as the latter are adversely affected by intense mutual hostility and sus-

picion among the states involved. In the past hardly any agreements have been reached and, even for those that have been concluded, no means of enforcement have been found and no supra-national combination of outside powers has proved willing or able to prevent substantial violation. The rewards of pre-emption have been too great (particularly – but not exclusively – for Israel) and the perceived swings in the balance of power, together with rapidly shifting political alignments, have tended to provide precisely those circumstances least conducive to any formal arms regime. Rather, they have placed a premium on military action as a means of solving political disputes, not least because all states have to some extent been cushioned against the worst consequences of failure in the military field by the certainty of great-power intervention.

Arms control is defined as any measure taken in the military security field which increases strategic stability in the relations of states involved in a conflict. Strategic stability is the diminution in the frequency of wars and, once they occur, their limitation in time, space and violence. A related objective of arms control is the limitation and reduction of defence expenditure, provided strategic stability is not harmed.

The structure of political relations in the Middle East is highly complex: it is a multi-polar system involving many regional powers, and it has a high level of super-power involvement and intervention. There are persistent conflicts, not only between Israel and several Arab states but also among the Arab states and between Arabs and other non-Arab states in the area or on its fringes. Lastly, there is the pervasive super-power competition. What aggravates this situa-

213

tion is that there is usually a potential for spill-over from one set of conflicts and competitions to others. Because of the volatility of the political forces acting in the region, the potential for escalation always exists. It is unlikely that all these conflicts and sets of competitions will be resolved. Nevertheless, the gradual defusing of conflicts could be initiated, and constraints could be developed which would deter potential aggressors and tend to decouple one set of conflicts from others in order to limit potential spill-over.

The relationship between arms control and inter-state politics in the Middle East is complex and multi-dimensional. Is it possible to achieve arms control in the Middle East in the present political context, or must political change precede arms control? The relationship is further complicated by the fact that one set of arms-control measures may be required before real peace can be achieved and a quite different set will probably be required to sustain that peace. A rather similar debate within the context of Soviet–American relations has persisted since the early 1960s, and three schools of thought have emerged which should be considered, since they will probably influence the dates of arms-control efforts in the Middle East as well. The first school argues that arms control can be decoupled from politics; that arms-control measures are possible even in situations of severe conflict without concomitant political relaxation; that arms-control measures and agreements can be achieved in such circumstances because they serve certain limited yet common interests of the adversaries. The second approach argues that there are links between arms-control agreements and changes in the political relationship between adversaries, but that agreements can be reached first and may even pave the way for political change by creating a new international climate. The third group accepts the existence of links between the realm of arms control and the realm of politics, but argues that political relaxation must precede arms-control agreements.[2]

The historical experience in the Middle East up to 1974 indicates that some tacit, unformalized arms-control measures can be agreed, even in a situation of severe political conflict. Moreover, because of the role played by external powers, such measures, independent of political relaxation, are perhaps more practicable than those

which affect the super-power relationship. At the same time, those past successes have contributed not to political relaxation but only to the postponement of wars or limitations on the use of force.[3] While this in itself may be a not inconsiderable achievement, something more durable must be sought. No direct, significant formal arms agreement between the regional powers took place between the signing of the Armistice Agreements in 1949 and the period after the 1973 war.

But what of the future? In theory it seems possible that the same *type* of arms-control measures could be applied again, either with or without prior formal political agreements. The Camp David Accords include, for example, quite specific proposals for the demilitarization of the largest part of the Sinai and rather less specific measures to be applied to the West Bank. Agreements among the suppliers about limitations on the supply of arms are also a possibility. Because Israeli occupation of the territory since 1967 has become the central issue of political aggravation, any Israeli withdrawal from these territories would bring about a considerable political relaxation, since it would diminish Arab motivation for another war and therefore stabilize relations in the region. The stabilizing effect of this proposed package of steps would probably be more considerable than in the past precisely because of the centrality of the territorial issue and because the wars of violence of the period since 1967 have proved the political unprofitability of war.

The link between arms control and politics in the Arab–Israeli region has two facets: first, to be stable and enduring, any political settlement will need to be supported by concomitant arms-control measures; second, a political settlement will depend to a large extent on a number of gradual steps, each of which will itself require the support of a considerable number of arms-control agreements and CBM. The political component, however, is important, not only to the defusion of the conflict, but also in furnishing a broad context for the various steps towards arms control. Herein lies a third link between arms control and the political process. The Israeli occupation of Arab territories since 1967 has so aggravated the conflict that it will be impossible to formulate far-reaching, formal arms-control agreements without linking them with gradual Israeli withdrawals from the territories conquered in 1967 (with some modifications agreed upon between the sides). Similarly, the Arab countries will have to agree to sign peace treaties with Israel and in general 'normalize' their relations with her. President Carter has endorsed this as official American policy, and President Sadat has accepted it completely and has called on other Arab states to follow his example. Jordan is known to be ready to accept normalization with Israel in principle, and Egypt's changed position only enhances this Jordanian posture, although Jordan remains at the moment in an uneasy position somewhere between Egypt and the 'rejectionists'.

The final political settlement (or settlements) will therefore have to include both political arrangements and formal arms-control agreements. Thus it appears that steps have to be taken simultaneously in the contexts of arms control and politics in order to facilitate the establishment of a stable relationship between Israel and her Arab neighbours. Indeed, the Israeli–Egyptian draft treaty (with the annexes) already follows this pattern. It includes both full normalization of relations and certain security arrangements such as demilitarization of most of the Sinai. It is unfortunate, however, that this demilitarization does not extend to the whole of the Sinai. However, the approach which emphasizes arms control as an instrument of political change or as creating a suitable context for political change has been more successful in practice and may remain so. Similarly, in analytical terms successful arms control would be central to the stability of the international political regime which would be created once the settlement was secured. For example, as has been noted, arms-control measures were cardinal in the three interim agreements reached between the combatants (the first Israeli–Egyptian agreement of January 1974, the Israeli–Syrian agreement in June 1974 and the Israeli–Egyptian agreement of September 1975) and are an important part of the draft treaty between Israel and Egypt. One of the reasons for the centrality of these measures in the past was that the Arab states preferred to focus on arms-control and security aspects in the agreements rather than on political contacts with Israel. Now, after Sadat's initiative, this preference has

less relevance. An additional reason was the nature of the military relations between the two sides following the 1973 war: anxiety concerning both general surprise attacks and limited attacks had to be gradually allayed. Since such concerns will persist, arms-control measures will be central to political development. Another related reason is that the asymmetries between Israel and the Arab world, in terms of manpower, geographical size and economic power, create permanent concerns in Israel regarding future development. Similarly, the present Israeli military superiority and the continued disunity in the Arab world are creating concern among Israel's neighbours. Lastly, a balance based on conventional arms is less calculable than the kind of well-developed bipolar nuclear balance which exists between the superpowers.

All these points lead to the conclusion that, as compared to East–West relations, arms control might (and certainly should) play an even greater role in the Middle East, not least because the possibility of conflict is measurably greater than, for example, in Europe. There is, therefore, a need for more deterrent constraints to be worked into any future settlement. There exist also the wider political and systemic concerns which provoke the observation that it is the relative *political* stability of Europe that has removed the urgency from a search for substantive arms-control agreement.

Extreme anti-Israeli sentiment will probably persist and must be countered. Then again, the potential for future political conflict, followed by crisis and war, is high in an area where there are many states with active foreign policies, where power blocs keep changing and shifting and where domestic instability is likely to continue. Indeed, even if the ideological component were to disappear and full peace, endorsed by diplomatic and economic relations, were to be established, other forces might provoke conflict between Israel and one or more Arab states. An arms-control regime could make the eruption of war resulting from such conflict less likely.

Indeed, it appears that were it not for the 1974 and 1975 Israeli–Egyptian agreements, President Sadat's visit to Jerusalem would not have been possible. These agreements, by their very existence and effectiveness, created a new context of mutual confidence. The fear of surprise attack had been somewhat reduced, and the fact that neither side has violated the agreements in any significant way has had a beneficial effect on the attitudes of both sides. At the same time, these agreements were far from adequate for the task of encouraging a feeling of mutual security. Thus, for example, President Sadat intimated that one of the *urgent* reasons for his decision to visit Jerusalem (other motives were long-standing and more general) was his concern about the possibility of unintended escalation along the Israeli–Egyptian border. At the time, Israel conducted certain military exercises in Sinai, and Egypt countered with large-scale military exercises of her own, and thus mutual anxieties increased. It was the concentration of Egyptian forces during these exercises that prompted Israel's Chief of Staff, General Gur, to warn, on the very eve of Sadat's visit to Jerusalem, that Egypt might in fact be preparing a military strike against Israel. The fear of surprise attack is a very potent destabilizing factor in the Israeli–Arab context. In addition, as the episode described demonstrates, there is concern about escalation as a result of accidents or misperception on each side about the intentions of the other.

*Confidence Building*
Confidence building is basically a process by which, first, mutual understanding of the political and strategic intentions of opponents in conflict is secured and, second, mutual concern about strategic and military behaviour of opponents is reduced. At one extreme of the confidence-building spectrum we have complete political accommodation. What, then, of the main measures which, in the context of the Middle East, might specifically serve to build confidence and hence contribute to the political process?

These seem to fall primarily into the following categories: first, those CBM that create mechanisms for inducing a better understanding of the strategic intentions of the other side; secondly, those that impose constraints on the side which is potentially more likely to try and change the *status quo* once a political settlement is secured; and, lastly, those that lessen the danger of 'misescalation', that is, an escalation resulting not from the deliberate intentions of the opponents, but as a result either of miscalculations about the intentions of the other side or of an undesired series of incidents or local confronta-

tions. The process of 'misescalation' might also result from the spill-over of a crisis between Israel and one Arab state into the relations of Israel and other Arab states.

## Demilitarization of Buffer-Zones and Restrictions on Deployment of Forces
*The Sinai*
The demilitarization of buffer zones and restrictions on deployment of forces will have central roles to play in the imposition of constraints and the reduction of the dangers of escalation. Most relevant in this context is Sinai, the tacit and partial demilitarization of which during the period 1957–67 was the major stabilizing factor in the Israeli–Egyptian relationship. The 1974 and 1975 agreements, by creating limited demilitarized buffer zones there, also contributed to stability, and the Israeli–Egyptian draft treaty and its Annex No. 1 provide for the demilitarization of most of the Sinai.[4]

The reasons for the stabilizing effect of the demilitarization of Sinai are, first, that it will supply both sides with an important strategic and tactical warning period after the indications of a surprise attack have been received. As the experience of 1973 (and those of Barbarossa and Pearl Harbour) demonstrated, these indications are potentially open to conflicting interpretations. On the one hand they may be ignored; on the other they may stimulate over-reaction when what appear to be military preparations on the part of the opponent are only military exercises. Only actual penetration of the demilitarized Sinai would provide unambiguous indication of an impending attack. This warning period is probably more important for Israel, because of the asymmetry between the structure of Israeli and Arab (and in this case, Egyptian) forces: the Israeli army is based primarily on a reserve system and a short period of mobilization is needed. The Arab forces are made up of standing armies which can – theoretically – be ready to move at shorter notice. Secondly, demilitarization would reduce the danger of accidental war or war caused by a series of miscalculations. Third, assuming that the two sides are not planning a war against each other, there are some advantages for both in having the Sinai demilitarized rather than policed by their own forces. From the Israeli point of view, if Egyptian forces begin to move across the Sinai with the intention of reaching the Israeli border, they would have to accept the mode of battle best suited to the Israeli forces – a quick, mobile campaign. Furthermore, if the Egyptian air-defence system had to move with the attacking forces across Sinai, they would have to be dispersed and hence would lose integrated command and control, as well as the aid of warning systems. Their effectiveness would diminish considerably and Israeli air superiority, which is a central component of the Israeli military capability, would be enhanced. The Israeli air force would be able to give efficient close support to their ground forces and to harass and disrupt the long 'tail' of the Egyptian forces.

The special strategic condition of Israel – her encirclement by actual (or, after a settlement, potential) opponents – dictated to Israel, until 1967, a strategic doctrine calling for attacks on one front at a time and the maintenance of defences on the others. This was possible because Israel's short interior lines enabled her to move forces quickly from one front to the other. The occupation of Sinai has diminished this important advantage, but demilitarization will restore it.

From the Egyptian point of view, it is also arguable that the demilitarization of Sinai will be preferable to the deployment of troops in the area. Two Israeli surprise attacks (in 1956 and 1967) ,have pointed to the vulnerability of an exposed forward Egyptian deployment. Such a deployment by Egypt in Sinai might again force Israel to strike first. However, if the agreement between Egypt and Israel is signed, Israel will have no motivation to attack first, while an Egyptian attack across a demilitarized Sinai would place Egypt at a great military disadvantage from the outset. It is therefore highly probable that demilitarization will act as a major constraint on military activity.

At Camp David Egypt and Israel agreed to the following formula for the demilitarization of Sinai: in an area lying approximately 30 miles east of the Suez Canal and the Gulf of Suez no more than one Egyptian mechanized or infantry division may be stationed; in the area adjacent to the Israeli border only UN forces and Egyptian police will be deployed; and in between these two zones – in the largest part of the Sinai – only Egyptian border patrol units, not to exceed three battalions, will be deployed. The issues of the settlements in the Rafah area and the two air-fields, Eitam in the Rafah area and Etzion south-west of Eilat, seem to have been resolved by the dismantling over time of the former and the reprovision of the latter in the Negev with United States funding. The deployment of a whole Egyptian division east of the Canal, however, seems excessive and will create difficulties.

The efficacy of UN buffer zones is also questionable. The UN has in the past lacked sufficient credibility in the Middle East, although the somewhat greater effectiveness of UNIFIL in the Lebanon may be changing that perception. The success or failure of the UN operation in the Lebanon will certainly affect the attitude of all parties to UN-patrolled zones. Nevertheless, it remains true that only the super-powers, and especially the United States, have both the vital interests at stake and the military power and 'reach' to back up their interests and commitments in the Middle East. Their power is, of course, not unlimited. They are constrained by their mutual competition and deterrent postures, by the power of the regional states and by domestic inhibitions. However, their ability to enforce their will and undertake credible commitments must remain superior to that of any other combination of outside powers or of the UN. Should the UN fail to inspire confidence, and should the necessity for an external presence in Sinai remain, it will have to be that of a super-power. In view of the political postures of Egypt and Israel, it appears likely that only the United States would enjoy the trust of both.

The creation of a system of early-warning stations in the Sinai is an additional CBM, in that such a system provides assurance that preparations for surprise attacks can be detected. The two sides have their own independent means for detection and surveillance (although their quality is unequal), but the stations in Sinai will have an additional role, that of serving as one component in a mechanism for crisis management. There are potentially three alternative systems for manning and controlling the stations: separate control by Israel and Egypt respectively; joint Israeli–Egyptian control of stations; and either system with American participation. The stations can be located either in different convenient places in the Sinai or according to the requirements of whoever is controlling them – those under Israeli or Egyptian control are located in the eastern or western sides of Sinai respectively. A new component now under discussion concerns UN observation of maritime traffic through the Straits of Tiran.

The main question is probably whether American participation would enhance confidence building and stability. Ideally, it would seem that joint Israeli–Egyptian stations *without* American participation would increase mutual trust and confidence. The two sides, directly and together, would have to monitor troop movements, demand explanations in case of threatening moves and gradually develop procedures for crisis management. On the other hand, there would also be important advantages to American participation and involvement: political crises might develop between the two countries, either because of direct clashes of interest or – more probably – because of a spill-over from the other conflicts in the Middle East; then again, at least during the first period, there could be misunderstandings about intentions and actual troop movements which the United States could resolve. Similarly, there might be disagreement regarding interpretation of information collected. Without a trusted third party (and the United States is such a party), such misunderstandings might lead to misperceptions and these to hasty and dangerous decisions. American participation in the early-warning system would probably not resolve serious and genuine political conflicts between the two regional powers, but it would resolve more limited misunderstandings and would contain 'misescalation'. A general guarantee of the demilitarization by the United States as well as by the UN would be a contributory factor in the prevention of political disagreements from escalating into conflict and crisis.

### The West Bank

The current Israeli–Egyptian negotiations are giving consideration to the future of the West Bank and the Gaza Strip, but it remains to be seen whether the resolution of the Sinai issue is really linked with the solution of these problems or not. At one time it appeared that unless Israel decided in principle eventually to return these areas (with some modifications agreed upon between the two sides) to Arab sovereignty, the chances for a separate Israeli–Egyptian agreement were meagre. Now it appears otherwise, despite the fact that it could be argued that continued Israeli control over the West Bank and Gaza would be destabilizing in the long run in any case.

The strategic situation in the West Bank is not at all like that which prevails in the Sinai. There are three major differences. First, the West Bank, unlike Sinai, protrudes into the very heart of Israel. The major threat to Israel lies in the possibility of a surprise attack by a concentration of Arab armour deployed on the West Bank and directed at the waist of Israel (which at some points is only 10 miles wide). This threat must be removed permanently if Israeli unease is to be allayed. The demilitarization of this area is therefore essential. But therein lies the second difference. Demilitarization of the West Bank, though essential, will not give Israel the same military opportunities which she could gain from a withdrawal from the Sinai and its subsequent demilitarization. Her deterrent posture against Arab attempts to remilitarize the West Bank would be weaker than in the Sinai. The West Bank is narrow, hilly, less suitable for mobile tank warfare and quite densely inhabited. On the other hand, it is relatively easy to cut it off from the eastern part of Jordan by a quick move along the Jordan valley. This option in some degree balances the other factors. The third difference between the two areas lies in the military capabilities which could be mustered on the West Bank by Arab forces. The Jordanian forces by themselves, though efficient, are too small to constitute a major threat to Israel. On the other hand, if Arab forces – those of Syria, Iraq and Saudi-Arabia – were allowed to operate from Jordanian territories, the situation would be very different.

The security measures which must accompany the return of the area to Arab sovereignty will have to answer legitimate Israeli security concerns arising from these differences. The first measure would be its complete demilitarization so far as Arab forces are concerned, except for small units with internal policing responsibility. This demilitarization would have a far-reaching political implication. Since no sovereign state is ready to demilitarize itself completely, it is hard to see an independent Palestinian state doing this. Therefore the logic of demilitarization dictates that it should be Jordan that should regain Arab sovereignty over the West Bank and Gaza. Both Egypt and the United States are trying to encourage a 'Jordanian solution' for these areas. The Camp David Accords regarding the West Bank envisage the continuation, for at least the five-year transitional period (and almost certainly for much longer), of an Israeli presence in some limited strategic positions on the West Bank as a further hedge against the possibility of a swift surprise remilitarization of the area by Arab forces. This will certainly be a contributing factor to security in the area. Two additional CBM appear necessary in order to increase the stability of the proposed system of security arrangements. The first concerns some limitation on the deployment of Jordanian forces on the *eastern* side of the Jordan river, in the (perhaps unlikely) event of Jordan entering into any arrangements over the West Bank. Thus, for example, large concentrations of armour and surface-to-air missiles should be banned in a wide strip of land along the river. The second measure concerns the creation of a *de facto* and, if possible, even *de jure* Israeli–Jordanian security bloc. This would have far-reaching political and strategic implications. In Israel's interests and those of stability such a measure should have two main components: first, an undertaking by Jordan not to permit the entry ·of foreign Arab forces into Jordan. Violation of such a commitment should be recognized as a legitimate Israeli *casus belli*. The second is the signing of a defence treaty or alternatively, a 'no use of force' treaty between Israel and Jordan. In this context it should be noted that on several occasions Israel has in fact acted as the *de facto* guarantor of Jordan against the intrusion of foreign Arab forces into that state (indeed, such an intrusion used to be one of Israel's *casus belli* until the 1967 war). Her most significant act in that role was the deterrent posture she assumed against the Syrian intervention during the 1970 civil war in Jordan. It is, therefore, just possible that Jordan could be interested in entering into some form of agreement along these lines as the price for an Israeli withdrawal from the West Bank. (Such a withdrawal would depend in the first place, ·of course, on the Israeli government's political decisions.)

The formation of an Israeli–Jordanian bloc would critically diminish the threat of escalation leading to war along Israel's eastern front and would thus increase stability in the area. It would be of primary importance as a CBM between these two states. As Jordan would most probably continue to enjoy strong support from Saudi Arabia (with whom she has significant political links), it is unlikely that her relations with Israel would lead her into greater dependence on Israel. More crucial will be the pressures that the radical states will try to exert on Jordan to induce her to join them in rejecting Camp David.

*The Golan Heights*
The Heights pose a particular problem for Israel, being a high plateau commanding the northern valleys inside Israel, which is very difficult of access from the Israeli side and easy of access from the Syrian side. Syrian forces would be able to re-occupy the Heights with a swift surprise move. Restrictions on deployment of Syrian forces and offensive weapons systems beyond a demilitarized Golan are therefore essential if confidence is to be built. Syrian forces would still be in an advantageous position if they decided to re-occupy the Heights, but peacetime deployment limitations would somewhat constrain their freedom of movement.

The super-powers may have a role to play in guaranteeing demilitarization of the Heights. It is not clear, however, whether the regional powers would welcome either a super-power or (if proposed) a UN military presence there to buttress the guarantee. If the present political conditions persist, it seems unlikely that Israel would relish a Soviet presence or Syria an American one (or a Soviet one, for that matter). One possible solution would seem to be joint American–Soviet forces on the Heights. Again, it is not clear whether the regional powers would welcome such an idea, nor whether the super-powers would be able to reach such a high level of co-operation (it seems very unlikely at present). In the past the Soviet Union has indicated that she might be interested in the idea of joint forces (that was in 1973 and on the Egyptian front), but it is not clear what her position would be now, and the United States has always been far from enthusiastic about such co-operation. Indeed, because of increased Soviet military intervention, direct or by proxy, on the periphery of the Middle East, such co-operation appears even less likely. The situation may change, however, in the more distant future.

The demilitarization of the Golan may serve as a CBM but it seems unlikely that it would have a very profound effect because of the entrenched hostility which exists between Israel and Syria. Stable relations between the two sides would have to rely primarily on a system of strong deterrence, coupled with a coalition structure in the Arab world which would impose severe constraints on any Syrian war initiative. Furthermore, as long as negotiations over the future of the West Bank continue (following an anticipated Israeli–Egyptian agreement) – probably five years – the problem of the Golan Heights will assume a lower priority.

*Limitations on the Arms Race and on Size of Forces*
Perhaps the most complex subject is the issue of limitations on the arms race. It is hard to reach conclusions about which arms-transfer limitations would be stabilizing and hence desirable – as difficult as it is to secure agreements. (The problem of verification on the other hand, though it is also a difficult one, appears to be somewhat less intractable.) We do not as yet have any accepted notion of what is a stable balance of conventional arms. In view of the many factors affecting such a balance and the many asymmetries involved in the Israeli–Arab relationship, the intellectual task of defining measures for a stable balance appear enormous. For example, should the limitations be quantitative or qualitative? Should they apply to all states in the Middle East, or just to those in the Arab–Israeli region? What are the criteria for a stable balance? And what mechanisms for arms control can be developed once such criteria are agreed upon?

There are, in fact, several arms races between Israel and various Arab states, and there are spill-over effects from one to the other. Arms races result not only from an action–reaction process, but from other causes as well. The vast accumulation of financial resources in the oil countries is both a stimulus for the purchase of arms and a temptation for the producers. As for the suppliers, is it possible to involve only some of them in arms-transfer agreements, or must all of them take part? In the latter case, what are the

possible political implications of a general agreement? Even a partial treatment of these problems goes far beyond the scope of this paper. Nevertheless, some brief comments related to the problem of confidence building are appropriate, particularly in the Israeli–Egyptian context.

To begin with, in view of the complex problems mentioned above, CBM would be easier to achieve and maintain than arms-transfer limitations, and they would have a greater potential for stabilizing the situation in the area. Secondly, because of the multiplicity of suppliers and the existence of a 'buyers' market' for arms in the Middle East, there is a strong likelihood of violations of a agreements. Such violations would lead to a breakdown in the mutual confidence that might have begun to develop as a result of other arms-control measures and a political settlement. The need for some limitations is nevertheless very pressing, primarily because of the destabilizing impact of some systems. However, such limitations must be applied with great caution and only after very detailed studies. Furthermore, they must be seen as part of a wider system of security measures and not as independent measures.

In general, it seems that an effective approach to some of these extremely difficult problems may be to emphasize (at least in the first phase) primarily qualitative limitations on the types of arms transferred. Those arms which have a high potential for destabilizing the strategic situation should be limited or restricted. These include, for example, weapons systems which give a significant advantage to the side that launches a surprise attack.

Within the Israeli–Egyptian context a further idea has recently been considered. Because of the asymmetry between the structure of the Egyptian forces (which are made up primarily of a standing army) and the Israeli forces (which consist primarily of reservists), strategic problems are created for Israel. A possible way to resolve this dilemma is partially to demobilize the Egyptian forces and turn them into well organized reserve units. This would operate as a CBM.

*The Egyptian–Israeli Military Commission*
The measures discussed above are proposed as part of a future political settlement. One mechanism which contributes to confidence building,

apart from the arms-control measures enshrined in the 1974 and 1975 agreements, is already in operation. This is the Joint Military Commission; created by Israel and Egypt at the summit meeting in Ismailia in December 1977, which started its meetings shortly thereafter in Cairo. Although these meetings eventually ceased, a small Israeli delegation continued to stay on in Cairo.

In the meetings between military leaders in Cairo (before the Ismailia summit), and in Ismailia during that meeting, the two sides probably initiated an exchange of views about the military situation and about possible security measures. One can speculate that these contacts have probably created a context within which a process of learning about the strategic doctrines of the two sides could be pursued. The meetings of the Military Commission in Cairo doubtless continued this process, with the two sides assessing each other during formal and informal contacts and, as a result, beginning to reach a better understanding of each other's concerns.[5] (A joint committee to supervise the implementation of the security arrangements is to be established in accordance with the Israeli–Egyptian draft treaty.)

Even before President Sadat's initiative, the United States served as a convenient channel through which both Israel and Egypt were able to inform each other about military moves which might provoke concern. It seems reasonable to assume that, under the auspices of a future military commission, such exchanges of information will become even easier. Moreover, this commission could be turned into a permanent organization for dealing with various security issues and possible future arms-control arrangements, even after the signing of a peace settlement. It could then fulfil tasks which fall within the first category of confidence building, that is, learning about the strategic intentions of the other side.

## Conclusion

Arms control in the Middle East seems to have a central role to play both in facilitating political changes and in maintaining a measure of stability following a settlement. Arms control can prevent a deterioration in political relationships from spilling over into military conflict. It also appears that it is precisely in these security-military realms (rather than on the level of politics) that a rational process of mutual understanding could develop. This is partly because the political realm is affected far more by ideological considerations, prejudices and emotionalism, and partly because the military establishments are aware of the threat posed by the present situation. Although this leads them, in the first place, to worst-case analysis, it also opens up avenues which may lead to an understanding of the security concerns of the other side.

Two dangers are associated with over-emphasizing the role of confidence building. The nature of inter-state relationships in the Middle East is such that changes, fast or slow, in the foreign policy of different states are a persistent phenomenon. A political settlement between Israel and an Arab state, even if accompanied by far-reaching political accommodation, might be reversed. Such a reversal must not be allowed to affect the arms-control arrangements between the two. To the extent that political accommodation is based on a feeling of mutual security and confidence, political animosity must be prevented from affecting attitudes in the security area. Too much emphasis on confidence building as a political instrument might therefore, in certain circumstances, be counter-productive. (Indeed, the arms-control measures proposed in this paper have a primary role to play in increasing the constraints on potential initiators of war and in reducing causes for war resulting from misperceptions and 'misescalation'. Although the confidence-building potential of arms-control measures is significant, it is nevertheless a by-product of their overall impact.)

An additional danger is that some arms-control agreements would perhaps be less stable than others. This is primarily the case with arms-transfer limitations. Violations of these agreements must not affect other arms-control agreements such as demilitarization of zones and restrictions on deployment. In a sense, these potentially less stable agreements should be decoupled – in their confidence-building role – from other arms-control agreements.

However, there are grounds for thinking that some of the arrangements which have already been introduced somewhat tentatively in Sinai, in Southern Lebanon and on the Golan Heights are capable of being applied more generally. It can be argued that the concept of buffer zones, coupled with surveillance arrangements which give both sides confidence that the unusual can be detected, have led not only to a military stand-off in Sinai, but also to the real possibility of peace between Egypt and Israel. The direct involvement of the United States in the monitoring arrangements on the Golan and in Sinai (and – to a much more limited extent – that of the UN through UNIFIL) does indicate that the presence of external powers can help to defuse situations of extreme tension. The possibility of using standing consultative bodies to resolve potentially disquieting developments by explanation and reassurance has begun to emerge in the committee established by Egypt and Israel as a direct result of the Sadat initiative. These are all, by definition, CBM and one might hope that their extension and development to other fronts and other sensitive borders could allay the very basic fears of the consequences of successful surprise attacks. The allaying of these fears could lead to political accommodation.

## NOTES

[1] On the 1975 agreement, see *inter alia* 'Memorandum of the Agreement between the Governments of Israel and the United States', in US Senate, Committee on Foreign Relations, *Early Warning System in Sinai*, Appendix to *Hearings*, 94th Congress, 1st Session (Washington DC: USGPO, 8 October 1975); *Early Warning System in Sinai*, Report [94–415] together with individual views (to accompany S. J. Res. 138) from US Senate, Committee on Foreign Relations, 94th Congress, 1st Session (Washington DC: USGPO, 7 October 1975).

[2] On these schools of thought (but differently defined) within the framework of MFR, see Christoph Bertram, *Mutural Force Reductions in Europe: The Political Aspects*, Adelphi Papers No. 84 (London: IISS, 1972).
[3] See Yair Evron, *The Role of Arms Control in the Middle East*, Adelphi Papers No. 138 (London: IISS, 1977).
[4] *New York Times*, 24 November 1978, p. A14.
[5] See, for example, the articles by the military commentator, Zeev Schief, *Ha'aretz*, 30 October, 21 and 25 December 1977.

# 7 EUROPEAN SECURITY AND CONFIDENCE-BUILDING MEASURES

JOHAN JØRGEN HOLST AND KAREN ALETTE MELANDER

This article sets out to examine the system of confidence-building measures (CBM) which was initiated by the Conference on Security and Co-operation in Europe (CSCE). First, however, it seems desirable to outline some of the key considerations involved in constructing arms control arrangements for Europe.

## The Function of Arms Control in Europe

The basic goals of arms control include:

(1) Reducing the probability of war
(2) Reducing damage and suffering if war should occur
(3) Reducing obstacles to a quick and equitable end to a war
(4) Reducing the costs and burdens of the arms competition
(5) Reducing the role of military force in international relations.

Such objectives as these can never be attained absolutely. They will in part pose conflicting policy requirements, so that the policy problem is to achieve optimized outcomes rather than simply to maximize single goals

Particular European arms control measures cannot be considered as politically neutral technical arrangements for enhancing stability; they are instruments for building and managing the evolving security order in Europe, and should be assessed in a political context. Arms control proposals have been advanced for constraining political change undesirable from a particular interest perspective. They have also been deployed as a means of exploiting favourable

asymmetries, blocking undesirable departures, and promoting political advantages. The ostensible commitment not to strive for unilateral advantage can eliminate neither political competition nor incentives and opportunities for exploiting ambiguities and spin-off effects. However, the whole concept of arms control is based on the notion of certain shared interests transcending the competition of the moment. International politics is not a zero-sum game, and the shared danger of nuclear holocaust has forced states to a significant extent to regard security as a shared value – an idea derived from notions of community and a regulated system of power balance, based on interdependence and reciprocal restraint. But such notions are not equally strong in the political traditions and outlooks of all the states in Europe. There are also competing traditions, emphasizing hegemonic ambitions and a commitment to struggle.

When we turn to assessing the goals of arms control we move inevitably into the realm of normative politics. However, normative prescriptions should be based on an analytical evaluation of the nature of the security problems in Europe. Here we shall not consider the five basic goals of arms control, but concentrate rather on concrete objectives derived from them and aiming at confidence building under present conditions in Europe. Thus, we postulate that the elimination or amelioration of pre-emptive instabilities constitutes a legitimate objective on the arms control agenda. Measures intended to enhance crisis stability need to be based on a detailed analysis of given force dispositions and the particular characteristics of the weapon systems involved. Therefore the urgency of the pre-emptive instability problem is to a considerable extent a function of technological developments and their introduction into the force structures, and of the impact of force structures on political relationships in the areas of immediate confrontation.

Johan Holst is Under-Secretary of State and Karen Melander is a member of the Norwegian Ministry of Defence. This is a revised version of a paper for the colloquium on 'The Belgrade Meeting within the Follow-up of the CSCE and the Military Aspects of European Security' organized by the Institute of International Politics and Economics in Belgrade, May 1977. The views expressed here are personal and are not attributable to the Norwegian government or the Norwegian Ministry of Defence.

We consider another objective of arms control to involve the blocking of surprise attack options. Again we have to deal with the incentives inherent in certain weapon characteristics, troop dispositions and deployments, and it is important that arms control efforts keep pace with the evolving nature of the security problem in Europe. Arms control negotiations tend to be rather prolonged, but the nature of the problem they deal with may be transformed much more rapidly than diplomats can construct agreements on the basis of initially dissimilar proposals. The emerging problem of security in Europe is closely connected with options for zero- or rapid-reinforcement attacks across the East–West division. From this point of view the manpower approach at the Mutual and Balanced Force Reduction (MBFR) talks is not ideal. Similarly, we have observed technological developments rupture some of the categories and distinctions upon which the Strategic Arms Limitation Talks (SALT) have been predicated till now.

In the European context arms control measures should provide reassurance about military activities and dispositions. This reflects recognition of the interdependent nature of the security of European states, which is structural and intrinsic to the nature of international society. Measures of reassurance can be unilateral, bilateral or multilateral and can reflect explicit agreements or tacit co-ordination.

An implicit objective of arms control in Europe is to reduce the impact of the military factor on the process of European politics. This involves curtailing the shadow rather than the substance of military power: reducing the political convertibility of the military currency and imposing constraints on the application of military force. Countries whose military power is small are likely to become ardent champions of such approaches, but those that are militarily powerful tend to be rather reluctant to concede their comparative advantages – verbal declarations to the contrary notwithstanding. However, from the point of view of the European political process, curtailing the *role* of military force is more important than reducing the *level* of military establishments *per se*; reduced levels may or may not result in a reduced role for military force, depending on the details of reduction. The so-called associated measures under consideration in the MBFR talks are there-fore as important as the aggregate force ceilings proposed, if not more so, and are functionally related to the CBM of the CSCE.

Arms control measures could also provide catalysts for political detente and co-operation in Europe beyond the sphere of military security. They are important for the purpose of maintaining momentum. A detente which did not extend to the military confrontation in Europe would, as we see it, inevitably grind to a halt.

## The Purpose of Confidence-building Measures

With respect to the military situation in Europe, confidence building involves the communication of credible evidence of the absence of feared threats. Since modern technological means of surveillance have long since penetrated the shells of secrecy traditionally surrounding the military preparations of the nation state, CBM can be but a minor supplement to the various means of intelligence collection. Nevertheless, they are of political and psychological import-ance, because they can only be implemented on the express initiatives and wishes of the states whose military activity is notified or observed. They establish a linkage between the political and military aspects of European security.

In the Final Act the participating states declared that they had a duty to refrain 'from the threat of use of force in their relations with one another' as well as from 'any manifestation of force for the purpose of inducing another participating state to renounce the full exercise of its sovereign rights'. The CBM provisions constitute an effort to give operational expressions to these general principles. They are in some sense prior to arms control and disarmament. Thus they do not aim at a direct reduction in the competitive military efforts. They form elements, rather, in a framework for the indirect alleviation and reduction of the incentives for competition which derive from uncertainty and possible mis-understanding. To this avail it is important that CBM also bring into focus some of the aspects of the security problem in Europe which are the most urgent from the point of view of stability.

A major objective of CBM, therefore, is to provide reassurance to the rest of the states in Europe. They should do this by reducing uncertainties and by constraining opportunities for exerting pressure through military activity. Ideally, they would shorten the shadows of

224

military force, and cofindeenc would be enhanced to the extent that the option of surprise military action receded into the background.

With respect to the pattern and practice of military activities CBM should serve to raise the threshold against military transgression of the rules of inter-state behaviour: rules such as those promulgated in the decalogue of the CSCE Final Act. A system of CBM for Europe need not be enshrined in formal agreements but could evolve through state practice over time, reflecting the will for continued detente. The incentives for expanding CBM will not only reflect the experience drawn from their initial implementation but will reflect, and also influence, the general atmosphere and substance of East–West detente.

In attempting to move from general principles to concrete measures of confidence-building potential, it is necessary to establish reasonable criteria for assessing the relevant parameters. What should be the numerical threshold for prior notification of manoeuvres? First of all, it is necessary to find a reasonable unit of account, since formations differ in size and nomenclature. The number of men seems the most simple and obvious solution. But how large a number? Here we have to assess the expected frequency of notification and the volume capable of constituting a threat. The answers may differ in the various regions of Europe, but, from the point of view of overall equity, it is important to establish uniform rules. There is little doubt that the current thresholds are somewhat high compared to the scale of feared threats in many regions of Europe.

Then we have the question of notification time. Clearly, there ought to be some relationship between the time actually spent in preparing for a manoeuvre and the required lead time for notification – otherwise observed preparations which are not notified could generate fears of actual preparations for attack. Political crises may erupt suddenly. Hence, it is important that military manoeuvres be announced well ahead of time, in order to allay fears that they are staged for purposes of influencing a domestic crisis situation. Most Western states in fact announce their military exercises well in advance of the 21 days stipulated in the CSCE Final Act. This practice has developed because of the need to inform the local communities which will be affected by the manoeuvres, the press and the outside world. It will lower the status of the CSCE provisions if Western notifications through diplomatic channels appear as an anti-climatic afterthought; hence we should probably envisage a period longer than 21 days for the prior announcement of major military manoeuvres.

But there is also another question. How can we guard against the use of official notification of manoeuvres to exert pressure on a given state or situation? Notification can be done very quickly, but it takes considerable time to stage manoeuvres. Could it be that notification according to CSCE rules could in some circumstances serve to amplify threatening or warning signals, thus enabling pressure to be exerted more quickly than in the absence of the system of prior notification? No final answer can be given, except to note that the proof of the pudding lies in the eating. Should the perception spread that the CBM system was being exploited for purposes inimical to the spirit of the Final Act, the whole system would very soon collapse.

The possibility of misusing CBM to exert military pressure has to be assessed also in relation to how notification is to be given and to whom. Should notification be confined to those immediately concerned because of geographical proximity, or should it include all the states in Europe? For the smaller states in Europe it is important to insist on universality, in order to reduce the danger of focused pressure. Attempts to sub-regionalize the security order in Europe to the advantage of the dominant military power have been resisted by the majority. It is in consideration of such dangers that the Western states have invited observers from other countries in addition to their immediate neighbours to attend manoeuvres. States which for practical reasons of capacity have not been able to invite everybody have chosen a representative sample of observers which can sustain the notion of an all-European security order among formally equal states. The Eastern practice has been somewhat different.

How much information should be communicated in notifying manoeuvres, and how much should invited observers be allowed to observe? Clearly, the information should be sufficient for outside powers to make a proper assessment of the nature of the exercise. Too little information can often be more destructive of confidence than no information at all, and observers who feel that their ability to obtain a clear picture of the exercise in question is unduly constrained may come to suspect that they are kept in the dark and that some important information is being hidden deliberately. On the other hand, access should not be so extensive as to stimulate illicit intelligence activities. Observers should be treated with confidence and not subjected to security harassments, bugging, covert surveillance, etc. It would clearly be in everybody's interest to develop a code of conduct for the treatment of observers. The long-term goal should be the emergence of practices consistent with the idea of a more transparent and open world in the military as well as civilian sphere of human activity. We should recognize that the barriers to such a state of affairs are more pronounced in some countries than in others. But they do exist everywhere.

How much should be formulated as a state's obligation, how much should be left to voluntary practice? Again we have to adopt an evolutionary perspective. It should be possible, by co-ordinated practice and proper publicity, for states to exert pressure on those least inclined to move beyond the minimum provisions. Hence, a fairly broad scope for voluntary implementation above and beyond the minimum requirements is an important precondition for organic growth.

Finally, we have the problem of defining the phenomena to be observed or notified. How do we define the extent of a given manoeuvre if it is part of a continuous series of exercises? What counting rules should then apply with respect to the obligation to provide prior notification? There are other problems too, like that of so defining a military manoeuvre as to distinguish it from a military movement. If such distinctions are difficult to make in the abstract, they may be even more perplexing to the states whose confidence depends on being able to know about major military activities in their immediate environment. It would seem logical to conclude that both major military manoeuvres and movements should be included under the umbrella of CSCE obligations. This is particularly true because military movements constitute a more flexible and potent means of pressure than land-force manoeuvres. We must also consider the salient anomaly in the fact that current CBM do not extend to naval forces, traditionally the forces which have lent themselves most easily to the exertion of political pressure upon states (gunboat diplomacy).

CBM concerning military manoeuvres do not legitimate such manoeuvres; they take cognizance only of the fact that such activities take place and that they affect the perceived security of several states in Europe. CBM need not be confined to the phenomenon of military manoeuvres, but should be focused on the particular aspects of military activity which tend to produce fears and uncertainty. Thus it would seem reasonable to focus future attention on the possibility of arriving at codes of conduct concerning the nature and pattern of military activities in national border areas. Special constraints might also be imposed on activities with particular offensive potential, provided one could avoid the interminable problems of definition which plagued negotiations about qualitative disarmament between the wars. Finally, another area of uncertainty and incentives for expanded competition is that of military budgets. There are at present great differences in the availability of information about how much various states are actually spending on defence, how they spend it, why they spend it the way they do, and how they envisage long-term budgets (particularly with respect to procurement). An accepted formula for providing verifiable information to some European agency, which would publish all budgets in the agreed detail, could presumably slow down one of the major engines of the arms competition: lack of knowledge about the programmes and ambitions of the potential adversary.

### The Record since Helsinki
Turning to a brief examination of the record of CBM so far, it must be recognized that this can be no more than an interim report, in view of the short time that has elapsed since Helsinki. It should also be borne in mind that shortcomings with respect to compliance and implementation may not simply reflect intrinsic weaknesses in the provisions of the Final Act; they may have been caused by institutional inertia as well as by a lack of political will. CBM have but a limited potential for influencing the political atmosphere in Europe, but their implementation in practice is likely to reflect in part the actual state of East–West relations

in Europe and beyond. These relationships are complex and very hard to unravel.

The Final Act is but an overture, suggesting themes to be developed in a new concert of Europe; the orchestration will be determined by state practice, *inter alia* in the field of CBM. The record of compliance with the provisions of the Final Act is somewhat dissimilar as between the different states in Europe. The Western states and neutral states have tended to go beyond the minimum provisions in order to generate confidence momentum. The Eastern states have stayed closer to a minimum implementation, and were slower to begin to notify manoeuvres (see Table 1). The institutional obstacles to increased openness may have been greater in the East (though the initial five-month period of silence over notifications did not constitute a failure to adhere to CSCE provisions but rather an apparent unwillingness to notify manoeuvres below the 25,000-man threshold.

According to our calculations a total of twenty-five manoeuvres have been preannounced

in accordance with the provisions in the Final Act: fourteen Western, six Eastern and five conducted by neutral countries (see Table 1). Half of the Western manoeuvres were below the threshold of 25,000 men as were four of the manoeuvres by neutral countries. In April and October 1976 Hungary did notify manoeuvres below the 25,000-man threshold, but in the first case the notification was given only one day before the manoeuvres began and in the second case on the same day.

The fact that the Eastern states have notified fewer manoeuvres than the West is not attributable to a larger number of Western manoeuvres, but to a greater willingness by Western states to notify manoeuvres involving under 25,000 men. In the Final Act the states recognize 'that they can contribute further to strengthening confidence and increasing security and stability, and to this end may also notify smaller-scale manoeuvres to other participating states, with special regard for those near the area of such manoeuvres'.

**Table 1: Notification of Manoeuvres and Invitation of Observers since Helsinki**

| | Sponsoring country | Name of manoeuvre | Size of manoeuvre | Observers invited | Countries invited to send observers | Observers invited from each country |
|---|---|---|---|---|---|---|
| | NATO *countries* | | | | | |
| *1975* | | | | | | |
| Sept | W. Germany | *Grosse Rochade* | 68,000 | No | | |
| Oct | USA | *Certain Trek* | 57,000 | Yes | All CSCE[a] | 2 |
| Oct/Nov | USA | *Reforger 75* | 53,000 | No | | |
| Sept | Turkey | *Deep Express* | 18,000 | No | | |
| Oct | Norway | *Batten Bolt* | 8,000 | No | | |
| Oct/Nov | Netherlands | *Pantsersprong* | 10,000 | No | | |
| *1976* | | | | | | |
| Sept | W. Germany | *Grosser Bär* | 50,000 | Yes | All CSCE[a] | 2 |
| Sept | USA | *Gordian Shield* | 30,000 | No | | |
| Sept | USA | *Lares Team* | 44,000 | Yes | All CSCE[a] | 2 |
| Feb/Mar | Norway | *Atlas Express* | 17,000 | No | | |
| Sept | Norway | *Team Work* | 13,500 | Yes | AUS, CA, DE, FIN, NE, PO, SWE, UK, USA USSR, WG, | 2 |
| Oct | Denmark/ W. Germany | *Bonded Item* | 11,000 | No | | |
| Nov | Britain | *Spearpoint* | 18,000 | Yes | AUS, CA, CZ, EG, FIN, IR, NE, PO, RO, SWE, SWI, USSR, YU | 1 |
| *1977* | | | | | | |
| May | USA | *Certain Fighter* | 24,000 | No | | |

**Table 1. – (contd)**[a]

| | Sponsoring country | Name of manoeuvre | Size of manoeuvre | Observers invited | Countries invited to send observers | Observers invited from each country |
|---|---|---|---|---|---|---|
| | *WP countries* | | | | | |
| *1975* | None | | | | | |
| | | | | | | |
| *1976* | | | | | | |
| Jan/Feb | USSR | *Kavkaz* | 25,000 | Yes | BU, GR, RO, TU, YU | 3 |
| Jun | USSR | *Sever* | 25,000 | Yes | EG, FIN, NO, PO, SWE | 2–3 |
| Apr | Hungary[b] | — | 10,000 | | | |
| Oct | Hungary[c] | — | 15,000 | | | |
| Sept | Poland | *Tarcza 76* | 35,000 | Yes | AUS, DE, FIN, SWE | 2 |
| | | | | | | |
| *1977* | | | | | | |
| Mar | USSR | — | 25,000 | No | | |
| | | | | | | |
| | *Neutral and non-aligned* | | | | | |
| *1975* | | | | | | |
| Oct | Yugoslavia | — | 18,000 | No | | |
| Nov | Switzerland | — | 40,000 | No | | |
| | | | | | | |
| *1976* | | | | | | |
| Oct | Yugoslavia | *Golilja* | 24,000 | Yes | 22 CSCE participants | 2 |
| Nov | Sweden | *Poseidon* | 12,000 | No | | |
| | | | | | | |
| *1977* | | | | | | |
| Mar | Sweden | *Vönn-77* | 10,000 | Yes | AUS, DE, EG, FIN, NO, PO, SWI, UK, US, USSR, WG, YU | 2 |

[a] This implies that in general all CSCE countries were invited. It could not be ascertained however, whether the invitees included countries with no military forces of their own, such as San Marino, Monaco, Iceland, etc.
[b] Notified one day before the manoeuvre.
[c] Notified the day the manoeuvres began.

KEY

| | | | | |
|---|---|---|---|---|
| AUS = Austria | DE = Denmark | IR = Ireland | RO = Romania | UK = Britain |
| BU = Bulgaria | EG = E. Germany | NE = Netherlands | SWE = Sweden | USA = United States |
| CA = Canada | FIN = Finland | NO = Norway | SWI = Switzerland | USSR = Soviet Union |
| CZ = Czechoslovakia | GR = Greece | PO = Poland | TU = Turkey | WG = W. Germany |
| | | | | YU = Yugoslavia |

The Final Act also contains a paragraph wherein the states recognize 'that they may notify other manoeuvres conducted by them'. However, to the extent that this observation was intended to refer to independent air or naval exercises, no states have preannounced any such manoeuvres according to the CSCE procedures.

The Eastern states have adhered to the practice of inviting observers only from neighbouring countries. This is not in contravention of the Final Act, where it is explicitly stated that it is up to the inviting state to 'determine in each case the number of observers as well as the procedures and conditions of their participation'. The Western states, along with the neutrals, have invited observers from a broader spectrum of CSCE participating states.

The Eastern states have not up to now accepted any invitation to observe Western manoeuvres, though the reasons for this are not known and have not been explained. (It should be observed that the exchange of observers according to the Final Act is to take place 'in a spirit of reciprocity'.) With the exception of Romania, they also declined to send observers to a manoeuvre in Switzerland in 1975. Their observers did, however, participate in a manoeuvre in Yugoslavia in 1976, and the Soviet Union, Poland and East Germany sent observers to a Swedish manoeuvre in March 1977.

The procedures and conditions which have determined the participation of observers during manoeuvres have also varied considerably. Generally speaking, Western and neutral states have granted the observers greater opportunities for direct observation and contact with the host nation's personnel than have the Eastern states. Participating states have differed in numbers of observers invited, whether or not they included imported experts from the observer countries in addition to the military attachés accredited to the countries observed, the rank of the observers, etc. They have also followed different practices with respect to the equipment which observers were allowed to bring with them, most notably photographic equipment. Furthermore, states have followed different patterns over the information they have provided about manoeuvres.

The Final Act states that the participating states recognize that they may at their own discretion and with a view to contributing to confidence building, notify their major military movements. No state has provided such notification since Helsinki.

According to the Final Act 'information about relevant developments, progress and results' in other negotiating fora should be 'proved on an appropriate basis' to other states participating in the CSCE. At the Vienna talks on mutual troop reductions the two sides have fulfilled that obligation through comprehensive statements delivered by their respective spokesmen at the end of each of the eleven sessions which have been held till now.

## Scope for Amplifying, Reinforcing and Expanding CBM

The participating states seem to have adhered to the formal requirements contained in the Final Act, but to have varied significantly in their discretionary practice. In order to ensure a more uniform practice, it would seem desirable for the threshold for notification of major military manoeuvres to be lowered to, say, 10,000 men. The frequency of such manoeuvres is not so high that the modification would produce practical problems, and continuing the present pattern of notification could give rise to the view that states which show reluctance to preannounce manoeuvres below the 25,000-men threshold are less interested in expanding confidence and mutual security than those who do not. Indeed, tensions could arise from an irregular pattern of implementation, particularly in view of the emphasis on reciprocity in the Final Act. Many of the smaller states in Europe never stage manoeuvres of a size which approach the current threshold, and, from the point of view of universality, it is important to ensure the participation, and include the concerns, of all the participating states.

In the absence of a decision to lower the threshold to 10,000 men, we believe that 'may' in the paragraph on small-scale manoeuvres should be replaced by 'will'. If the fixed threshold were lowered to this figure, it would seem desirable to focus more specifically on below-threshold notification of military manoeuvres in the immediate vicinity of national border areas, in order to strengthen mutual confidence in the areas where the potential for fear and misjudgment is greatest.

Since states have differed in their propensity to invite observers, in the selection of countries from which they invite them, and in the way they treat them, consideration should be given to amplifying and strengthening the provisions concerning observers, so as to produce a more equal and consistent pattern of implementation. It is important, however, to preserve the basic principle that observers be invited at the discretion of the host country. They should not constitute externally imposed agents of control; they are observers at the disposal, so to speak, of a host country desirous of demonstrating the absence of aggressive designs. It is possible also to envisage the eventual growth of the observer institution to include special surveillance teams which could be on call whenever a state in a crisis situation wanted to be able to provide a convincing demonstration of the absence of aggressive preparations.

The Final Act already states that participating states 'will' invite other states to send observers, and that this should be done 'voluntarily and on a bilateral basis, in a spirit of reciprocity and goodwill'. The obligation is general and not tied to major military manoeuvres only, and indeed Western and neutral states have invited observers to manoeuvres smaller than 25,000 men. The general obligation is therefore clear enough. However, in order to avoid subregionalized implementation by the invitation of observers from neighbouring and small states only, it would seem useful to include a provision stipulating that observers from a representative group of participating states will be invited. Furthermore, it is desirable to consider the formulation of common criteria for the treatment of observers. For example, this could include provisions designed to ensure their ability to observe adequately by guaranteeing them a reasonable freedom of movement in the manoeuvre area under escort. They should be given adequate briefings on the scenario, forces, objectives and terrain of the manoeuvre. The observers should have the right to use binoculars and cameras, subject, perhaps, to exceptions for particularly sensitive areas. Such a code would be designed to produce a greater uniformity of practice and to enable the observers to fulfil their confidence-building functions.

It is worth re-emphasizing that the exchange of observers is primarily an instrument affecting perceptions of the political climate and is of rather limited military utility. However, out of the observer practice in the CBM context could grow more ambitious schemes for mutual observation and control in connection with agreements on arms control and disarmament: for example any MBFR agreement reached at the Vienna talks.

As it was observed above the 21 days minimum time for notification of major military manoeuvres should be extended to coincide more realistically with the preparation time needed for major military manoeuvres. A period of 60 days would seem reasonable and would provide increased insurance against the interpretation that a given manoeuvre was being organized so as to exercise pressure in a political crisis. Consideration might also be given to broadening the content of notification to include more information about participating units – particularly their use of heavy equipment, such as tanks, armoured combat vehicles, etc. – the naval and air components in combined manoeuvres, and possible links between the manoeuvre in question and previous or subsequent manoeuvres.

No states have yet chosen to notify military movements. Such activity may be hard to distinguish from a manoeuvre, since all manoeuvres imply movement of forces. However, not all movements involve a structured phase of two-sided activities which characterizes a military manoeuvre. The ambiguities involved, and the fact that manoeuvres are almost invariably preceded by movements and build-ups of forces, point in the direction of rewriting the provisions on military movements so as to create conditions governing their notification which are analogous to, or indeed congruent with, those that apply to major military manoeuvres. However, military movements do not require the same preparations as military manoeuvres, so that the lead time for notification should probably be shorter, say 15 days. Moreover, some states are dependent on the rapid transfer of allied forces in an emergency in order to deter or repel aggression. There should therefore be an escape clause covering the case when extraordinary events threaten to jeopardize the supreme interests of a participating state.

Such suggestions as we have made in this section are in consonance with the text of the Final Act, in which the participating states recognize that the experience gained by the implementation of its provisions, together with further efforts, 'could lead to developing and enlarging measures aimed at strengthening confidence'. In order to sustain this process it appears desirable to consider additional CBM for subsequent incorporation into the text. Several states have drawn attention to the fact that they consider naval and air exercises particularly worrisome. It would therefore be useful to study possible parameters for the definition of thresholds for notification of such manoeuvres as well, though obviously a straight manpower criterion will not be very applicable. In addition, several states have expressed the view that particular constraints should be considered in relation to military activity in immediate national border areas – e.g., within 25 km of borders – and the possibility of establishing ceilings on the forces manoeuvring in such areas may be considered. It is conceivable also that it might be possible to identify certain military activities which would be considered particularly offensive in such areas. The participating states could then adopt a pledge to refrain from such activities.

CBM-type arrangements associated with agreements on mutual force reductions in Central Europe could include, for instance, prior notification of movements into or major exercises in the force-reduction area, agreed rules governing the rotation of stationed troops, limitations on the size, number and duration of exercises in the force-reduction area, and the exchange of observers during exercises. Constraints on movements and dispositions in the immediate vicinity of the MBFR area and the establishment of fixed observation posts at major communication nodes might also be included. CSCE arrangements could provide a general framework for the integration of such particular constraints into a broader context. Hence, a certain overlap between CBM arrangements under both CSCE and MBFR could serve the function of preserving the coherence and cohesion of the security order in Europe at large.

Finally, it seems to us that a commitment on behalf of the participating states to publish data about military expenditures and procurement according to accepted definitions and formats would contribute substantially to reducing the uncertainty and competition which is generated by inadequate information.

We have attempted to suggest various ways in which the provisions of the Final Act with respect to CBM could be amplified, strengthened and expanded so as to shorten the shadows of uncertainty and fear too often associated with military activity on 'the other side of the hill'.

We do not envisage a renegotiation of the Final Act. Nor do we advocate any changes in its formal status. What we would envisage is a separate document in which the participating states reconfirm their commitment to the principles embedded in the Final Act and declare their intent to implement the provisions contained therein in a consistent and enlightened manner. It would be desirable that the declarations constituting the Belgrade document encompass a commitment to the amplifications on CBM outlined above. There might also be initial discussion of new measures aimed at strengthening confidence, and their possible referral to a post-Belgrade working group of experts under a precise mandate. The Final Act contains several ambiguities reflecting the compromises which had to be made in order to produce the necessary consensus. The follow-up process should aim at a gradual reduction of the ambiguities in the Final Act through the introduction of greater precision in the voluntary commitments undertaken by the participating states CBM are important to the general process of detente also because they can be made precise and specific, thus lending substance and precision to the process of multilateral construction of a peaceful and co-operative order in Europe.

# 8 NEW MILITARY TECHNOLOGIES

While technological innovation is a constant process, many of the strands of recent technological development seemed to come together in 1974 in a way which could deeply affect not only military tactics and force structures, but also arms control arrangements and alliance politics in the near future. If there was one common characteristic, both in the nuclear and in the conventional military field, it was the greater vulnerability of fixed targets and its consequences for the relationship between offence and defence.

## NEW CONVENTIONAL WEAPONS

A new range of weapons, employing a wide selection of new guidance, target-acquisition and command-and-control techniques, promises to give conventional forces vastly increased firepower. The United States, the Soviet Union and the West European powers are moving quickly to deploy the new systems. The United States alone is funding thirty new programmes which incorporate new guidance and command technologies.

### The New Technologies

Weapons now being deployed or developed incorporate improvements in a variety of capabilities.

PRECISION GUIDANCE. Probably the most striking attribute of the new systems is the increased accuracy obtainable by the technologies of mid- and terminal-course guidance. Precision guided munitions (PGM) comprise a growing class of bombs and missiles with dramatically increased single-shot kill probabilities (see Table 7).* With accuracies expressed in terms of circular error probable (CEP), as low as 10 ft, these systems vary widely in role and sophistication – from glide bombs that home on the energy reflected from a target illuminated by a laser to wire-guided anti-tank missiles, like the American *TOW* or the Franco-German *HOT*. These last possess semi-automatic tracking features, which means that unlike earlier anti-tank systems (the Soviet *Sagger* AT-3, for example) the missile need not be tracked by the operator after the target has been acquired. PGM now being deployed on strike aircraft have still more sophisticated guidance systems and can deliver larger charges. The American *Maverick* AGM-65A is steered towards its target by television signals, enabling the aircraft to leave the launch area immediately after firing (infra-red homing and laser-guided versions are under development).

Other PGM not yet deployed but under development in the United States include laser-guided artillery projectiles and multiple independently manoeuvring sub-munitions (MIMS), a small anti-armour warhead dispensed from a cluster bomb which would use a terminal guidance system to attack individual targets. American and, reportedly, Soviet research efforts are also concentrating on the development of high-powered lasers as destructive weapons; in tests in the United States lasers have been used to shoot down airborne targets. Ranges of 100 km are believed to be possible for systems of this type which could be deployed in the mid-1980s.

STAND-OFF GUIDANCE AND CONTROL. Already in use for reconnaissance, remotely piloted vehicles (RPV) will probably have the greatest impact in strike and electronic warfare roles. Recoverable RPV can be used as support jammers and chaff dispensers to degrade an

---

* For the effectiveness of 'smart' weapons in comparison with traditional ordnance, see Kenneth Hunt, *The Alliance and Europe: Part II: Defence with Fewer Men*, Adelphi Paper no. 98 (London, IISS, 1973), p. 15, note 27.

**Table 7: Selected Precision-guided Munitions (in service or advanced development)**

| Type | Developed by | Range (metres) | Guidance |
|---|---|---|---|
| **Surface-to-Air** | | | |
| SA-6 | Soviet Union | 30,000 | Optical or radar |
| SA-7 | Soviet Union | 3,500 | Infra-red (optical aiming) |
| *Roland* | France/Germany | 8,000 | Optical |
| *Rapier* | Britain | 5,500 | Optical |
| *Redeye* | United States | 2,000 | Infra-red (optical aiming) |
| SAM-D | United States | n.a. | Semi-active radar homing |
| **Surface-to-Surface** | | | |
| *HOT* | France/Germany | 4,000 | Semi-automatic command |
| *Cobra* | Germany | 2,000 | Manual command |
| *TOW* | United States | 3,750 | Semi-automatic command |
| *Dragon* | United States | 1,500 | Semi-automatic command |
| *Sagger* AT-3 | Soviet Union | 3,000 | Manual command |
| *Swingfire* | Britain | 4,000 | Optical |
| **Air-to-Surface** | | | |
| *Martel* | France/Britain | 60,000 | Radar seeking |
| *Maverick* | United States | 22,000 | Television tracking |
| *Rockeye* | United States | free fall | Laser homing |
| *Shrike* | United States | 16,000 | Radar seeking |
| *Condor* | United States | 110,000 | Television tracking |

n.a.=not available.

adversary's surface radar network, while strike RPV, armed with PGM, could be used against a variety of fixed targets, such as defence sites, command centres and air fields, and – further into the future – against mobile targets. Advanced RPV now under development include the American Army's 'mini RPV' – a propeller-driven, battlefield reconnaissance vehicle and laser target designator, which is capable of remaining aloft for hours – and a more exotic system, the *Firebee II* (BGM-34A/B/C). A testbed for systems which could be operational by the early 1980s, the *Firebee II* has been developed to evaluate the feasibility of RPV for defence-suppression roles.

TARGET ACQUISITION/COMMAND AND CONTROL. Accurate detection, location and targeting are essential to the new generation of weapons now entering service with several states. These tasks have been facilitated by the development of 'precision positioning' systems, which enable forces to be accurately deployed. Examples are the United States Air Force's Precision Locator and Strike System, which uses a ground station, ground beacons and relay air-craft both to locate and identify radar-emitting targets and to guide weapons to them, and the *Pave Tack* programme, which uses a forward-looking infra-red and laser designator system for delivery of munitions in bad weather and at night. An important feature of these programmes is the use of common ground and air grids which, coupled with an immediate (real-time) reconnaissance capability, enable commanders to make prompt decisions; using satellites, the United States will possess a global grid in the late 1970s which will allow naval units, aircraft and land forces to employ common positioning references. Such capabilities, however, require communications systems able to assemble and transmit vast amounts of information. Developments in computer software design are now under way among NATO nations to provide improved information distribution.

On the battlefields, developments in 'infyonics' – the application of sensor and communication technologies to land forces – offer the most striking command-and-control possibilities. Close combat has traditionally been an area where technology has been least exploited, but a number of developments not only promise to increase the firepower of small units, they also promise to provide them with a better sense of the battlefield environment. Night-vision devices, thermal imagers and remote sensors improve surveillance and target location, while transmission of information from ground units to command centres by means of microwave and digital-burst techniques enhances command and control.

## Consequences in Europe

The marriage of these various technologies has led to suggestions that conventional war is on the verge of a major qualitative change. Because of the increasing firepower available to small units, it is argued that the concentration of forces on the battlefield is less desirable, and that larger and expensive systems – such as battle tanks and aircraft – have become increasingly vulnerable to far less expensive weapons carried by small units. Because concealment of forces is important under these conditions, and the massing of forces risky, it is then maintained that the balance between offence and defence could swing to the latter – *if* the defence takes advantage of the opportunities afforded by new technologies and moves towards new concepts of force structuring. Since these developments appear to favour the defence, and since improved accuracy provides the opportunity to reduce damage to civilian structures and population, the introduction of large numbers of PGM and associated systems is thought especially relevant to central Europe, where the primary military problem has long been seen as that of defence against a concerted attack by Warsaw Pact armoured forces.

These arguments must be examined with great care, not only because the potentials of the new systems are in some cases not fully known, but also because a variety of factors will influence their ultimate military and political impact. The ability of states to exploit these systems to alter existing force balances will, to a large extent, depend on the quantity procured. And while the 'life-cycle' costs of many of the new systems may be lower than those of the systems now deployed, growing constraints on Western economies may preclude their abundant supply. This may be particularly important, given the suggestion that, widely spread among numerous units, munitions for the new systems will be rapidly exhausted in battle, and that even a NATO defence posture very well – if not abundantly – equipped with PGM could be swamped by superior numbers and eroded by attrition. Claims about the procurement costs of new weapons must also be treated with care; it is often noted that a *TOW* anti-tank guided weapon costs $3,000, but the unit used to guide the missile to its target costs $20,000.

There are also possible technical and tactical limitations attached to the new systems. PGM are subject to a variety of potential operating problems and, though efforts are being made to develop infra-red and anti-radiation sensors that can operate at night and in poor weather, most of the guidance systems require clear daylight to function properly. Even under these conditions, PGM may not perform as required in urban areas, where extraneous energy sources and obstructions could inhibit their effectiveness.

A more important caveat is the possible impact of countermeasures on the performance of the new systems and the effect of the Soviet Union's acquisition of a similar class of weapons. Only speculation is possible at the moment, but it should be noted that, while certain countermeasures to PGM and associated systems (such as electronic jamming) would be expensive, others (like the use of smoke or camouflage) may provide inexpensive solutions to the problem of defeating 'smart' technology. Moreover, while the acquisition of the new systems by Western forces should lead to enhanced conventional capabilities, the impact of a parallel move by the Warsaw Pact forces is by no means clear. The new systems appear to favour the defence, but this advantage is dependent on their abundant procurement and optimal use.

A further problem – and one that could lead to much speculation and conjecture – concerns the relationship of the new systems to tactical and strategic nuclear-weapons doctrine and arms control. In certain roles and missions advanced conventional weapons might provide some alternatives to the use of tactical nuclear systems. If this were in fact possible, the United States might then substitute conventional weapons for some of the 7,000 warheads now deployed in Europe. Such a shift in posture would seem to have the advantage both of raising the nuclear threshold in time of war and of facilitating an agreement on mutual force reductions by incorporating reductions in nuclear weapons in a NATO–Warsaw Pact accord. At the same time, however, many of the new systems are 'dual-capable' and provide opportunities for more efficient delivery of a new generation of nuclear weapons, both tactical and strategic; as a result, traditional distinctions between conventional, tactical nuclear and strategic nuclear forces could become increasingly blurred. With conventional weapons able to take on some of the traditional missions of tactical nuclear systems, and with the present American strategic doctrine holding out the possibility that strategic forces could be used in theatre roles, it could become difficult to differentiate levels of conflict escalation or to structure arms control agreements in terms of the nature of the weapons employed.

## NEW STRATEGIC TECHNOLOGIES

An important consequence of new strategic technologies is the increasing vulnerability of fixed-site land-based missiles. New technologies will permit missile silos of given proportions to launch substantially larger missiles, and attacking missiles to deliver a greater weight of warhead (and producing a nuclear burst of higher yield for a given weight of warhead) far more accurately. The prospect of ballistic missiles far more lethal against hardened targets, and the logical consequence of greater vulnerability for silo-housed missiles, has already begun to have a profound effect upon force planning and programming, strategic doctrine and the value of arms-control schemes that have hitherto seemed unattractive.

### Accuracy

The accuracy with which a warhead is delivered is the single most significant factor governing the effectiveness of a delivery system when used against hard targets (as a rule of thumb, halving the distance by which a missile is expected to miss its target is equivalent to increasing the yield of the warhead eight-fold). The success of an attack on a missile force deployed in underground silos is primarily a function of the reliability of the attacking forces' delivery system, accuracy of delivery, the number of warheads delivered and their yield – as opposed to the hardness and number of silos attacked and the adversary's firing doctrine.* The most accurate strategic missile presently in the inventory of either super-power is believed to be the American *Minuteman* III, which has a circular error probable (CEP) of approximately 1,300ft.† When fitted with Mk 12 warheads, which give a yield of 170 KT this CEP is grossly inadequate for hard-target counterforce strikes, since it gives a single Mk 12 warhead a single-shot kill probability of only 44 per cent against a silo hardened to withstand blast overpressure of 300 lb per square inch (psi). Hence more than one warhead would have to be fired for the United States to be confident of destroying the target. The ratio of attacking

---

* The firing tactic of 'launch on (radar) warning' does confront the intending assailant with the possibility that he will be striking at empty holes.

† The CEP is the estimated radius of a circle within which 50 per cent of the re-entry vehicles are expected to land.

warheads to attacked silos is so unfavourable – given the characteristics of the Mk 12 warhead – that a large counterforce attack would progressively disarm the attacker.

The United States is pursuing a host of programmes designed to reduce missile CEP. Most significant for the next decade is the development of the Advanced Inertial Reference Sphere (AIRS), due to be flight-tested in 1976. Developed as an integral part of the Missile Performance Measurement System, it is a single instrumentation package that reduces the cumulative navigational errors that stem from many separate instruments to but one source of error. Through miniaturization, the instruments that monitor the trajectory of a missile will be co-located within the sphere, thereby drastically reducing the gyroscopic drift which increases CEP. Duly transformed from its initial prototype into a full-fledged guidance system, this technology could, on a conservative estimate, reduce the CEP of an ICBM initially to 700 ft (and quite possibly eventually to some 400 ft) without benefit of terminal guidance.

Terminal guidance attracted considerable public interest in 1974, with Mr Schlesinger's announcement that $20 million was being requested for the development of this technology in the Advanced Ballistic Re-entry System programme. The most promising terminal-guidance technology is terrain contour matching (TERCOM). This involves the translation of target topography into computer language and the location of the missile in flight, optically or by radar, so that late guidance corrections can be affected.* It raises a number of complex technological problems. First, the terminal guidance sensor in an ICBM warhead must be designed to survive the shock of re-entry into the earth's atmosphere from space. Secondly, target recognition is difficult to achieve in the face of active and passive countermeasures (not to mention poor visibility) without real-time human assistance.† Thirdly, terminal-guidance technologies will use up precious weight and space in a missile.

Accuracy is also being improved by stellar navigation aids to effect mid-course correction of missile trajectories directed by inertial guidance instruments. By the mid-1980s these will be supplemented by course-correcting data obtained by reference to the Navstar, Global Positioning System. Consisting of 24 satellites in synchronous orbit,‡ it will permit determination of a missile's position to within 20 ft in latitude, longitude and altitude. Finally, missile accuracy will improve as more precise geodesic knowledge is gained and as local variations in the earth's gravitational field are appreciated.

There will, however, be limits beyond which the accuracy of inertially-guided inter-continental missiles cannot and need not be improved. With inertial guidance zero CEP§ is impossible to achieve over inter-continental ranges, because of incurable geodesic error and unpredicted gravitational anomalies. Although terminal guidance – for instance with manoeuvrable re-entry vehicles – could increase accuracy further, it is far from certain that this development would be worth the cost or the proportion of the missile's payload and carrying space that would have to be sacrificed – particularly since zero CEP is not necessary for nuclear weapons to destroy a missile in its silo.

### Throw-Weight, Yield and MIRV

The payload and the weapon yield 'thrown' by a missile of given dimensions, or from a silo of a given diameter, may be increased in three principal ways. First, the so-called 'cold'

---

* TERCOM is almost certain to be the first terminal guidance technology fitted to strategic offensive weapons, assuming the United States decides to proceed with one or more of the long-range cruise-missile programmes at present being funded.

† Real-time information refers to data transmitted, received and processed as the events concerned take place. 'Historic' data, in contrast, is passed only after a delay.

‡ A satellite so stationed has an orbital speed the same as the rotation of the earth, so that the position of the satellite relative to the earth does not vary.

§ The possibility of one warhead hitting a given point with perfect accuracy.

or 'pop-up' launch may be adopted; secondly, new warhead technologies may be devised for improving the yield-to-weight ratio; thirdly, more efficient rocket propellants greatly improve thrust-to-weight ratios, enabling a given weight of fuel to throw a far greater weight of warhead.

Cold-launch canisters eject an ICBM from its silo by means of low-pressure gas before the first-stage rocket motor is fired (the same principle is used to launch SLBM). This permits an increase of about 15 per cent in the usable diameter of an ICBM silo, compared with the conventional method of launching since internal shielding can be removed.* In principle, at least, cold launching permits rapid reloading of a missile silo, and the cold-launch canister also serves to protect ICBM deployed in land-mobile mode. Cold-launch canisters are already deployed with Soviet ICBM, and a variety of alternative cold-launch techniques are under study in the United States.

The micro-miniaturization of electronic components and circuits, together with the development of new fusing mechanisms, mean that far higher yields can be obtained from warheads of given proportions. The United States is at present planning to fit *Minuteman* III with the Mk 12A warhead in the late 1970s. This will have the same weight and shape (and hence the same ballistic characteristics) as the present Mk 12 warhead, but the yield of each of its three warheads will be approximately 340 KT as opposed to 170 KT.

Research in progress on new high-energy rocket fuels suggests increases of up to 70 per cent of the throw-weight deliverable by existing propellants should be feasible.

Greater throw-weight permits the fitting of more or larger warheads upon a missile force. While both super-powers are at different levels of competence in missile and computer technologies, both are planning the improvements mentioned above, and as a result missile throw-weight is rising, CEP is falling and the miniaturization of warhead components is being pursued very successfully. While the American Mk 12A warhead will be in the 300 KT range, there is the possibility of the Mk 20 warhead for *Minuteman* III which (if developed) will be in or above the 400 KT range.† In the *Pave Pepper* programme, the United States Air Force is studying the design of warheads smaller than the Mk 12 (such a system would probably be designated *Minuteman* IV), but which – married to AIRS, stellar navigation aids and/or terminal-guidance technology – could provide a very substantial hard-target counter-force capability in the 1980s.

The Soviet missile force currently has a throw-weight advantage over that of the United States in excess of 4 : 1 – and hence, theoretically, considerable latitude in terms of warhead design and MIRV numbers. The new ICBM systems entering the Soviet inventory can throw a payload of 16,000–20,000 lb (the SS-18) and 4,500–6,000 lb (the SS-19), whereas the current throw-weight of *Minuteman* III is 2,000 lb. However, this advantage at present compensates for what is believed to be *relatively* low accuracy and a considerable Soviet lag in electronics technology. It is worth noting that, while warhead yields can vary from expected values, they are not subject to anywhere near the same degree of uncertainty as is CEP – which is in any case an estimate of where 50 per cent of the warheads should fall. The United States is going to be far more dependent on accuracy than on yield for the effectiveness of her strategic weapons.

### Command, Control and Communications

A major problem of strategic communications has been posed by the nuclear-powered ballistic missile submarine (SSBN): how could communications be made both reliable and

---

* The diameter of all *Minuteman* silos is 12 ft. A cold-launched ICBM could occupy up to 10 ft of that diameter. A 'common understanding' of SALT I was that the dimensions of ICBM silos were not to be increased by more than 10–15 per cent. Exactly what this means has been a subject of contention since May 1972.

† The threshold treaty on underground nuclear tests (signed in Moscow in July) would, of course, foreclose upon the testing of any warheads at yields greater than 150 KT after March 1976.

undetectable? An important step towards more reliable communications is being taken with the development of the *Sanguine* extremely-low-frequency (ELF) system by the United States Navy. At present, communications with submerged SSBN operate on very low frequency (VLF), but ELF penetrates seawater to twenty times the depth of VLF and is very much more difficult to jam. The virtual immunity of *Sanguine*'s shore facilities to such nuclear effects as blast and electro-magnetic pulse (EMP),* combined with the system's ability to communicate with deeply-submerged submarines, should contribute to the relative invulnerability of SSBN and to the confidence with which they may be used. (*Sanguine* installations, however, need a lot of land, and so have encountered political opposition.)

The rapid retargeting† of ICBM, providing much greater strategic flexibility, is now becoming possible with the introduction of the Command Data Buffer System (CDBS). Each launch-control centre (LCC) can retarget the *Minuteman* III it controls by passing electronic instructions along buried landlines (previously, computer tapes had to be transported physically to individual missile silos). New computer target programmes are now passed to the LCC from Strategic Air Command headquarters, by means of special communication lines, all of which are designed to withstand nuclear effects (and particularly EMP). CDBS offers some hope that in a nuclear war ICBM can be used more selectively and flexibly than before.

In order to arrive at real-time information on the course of nuclear events, an Attack Assessment System (AAS) is in development in the United States. Combining the collection of real-time information from all available sources (for example, early warning satellites and ground-based radars), with the immediate and continuous computerized analysis, integration and presentation of that information, the AAS is intended to provide data on the source of an attack (possibly down to individual silos), the precise targets (involving missile trajectory prediction), the scale of the attack, the expected time-scale of weapons arrival and the exact character of actual nuclear explosions. This is a very ambitious project, but it is addressed to questions that would need to be answered at very short notice if both timely and measured nuclear responses are envisaged.

Probably the most important intelligence-gathering technologies are those designed to give early warning of missile launches. Satellites 'parked' in synchronous equatorial orbit today provide real-time information on missile launchings by means of infra-red sensors which measure the energy in the exhaust plume of a rocket motor. Information on missile firings is then passed instantaneously, via ground relay stations and military communication satellites, to military and political authorities. Unfortunately, the sun's rays shining upon the upper surface of clouds can be mistaken for a rocket plume, and, in addition, the necessity for equatorial orbits means that the curvature of the earth precludes adequate coverage of the higher latitudes. These satellites are complemented by the three-site Ballistic Missile Early Warning System for accurate line-of-sight radar warning, and by the much less accurate over-the-horizon forward-scatter radars of the 440L Warning System. The satellites are vulnerable to attack, but, for one thing, it would take several hours for a satellite-killer from Soviet missile-launching latitudes to approach a satellite in synchronous equatorial orbit, and, for another, satellite-killing, in terms of warning of hostile intent, would be to the late 1970s and 1980s what mobilization was to the early 1900s.

## Protecting ICBM

Improvements in yield and accuracy and increased numbers of re-entry vehicles combine to produce kill ratios prospectively fatal for the fixed-site land-based ICBM, although it is likely

---

* A nuclear explosion produces electrical and magnetic fields which, if they penetrate an unshielded missile silo can destroy electronic equipment and wipe clean computer memories.

† New target programmes can be fed into ICBM in 36 minutes with the CDBS. Previously, to change the target tape on a missile could take between 16 and 24 hours.

to be some years before all of these prospective technologies are perfected and deployed. The simplest and most obvious solution to the problem would be to phase ICBM out of the strategic arsenal. However, for reasons of cost, secure command and control, accuracy of delivery, flexibility (as a result of relative reliability of communication) and political balance, fixed-site land-based missiles will probably continue to form a major part of the strategic forces of both super-powers. Both are therefore seeking ways to protect their ICBM against the new technologies.

Under the Upgraded Silo Programme, the United States Air Force is housing all its *Minuteman* ICBM in silos redesigned to withstand blast overpressures of 1,000 psi, instead of the former value of 300 psi – this programme is almost completed. The reinforced silos are also designed to resist the EMP of a nuclear explosion: sensors close down electronic circuitry for milliseconds, the duration of the EMP surge, while large electronic capacitors electrically seal the silo. The USP is adding 10 in. of concrete to the silo doors and providing a 'debris catcher', so that earth or snow heaped on the doors does not drop on the missile at the moment of firing. ICBM could also be housed in new 'hard rock' silos in mountainous areas, built to withstand overpressures of 3,000 psi, but such silos would be very expensive to construct and would not provide protection against eventual improvements in missile accuracy.

As an alternative to silo protection, both super-powers are investigating the possibility of mobile ICBM, which would be more difficult for an attacker to detect and target accurately. The following land-mobile concepts are currently being considered: road- and rail-mobile ICBM (capable of firing from cold launch canisters); an off-road countryside-wandering system; a garage-mobile system (an ICBM would move at random from the hub of an underground 'wheel' along the spokes – covered trenches – to one of 13 silos around the rim of the firing complex); and deployment in complexes of ponds, 40 ft deep, with the missiles rotated at random between the ponds. All these concepts will require a major investment of time and money, and it is too early to judge which will finally be adopted, if any.

Air-mobility has also attracted attention and some funds. ICBM could be dropped from large aircraft (for example, modified versions of the Boeing 747 or the C-5A *Galaxy*) and would then ignite their first stage motors and pursue a normal ballistic trajectory – subject to course corrections provided by stellar navigation aids and AIRS. A first successful test of this kind was reported in September 1974 when the United States launched a test missile from a C-5A.

In principle, both air- and land-mobile ICBM could be neutralized by 'barrage bombing', but such an extravagant tactic would function effectively only against a rail-mobile system. Mobile missiles could experience a loss of accuracy and reliability; but independent canister-contained missile support systems and likely improvements in the technologies for mid- and late-course correction could offset these deficiencies.

# 9  NEW TECHNOLOGY AND DETERRENCE

In recent years there has been increasing concern in the West about the future stability of the global strategic balance. The counterforce capabilities of both the United States and the Soviet Union are improving significantly, threatening the survivability of fixed strategic installations and challenging the role of the land-based components of national deterrent forces. By the mid-1980s deployment of the new technologies now being developed will seriously erode the second-strike capability of land-based missiles. Although much of the recent debate has centred on this question, it may by then no longer be relevant. Not for many years has technological change been as volatile as it is at present. With many applications of new technologies under development, others 'in the pipeline' and still more being researched, it can no longer be assumed that the premises upon which the present strategic stability are based are assured.

## Recent Developments

Of primary significance for the future of the strategic balance, at least in terms of the next ten to fifteen years, are a number of developments in strategic technologies – in engines, warheads and guidance systems.

The greatly enhanced precision-guidance capacities which are now, or soon will be, available offer extraordinary accuracy. These guidance systems use for homing either those characteristics of a target which distinguish it from its surroundings (e.g. optical, infra-red, radio-wave or acoustic signatures) or highly accurate navigation to strike fixed targets with known locations (or passing known locations) by such means as terrain contour matching (TERCOM), advanced inertial navigation systems or navigation satellites. Although both the United States and the Soviet Union have made progress in this field, American ballistic-missile guidance systems are generally considered to be a generation ahead of their Soviet counterparts. Judging from the varying estimates of accuracy that have been given, the current circular error probable (CEP) of the *Minuteman* III ICBM seems to be as low as 600–800 ft. Software improvements in the NS-20 guidance system, now being incorporated in all *Minuteman* III, will reduce this margin even further. The advanced inertial reference sphere (AIRS), a 10·3-inch diameter gimbal-less inertial guidance system being developed for the US Air Force's MX ICBM, is expected to produce a CEP of around 200–300 ft, the lower figure probably being the limit attainable with purely inertial systems. Although the United States is investigating the application of various techniques of terminal homing to ICBM, it seems doubtful, given these very low CEP, that they will increase accuracy enough to justify their deployment. By comparison, the CEP attributed to the latest generation of Soviet ICBM – the SS-17, SS-18 and SS-19 – range from about 1,200 to 1,600 ft and are not expected to come below 1,000 ft until the early 1980s.

Increasing accuracy is also a feature of the American submarine-launched ballistic missile (SLBM) systems. The CEP of the *Poseidon* SLBM is currently about 1,500 ft at its maximum range of 2,500 nautical miles, and the Improved Accuracy Programme (IAP) is expected to reduce this to about 1,000 ft by the early 1980s. The *Trident* I (C4) missile, expected to be operational before the end of this decade, will carry a full payload 4,000 nm while maintaining accuracy equivalent to that of the *Poseidon* missile, primarily by using a stellar sensor to take a star sight during the post-boost phase of the missile flight to correct the flight path. It is, of course, not necessary for this missile to be launched over its maximum range, and shorter flight paths produce correspondingly lower CEP:

a *Trident* missile with a CEP of 1,200 ft at maximum range would have a CEP of under 1,000 ft if limited to the range of the existing *Poseidon* SLBM. These low CEP give existing and forthcoming American SLBM a substantial capability against all but the most hardened military targets; furthermore, the introduction of the *Trident* II (D5) missile, planned for the late 1980s, would give the American SLBM a true counterforce capability. Soviet SLBM – including the SS-N-8, which has a range of nearly 5,000 nm and uses a stellar inertial guidance system – are reported to have achieved CEP of under 1,500 ft, giving them a marginal counterforce capability.

Several important research and development (R&D) projects on propulsion are on the verge of yielding greatly improved efficiency in the use of fuel, weight and space. They include improved solid-propellent rocket booster motors and relatively small but highly efficient turbo-fan and turbo-jet engines – for use in, for example, strategic and tactical cruise missiles. While developments in modern guidance systems, and particularly 'area correlation' techniques such as TERCOM, have excited strategic analysts and planners the most with regard to cruise missiles, they could not have been fully utilized without the development of small (100–150lb) engines capable of powering missiles over a range of 600–2,000 miles.

The technology of explosives and warheads has also changed greatly in recent years. Not only has the destructive potential of a given warhead volume and weight increased, but a variety of new warheads have been developed to meet specific requirements, particularly for theatre use. The United States has developed the B-61 variable-yield ('dial-a-yield') bomb; the three-choice full-fusing option bomb with a device which, at the discretion of the bombardier, enables detonation of the free-fall bomb either in the air, on impact or by delayed action; a series of low-yield nuclear artillery shells for the 155mm and 8-in. guns of the US Army in Western Europe; and the enhanced radiation or neutron bomb. This increased ability to control the timing, size and type of explosion will permit greater use of these munitions where considerations of the safety of one's own troops or population centres become paramount. Although the applicability of these developments for strategic nuclear use is less clear, they have the potential to increase further the options in scenarios of counterforce and limited strategic warfare. A range of conventional explosives and warheads with potential strategic implications have also been developed recently. It is possible that non-nuclear weapons, including fuel-air explosives, improved cluster munitions for area targets, and hard structure munitions, when combined with highly accurate, long-range ballistic or cruise missiles, could be used against targets which can now be destroyed only by nuclear weapons.

Other technological developments, although outside the sphere of weapons, may also affect the strategic balance: developments in command, control and communications ($C^3$) technologies (including real-time satellite observation and warning), considerable improvements in data processing, and re-targeting capabilities for both ICBM and SLBM systems. All three have greatly increased the ability of both the US and the USSR to launch strategic nuclear strikes of a very limited and selective nature, so as to permit the fighting of an extended war involving controlled sequential exchanges. Although the United States has possessed a rather extensive capability for such controlled strategic warfare since at least 1961, Soviet developments are much more recent. It was not until July 1974 that the Soviet Union was able to launch her first geostationary satellite, and she now has at least two military communications satellites operating at geosynchronous altitude. An over-the-horizon radar system (which began test transmissions in July 1976) is being developed as an alternative long-range early-warning system. Hardened command and control installations have purportedly been constructed both in the Moscow area and within ICBM deployment fields. Interestingly, the introduction of a new technology for crisis prevention – the Moscow–Washington satellite hot-line – even provides for continuous communication between the White House and the Kremlin during a nuclear exchange, thus making a controlled nuclear war on a limited level feasible. It should be noted, however, that these supportive systems providing flexibility to existing nuclear forces are themselves vulnerable. Many of them – early-warning radars, communications links, the very-low-frequency command system of the ballistic missile submarine fleet – are large and easily attacked. Their destruction would not only rule out further controlled exchanges but would also seriously affect certain strategic capabilities. American counter-force capabilities would suffer most in this respect, since American ability to attack hard targets and the associated American strategic policy of target discrimination is much more dependent upon supportive systems than upon the large throw-weights that Soviet designers prefer. To the extent that actual war-fighting scenarios become increasingly accepted, one can expect further hardening or protection of these potential sub-systems of control against nuclear weapons effects.

## Implications of Available Technology

The collective impact of more accurate, powerful and discriminating offensive weaponry has two major implications for the maintenance of strategic stability. First, the continued viability of a basic component of contemporary strategic forces – fixed-site land-based missiles – has been called into question; second, the greater theoretical ability to fight a strategic nuclear war at controlled levels may increase pressures to launch a pre-emptive counterforce strike in a crisis.

These developments are principally a result of the very high single-shot kill probabilities (SSKP) which can be achieved by ballistic missiles with the high accuracies described above. Even against targets hardened to withstand 1,000 psi blast overpressure, the present Mk 12 re-entry vehicle of the *Minuteman* III (with a 170KT warhead) could achieve an SSKP estimated to be between 45 and 60 per cent with a CEP of 700ft. By comparison, the Mk 12A warhead (designed to replace the Mk 12), with its 350KT warhead and a CEP of 500ft, is expected to have an SSKP against the same target of up to 90 per cent. More significantly, an American decision to deploy a force of 300 MX ICBM would give the United States a first-strike potential of destroying well over 90 per cent of the fixed land-based Soviet missiles. Before that time – by the mid-1980s – improvements in the accuracy of Soviet ICBM will give the Soviet Union the ability to destroy a substantial proportion of the American ICBM force. However, since a greater proportion of Soviet deterrent forces consists of ICBM than is the case for the United States, ICBM vulnerability will have a greater impact on the Soviet Union than on her Western rival.

Yet at the same time that technology has increased the vulnerability of these missiles, it has also provided options which either increase their survivability or provide alternative choices for strategic forces. One possibility is to accelerate the hardening of ICBM silos, so as to reduce their vulnerability to attack. About half the present American ICBM force is hardened to withstand about 1,000 psi blast overpressure, and a number of the new Soviet ICBM are reportedly being deployed in 2,000 psi silos. But silo hardening has its limits. In normal engineering practice, the maximum compressive strength of concrete is estimated to be 3,000 psi. Such hardening is very expensive (a 3,000 psi silo costs more than $15 million) and is feasible only in special geological environments. More important, if missiles with CEP as low as 600 ft are used, hardening to 2,000–3,000 psi reduces SSKP by only a few percentage points.

A second and much discussed means of reducing the vulnerability of land-based missiles is to make them mobile. The Soviet SS-16 ICBM was designed for land mobility, and the SS-20 IRBM (which comprises two stages of the SS-16) is already operational in a land-mobile mode. In the United States, the MX ICBM, if approved, will probably be deployed in some mobile form, although the specific configuration remains to be decided. Primary basing concepts now being considered for the MX consist of concealing mobile missiles in either underground trenches or multiple hardened shelters. But while the MX offers an apparently useful technical response to the threat posed by the new generation of offensive Soviet missiles, it also promises to be controversial. Not only will the cost be considerable (about \$30 billion for the programme, comprising 300 MX tunnel-based mobile launchers), but the system, although less vulnerable than fixed ICBM, may still not be absolutely invulnerable to an accurate Soviet strike with high-yield warheads. Moreover, the introduction of an American mobile system might accelerate the Soviet move to mobility on a much wider scale, thus making verification of any arms-limitation agreement highly imperfect.

A third response option is to adopt a launch-on-warning (LOW) strategy, which calls for launching one's own offensive missiles as soon as radar confirms that the adversary has launched his. This would remove the need for survivable systems, or redundant systems in order to ensure sufficient retaliatory, second-strike capability. However, nearly all analysts reject LOW as inherently destabilizing and lacking credibility. It is argued that a LOW posture would increase the potential for accidental war, while at the same time placing difficult, if not impossible pressures upon decision-makers in times of crisis. More feasible might be a launch-through-attack (LTA) strategy: missiles would be launched when the full scope of the attack became clear. But the utility of an LTA posture diminishes as the synchronization and the success of the attack rise, and it remains a highly risky solution to ICBM vulnerability.

Before any of these responses is seriously considered – and none of them is either cheap or fool-proof – it will be important to put the emerging vulnerability of land-based strategic missiles in perspective. Much of the American debate on this issue has tended to draw strategic consequences from technological capabilities: because ICBM are becoming more vulnerable, it is argued, the Soviet Union could see an advantage in destroying them, thus leaving the United States in an inferior strategic position from which to respond. For both political and technical reasons, this is a scenario of questionable plausibility, and thus does not provide a basis for serious assessment of the significance of ICBM vulnerability. First, it assumes that the United States will indeed recognize a massive Soviet attack on her land-based missile installations as a limited – as opposed to an all-out – nuclear strike and will be willing to respond only in kind. In his FY 1979 Defense Posture Statement, however, Secretary Brown cast doubt on this assumption: 'The Soviets might – and should – fear that, in response, we would retaliate with a massive attack on Soviet cities and industry'. Second, such a strike only makes sense if the attacker has complete confidence in the reliability of his counterforce systems and can be assured that a complex co-ordinated salvo at intercontinental range will work to perfection. Phenomena such as 'fratricide' (exploding warheads creating an environment in which other incoming warheads do not function properly) must reduce confidence in any such projection. Secretary Brown also raised this question in the Posture Statement, arguing that 'the Soviets would face great uncertainties' in planning a first strike, and 'they must recognize the formidable task of executing a highly complex massive attack in a single cosmic throw of the dice'. Most important of all, constantly deployed submarines (SSBN), bombers, cruise-missile carriers, besides surviving ICBM, would provide a retaliatory or second-strike capability for considerable counterforce, as well as for all-out, response. By the mid-1980s, the United States can expect that over 6,000 warheads will survive a surprise Soviet first strike – and perhaps as many as 10,000 if she were on full alert before the attack. Despite the unquestioned fact of growing ICBM vulnerability, a more sober assessment of its implications is needed before decisions can be taken on the most suitable response.

## The Dimmer Future

Technologies affecting land-based missile vulnerability are not the only qualitative developments affecting strategic stability. By the time that this vulnerability becomes a reality, it may no longer be the crucial issue in determining what is an effective balance of deterrence. Potentially even more influential are technologies being researched and developed that could affect the survivability of satellites and submarines, and (most fundamentally) the ability of offensive missiles to penetrate to their intended targets.

To date, greatest attention in this area has been given to satellites and the growth of anti-satellite satellites which can interfere with verification and reconnaissance, early warning, and $C^3$. During 1977, the Soviet Union continued her programme of actively testing interceptor satellites, bringing the total number of tests to fifteen, of which eight involved manoeuvring the interceptor near the target satellite, which was then destroyed by the 'explosive destruction' of the interceptor. One Soviet test in 1977 involved intercepting a target satellite at an altitude of over 620 m – a capability which, if perfected, would threaten the US Navy's transit navigation link. However, the Soviet Union has yet to demonstrate a capability to intercept satellites at higher altitudes – essential if the geo-stationary satellites at 22,300 miles critical to American early-warning and $C^3$ functions are to be made vulnerable. The United States has responded to the Soviet effort by beginning her own anti-satellite programme, based on the principle of destroying the target satellite by collision. The first tests of this American hunter-killer satellite are scheduled for 1980, and an initial operational capability is set for 1982. At the same time, the United States is improving techniques to counter Soviet advances in anti-satellite weaponry. These steps include increasing the protection of sensitive components in satellites, the development of detection and evasion capabilities, and even the use of lasers to destroy enemy interceptors. (Both countries are exploring the use of lasers and charged-particle beams to blind or destroy each other's satellites.) A third American response is political rather than technical: the proposal first made in March, that negotiations should begin to control the development and deployment of this new category of anti-satellite weaponry, so as to nip this newest 'space race' in the bud.

Less advanced, but of equal if not greater potential significance for strategic stability are R&D efforts in anti-submarine warfare (ASW). Although no breakthroughs have occurred or seem imminent, the United States continues to make progress in her mostly acoustic ASW programme. More speculative and exotic are several Soviet investigations into various 'hydrodynamic signatures' (including heat, radiation, gas, magnetic and wave) made by passing submarines and potentially detectable by satellites, surface ships and other submarines. These efforts notwithstanding, the basic ASW problems of detection and destruction remain formidable. In addition, the increased range and reduced noise and cross-section of the new generation of American SSBN will increase the problems facing Soviet ASW experts, as will the establishment of new $C^3$ procedures (notably the planned extremely-low-frequency *Seafarer* system), which will eliminate the need for submarines to reduce speed and approach the surface to communicate.

No single technological breakthrough would be as far-reaching as the development of a viable ballistic missile defence (BMD). The introduction of a comprehensive BMD system would undermine the fundamental 'deterrence through mutual vulnerability' concept of contemporary strategic stability. The 1972 ABM Treaty between the Soviet Union and the United States effectively prohibits the deployment of BMD, both of then-existing and future technologies, and is of indefinite duration. But the Treaty does permit continued research and development, and there are indications that Soviet and American R&D programmes continue unabated. The most interesting avenue of research involves generating streams of charged, sub-atomic particles and directing them with electromagnets at a target. While theoretically such charged-particle beams could be used to destroy incoming missiles, certain basic problems exist: the earth's atmosphere is difficult to penetrate, and its magnetic field interferes with guidance. The technology is still primitive, and the allegations of General Keegan and others that the Soviet Union has had considerable success in this field are premature. All the same, the potential development of a BMD system based on charged-particle beams or an alternative technology is a disquieting prospect.

# 10 MILITARY COMPETITION IN SPACE

If either the United States or the Soviet Union were to be deprived of the use of military satellites in a time of crisis she would find herself at a marked disadvantage. Both have come to rely on the capabilities of satellite systems to provide the instantaneous warning and information needed in a contemporary war. Even in peacetime, the use of space for reconnaissance, communications, electronic intelligence, ocean surveillance and navigation has burgeoned. Surveillance satellites – the so-called 'national technical means' of verification – are essential to each superpower in order to ensure that it has detailed information on the other's strategic weapons, and they are thus the vital underpinning for agreement in arms control. Early-warning satellites are relied upon to identify missile launches, and electronic intelligence satellites can then track the missile to determine its ultimate impact area, thus assuring each side of the other's intentions. Communications satellites are vital for the near-instantaneous transmission of commands to units all over the world. Navigation satellites are already necessary for naval units (particularly strategic submarine forces), and in the near future missile guidance will come to depend on satellites. Even fighting units on land and in the air will come to rely on satellite data for precise position definition.

Both powers have become deeply conscious that space-based systems are extremely vulnerable to counter-action. New technologies have raised the possibility of serious interference with, and even the destruction of, satellites, and this has forced both sides to examine ways of defending their space-based systems against a pre-emptive attack.

Events in 1978 drew attention to different aspects of the military use of space. On 24 January the Soviet ocean surveillance satellite *Kosmos* 954 crashed in a fortunately uninhabited area of the Canadian North-west Territory, spewing radioactive fragments of its nuclear reactor over a large area; and two days later the People's Republic of China launched its second reconnaissance satellite. During the year, public attention was drawn to the continuing research and development that both the United States and the Soviet Union were conducting into anti-satellite (ASAT) measures, ranging from exploding killer satellites close to their targets, via the launching of impacting fragments into a target satellite's orbit, to exotic techniques based on lasers and charged-particle beams.

As the launch of the Chinese reconnaissance satellite makes clear, it is not only the super-powers which are involved in military competition in space. The number of states which maintain their own space programmes, and of those which intend to use these programmes for military purposes, is growing and will continue to grow in the coming years. Although China is only the third power to launch her own military satellites, the time is not far off when this small club will be joined by others. India plans to make the first of her own launches, using her SL-B-3 rocket, in July 1979 (two Indian satellites have already been launched by the Soviet Union). One of the satellites to be launched is a remote sensing satellite, though whether its camera resolution will be sufficient for military application remains to be seen. NATO and British communications satellites have been launched by the United States, but no other NATO power has yet carried out a launch of its own. In 1983 France plans to launch a remote sensing satellite with some military reconnaissance capability (*SPOT*) and is preparing a dedicated military reconnaissance satellite which will be put into orbit in 1985. Japan has launched more non-military satellites than any other state except the USSR and the US, and certainly has the capability to build and launch military satellites if she ever felt it were necessary. The private German firm OTRAG is developing satellite launchers and testing them in a large rented area in Zaire; it intends to place its first small payloads into orbit within the next two years and hopes to achieve geosynchronous altitudes in the early 1980s. These new abilities to launch reconnaissance and communications satellites will soon compound the problem, since satellites which can be used to verify arms control can also direct a military attack.

## Ocean Satellites

The crash of *Kosmos* 954 called attention to ocean surveillance satellites, an area of space technology in which the Soviet Union has followed a different path from that of the United States and in which she now has a significant lead. In December 1967 the Soviet Union began to launch satellites that exhibited very peculiar behaviour: after remaining in a low orbit of about 250–300 km for some days (and later for as much as two months), they split into two, one part burning up on re-entry into the atmosphere and the other being raised to a higher circular orbit of about 900–1,000 km. The reason was that the satellites contained an active sideways-looking surveillance radar which required a small nuclear reactor (containing about 50 kg of enriched uranium) for a power source. Once it ceased to produce enough power for the radar, the reactor was separated and boosted into high orbit, where it was supposed to stay for up to 900 years while the reactor materials decayed to safe levels.

The Soviet ocean satellite surveillance system appears to have become operational in May 1974, when for the first time satellites were used in pairs, with the second satellite following the first into the same orbit half an hour later. Not only could ships' positions be plotted but, by monitoring changes in the plot occurring within this time span, their speed and direction could be ascertained. Even the types of vessels could be deduced to a certain extent from their radar cross-sections. One such pair of satellites has been launched every year since 1974, with the exception of 1978 when, probably due to the *Kosmos* 954 accident, two pairs were launched. In 1974 the launches coincided with the NATO naval manoeuvre *Dawn Patrol*, and in 1975 with the Warsaw Pact manoeuvre *Okean 75*. If developed further, this system may provide real-time targeting information on US ships.

The United States is developing a comparable radar satellite system under the code name *Clipper Bow*, which is expected to be operational by 1983. Hitherto she has relied on maritime patrol aircraft and on passive electronic intelligence satellites under a programme known as *White Cloud*. These satellites are launched in clusters of four (two such clusters have been launched to date), and it is believed that one 'mother satellite' co-ordinates the information gathered by the three 'daughters' which monitor radar transmission from ships. Differences between the signal strengths received by the three 'daughter satellites' give the location of the ship, and the signal characteristics, or combinations of certain signals, will help to identify the kind of naval vessel. It is possible, for example, to identify *Nanuchka*-class missile corvettes from their radar emissions, because their radar system is not known to be used by any other Soviet naval vessel. However, since the system depends on detecting radio emissions, detection can easily be avoided by maintaining radio silence for the period of overflight.

## Navigation and Guidance

The American Global Positioning System (GPS) is a system of twenty-four *NavStar* navigation satellites, to be placed in groups of eight at 20,000 km altitude, which is expected to be operational from the mid-1980s. Satellite navigation information is currently provided by four *Transit* satellites in polar orbits at about 1,000 km altitude. By monitoring two standard frequency signals and the orbital data they transmit, the position of a receiver can be determined during each overflight with an accuracy of some hundreds of metres. The main purpose of the *Transit* system is to update inertial navigation systems of nuclear ballistic missile submarines so as to ensure sufficient missile delivery accuracy, but other naval units also use the signals for navigation.

The limitations of the *Transit* system are that it only provides two-dimensional information, and this can only be updated on each satellite pass. Moreover, because the position-fixing depends on exact measurement of a frequency shift, the system cannot be used by fast-moving receivers like aircraft and is very vulnerable to electronic countermeasures (ECM). Also, it relies on only four satellites, and these are within range of the Soviet ASAT system.

All these problems will be solved by the GPS, which will enable military receivers to locate their position in three dimensions at any time and at any place in the world (including space, up to altitudes of a few thousand kilometres) with an accuracy of 10 metres. Velocity, it is claimed, can also be determined with an accuracy of 6 centimetres per second. The satellites' transmissions are protected against ECM and unauthorized use (by so-called spread-spectrum pseudo-random-noise signals), although another signal, providing a less accurate fix, will be made available to civil airlines and shipping. The GPS will improve the performance of all forces to a remarkable extent. For the first time there will be a common reference grid world-wide, which can be used for determining the exact relative position of all users. GPS receivers can be used not only by naval forces but also by ground forces or aircraft. Thus a target of which the co-ordinates are known can be attacked by aircraft flying blind, and reconnaissance aircraft will be able to correct navigation errors and drifts and follow predetermined flights paths with great accuracy. Moreover, there are no difficulties in principle to using GPS guidance even for ballistic missiles (including those launched from submarines), which would reduce their circular error probable to a few tens of metres over intercontinental distances. The GPS thus promises to be one of the most significant recent improvements in military technology.

## Anti-Satellite Systems

The vulnerabilities of the US and Soviet satellite systems differ. On the whole, the Soviet Union deploys more satellites in low orbit, because she is unable, for geographic reasons, to launch the very high geostationary satellites used by the United States. In addition, the United States tends to use fewer satellites because she can use one vehicle to fulfil several functions. This makes US systems more vulnerable and has caused the United States to be very concerned about the continuing Soviet anti-satellite programme.

Tests of Soviet satellites designed to seek out and destroy other spacecraft were begun in 1967. The initial phase of the programme ended in 1971, but extensive testing was resumed in 1976. Most of the tests have been simulations. The one on 19 May 1978 was typical: *Kosmos* 1009, launched from Tyuratam, was initially placed in a transition orbit, but before completing a full revolution it was shot up towards its target satellite *Kosmos* 967, passing it at a distance of 1 km at an altitude of about 1,000 km. In some of the tests the interceptor has exploded into a large number of fragments in close proximity to the target, which is then destroyed by the impact. It is believed, in addition, that the Soviet Union is making preparations to launch a satellite-mounted high-energy laser which could be used to destroy other satellites.

The 19 May test illustrates both the capabilities and the limitations of the Soviet interceptor system. Although the orbits of interceptor satellites can reach altitudes of 2,000 km, all interceptions have taken place at altitudes of less than 1,000 km. Current American reconnaissance, electronic intelligence, meteorological, ocean surveillance and *Transit* navigation satellites are thus all threatened by the Soviet system. The time between the launch of the interceptor and the interception is very short (1–2 hours). Because the number of American satellites normally operational for these purposes at any one time is usually small (15) the number of interceptors needed is not great. Another group of satellites within the range of the Soviet interceptor system is the Satellite Data System (SDS), consisting of three spacecraft which provide communications over polar areas and are believed to act as relay stations for reconnaissance satellites flying over the Soviet Union. They are placed in highly eccentric orbits, which reach an altitude of nearly 40,000 km over the northern hemisphere, but come as low as 300 km at their perigee over the southern hemisphere, where they are vulnerable to interception. Also theoretically vulnerable is the American *Space Shuttle*. This can reach altitudes up to 1,200 km, but its usual operational altitude for placing spacecraft into orbit will rarely exceed 500 km.

There are, however, important limitations to the Soviet ASAT system. It is still impossible to reach the *NavStar* GPS satellites, which will orbit at 20,000 km, or the US communications and early-warning satellites, which are in geostationary orbit at 36,000 km. The interceptors cannot change their orbital plane and therefore can only be launched when the launch site lies in the orbital plane of the target satellite, and this only happens twice a day. But in only a fraction of these passes can the target satellite be reached by the interceptor within a few hours, since in the majority of cases when the orbital planes coincide the distance between target and interceptor is too great. Thus an interceptor launch is possible only once in several days. This has the important consequence that, whereas a single satellite might be intercepted by surprise, degrading a satellite system which uses several spacecraft might take a matter of weeks.

The United States has now begun to develop her own ASAT capability. The most promising project uses a small manoeuvrable warhead developed from anti-ballistic-missile technology. This is propelled by a relatively small rocket into the flight path of a satellite, where it releases a number of small missiles which home on the target using an infra-red terminal guidance system. The system differs from the Soviet one principally in that it is planned to be launched from an aircraft, which offers much greater flexibility of use. The launching aircraft can be flown into positions from which the targets can be intercepted at almost any predetermined time. A first test of the warhead in space is planned for 1981.

The range of this weapon is expected to be comparable to that of the Soviet system, which means that satellites can be intercepted at up to 1,000 km but that those in geosynchronous orbits cannot be reached. This limitation is less important for the United States, since the Soviet Union's more northerly position dictates that she cannot make use of geostationary orbits but must place her early-warning satellites and most of her civil and military communications satellites in highly eccentric orbits. Because of their high apogees, some 40,000 km above the northern hemisphere, they are visible from the Soviet Union for some 80% of the time, but the corollary is that during their perigees, low over the southern hemisphere, they will be within range of the American ASAT system. The Soviet Union normally maintains 16 *Molnya* communications satellites and three early-warning satellites in space at any one time, and all have to pass through the low perigee every twelve hours. If the American ASAT system becomes operational in the 1980s, it promises to be far superior to the present Soviet system, partly on account of its greater flexibility and partly on account of the greater vulnerability of the Soviet satellites.

**Directed Energy Weapons**
Both the United States and the Soviet Union are becoming increasingly interested in directed energy weapons, both high-energy laser (HEL) and particle-beam weapons (PBW). Some of the fundamental research on these is directed towards their use for controlled nuclear fusion or nuclear weapons simulation, so that the funding which appears in defence budgets is only a small part of the money actually being spent. Even so, the US defence budget for FY 1979 includes $184.1 million for laser weapon development and $11 million for particle-beam weapons (which makes it clear that US planners have better hopes for the former than for the latter).

*High-Energy Lasers*
Research into the military applications of high-energy lasers was initially undertaken by the US Defense Advanced Research Projects Agency (DARPA), but development has now been handed over to the services.

The properties of laser weapons (a straight beam moving at the speed of light, with short reaction times and high aiming accuracy) make them particularly suitable against aircraft, cruise or guided missiles or ballistic re-entry vehicles. The main problem with mobile, ground-based lasers (such as might be used for defence against incoming missiles, for example) is that, in anything other than clear weather, water and other particles in the atmosphere absorb so much of the beam's energy that the range at the moment is less than 10 km. This limitation can be avoided in the case of ground-based ASAT lasers; such weapons could be static, and this would allow use of larger, more powerful beams and they could also be set up in areas where clear weather is likely. This should enable them to achieve the 'lethal' range of about 700 km. Lethal ranges of space-based sys-

tems against satellites are difficult to estimate, and depend in part on the target satellite's vulnerability to laser radiation. Although a laser beam in the vacuum of space is not weakened by absorption, the beam spreads, and thus decreases in intensity, with distance. It is therefore difficult to envisage space-based ASAT laser systems with very long ranges. This difficulty is particularly important for a projected anti-ballistic-missile (ABM) system using high energy lasers which is being considered by the US Army. A space-based system would have the advantage that ICBM could be intercepted over Soviet territory in the boost phase, while they are large and vulnerable, with their propellant stages still attached. However, the limited range of lasers would not permit them to be placed in those high geostationary orbits from which a few could cover all the areas through which ICBM must pass; beam intensity would have decreased too much with distance to be certain of damaging the target. But if space-based ABM systems were placed in lower orbits from which they could inflict damage, e.g. at 1,000 km, they would only occasionally pass over areas where ICBM could be intercepted and would therefore spend most of their time in the wrong place. In order to overcome this, a large number of lasers would have to be maintained in orbit, which, apart from being very expensive, would create a highly exposed and vulnerable system.

As far as laser weapon systems are concerned, therefore, not only are there fundamental technical problems to be solved, but also it remains uncertain whether in the end they will be competitive with other weapon systems which are intended to fulfil the same function, such as missiles.

*Particle-beam Weapons*
This uncertainty is even greater with particle-beam weapons. It is known that the Soviet Union has been active in particle-beam research for many years, particularly with respect to controlled nuclear fusion and for industrial applications. Soviet particle-beam research is believed to be concentrated at Sarova, near Gorki, and at Semipalatinsk. Extensive activities (particularly at the latter facility) have led some

to conclude that a major Soviet break-through in beam weapons development has already been achieved. But this conclusion is doubtful.

Charged-particle beams consist of streams of sub-atomic particles (protons or electrons) accelerated to very high velocities in an electromagnetic field and then released in the direction of a target. Hydrogen ions can also, in theory at least, be used to form hydrogen atom beams. In both cases, the power required is enormous. Yet, compared to lasers, particle-beam weapons have the advantage of higher efficiency and less attenuation by atmospheric water content. They are therefore less dependent on weather conditions, and, even if the beam intensity is insufficient to damage a target structurally, the target's electronic components may be affected by the ionizing radiation produced by high-energy particles hitting its surface. Targets might therefore be more vulnerable to particle beams than to lasers.

But particle beams, too, have several inherent problems. Used within the atmosphere, the beam interacts with the air, causing a loss of energy and instabilities which make precise aiming difficult. The earth's magnetic field bends charged-particle beams and this adds to the deviation. In addition, the mutual repulsion of the beam's charged particles increases beam-spread and the beam thus loses intensity with distance.

American particle-beam programmes are now being co-ordinated under the auspices of DARPA, in order to investigate whether some of the basic technical problems can be overcome. Thus far American efforts have been concentrated on three possible areas of application. Most advanced is the US Navy's *Chair Heritage* programme, which by the mid-1980s might lead to a first prototype electron-beam weapon of short-range (a few kilometres) for defence against cruise missiles. This might be based on large ships such as aircraft carriers. The US Army has been pursuing a concept aimed at developing a space-based electronically-neutral particle-beam weapon for ABM purposes. Such a system would also have ASAT capability. As with space-based laser systems,

however, a large number of these would have to be deployed. Moreover, because of their considerable size, each satellite carrying such a weapon would have to be assembled in space by means of several *Space Shuttle* flights. This would be a conspicuous and time-consuming operation which might allow the Soviet Union to act diplomatically, or even militarily, to prevent it. Such satellites would be very vulnerable to ASAT attack.

The third system, also under consideration for the US Army, is a ground-based proton-beam ABM system. This programme is still in a very early stage, and it is uncertain whether it will prove technically feasible.

Indeed, the technical problems associated with both laser and particle-beam research are such that it is not yet possible to forecast whether any of these ideas will in the end lead to weapons systems. If the problems (mainly, but not only, in the area of particle-beam weapons) can be solved, effective self-defence systems may prove feasible for ships and aircraft large enough to carry the heavy devices and the corresponding power facilities. In any event, laser weapon systems seem unlikely to be operational before the mid-1980s, and particle-beam weapons could not be ready until a good deal later than that – well into the 1990s.

## Protective Measures

In parallel with the development of ASAT systems, countermeasures to the threat from the other side are being developed, tested and deployed on US spacecraft. To reduce a dependence for power on the very vulnerable solar paddles, two experimental communication satellites were launched in March 1976 (LES 8 and LES 9) which used radio-isotope thermo-electric generators. Efforts are being made to reduce electronic circuit sensitivity by shielding, by the choice of less sensitive components and by built-in redundance. So-called 'dark' satellites are being developed to reflect less light and reduce radar echoes, thus reducing the danger of detection. Impact sensors are being attached to US satellites to distinguish between interference by an aggressive act and an accident. Radar detectors have been built which warn against possible radar emissions from the terminal guidance systems of interceptor satellites. Horizon sensors used for altitude control can be protected by a shutter, and satellites under warning of attack can use additional propellant to manoeuvre away from the interceptor. A system for ejecting decoy satellites is also being developed.

This is an impressive list of safeguards, yet none of them ensures survivability of satellites. Rapid replacement may therefore be necessary. The US *Space Shuttle* could be used to place satellites in orbit, but in wartime conditions would itself be vulnerable. The USAF therefore plans a limited silo-launched capability for rapid satellite replacement by early 1980. To establish this capability, it is planning the trial launch of a satellite using a *Minuteman* III or *Titan* II missile.

## Arms Control

Efforts to protect satellites include political as well as technical initiatives. On 8 June in Helsinki, the United States and the Soviet Union began talks on ways of restricting anti-satellite weapons. (The 1967 Outer Space Treaty only banned space-based nuclear and other weapons of mass destruction. It did not prohibit the use of a satellite or other space-based system to destroy another orbiting system.) The recent negotiations are an indication of the mutual recognition of the importance of space systems to the strategic balance; at the same time, the inability thus far to reach any form of settlement is a reflection of the political and technical problems confronting the negotiators. Yet the prerequisites exist for an agreement: neither country has a commanding lead in the relevant technology, which in any case is rudimentary and barely deployed, and technological breakthroughs are still a decade or more away. As a result, it is quite possible that both the United States and the Soviet Union might want to avoid the risk of falling far behind in this crucial technology more than they want to compete for the advantage a lead would bestow.

The primary obstacle to a comprehensive ban on anti-satellite capabilities is verification. Lasers can be easily concealed, and in some cases 'killer satellite' systems can be tested under the disguise of a normal satellite launch. Nor is there a clear line separating military activity from any other – the *Space Shuttle*, for example, could be used to place both military and civil satellites in orbit, and may have the capacity to capture or destroy enemy satellites. But there is a fundamental difference between the ability to take out one or two satellites without warning and the capability to destroy most or all of an adversary's satellites simultaneously. While the former would cause a serious political crisis, only the latter would threaten to give a clear advantage to one side. Neither super-power is as yet close to such a capacity. It is this which may induce both to seek an agreement before the other side has moved beyond the technological constraints which still apply today.

# INDEX

ABM (anti-ballistic missile) systems: and laser technology, 249; limitations on, 15, 135, 147-8; and particle-beam technology, 250; in SALT I, 44, 45, 46, 47

ABM (Anti-Ballistic Missile) Treaty: details, 168-70, 173; and national technological means, 127; and political stability, 157, 198; and technological development, 169, 244; see also 124, 125, 149, 160

AIRS (Advanced Inertial Reference Sphere) 236, 239, 240

ALCM (air-launched cruise missile) 136, 140

ASW (anti-submarine warfare) 18, 160, AWACS (Airborne Warning and Control System) : in Israel, 80

Aerial reconnaissance, 131

Agreement on the Prevention of Incidents on and over the High Seas, 208

aircraft: deployment restrictions on, 23

aircraft carriers: as forward base systems, 54-5; limits on, 19, 23

aircraft reconnaissance: in verification, 131-2

Algeria: western bases in, 21

amphibious troops: deployment restrictions on, 23

Arab Defence Procurement Organisation, 82

Arab-Israeli conflict: and arms control, 66, 67-77, 81-94, 101-3, 213-6; and arms race, 77-81, 90-2; and confidence-building measures, 213-222; and demilitarised zones, 75-6, 82, 84-6, 93-4, 216-221; politics of, 101-3, 213-6; UN limitations on supply of arms to, 67; wars of, 71, 73-4

armed forces: advance notice of manoeuvres of, 25, 26, 29, 83-4, 187, 189, 190-1, 225-31; limitations on, 7-20, 21, 28

arms control: of ABM Treaty, 168-70; and anti-satellite capabilities, 251; and conventional weapons systems, 235; in

Europe, 4-6, 223-4; and grey area weapons, 2, 110, 134-43, 145, 154-7; and MIRV on IRBM, 121; means of, 5-6; method of: by area restriction, 23-4, 84-6; through confidence-building, 184-222; through demilitarised zones, 75-6, 83, 84-6, 93, 95, 96-9; by deployment restrictions, 21-7, 29, 84-6, 95, 216-21; by forces control, 7-9, 10-11, 17-8, 28, 84-6, 223; by limits on testing, 162-4; by military budget constraints, 11-4, 19-20, 28, 129-30, 159-60, 223; by military mission limitations, 168-75, 177-81; by naval force limitations, 10-11, 23, 28, 206-12; by nuclear disarmament, 199; by precluding new bases, 21-3, 29; by research and development restrictions, 13, 14-6, 20, 28, 130, 161-2; by weapon type restrictions, 9-11, 18-9, 28; by weapons procurement restrictions, 164-5; in Middle East, 66-103, 213-22; negotiated reductions in, 114-5; and politics, 101-3, 144-5, 213-6; purpose of, 5-6, 66-7, 223-4; rationale of, 157-61, 223-4; and stability, 157-8; support for in US, 115; and technological developments, 152-83, 198, 232-40; and war damage limitation, 158-9, 223; and weapon fashions, 113, 122; see also armed forces, MBFR, SALT

atomic weapon, 1

Baghdad Pact, 1955, 68

'bargaining chip', 175

bases: arms control by restrictions on, 21-3, 29; Western attitude to, 27; see also FBS (forward based systems)

bombers: roles of, 136; Soviet Backfire bomber and SALT, 120, 127-8, 136, 137, 138-9, 155-6; in strategic balance, 117-8, 120, 137; verification of, 128; under Vladivostock agreement, 135, 138-9

CBM (confidence-building measures): and CSCE, 231; early, 1; in Europe, 187-96, 223-31; and FBS, 194; future, 229-31; history of, 226-9; in the Middle East, 213-33; and naval arms control, 206-12; and observers, 187-8, 193-4; purpose of, 196, 198, 208, 210, 216, 224-6; in SALT, 197-205

CCD (Conference Committee on Disarmament) 147

CENTO (Central Treaty Organisation): and arms control in Middle East, 69

CEP (circular error probable) 232, 236, 240-1

CSCE (Conference on Security and Co-operation in Europe): and CBM, 184, 188, 208, 211, 223, 231

CTS (Comprehensive Nuclear Test Ban) 202

China: satellites of, 245, 246

cruise missile: and aerial reconnaissance, 131; air-launched, 136, 140; 'bargaining chip' use of, 175; grey area weapons, 134, 135, 140-2, 155; ground-launched, 140; long range, 136; as multi-mission weapon, 155; and SALT, 120, 121, 140-2, 145, 156; sea-launched, 18-9, 28, 140; and strategic stability, 110; and TERCOM, 241; technological developments of, 241; and USSR, 148; verification of, 128-9, 131, 140, 145; under Vladivostock agreement, 135, 197

Cuba, as USSR base, 22

DARPA (Defence Advanced Research Agency) : and HEL, 249; and PBW, 250

demilitarised zones: in Black Sea, 206; and CBM, 192-3, 195; in Great Lakes, 206; in Middle East, 75-6, 83, 84-6, 96-9, 103, 216-21; and PGM, 93

ELF (extremely-low-frequency) system, 238

Egypt: alliance with USSR, 71; arms production in, 82; and CBM, 213-22; and demilitarised zones, 75-6, 82, 84-6, 93-4, 216-21; forces of, 220; and nuclear proliferation, 74; PGM of, 92, 94; politics of and arms control, 213-16; and Sinai, 84-6,

93, 216-18; US embargo on arms to, 68; USSR arms to, 70, 71, 72, 73, 77, 78; and West Bank, 218-9, 220

Europe: as arena for superpowers, 4, 22, 26, 42-3; confidence-building in, 187-96, 223-31; conventional war in, 234-5; and cruise missiles, 140-2; and FBS, 31-3, 38, 136-7; inclusion of strike forces of in SALT, 41, 44, 140-2; military strength of, 4; and NPT, 6; PGM in, 234; reservists in, 8; and SALT, 40, 45-6, 140-2; security of, 4-5, 26, 28-30, 57, 140-2, 158, 160, 223-31; as theatre of war, 59-60, 42-3, 136-7

Euro-strategic balance, 136-7

FBS (forward based systems) : aircraft carriers as, 54-5; and CBM, 194; categories of, 52-6; definition of, 49-52; in Great Britain, 52-3; NATO and, 58-60; in SALT, 31-3, 42-3, 46-7, 52-6, 135, 145; in Turkey, 53-4; USSR and, 26; USSR's use of in negotiations, 63, 120, 121, 136; Warsaw pact and, 26; West Europe and, 38, 47

FROD (Functionally Representational Observable Differences) 192

fishing rights: and restrictions on naval forces, 26-7

France: embargo on arms to Israel, 72; and MBFR, 143; and modernisation of forces, 61; satellites of, 246; and supply of arms to Arabs/Israel, 67-8, 69

GLCM (Ground-launched cruise missile) 140

GPS (Global Positioning System) 247

gases, nauseating, 14

Great Britain: and Comprehensive Nuclear Test Ban, 202; modernisation of forces, 61; role of RAF, 52; satellite of, 246; supply of arms to Arabs/Israel, 67-8; US FBS in, 51, 52-3

grey area weapons: Backfire bomber as, 120, 127-8, 136, 137, 138-9; cruise missile as, 140-2; definition of, 110; Multi-mission weapons, 154-7; multi-purpose weapons, 235; problems of, 134-43; technology of, 235

'gunboat diplomacy', 206

PBV and, 134, 135; technology of, 236-7; verification of, 128-9, 131, 139; under Vladivostock agreement, 116, 117-8, 135
MLF (multi-lateral force) 135
MRBM (medium range ballistic missile): attacks on, 42; distinguishing from ICBM, 45; as grey area weapon, 140, 142; limitations on, 39; and SALT, 135-6, 142; of USSR, 137
MRCA (multi-role combat aircraft): European-built, 36; Great Britain and, 52-3
Mediterranean: super power presence in, 22
Middle East: arms control in, 66-103, 213-22; arms race in, 77-81, 90-2; CBM in, 213-22; crisis of 1973 in, 65; demilitarised zones in, 75-6, 82, 84-6, 93-9, 216-21; France and, 67-8, 69, 72; Great Britain and, 67-8; military intelligence in, 83-4; nuclear proliferation in, 74; politics of, 213-6, 221-2; US and, 69, 70, 71-4; USSR and, 69-71, 72, 73-4; wars, 54, 78-9, 87-8
military exercises: advance notice of, 25, 26, 29, 83-4, 187, 189, 190-1, 225-31; and confidence-building, 187-96, 225-31; restrictions on, 24, 189, 195, 230
Montreux Convention 1936, 206
Morocco: US embargo on arms to, 7

NATO: ASW of, 18; arms reduction in, 6; attitude to defence, 190; and CBM, 193, 195; and communication technology, 233; conventional weapons, 61-2; co-ordination of policies of, 33-41; cruise missiles of, 140-2; definitions of strategic and tactical, 136; and FBS, 26, 31-3, 34-7, 46, 47, 58-60, 120-1; and force-ceilings, 17; and future negotiations of SALT or MBFR, 63-4; grey area weapons of, 134, 140-2, 156; and IBM/MRBM of USSR, 135-6; and military exercise limitations, 195; and MBFR, 49-50, 55, 159; and multi-mission weapons, 156; naval forces, 11, 17; nuclear weapons, 31, 32-3, 56-63, 64-5, 140-2; and SALT, 32-4, 45-7, 49, 135-6, 140-2; satellites of, 246; weapons and security, 3
NCAT ('No Counter-city Attacks' Treaty) 87-90, 99, 103

NFUFT ('No First Use of Force' Treaty) 86-7, 99
NPT (Non-Proliferation Treaty) 6, 33, 61, 74, 115, 138
NTM (national technical means): alternatives to, 129; application of, 146, 202; definition of, 124-8; and mobile ballistic missiles, 130, 131; and SS – 20, 139; and satellites, 124, 245
naval exercises: advance notice of, 208, 209, 210, 211; restrictions on, 24
naval forces: arms control and, 10-1, 23, 24, 26-7, 28, 206-7; and CBM, 206-12
Netherlands: nuclear strike role of, 50
'Nixon Doctrine' for the Pacific, 21
nuclear proliferation: and CTB, 202; in Middle East, 74; and SALT, 115, 122; and super powers, 160-1
nuclear weapons: and conventional weapons, 61-2; deployment restrictions on, 22; peripheral, 137-43; spread of and SALT, 115; US budget for, 11; USSR budget for, 11-2
nuclear-free zone, 26, 31

Oil: and arms build-up in Middle East, 66; use of to obtain arms, 90

PAR (Programmed Assured Restraint) 201-5
PBV (post-boost vehicle) 134, 136
PBW (particle-beam weapons) 249-50
PGM (precision guided munitions): in Europe, 234; as grey area weapon, 136; in Middle East, 79, 80, 92-4; operating problems of, 234; production of, 91; in service, 233; technology of, 232-3, 240; in Vietnam war, 136
para-military units, 8
Pershing missiles: limitations on, 39-40, 43, 141; in MBFR, 143; in NATO's forces, 31, 34, 61, 136, 141; US supply to Israel, 74; USSR and NATO's, 31, 34
Persian Gulf: arms build-up in, 66; USSR navy in, 21, 22, 23

RPV (remotely piloted vehicle): as grey area weapon, 134; technology of, 232
research and development: control area for